CREATING THE CHILD

Creating the Child

The Ethics, Law and Practice
of Assisted Procreation

Editor

DONALD EVANS

Director, Centre for Philosophy and Health Care
University of Wales, Swansea
Swansea, Wales

Assistant Editor

NEIL PICKERING

Centre for Philosophy and Health Care
University of Wales, Swansea
Swansea, Wales

Martinus Nijhoff Publishers

The Hague / London / Boston

Library of Congress Cataloging-in-Publication Data

ISBN 90-411-0207-8
ISBN 90-411-0209-4 (Set)

Published by Kluwer Law International,
P.O. Box 85889, 2508 CN The Hague, The Netherlands.

Sold and distributed in the U.S.A. and Canada
by Kluwer Law International,
675 Massachusetts Avenue, Cambridge, MA 02139, U.S.A.

In all other countries, sold and distributed
by Kluwer Law International,
P.O. Box 85889, 2508 CN The Hague, The Netherlands.

Printed on acid-free paper

All Rights Reserved
© 1996 Kluwer Law International
Kluwer Law International incorporates the publishing programmes of
Graham & Trotman Ltd, Kluwer Law and Taxation Publishers,
and Martinus Nijhoff Publishers.

Printed in the Netherlands

To the memory of Patrick Steptoe

Clinician and pioneer of IVF services

CONTENTS

ACKNOWLEGEMENTS

Most of the chapters in this volume and in its companion volume *Conceiving the Embryo* were written in the course of a concerted action, executed from 1992-1995 and financed by the European Commission BIOMED I project, entitled *Fertility, infertility and the human embryo: the ethics, law and practice of assisted procreation* and an extension to that action involving East and Central European scholars financed by the PECO funds of the European Commission.

I was privileged to coordinate this action and wish to record my thanks to all the scholars who participated in it, not all of whom are represented on the pages of these volumes. Those whose writings appear here gained much from discussion with those who have not contributed chapters but who attended research conferences and gave generously of their time and expertise.

Some additional chapters have been provided by scholars who were consulted during the concerted action and others who learned of it and offered assistance in providing complementary material.

The action was coordinated from the Centre for Philosophy and Health Care at the University of Wales Swansea from which the impetus for the study originated. This was in no small part due to the collaboration between the Centre in its early days and Dr. Patrick Steptoe the pioneer of IVF treatment. As a clinician he was always concerned about the ethical dimensions of his practice and sought advice from a wide range of people outside medicine. He discussed his worries with staff and students at the Centre in the mid nineteen eighties and in so doing stimulated interest in this novel and challenging area of clinical practice. The two volumes are dedicated to his memory.

Thanks are due to the administrative staff of the Centre, Mrs. Anne Edwards and Miss Gwyneth Abbott, who worked extremely hard to conquer the daunting challenges presented by the coordination of the work of over fifty researchers in some twenty countries.

Some of the material presented in this volume has appeared in some form elsewhere and thanks are due to the following for permission to republish:

The Cambridge University Press for permission to reprint parts of Arlene Judith Klotzko's 'Commentary on "Immortality through the fertility clinic"' from *Cambridge Quarterly of Health Care Ethics* 4 (3), Summer 1995, pp.380-383, and to reprint the case study of Mr X 'Immortality through the fertility clinic' *ibid*. p.375.

I should like to acknowledge the support of the University of Wales Swansea which has enabled both the coordination of the concerted action and the editing of this volume and

xii

its companion.   The process of editing would have been impossible without the dedication of my able Assistant Editor, Neil Pickering.   Finally thanks are due to my wife Ann who has seen much less of me during the past three years than either of us would have chosen and without whose understanding these books would never have materialised.

Donald Evans
Swansea January 1996

CONTRIBUTORS

Erwin Bernat, Department of Civil Law, Graz Law School, Heinrichstrasse 22, 8010 Graz, Austria.

Judge Christian Byk, Associate Professor of Law, University of Poitiers, France.

Gaetano Caserta, Centre of Prenatal Medicine, Institute of Obstetrics and Gynecology, University of Perugia, Italy.

Ermelendo V. Cosmi, II Institute of Obstetrics and Gynecology, University of Rome "La Sapienza", Italy.

Panagiota Dalla-Vorgia, Department of Hygiene and Epidemiology, University of Athens Medical School, Greece.

Prof. Dr. Drs. h.c. Erwin Deutsch, Faculty of Law, University of Göttingen, Germany.

Gian Carlo Di Renzo, Centre of Prenatal Medicine, Institute of Obstetrics and Gynecology, University of Perugia, Italy.

Maria Dolanska, Genetic Counselling Centre, Thomayer University Hospital, Prague, Czech Republic.

Donald Evans, Centre for Philosophy and Health Care, University of Wales, Swansea, Singleton Park, Swansea, Wales.

Martyn Evans, Centre for Philosophy and Health Care, University of Wales, Swansea, Singleton Park, Swansea, Wales.

Gilda Ferrando, Associate Professor of Private Law, University of Genoa, Italy.

Søren Holm, Department of Medical Philosophy and Clinical Theory, University of Copenhagen, Blegdamsvej 3, DK-2200 N, Copenhagen, Denmark.

Joseph H. Hubben, Professor of Health Law, Nijmegen University, The Netherlands.

Dr. Ivanyushkin Alexandr Yakovlevitch, Principal Scientific Researcher, Institute of Man, Russian Academy of Sciences, Moscow, Russia.

Arlene Judith Klotzko, J.D., Research Fellow in Medical Law and Ethics, The London Hospital Medical College, England. Research Fellow, The Center for Bioethics and Health Law, Utrecht University, The Netherlands.

Dr Jean Martin, Médecin cantonal (Cantonal Medical Officer), Lecturer at the Faculty of Medicine, Cité-Devant 11, CH-1014 Lausanne, Switzerland.

Jaime Vidal Martínez, Profesor Titular de Derecho Civil, Departmento de Derecho Civil, Universitat de València, Spain.

Maurizio Mori, Politeia. Centro per la formazione in politica ed etica, Milano, Italy. Editor *Bioetica. Rivista Interdisciplinare*.

Demetrio Neri, Full Professor of History of Philosophy, University of Messina, Italy.

Associate Professor of Law Linda Nielsen, Dr. juris, Faculty of Law, The University of Copenhagen, Denmark. Member of the Danish Council of Ethics.

John Parsons, Senior Lecturer/Honorary Consultant, Kings College Hospital, Denmark Hill, London SE5 8RX, England.

Neil Pickering, Centre for Philosophy and Health Care, University of Wales, Swansea, Singleton Park, Swansea, Wales.

Knut W. Ruyter, Center for Medical Ethics, University of Oslo, Norway.

Judit Sándor, J.D. LLM, Central European University, Budapest College, Hungary.

Karoly Schultz, Consultant Paediatrician, Tolna County Teaching Hospital, Department of Paediatrics, Szekszard, Hungary.

Jean-Marie Thévoz, Fondation Louis Jeantet de Médecine, C.P. 277, CH-1211 Genève 17, Switzerland.

Erich Vranes, Department of Civil Law, Graz Law School, Heinrichstrasse 22, 8010 Graz, Austria.

LIST OF FIGURES AND TABLES

Introduction

1. CREATING THE CHILD

Donald Evans
Centre for Philosophy and Health Care
University of Wales, Swansea
Singleton Park
Swansea
Wales

'The Lord gave and the Lord hath taken away' run the words of the traditional funeral service. They tell us a great deal about peoples' perceptions of the beginning and end of human life which have been shrouded in mystery and regarded with awe throughout history. But medical technology has done much to transform such perceptions in recent years. Our ability to intervene in biological processes and manipulate human life has raised new questions about the nature of life and death and has brought novel ethical questions into the world of clinical practice. Amongst these are the problems of who should and who should not have access to such innovative therapies and the question of whose interests are served by such procedures. Further, given the profound implications of the technologies for public perceptions of the nature of human life and relations, we might ask whether medicine exhibits hubris in its employment of them and whether the activities of clinicians should be subject to wider public controls than hitherto with respect to them.

Such questions arise in the field of assisted reproduction and it is with these that the essays in this volume are concerned. The creation or production of a human embryo *in vitro* opened the door to a range of techniques which could be employed to relieve the distress of the infertile but it also separated procreation from sexuality and normal social relationships. In so doing, while it has made it possible to investigate the earliest stages of the development of human lives more closely than hitherto (resulting in a series of discoveries with which we are still coming to terms), it has also tended to elevate the biological facts to a position of definitive authority in accounts of what the origins of human life are and how they ought to be handled. This shift or at least the tendency to shift in this way has considerable implications for the interests and rights of all the parties concerned, including commissioning parents, genetic parents, neonates born by means of such technologies, single women, post-menopausal women, homosexual people, doctors and society in general.

These changes and the important questions arising out of them were the subject matter of a phase of the concerted research action sponsored by the European Commission in which most of the contributors to this volume played a part. Doctors, social scientists, lawyers and philosophers together examined the ethics, law and practice of assisted

D. Evans (ed.), Creating the Child, 3–11.

procreation in member states of the European Union and countries beyond. They were concerned to compare the perceptions and regulation of assisted conception practices and determine whether there was a need to seek harmonisation of legislation to regulate the practices across national borders. The essays in this volume are some of the fruits of that research.

There is now a considerable variety of assisted conception procedures which have been well-proved in practice.[1] Technological advances in methods of handling infertility continue to occur. For example, most recently techniques of micro-manipulation of sperm and oocytes have held out hope for many infertile couples in whom male-factor infertility is the cause of their inability to conceive. Many such couples might now enjoy the possibility of begetting children who are the genetic product of both partners, so avoiding the necessity of employing donor gametes with all the attendant ethical and emotional problems which such employment might involve.[2] It is possible that further developments might render unnecessary other procedures which present moral difficulties. For example, whilst the cryoconservation of oocytes is currently impossible, in that there is no guarantee that the process will not damage the oocyte and make it unusable or dangerous to employ in the production of a pregnancy, things might alter. Should such a process be perfected then the need to fertilise ova and cryonconserve pre-embryos would disappear and with it problems which have exercised many who have objected to the production of 'spare embryos' or who have worried about storage limits and the ultimate destruction of unused embryos. On the other hand further developments might create additional moral problems. For example, the shortage of donor oocytes has encouraged researchers to consider the possibility of harvesting immature oocytes (oogonia) from foetal ovarian tissue.[3] If technological developments make it possible to mature such occytes *in vitro* without damage then, given that there are millions of them in a normal foetal ovary, the attractions are obvious. However the availability of such a supply will present a number of ethical problems including the problem of whether children should be created whose genetic mother was an abortus.

That such medical interventions are now possible does not in itself show that infertility is properly to be regarded as a condition with which medicine should concern itself or that health care resources should be devoted to the treatment of it. Indeed it has been argued that the medicalisation of the condition has simply occurred as a strategy for increasing the power of the male dominated medical profession at the cost of the disempowerment of women who are the focus of the interventions with all their attendant risks and costs. This is achieved by the use of the apparently value-free language of biology in terms of which infertility and assisted procreation are described.[4] The doctor is not saved by his appeal to resolving the problem of infertility for his patients or meeting their needs for the very identification of infertility or childlessness as a problem or a need betrays a value orientation which manifests a gender bias. This is a fairly extreme critique of infertility medicine but it is one which calls for an answer.

However we do not have to look so far for critics of assisted conception services

making demands on health care resources. Numbers of purchasing health authorities in the United Kingdom are on record as refusing to purchase such services because infertility is not an illness.[5] Yet health services are concerned with other conditions which do not in themselves constitute a disease condition. Biological dysfunctions which are socially debilitating, such as deafness, are certainly regarded as the proper business of medicine to cure or alleviate. It is indeed ironic that health planning policies will make resources available to produce the biological dysfunction of sterility in men and women for clinical and social reasons when they will not invest in services to resolve such dysfunctions.[6] In so doing the perceptions of some patients of their fertility are taken seriously as constituting a health need when the perceptions of other patients of their infertility are ignored, even though infertility touches something at the centre of the wellbeing of most people, namely, living in and rearing families. A strong case can be made for regarding infertility as a health need even though it may not constitute such for all who experience it.[7]

But infertility medicine rarely seeks to cure the condition of infertility. Indeed assisted procreation never does. Rather it circumvents the dysfunction and facilitates pregnancy but leaves the couple as infertile afterwards as they ever were. The need it addresses is rather childlessness and this has been labelled a social rather than a medical need.[8] That it can cause significant psychological distress is well documented and as such it merits the concern of society to alleviate it.[9] Some will argue that this is better done by social methods such as adoption whereas others argue that now medicine has developed the techniques to address the problem it is properly identified as a clinical need.[10]

Opposition to assisted procreation procedures is often voiced in terms of the interference with natural processes which they entail. The artificiality is said to undermine the dignity of human life by moving away from the traditional givenness of life to its commodification.[11] As such it constitutes a threat to established moral conceptions and ought to be resisted for this reason. This conservative view is held most clearly by the Roman Catholic church and has a long history.[12] It holds that the natural teleology of the reproductive process is something which ought to be protected as an absolute duty. Thus any interference with it either in the form of contraception, sterilisation, abortion, homosexuality or assisted conception, even by AIH, ought to be prohibited. This absolute regard has traditionally been protected by the institution of marriage which was regarded as indissoluble and marking the acceptable boundaries of sexual relations. Anyone born outside of this context was regarded as illegitimate. This ensured that legitimate children were not seen simply as biological products but rather as the results of marriage; parenthood was seen not as a biological relationship but as a social one; it could only occur in the context of the social institution of marriage. Such a view has profound implications for people in terms of their duties and rights *vis-a-vis* parenthood. But a consideration of the historical changes in the status of marriage since the sixteenth century and the widespread acceptance nowadays of contraception suggests that the view no longer enjoys general support.[13]

The claim that the unity of the sexual act of procreation is essential to our humanity

may also be subjected to critical scrutiny. Whilst its authority might not be assailable, in the sense that it might not be susceptible to refutation by argument, neither can it be established by these means. This can be seen by comparing the natural procreation and humanness view outlined above with another related, but importantly different, view of what is natural in human procreation. This construal of the natural is bound up with the dominant values in a society which regards heterosexual monogamous procreation as natural and consequently wishes to restrict access to such services to those who fall under the necessary social descriptions.[14] Each of these views employs the notion of naturalness to combat threatening variations from the norm they espouse. But the notion of naturalness itself is subject to rival construals.

The notion of naturalness might also be employed to further the provision of assisted procreation techniques - indeed to make a case for both unrestricted access to them and unrestricted practice of them. If we could establish a natural right to procreate then this would rule out interference with those who chose to exercise that right and, maybe, impose a duty on others to facilitate the claiming of that right by people who are impeded from so doing by the biological dysfunction of infertility. But there are serious difficulties in the way of establishing such rights.[15] In any case given that third parties are necessarily involved in assisted procreation and that society itself might be called upon to satisfy the claims of those armed with such rights the question of justifying such provision would arise with respect to the rights and interests of others. Most prominent amongst these are the interests of the children produced by such techniques.[16]

Whilst it might not be possible to establish a natural right to procreate we shall certainly have to consider the balance of rights between parents and child in any regulation of assisted procreation services.[17] Here we will find disagreement about which sets of rights should predominate. The separation of procreation from sexual relations has made it possible for there to be as many as three women with some claim to be the mother of a child born by assisted procreation i.e. where donor oocytes, surrogate womb and commissioning woman are involved. Thus there may even be a conflict between the rights of each of these women both in isolation from the rights of the child and in relation to them.[18] The emergence of the right of a woman to choose whether to continue with a pregnancy since the *Roe v. Wade* case has highlighted the tension between a woman's right to self-determination and the rights of a prospective child. It is not straightforward to interpret the significance of this right in relation to the situation just referred to. This becomes a matter of considerable concern to lawyers who point out internal conflicts in legal rights as embodied in the laws of given countries. For example, in Austrian law the provisions of the Act on Procreative Medicine are in tension with the constitutional rights of citizens.[19]

Some legislatures have placed the interests of the child at the centre of decisions concerning access to assisted procreation services.[20] This prioritising of rights has been supported in some quarters by an appeal to the analogy of adoption where society has the responsibility as a third party to provide a family for an orphaned or abandoned child.[21] All western European countries have strict vetting rules for prospective adoptive parents to determine their suitability to parent children - rules which are

designed primarily to ensure the welfare of the children. So, the analogy runs, as society provides assisted procreation services or permits their provision it has a similar responsibility towards the children who result indirectly from this third party intervention.[22] But there are important dissimilarities between the analogues which weaken the claim that prospective parents by assisted procreation should be subject to the same rigorous controls of access to parenthood as prospective adoptive parents.[23] Thus, for example, many would not agree that it is clear that children who result from assisted procreation procedures should at some time in their lives have access to the identity of their genetic progenitors, though this is guaranteed in Swedish regulations on the basis of the analogy with adoption.[24] However it would be a mistake not to take the similarities highlighted by the analogy seriously as this may lead to certain valuable controls and positive elements being introduced to assisted procreation programmes which properly protected the interests of children without subjecting prospective parents to unjustifiable invasions of privacy and inequalities of treatment with those who conceive children normally. In this way the analogy could prove to be useful.

One positive element which comes out of the analogy concerns the question of openness in the parent-child relationship. Experience of adoption has shown that secrecy in parent-child relationships can be destructive of the interests of the child and of the family in general.[25] Similarly it is claimed that ethnological research and both psychiatric and psychoanalytic clinical experience support the view that openness in family relationships involving children is to be encouraged - indeed that secrecy produces pathogenic effects.[26] Others take the view that the jury is still out on this matter.[27] As the lack of an absolute right to knowledge of the identity of its genetic progenitors does not displace the importance of the interests of a child in assisted procreation it would follow that any legislation which placed an absolute barrier to information of any kind, including genetic data of the progenitors as well as their identity, would put the welfare of the child at risk. It might nevertheless be the case that only in very extreme circumstances could the knowledge of the identity of a progenitor be of crucial significance to the welfare of a child. A case could therefore be made to be sparing in the extreme with absolute bans on information to the products of assisted conception procedures.[28] In fact, it is claimed that in some jurisdictions the absolute barrier to information about the identity of the gamete donor contained in assisted procreation legislation is contrary to the inherent and inviolable constitutional rights of the child.[29]

There is a related problem with the issue of the secrecy of the commissioning couples' infertility and employment of assisted procreation services. Even if access to genetic data of progenitors is to be made available to children of such couples they will not know their potential need for such information if they are completely ignorant of the fact that they were conceived in this way. Empirical research conducted in the European Commission project showed that only small minorities of couples intended to inform their children that they were the result of assisted conception procedures, suggesting that guarantees of provisions of access to genetic information are likely to be rendered ineffective.[30] It would constitute a breach of medical confidentiality to

insist that such information was shared with offspring by third parties in the event of parents' unwillingness to do so. In any case it would probably be unworkable and destructive of other valuable features of the family relationship. Nevertheless the need for openness could be made an important feature of the counselling offered to prospective parents. The Dutch draft of an artificial insemination act provides a useful example of a sensitive way legislatures can attempt to tackle this difficult problem.[31]

Given that the production of legislation to control assisted procreation procedures produces the kinds of difficulties alluded to above we may be moved to ask whether we could dispense with regulatory controls altogether. There are numerous reasons why we must answer no to this question. The first of them concerns the prioritisation of health needs and the allocation of scarce resources. Here we are not so much concerned with legal controls which might proscribe certain activities which are thought to be contrary to human dignity or the public interest as with matters of health policy, though these might coincide. Various features of the ability to have children and to enable others to do so are important from a public health perspective.[32] For example, the opportunity for prospective parents to select the gender of their children could, in principle, have serious effects on the sex ratios in the population which would have serious implications for public health[33], though the indications of the empirical survey referred to earlier suggest that this is an unreal fear.[34] On the other hand, as was pointed out by the 1992 Dutch Report *Choices in Health Care*, it would be difficult to establish infertility as a community health issue because it does not threaten the normal functioning of society. Nevertheless that same report noted that *in vitro* fertilisation may be necessary care for individual patients.[35] Thus it would be sensible to ensure that there was no blanket refusal to make such services available without making the procedures available to all and sundry as of right.

There are pressing reasons for more general controls to be imposed by the state either in the form of statutory regulation or legal sanctions. The example of Italy is a salutory reminder that if something can be done, and people are willing to pay enough, then it will be done whatever its implications may be for peoples' welfare. Whilst professional groups have issued guidelines to guard against improper exploitation of assisted procreation techniques with respect to criteria of access to services and the commercialisation of gametes, for example, such regulation has proved to be inefficient and possibly unjust.[36] (A similar claim has been made about the lack of state control in Greece[37], while in Spain legislation passed in 1988 has not been fully enacted.[38]) The injustice lies often in the application of inappropriate laws to resolve problems specific to procreative techniques.[39] In the absence of legal sanctions it is felt that market forces will encourage further exploitation of the grief of infertile couples and disregard for the rights of women and the interests of children in Italy, especially as restrictions elsewhere encourage patients to take advantage of the laissez-faire approach to assisted conception in that country.

However the need for regulation does not guarantee that satisfactory laws can readily be devised. It has been argued that the regulators will need to take serious account of the moral pluralism to be found in the countries concerned (though this has not always

occurred where legislation has been enacted) and allow some flexibility into the system to cater for the volatile state of public opinion about many of these issues.[40] They must also be informed by adequate reflection on the ethical issues in question in order to produce satisfactory controls, a lack which is alleged in the legislative control of reproductive medicine in Russia.[41]

The production of satisfactory legislation in any given country is difficult enough. But we have already referred to the movement of citizens between countries to obtain services which are proscribed in their own countries. This phenomenon has been labelled 'procreative tourism'. Whether such a practice ought to be discouraged or not is debatable. Certainly where there is dissonance in regulation such activities can produce legal and practical problems as the rights of individuals will vary from place to place. This has already resulted in difficult court proceedings where the child of a Swedish woman, produced by means of donor sperm she obtained in Denmark, wishes to establish the identity of his genetic father.[42] A quick comparison of the differences between the conservative legislation of France[43], Germany[44] and Austria[45] with the more liberal legislation of the United Kingdom[46] will facilitate the construction of further possible complicated cases. Harmonisation of regulation across national boundaries would obviate these problems though in the absence of the same some method of mediation between jurisdictions in such cases is called for. The possibility of harmonisation has been explored with some positive results which suggest that on general issues such as the non-commercialisation principle, informed consent and eugenic policies, it is both desirable and possible leaving room for national differences on other issues according to local culture and legal and medical traditions.[47]

Notes

(All references, unless otherwise indicated, are to authors' works in this volume.)

1. See Parsons, J. p.15ff and Di Renzo *et al* p.29ff.

2. See Parsons, J. p.21.

3. Di Renzo *et al*, p.34.

4. Pickering, N., pp.80-88.

5. Evans, D., p.57 and Soren Holm pp.66-71.

6. Evans, D., 'Infertility and the NHS' *British Medical Journal* Vol. 311, No. 7020, December 1995, p.1586.

7. Evans, D., pp.47-61 and Martin, J., p.248 and p.250.

8. Holm, S., p.65.

9. Holm, S., p.74.

10. See Holm, S., p.75 and Evans, D., p.58 and 'Infertility and the NHS' *op.cit.*, for these opposing positions.

11. Neri, D., pp.148-150.

12. Mori, M., pp.102-106.

13. Mori, M., pp.102-105.

14. Pickering, N., pp.111-123.

15. Evans, M., pp.128-132.

16. Evans, M., pp.132-143.

17. Neri, D., pp.145-148.

18. Sándor, J., pp.162-164.

19. Bernat, E., pp.327-28.

20. Klotzko, A.J., p.343.

21. This is the case in Sweden. See Ruyter, K.W., p.179.

22. Evans, M., p.141.

23. Evans, M., p.142; Ruyter, K.W., pp.180-82.

24. Ruyter, K.W., p.192, note 10.

25. Ruyter, K.W., p.177, p.183 and pp.185-189.

26. Thévoz, J.-M., p.201.

27. Schultz, K., pp.232-236.

28. Thévoz, J.-M., p.205.

29. Martínez, J.V., pp.222-223.

30. Dolanska, M. and Evans, D., pp.295-296.

31. Hubben, J., pp.211-216.

32. Martin, J., pp.241-242.

33. Martin, J., p.246.

34. Dolanska, M. and Evans, D., pp.298-299.

35. *Choices in Health Care* Report by a Government Committee. Ministry of Welfare, Health and Cultural Affairs, P.O. Box 5406, NL-2280 HK Rijswijk, 1992, p.87.

36. Ferrando, G., pp.255-257.

37. Dalla-Vorgia, P., 279-286.

38. Martínez, J.V., pp.287-289.

39. Ferrando, G., pp.259-261.

40. Ferrando, G., p.263.

41. Ivanyushkin, A.Y., pp.270-272, and p.274.

42. Dolanska, M. and Evans, D., pp.299-300.

43. Byk, C., pp.347-349.

44. Deutsch, E., pp.333-339.

45. Bernat, E. and Vranes, E., pp.325-332.

46. Klotzko, A.J., pp.341-347.

47. Nielsen, L., pp.305-324.

PART ONE

Infertility and the Role of Medicine

2. ASSISTED CONCEPTION: THE STATE OF THE ART

John Parsons
Senior Lecturer/Honorary Consultant
Kings College Hospital
Denmark Hill
London SE5 8RX, England

The term 'assisted conception' or 'assisted reproduction' was coined in the mid-1980s to describe techniques involving the manipulation of sperm, eggs or embryos. These techniques are used to help women or men, for a variety of medical and social reasons, to have healthy children. Assisted conception is used most commonly to help couples with difficulty conceiving to have a child. It may also be used to help women with medical problems that would make pregnancy unsafe for them, and couples at risk of transmitting a serious congenital disease. Social reasons for the use of assisted conception include single women and lesbian couples wishing to have a child without the involvement of a man, and the wish of a couple to have a child of a particular gender.

1. Infertility

Infertility is defined as the failure to conceive after twelve months unprotected intercourse.[1] This terminology suggests total inability to conceive, whereas in fact a very significant number of women conceive spontaneously after the defined time period. Thus the term 'subfertility', though aesthetically rather unappealing, may be preferred to 'infertility'.

1.1. INCIDENCE

In the United Kingdom two surveys of women past their reproductive years (48-50)[2] have shown that 4-7% of women remain childless voluntarily. Another study[3] showed that one in six couples experience problems conceiving at some time during their reproductive lives.

1.2. CAUSES OF INFERTILITY

In approximately one quarter of couples complaining of infertility there is a semen abnormality, and in about a fifth the woman is not ovulating an egg each month.[4] The

15

D. Evans (ed.), Creating the Child, 15–27.
© 1996 Kluwer Law International. Printed in the Netherlands.

incidence of Fallopian tube damage, commonly caused by sexually transmitted infection, varies and is dependant upon the sexual practices in the community studied. In the United Kingdom 14% of women with infertility have tubal damage.[5] In a very significant percentage of patients, in spite of adequate investigation, the cause of the failure to conceive remains unexplained. Spontaneous pregnancies occur in all these categories. Couples with a history of two-three years unexplained infertility have an 80% chance of conception over the subsequent two years.[6] Even men with very low or even zero sperm in their ejaculate appear to father pregnancies.[7] It is therefore important to avoid treating patients too early.

1.3. FACTORS INFLUENCING RESULTS OF TREATMENT

The most important factors influencing the results of treatment are the quality of the gametes (sperm and eggs) and the expertise of the laboratory handling those gametes. The clinical management of the patients is now so standardised that it has ceased to become an important variable. Egg quality is very age dependant. A woman's fertility falls steadily from her early twenties but particularly after the age of 35 years.[8] Conceptions in older women are much more likely to miscarry[9] or lead to the development of a congenitally abnormal foetus.[10]

1.4. COUNSELLING

That counselling should be available and accessible to couples finding themselves in need of fertility treatment, before during and after treatment, is recognised to be important.[11] Couples must understand the implications of the treatment and be able to obtain support during treatment if necessary. The option to cease treatment and accept childlessness or seek adoption must always be open to them.

2. Assisted Conception Techniques

2.1. OVULATION INDUCTION

Drugs that stimulate the production of eggs have been available since the late 1950s. These drugs (human menopausal gonadotrophins) are extracted from the urine of postmenopausal women. They are therefore impure, of variable potency, and difficult to use. The incidence of multiple pregnancy when using these drugs is significant even when treatment is carefully monitored. High multiple pregnancies (three foetuses or more) are much more likely to lead to premature delivery and handicap than single or even twin pregnancies.[12] Women with a high multiple pregnancy may wish to increase the chance of one or two of their foetuses being delivered safely by sacrificing the excess (see below).[13]

2.2. ARTIFICIAL INSEMINATION OF SPERM

This technique involves the mechanical placement of semen or separated sperm into the female partner's genital tract. The sample may be from the woman's partner or from a donor. It may be placed in the vagina, in the cervix, or in the uterine or abdominal cavities.

Artificial insemination by the woman's partner's semen would be indicated where intravaginal ejaculation was not possible. Examples include men with retrograde ejaculation, whose sperm must be retrieved from their bladder or urine[14] and inseminated into their partner, and paraplegic men who may produce semen only by rectal electroejaculation.[15] Artificial insemination may be required for psychological reasons; some men are unable to have an intravaginal orgasm, some women are unable to tolerate sexual intercourse. Artificial insemination with the partner's sperm may also be used, with controlled superovulation (drug therapy to cause the ovulation of three eggs rather than one), to treat unexplained infertility.[16] Controlled superovulation may, like ovulation induction, lead to a grand multiple pregnancy.

Where the man has no or very few sperm, treatment with donor sperm may be requested. Single women or lesbians may prefer anonymous sperm donation to the alternative of obtaining semen from friends. Donors may donate altruistically or be paid. They may donate anonymously or be known to the recipient - perhaps a relative or friend. Paid donors may receive 'expenses' or truly sell their semen. In the United Kingdom, anonymous donors may receive only expenses and must be registered with the Human Fertilisation and Embryology Authority; non-identifying information will be available for the children on request at the age of 18 years. Donors are excluded if their semen quality is poor or cryopreserves (freezes) unsatisfactorily, or if they give a history of significant hereditary disease or infection. The donor sperm is cryopreserved in liquid nitrogen (-192°C) until the donor has been shown to be free from Human Immunodeficiency Virus. The sperm is thawed and artificially inseminated at the appropriate time in the woman's menstrual cycle.

2.3. TECHNIQUES INVOLVING MANIPULATION OF SPERM AND EGGS

These techniques all require the early part of the woman's menstrual cycle to be monitored so that the collection of an egg or eggs from her ovary may be timed appropriately. Monitoring consists of the serial measurement of hormones in her urine or blood, and/or the serial measurement of the ovarian follicle or follicles, which contain the eggs, using ultrasound. The woman's unstimulated cycle may be monitored with a view to the collection of a single egg just before ovulation or she may be given hormones which stimulate egg production in her ovaries. Generally the more eggs available for manipulation, the higher the chance that conception will occur. However, some women conceive easily and one egg from an unstimulated 'natural' cycle may give them an adequate chance of success. There are concerns regarding the long-term effect of ovarian stimulation on the incidence of ovarian cancer.[17] Overstimulation of the

ovaries may lead to severe ovarian hyperstimulation syndrome which is very uncomfortable, requires hospital admission and can lead to thromboembolism which may cause serious morbidity or even death.[18]

When the eggs are judged to be mature, either following the natural midcycle increase in hormone levels or following the injection of an artificial surrogate hormone, they are collected by needle aspiration of the follicular fluid, usually under ultrasound guidance. In the natural cycle there is approximately 90% chance of an egg being collected[19], in a stimulated cycles 75% of follicles yield an egg giving an average 10-12 eggs per patient.[20] Older women produce less eggs than younger women and their egg quality is poorer. The risks related to egg collection are haemorrhage and pelvic abcess, though such serious complications are rare.

2.4. CRYOPRESERVATION OF EGGS

The ability to cryopreserve eggs would be particularly beneficial to women, who have not completed their families, facing drug or surgical treatment (usually for cancer) known to be damaging to ovarian function. A woman's ovarian reserve of eggs decreases with age, so egg cryopreservation might be used by women wishing to delay pregnancy into their late thirties, forties or even later.

Unlike spermatozoa, mature human eggs are very delicate and do not cryopreserve well. Live deliveries after cryopreservation, thawing and embryo transfer[21] have been reported but these have proved difficult to emulate.

However, immature eggs may be more resistant to cryodamage. Immature eggs collected from stimulated ovaries during IVF treatment have been successfully cultured after cryopreservation and thawing.[22] In mice immature eggs within their follicles have been cryopreserved, thawed, cultured, fertilised and transferred to a recipient female mouse to give live young.[23] In sheep, a live birth has occurred following an experiment where ovarian tissue was removed, cryopreserved, thawed and replaced into the same animal.[24]

In the future, women wishing to delay childbearing, for whatever reason, may have ovarian tissue removed and cryopreserved for later use. The ovaries of aborted female foetuses or fertile women dying accidentally might be used to stock donor egg banks.

2.5. EGG DONATION

A woman may need to consider using the eggs of a donor for a number of reasons. She may be born with no eggs, she may spontaneously run out of eggs before she has had the children that she wants, or her ovaries may be damaged by disease, drugs or surgery. Occasionally she may not wish to use her own eggs because she knows that to do so would put any resultant child at a high risk of a significant genetic disease.

Egg donors may be known to the person(s) using infertility services or anonymous, paid or unpaid. Known donors are usually relatives or friends who wish to donate for altruistic reasons, but they could also be women giving their eggs for financial gain.

Donors may give anonymously in response to publicity detailing the plight of women who require eggs, or by donating into a pool from which a friend may be given the eggs she needs. Women going through assisted conception may be willing to give a number of eggs to less fortunate women. Women may be offered inducements, such as free or reduced cost treatment for themselves, to do this. Prior to elective surgery that allows access to the ovaries, a woman may be recruited to undergo superovulation so that eggs for donation may be collected at the time of the planned procedure. Women may be encouraged to do this by inducements such as shorter waiting lists or treatment in a private hospital. In the future it may be possible to culture immature eggs *in vitro* to maturity from the ovaries of aborted female foetuses and dead women or ovarian tissue from women willing to donate during a gynaecological operation.

The mature donated eggs are inseminated with the sperm of the recipient's partner and resultant embryos transferred fresh into the recipient whose cycle has been synchronised or cryopreserved and transferred at a later date. Fresh transfer is likely to be more successful than transfer after cryopreservation. However, fresh transfer does carry a small risk that the donor has recently been infected with the AIDS virus. Cryopreservation allows the embryos to be quarantined until an HIV test six months later has been shown to be negative.

2.6. SPERM PRODUCTION

Semen is usually produced by masturbation. Some men may find ejaculation on demand difficult and they may need to produce a sample by coitus interruptus or by using a vibrator. Men with spinal injury may need rectal electroejaculation.

2.7. SPERM PREPARATION

Freshly ejaculated semen consists of seminal fluid, sperm, white cells and debris. From this mixture sperm which exhibit rapid progressive motility must be selected for assisted conception. In the 'swim up' technique the semen is diluted with culture medium shaken then centrifuged. The supernatant fluid is removed and the pellet of sperm and debris at the bottom of the tube carefully over-layered with culture medium. The most active sperm will swim out of the pellet into the culture medium. Another commonly used technique involves centrifuging the semen with fine particles (Percoll). The best sperm may be found at a particular level in the test tubes predetermined by the size of the particles. Attempts to separate x (female) from y (male) sperm have not been shown significantly to affect the chance of having either a male or a female child.

2.8. DAY 0 TRANSFER TO THE FALLOPIAN TUBES

Fertilisation *in vivo* occurs in the Fallopian tube. In couples with unexplained infertility, where the man has normal semen and the woman ovulates eggs and has healthy undamaged tubes, placement of eggs and sperm together in the Fallopian tubes

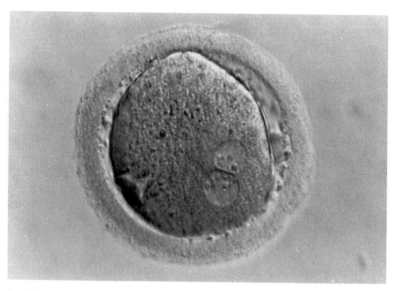

Fig. 1: Two pronuclei may be seen within the cytoplasm of the egg (photograph: Mr. Mark Howard)

(Gamete Intrafallopian transfer; GIFT) increases the chance of pregnancy significantly.[25] The gametes may or may not be mixed together before they are placed in the Fallopian tubes. They are transferred using a catheter passed either abdominally through the lateral ends of the tubes using a laparoscope (an endoscope used for viewing the abdominal organs via a small cut in the navel) under general anaesthesia, or through the medial ends of the tubes via the vagina, cervix and uterine cavity.

The number of eggs transferred should be limited to three to reduce the risk of multiple pregnancy.

2.9. *IN VITRO* INSEMINATION

Alternatively the egg and sperm may be mixed together *in vitro*, in either a tube or dish. Approximately 100,000 spermatozoa are added to each egg several hours after egg collection. Higher concentrations of sperm may be used when the sperm quality is poor.

2.10. *IN VITRO* FERTILISATION

The eggs are examined 12-18 hours after insemination for the presence or absence of pronuclei (figure 1 above). Two pronuclei confirm fertilisation and represent the male and female genetic material. At this stage there is no way of assessing the quality of these early embryos.

Some 55-65% of inseminated eggs fertilise.[26] If a small number of eggs fail to fertilise, it is likely that the eggs were not fertilisable. If the majority or all of the eggs fail to fertilise, it is likely that there is a sperm problem. Microscopic assessment of sperm number, shape and motility are used to estimate sperm quality but correlate poorly with ability to fertilise eggs. Fifty per cent of couples experiencing failed fertilisation will achieve fertilisation on a subsequent attempt[27] so there appears to be a variability in gamete quality and/or laboratory culture conditions.

2.11. MICROMANIPULATION

Where the sperm assessment suggests a very poor chance of fertilisation or there is a history of previous failure of fertilisation, single sperm may be picked up in a fine glass tube and injected into each egg (Intracytoplasmic sperm injection).[28] This technique gives fertilisation rates of between 60% and 70%.

The semen collected from men just prior to chemotherapy for testicular or other cancer, and from men with spinal injuries, is usually poor. Microinjection of sperm from such semen significantly increases the chance of fertilisation and pregnancy.

Azoospermia, that is the absence of sperm in the ejaculate, may be due either to a blockage in the male tubes (*vasa deferentia*) or a testicular problem. In the former situation, small numbers of spermatozoa may be obtained by surgically collecting sperm between the blockage and the testis. In the latter situation it may be possible to biopsy the testicle (either at open operation or using a needle) and find a few spermatozoa suitable for microinjection.

Many men who previously had no chance of having their own children may now be offered treatment with a reasonable chance of success. However, the risk of passing their fertility problem to their sons is unknown.

2.12. DAY 1 EMBRYO TRANSFER TO THE FALLOPIAN TUBE

Fertilised eggs (zygotes) may be transferred to the Fallopian tubes the day after insemination. Zygote intrafallopian transfer (ZIFT) may be achieved - as with GIFT - abdominally using a laparoscope or via the vagina cervix and uterine cavity. It is only suitable for women with normal Fallopian tubes. It has not been shown to be more successful than Day 2 transfer into the uterine cavity.[29]

2.13. PRE-IMPLANTATION DIAGNOSIS

Patients known to carry significant single gene defects or chromosomal abnormalities may prefer to have preimplantation diagnosis performed on embryos generated *in vitro* rather than face a later procedure with the prospect of a termination of pregnancy if the foetus is affected. The embryo may be biopsied during the cleavage (figure 2 overleaf) or blastocyst (figure 3 overleaf) stages without necessarily damaging its development. Embryos found not to carry the disease causing concern are transferred to the woman's

John Parsons

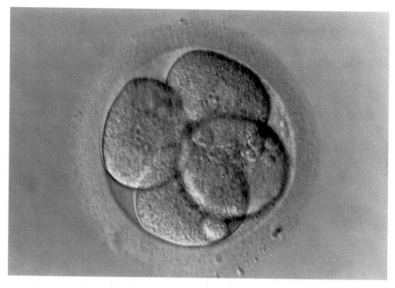

Fig. 2: A four cell (cleaving) embryo (photograph: Mr. Mark Howard)

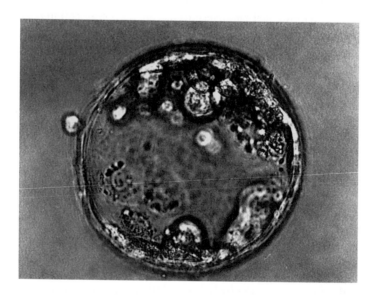

Fig. 3: A blastocyst (photograph: Dr. Virginia Bolton)

uterine cavity. Some (x-linked) congenital diseases are carried by women but expressed in men. Affected embryos may not be easy to identify, in which case only female embryos are replaced. The selection of embryos of a particular sex for purely social reasons could be performed using the same technique.

2.14. CLONING

Initially each cell of the cleaving human embryo has the potential to form a complete individual. Thus, early cleaving embryos could be disaggregated and each cell used as a separate embryo. All the embryos from each cleaving embryo would be identical. Fortunately mammalian embryos loose their totipotentiality early in their development so the prospect of many identical individuals being produced from a single embryo is not realisable. It has been suggested that splitting embryos in this manner might, by increasing the number of embryos available for transfer, increase pregnancy rates.

2.15. TRANSFER OF CLEAVING EMBRYOS

Cleaving embryos are usually transferred on day 2, the day after the pronuclei have been identified, at which stage they have divided once to two cells or twice to four cells. Embryo transfer may be delayed a further one to four[30] days without there being an adverse effect on pregnancy rate. Embryo transfer is usually to the uterine cavity by means of the tip of a fine catheter passed through the cervix. In the majority of cases this is a simple, painless procedure but if difficulties are encountered it may be necessary to inject the embryos into the uterine cavity using an ultrasound guided needle[31] or if the Fallopian tubes are healthy to place them in the tubes laparoscopically.[32]

The combination of egg collection, *in vitro* fertilisation and embryo transfer to the uterine cavity is referred to by the term '*in vitro* fertilisation and embryo transfer' (IVF and ET). Although developed for women with irreparable tubal damage[33], this combination of procedures, because it circumnavigates spontaneous ovulation, egg pick-up by the Fallopian tubes and transport of the egg/embryo to the uterus, is suitable for all categories of patients with infertility.

2.16. IVF SURROGACY

The embryo of an infertile couple may be placed and implant in the womb of a surrogate. This approach may be used to treat couples where the woman was born with no uterus or it was removed for some reason (for example, hysterectomy for severe haemorrhage following childbirth or for cervical cancer), or where the uterus has been unable to hold pregnancies long enough for the foetus to survive or where the woman is medically unfit to carry a pregnancy (for example, because of heart disease or atendency to form blood clots). To these medically significant reasons could be added the less compelling wish of the woman not to carry a pregnancy herself. The surrogate

may help the infertile couple altruistically, with or without receiving expenses, or receive full payment for her services. She may be a relative, a friend or a woman volunteering in response to word-of-mouth information or frank advertising.

The infertile woman is superovulated, her eggs are collected and inseminated with her partner's sperm, and resultant embryos either transferred into the synchronous womb of the surrogate or cryopreserved and transferred later.

2.17. EMBRYO CRYOPRESERVATION

Embryos, like sperm, may be cryopreserved in liquid nitrogen. It is not known how long they remain viable following cryopreservation but other mammalian embryos have been thawed after more than 14 years with no reduction in their ability to survive, implant and produce healthy live young.[34] It is likely that, protected from radiation, such embryos would survive for ever.

Only the best quality embryos survive cryopreservation so it tends to be the younger women, from whom large numbers of eggs may be collected, who have excess embryos available for preservation for transfer some time later. Embryos that survive thawing are as likely to implant as fresh embryos.[35]

Cryopreservation may be used therapeutically to avoid embryo transfer in women at risk from ovarian hyperstimulation syndrome, which is aggravated by pregnancy. Eggs for donation may be inseminated by the recipient partner's sperm and resultant embryos cryopreserved for transfer at a convenient time.

2.18. EMBRYO DONATION

Where couples have both sperm and egg problems they may want to use embryos from the gametes of another couple. These may be fresh embryos excess to the donor couple's needs at the end of a treatment cycle or frozen embryos after they have had all the children they desire. Embryos may also be generated from eggs and sperm from unrelated donors.

The donor embryos are transferred into the recipient at the appropriate time in either her own spontaneous cycle or during hormone replacement therapy.

2.19. FOETAL REDUCTION

The treatment of infertility with any of the assisted conception techniques is stressful and has, per cycle of treatment, what seems like a low chance of success. In order to increase the chances of success, ovulation induction is performed with more than one large follicle, GIFT is performed with more than one egg and after *in vitro* fertilisation more than one embryo is transferred. The inevitable corollary is an increase in the number of twin and grand multiple pregnancies. Regardless of the social problems that grand multiple pregnancies cause, the perinatal mortality rate associated with triplet and higher order pregnancies is very much higher than in singleton or twin gestations.[36]

Couples facing a grand multiple pregnancy having considered the social consequences and medical risks may request that the number of implantations be deliberately reduced. At between 7-11 weeks gestation a needle may be passed under ultrasound control either through the wall of the vagina or the skin of the abdomen into the heart of the foetus selected. A small quantity of a concentrated solution of potassium causes the heart to stop. The foetus and placenta shrink and are barely identifiable at the delivery of its sibling(s). This technique is not without risk; all the pregnancies may quickly miscarry, or after a delay deliver prematurely.

3. Conclusion

Since the end of the 1970s there has been a dramatic increase in our technical ability to help couples having difficulty conceiving. With this increased expertise has come a multitude of ethical and legal dilemmas which will be resolved only by education, consultation and discussion.

Notes

1. Tietze, C., 'Statistical contributions to the study of human fertility' *Fertility and Sterility* 7, 1956, pp.88-95.

2. Johnson, G., Roberts, D., Brown, R., Cox, E., Evershed, Z., Goutam, P., Hassan, P., Robinson, R., Sahdev, A., Swan, K. and Sykes, C., 'Infertile or childless by choice? A multipractice survey of women aged 35 and 50' *British Medical Journal* 294, 1987, pp.804-806; Templeton, A., Fraser, C. and Thompson, B., 'The epidemiology of infertility in Aberdeen' *British Medical Journal* 301, 1990, pp.148-152.

3. Hull, M.G.R., Glazener, C.M.A., Kelly, N.J., Conway, D.I., Foster, P.A., Hinton, R.A., Coulson, C., Lambert, P.A., Watt, E.M. and Desai, K.M., 'Population study of causes, treatment, and outcome of infertility' *British Medical Journal* 291, 1985, pp.1693-1697.

4. *Ibid.*

5. *Ibid.*

6. *Ibid.*

7. Hargreave, T.B., 'Laboratory assessment of male fertility' in Hargreave, T.B. and Soon, T.E. (eds), *The Management of Male Infertility* Singapore, PG Publishing, 1990, p.92.

8. Virro, M.R. and Shewchuk, A.B., 'Pregnancy outcome in 242 conceptions after artificial insemination with donor sperm and effects of maternal age on the prognosis for successful pregnancy' *American Journal of Obstetrics and Gynaecology* 148, 1984, pp.518-524.

9. Stein, Z.A., 'Reviews and commentary: a woman's age: childbearing and childrearing' *American Journal of Epidemiology* 121, 1985, pp.327-342.

10. Hassold, T. and Chiu, D., 'Maternal age-specific rates of numerical chromosome abnormalities with special reference to trisomy' *Human Genetics* 70, 1985, pp.11-17.

11. Cf. *Human Fertilisation and Embryology Act 1990*, S.13(6); Schedule 3, para. 3(1)(a), London, Her Majesty's Stationery Office.

12. Botting, B.J., MacFarlane, A.J., Bryan, B., Murphy, M.G.F. and Richards, M.P.M., 'Background' in Botting, B.J., MacFarlane, A.J. and Price, F.V. (eds), *Three, Four and More: A Study of Triplet and High Order Births* London, Her Majesty's Stationery Office, pp.15-30, p.23 (Table 1.2).

13. Lipitz, S, Reichman, B, Uval, J., Shalev, J., Achiron, R., Barkai, G., Lusky, A. and Mashiach, S., 'A prospective comparison of the outcome of triplet pregnancies managed expectantly or by multi-fetal reduction' *American Journal of Obstetrics and Gynaecology* 170 (3), 1994, pp.874-879.

14. Braude, P.R., Ross, I.D., Bolton, V.N. and Ockenden K., 'Retrograde ejaculation: a systematic approach to non-invasive recovery of spermatozoa from post-ejaculatory urine for artificial insemination' *British Journal of Obstetrics and Gynaecology* 94, 1987, pp.76-83.

15. Buch, J.P. and Zorn, B.H., 'Evaluation and treatment of infertility in spinal cord injured men through rectal probe electroejaculation' *Journal of Urology* 149 (5 part 2), 1993, pp.1350-54.

16. Hovatta, O., Kurunmäki, H., Tiitinen, A., Lahteenmäki, P. and Koskimies, A.I., 'Direct intraperitoneal or intrauterine insemination and superovulation in infertility treatment: a randomized study' *Fertility and Sterility* 54, 1990, pp.339-341.

17. Whittemore, A.S., Harris, R., Itnyre, J. and the Collaborative Ovarian Cancer Group, 'Characteristics relating ovarian cancer risk: collaborative analysis of 12 U.S. case controlled studies' *American Journal of Epidemiology* 136, 1992, pp.1184-1203.

18. Waterstone, J.J., Summers, B.A., Hoskins, M.C., Berry, J. and Parsons, J.H., 'Ovarian hyperstimulation syndrome and deep cerebral venous thrombosis' *British Journal of Obstetrics and Gynaecology* 99, 1992, pp.439-440.

19. Lenton, E.A., Cooke, J.D., Hooper, M., King, H., Kumar, A., Monks, N., Turner, K. and Verma, S., '*In vitro* fertilization in the natural cycle' *Baillière's Clinical Obstetrics and Gynaecology* 6, 1992, pp.229-245.

20. Waterstone, J.J. and Parsons, J.H., 'A prospective study to investigate the value of flushing follicles during transvaginal ultrasound-directed follicle aspiration' *Fertility and Sterility* 57, 1992, pp.221-223.

21. Chen, C., 'Pregnancy after human oocyte cryopreservation' *The Lancet* 2, 1986, pp.884-886.

22. Toth, R.L., Baka, S.G., Veeck, L.L., Jones, H.W. Jr., Muasher, S. and Lanzendorf, S.E., 'Fertilization and *in vitro* development of cryopreserved human prophase 1 oocytes' *Fertility and Sterility* 61 (5), 1994, pp.891-894.

23. Carroll, J., Whittingham, D.G., Wood, M.J., Telfer, E. and Gosden, R.G., 'Extra-ovarian production of mature viable mouse oocytes from frozen primary follicles' *Journal of Reproduction and Fertility* 90, 1990, pp.321-327.

24. Gosden, R.G., Baird, D.T., Wade, J.C. and Webb, R., 'Restoration of fertility to oophorectomized sheep by ovarian autografts stored at 196°C' *Human Reproduction* 9, 1994, pp.597-603.

25. Kovacs, G.T., 'The likelihood of pregnancy with IVF and GIFT in Australia and New Zealand' *Medical Journal of Australia* 159 (9), 1 November 1993, pp.637-638.

26. Capmany, G. and Bolton, V.N., 'Polypeptide profiles of human oocytes and preimplantation embryos' *Human Reproduction* 8, 1993, pp.1901-1905.

27. Molloy, D., Harrison, K., Breen, T. and Hennessey, J., 'The predictive value of idiopathic failure to fertilize on the first *in vitro* fertilization attempt' *Fertility and Sterility* 56, 1991, pp.285-289.

28. Nagy, Z.P., Liu, J., Joris, H., Verheyen, G., Tournaye, H., Camus, M., Derde, M.-P., Devroey, P. and Van Steirteghem, A.C., 'The result of intracytoplasmic sperm injection is not related to any of the three basic sperm parameters' *Human Reproduction* 10, 1995, pp.1123-29.

29. Tournaye, H., Devroey, P., Camus, M., Valkenburg, M., Ballen, N. and Van Steirteghem, A.C., 'Zygote intrafallopian transfer or *in vitro* fertilisation and embryo transfer for the treatment of male factor infertility: a prospective randomized trial' *Fertility and Sterility* 58, 1992, pp.344-350.

30. Cf. Dawson, K.J., Conaghan, J., Ostera, G.R., Winston, R.M. and Hardy, K., 'Delaying transfer to the thrid day post-insemination, to select non-arrested embryos, increases development to the fetal heart stage' *Human Reproduction* 10 (1), 1995, pp.177-182; and Bolton, V.N., Wren, M.E. and Parsons, J.H., 'Pregnancies following *in vitro* fertilization and transfer of human blastocysts' *Fertility and Sterility* 55, 1991, pp.830-832.

31. Parsons, J.H., Bolton, V.N., Wilson, L. and Campbell, S., 'Pregnancies following *in vitro* fertilization and ultrasound directed surgical embryo transfer by perurethral and transvaginal techniques' *Fertility and Sterility* 48, 1987, pp.691-693.

32. Yovich, J.L., Yovich, J.M. and Edirisinghe, W.R., 'The relative chance of pregnancy following tubal or uterine transfer procedures' *Fertility and Sterility* 49, 1988, pp.858-864.

33. Steptoe, P.C. and Edwards, R.G., 'Birth after the reimplantation of a human embryo' *The Lancet* 2 (8085), 1978, p.366.

34. Glenister, P.H., Whittingham, D.G. and Wood, M.J., 'Genome cryopreservation: a valuable contribution to mammalian genetic research' *Genetic Research, Cambridge* 56, 1990, pp.253-258.

35. Veeck, L.L., Amundson, C.H., Brothman, L.J., DeScisciolo, C., Maloney, M.K., Muasher, S.J. and Jones, H.W. Jr., 'Significantly enhanced pregnancy rates per cycle through cryopreservation and thaw of pronuclear stage oocytes' *Fertility and Sterility* 59 (6), 1993, pp.1202-1207.

36. Botting *et al*, in Botting *et al* (eds), *op.cit.*

3. CONTROL OF HUMAN REPRODUCTION

A Clinical Perspective on Bioethical Problems

Gian Carlo Di Renzo
Centre of Prenatal Medicine
Institute of Obstetrics and Gynaecology
University of Perugia, Italy

Ermelendo V. Cosmi
II Institute of Obstetrics and Gynaecology
University of Rome "La Sapienza"
Italy

Gaetano Caserta
Centre of Prenatal Medicine
Institute of Obstetrics and Gynaecology
University of Perugia, Italy

Man's dominion in financial terms or in terms of impositions of power has already been achieved. A specific genotype can be forced on the free and casual distribution of the genes through merely financial or other authority criteria.

1. Infertility Versus Fertility

Infertility affects about 8% of people in the developed countries and about 30% of people in the developing countries, representing 500-900 million people in the world.

Infertility is a much abused term. Patients and physicians use the term in a multitude of ways, and this often interferes with proper and coherent communication. In practice, a couple with relatively normal fertility will conceive in the course of one year of regular coitus if no contraception is being used. Failure to conceive within one year of trying implies infertility, but if evidence is gathered indicating that, for all intents and purposes, conception is impossible, then the proper term is sterility.

Measuring the probability of conception per cycle is one of the more meaningful ways to evaluate the performance of couples who have undergone a particular infertility treatment. This is usually described as cycle fecundity or fecundability. However, even if the definition of fecundability is agreed on and used in assessment of infertility treatments, this parameter is a population-based measurement. It is difficult directly to

29

D. Evans (ed.), Creating the Child, 29–45.
© 1996 Kluwer Law International. Printed in the Netherlands.

apply such a measure to an individual couple.

2. Definitions of Terms Used in Human Fertility[1]

Fertile/fertility
  Capable of conceiving and bearing young
    Spontaneous conception in less than one year; usually implies progression of
    pregnancy beyond the first trimester; may imply delivery of living infants.

Sterile/sterility
  Bearing no progeny
    Incapable of conception

Infertile/infertility
  Diminished or absent fertility; does not imply as irreversible condition as sterility
    No conception in one year or more

Fecund/fecundity
  Pronounced fertility; capable of repeated fecundation (impregnation)
    Probability of achieving pregnancy each menstrual cycle; also called cycle of
    fecundity or fecundability

Prolific/prolificacy
  Bearing many children
    Number of foetuses (or living infants) per conception.

3. Assisted Reproduction Techniques

3.1. GENERAL THOUGHTS

Avoiding questions such as 'did the doctor have a right to make that decision?' and so
on, which are questions about who should decide, not whether the decision is the
morally correct one, a utilitarian (consequentialist) might decide in favour of the
treatment, a Kantian against it.

  Thus, a medical objective might be to cure infertility. Yet when *in vitro* fertilisation
or other technologies are introduced, we are in fact admitting that infertility, in the case
of a specific couple, is not curable, thus we have to have recourse to other measures.
Until recently, only legal remedy was available in such a case (i.e. adoption) for the
couple's so called right to have offspring. It is possible that it is a mistake even to
consider medical interventions into what is an existential, or a social problem, rather
than a medical one. In essence, does everybody have the right to have a child? Do
single persons? Homosexual couples? Do we 'medicalise' a complex human problem,

thus reducing it to a one-dimensional technological problem, possibly obscuring its deeper ethical and social dimensions in the process?

The use of technological interventions which are not directly indicated as a cure of a disease or the alleviation of pain, is problematic as such, aside from its specific applications. Science and technology are, by their very nature, manipulative, and manipulation reduces humans to the status of objects: a situation clearly in conflict with the respect due to the dignity of all humans. It is the latter which is deemed primary by most ethical doctrines, so the conflict is both basic and unavoidable.

With the birth of Louise Brown, in July 1978, Patrick Steptoe and Robert Edwards ushered in a new era in the management of human reproductive failure. To date, thousands of babies have been born as the result of *in vitro* fertilisation and embryo transfer (IVF-ET) and the procedure is now an important and accepted component of infertility specialists' therapeutic armory. The co-development of ancillary techniques such as embryo and gamete cryopreservation, oocyte micro-manipulation, and oocyte donation has further improved the chance of conception of the involuntarily childless couple. Further, IVF-ET has provided an unprecedented opportunity for the scientist to acquire a greater understanding of human reproductive biology, particularly in the areas of reproductive endocrinology, gamete interaction, early embryogenesis and implantation.

The problems arising from the use of so-called assisted (non-coital) human fertilisation are familiar, with controversial questions pertaining directly to medical technologies used to achieve the birth of a child. There are groups of dilemmas, such as whether legally to admit donation of gametes or embryos, whether to banish lavage, whether to punish surrogacy, advertising and negotiation, what to do with spare embryos, or whether research or experimentation on early human embryos should be left to develop within certain limits. As to maternity, the law emphasises the maxim *fructus ventrem sequitur*; that is, gestational maternity is considered decisive. This is so generally, even if an important exception may be met in surrogacy, in cases both where a surrogate gestational mother and where a surrogate mother are involved (the distinction between these two kinds of surrogacy is given below). In these cases, by a pre-conceptual agreement in writing between the parties, the mother who bears the child does not become the mother who rears it, unless the contract is refused.

Actually, several procedures and concepts in assisted reproduction are of concern:
gamete donation;
gamete cryopreservation (spare ova and sperm);
embryo cryopreservation and donation;
surrogacy, surrogate motherhood (either surrogate gestational mother or surrogate mother. The surrogate gestational mother provides only the gestational component; the surrogate mother provides both the gestational and the genetic components of reproduction);[2]
research on pre-embryos;
selective reduction of multiple pregnancy

3.2. GAMETE DONATION

3.2.1. *Sperm Donation*

The availability of sperm donors has enabled couples with refractory male factor infertility to achieve pregnancy through different procedures.

Procedural selection could be related to a woman's relative fertility and ranges from a simple approach, such as donor insemination (DI) to IVF-ET and on to procedures that combine IVF with the intrafallopian transfer of fertilised oocytes. However, the criteria for the evaluation of sperm, such as count, morphology and functional aspects required in the case of *in vivo* fertilisation are markedly different from those necessary in an IVF program, where a direct contact between the gametes, in an *in vitro* environment often allows the bypassing of some basic steps of spontaneous reproduction.

So, in some cases of male factor infertility, Assisted Reproductive Techniques (ART) and particularly the new micro-manipulation techniques might overcome the need for a donor and allow a progeny with a lineal genetic link to both partners. However, where donor gametes are employed, the use of cryo-stored donor semen rather than fresh semen is advisable, because the storage allows time to perform a complete medical screening of the donor (that must include a thorough history, physical examination, a detailed genetic and infectious disease evaluation) and to match the phenotype characteristics of the donor with the specific need of the prospective parents. Moreover, the donor can be retested for infectious diseases (HIV, Hepatitis B-C, CMV, etc.) six months later, to allow an appropriate 'window period'.

The rationale of donor semen use is that it grants the possibility of rearing a child with a genetic link to the woman and a legal one to the couple. In fact, the prospective parents must give an informed consent in writing before any procedure, so that the future infant is considered to be the legitimate child of the recipient and her consenting partner.

However, concerns about donor semen use include the following.

(a) The introduction of a third party in the exclusive couple relationship is seen by some as making it in fact comparable to adultery. However, the techniques involve no personal relationship between the woman and the donor, and the identity of the biological father is normally unknown to the mother. (It is advisable that the physicians should maintain a permanent record of contractors and resulting children.)

(b) The mother's feeling the child to be more hers than it is her partner's (her husband, for example) and the partner's experiencing a sense of inadequacy and of exclusion. This might constitute a threat to the couple's relationship or marriage.

(c) The existence of possible psychological dangers to the child. It is open to discussion whether the resulting child should or should not know the circumstances of his conception.

(d) The possibility in donor semen use of the occurrence of abnormalities in the offspring or transmission of infectious diseases to both the woman and the child. It

appears that appropriate donor screening should decrease the chances of such eventualities.

(e) The possibility of cryo-injury. This is considered separately.

(f) The possibility of the excessive use of the same donor. The danger of consanguinity dictates that a donor should not be allowed to be the father in more than ten cases. If the donation is taking place in a very restricted area, then even this figure may need appropriate reduction.

However the same techniques (especially DI) that enable infertile couples to procreate, may make pregnancy possible in the case of non-traditional couples, such as lesbian couples, and single women. Obviously, in such cases, on the one hand, male factor infertility is absent; but, on the other hand, as with heterosexual couples who require DI, a separation between sexual intercourse and reproduction already exists. But in non-traditional couples a member of one gender is lacking, thus the environment presents some differences with the conventional concept of family (the archetype of family). So, important social concerns may follow.

Further, today in Western countries, it is possible to acquire a self-insemination device that eliminates any form of control (by regulations, for example, of clinics) and gives rise to many new, unsolved questions.

To date, the use of the partner's cryo-preserved semen after his death or of sperm retrieval from the dead partner, are rare. Even if such procedures cannot be considered truly to be an example of semen donation, they resemble a form of bequest, or even, especially in the latter case where consent is absent, an embezzlement.

3.2.2. Oocyte Donation

This procedure may be used when: there is an ovarian failure (owing to premature menopause, ovarian dysgenesis or medical/surgical treatment), or when egg recovery is impossible because the ovaries are inaccessible (even though such cases are on the decrease as technology improves) because the woman suffers from genetic disorders or a resistant ovarian syndrome.

A precise timing of the menstrual cycle between the donor and the recipient is necessary in order immediately to transfer the oocyte(s) recovered. These are difficult to freeze and store, and close endometrial synchrony is also important. As compared to the case of donated semen, this leads to a greater physical and psychological involvement of the donor.

Oocyte donors may be known to the patient, as in the case of friends or relatives. Otherwise, anonymous donors are used, including women who have undergone oocyte retrieval at the time of pelvic surgery and, more commonly, IVF patients who are willing to donate excess eggs (even if, with the increased use of cryo-preservation, there will probably be fewer oocytes from this source) or volunteers who electively undergo stimulation and oocyte retrieval exclusively for the purpose of egg donation (payment induced?). Donor screening must include a thorough history and physical examination, including a detailed genetic and infectious disease evaluation identical to that used for

sperm donors. Obstetric history and blood-typing are necessary, as is a psychological assessment. Extensive counselling regarding emotional and physical risks (the latter can be present only in the cases of ovarian stimulation and oocytes retrieval for an elective donation purpose, since in the other situations the risks are exclusively related to the IVF program or to the surgical approach) and informed consent are mandatory.

There are no gestational risks to the recipient over and above the risks commonly associated with pregnancy, if the woman is within the usual range of child bearing age. However, it is important to underline the fact that obstetrical risks are an age related phenomenon, and this becomes particularly relevant for women above the normal upper limit of the human reproductive span. In such a context, special concern may be felt for the child of individuals 'mature' couples or mothers likely to be affected by age-related disabilities. Further concern for the child centres on the risk of genetic abnormalities that may be related to the age of the gamete providers. A decrease of risk can be obtained by the use of young donors.

Other unsolved questions involve the introduction of a third-party in to the couple's relationship, and the rearing responsibilities and duties after birth. A further recent worry is of infectious diseases such as HIV. To date, no practical method has been found to store, and thus quarantine, oocytes before their use (which can, by contrast, be done with donor sperm). A practical solution could be to fertilise oocytes, store the resulting pre-embryo, re-test the donor after six months, and only then undertake embryo transfer. But this suggested method may also be defective from a bioethical point of view, since it produces spare embryos.

Finally, in the face of the growing demand for donated oocytes and the relative difficulty of finding donors, there is the need to look for new possible oocyte sources. An important advance would be the *in vitro* maturation of immature human oocytes, their fertilisation and subsequent transfer. There have been cases reported of the recruitment of oocytes from unstimulated ovaries, surgically removed for gynaecological indications, being then transferred to a donor oocyte program. Obviously, the development of such a method might meet a very large demand, since even a fragment of a young woman's ovaries contains hundreds of primordial follicles. However, at present, there are some doubts as to the constancy and effectiveness of zygote development from oocytes matured in such conditions. Moreover, it has to be remembered that, when there is a gynaecological problem justifying an ovariectomy or other gynaecological intervention, the ovaries are probably already old. Gynaecological patients, that is, are usually in an age group where the genetic risk of oocyte abnormality is increased.

Another possible source of oocytes (but also of moral concerns) is the foetal ovary, which contains millions of immature oocytes (called oogonia). The use of aborted human foetal tissue in this way can be envisaged, although it is not yet known whether oogonia recovered immediately after an abortion can develop into mature oocytes. Another use for such foetal material might be to repopulate adult ovaries in a graft programme.

3.3. CRYOPRESERVATION

3.3.1. *Background*

Prior to the availability of cryopreservation, the recruitment and aspiration of multiple follicles for IVF led to a serious dilemma: how to deal with 'excess' oocytes or embryos. In cases in which more than three or four oocytes are inseminated, there is a chance that the number of embryos obtained will exceed the programme's maximum number for transfer. Here, the excess of embryos may be either transferred, with increased risk of high-order multiple gestations, or discarded. The latter option would appear, at the very least, to be wasteful. Alternatively, programmes could limit the number of embryos to three or four. This approach is also imperfect. In fact, if the percentage of eggs that fertilise is lower than expected, fewer than three embryos may be transferred, thus compromising the patient's prospects for pregnancy. Further, it is not always possible to identify the 'best' oocytes for insemination. The advent of human embryo cryopreservation has allowed programs to inseminate all oocytes, thus maximising the chances of transferring three or four healthy embryos. Any healthy concepti in excess of this number may then be frozen for eventual transfer in a future, natural cycle. This practice increases the patient's cumulative pregnancy rate per oocyte retrieval procedure.

Cryopreservation of human embryos may be performed at virtually any developmental stage, from pronuclear to blastocyst. Most efforts have concentrated on four- to eight-cell embryos. Freezing and thawing protocols differ with stage, and different cryoprotectants are used. Necessary equipment includes a controlled biologic freezer capable of cooling in increments of 0.1 to 0.5 per minute, and a liquid nitrogen supply and storage facility. The embryologist should be thoroughly familiar with cryobiology.

Cryoprotectants are agents that are used - depending on embryo stage - to replace cellular water, and thus protect the embryos from the potentially lethal effects of freezing. Cellular dehydration is necessary in order to minimise the damage caused by intracellular ice crystals formation during the freezing and thawing process. The potential applications of cryopreservation are not limited to the storage of 'excess' embryos after IVF-ET. The technique might be considered in patients who are about to undergo chemotherapy or radiation therapy for malignant neoplasia, given the high risk of ovarian failure after such treatment. Additionally, egg or embryo freezing might help to overcome some of the donor-recipient synchronisation difficulties that arise in donor egg programmes.

3.3.2. *Gamete Cryopreservation*

Sperm cryopreservation. Some pathologies (such as neoplasia) and some therapies (such as surgery, radiotherapy, and chemotherapy) may cause irreversible damage to the testes or to spermatogenesis, so that it is necessary to cryopreserve seminal fluid to make future parenthood possible. Seminal fluid cryopreservation is necessary for DI because

it allows the storage of samples from many donors over a long time.

Regarding the risk that frozen or thawed semen could suffer damage (cryo-injury) leading to the birth of babies with structural or functional abnormalities, long experience in both animal and human fields is reassuring. However, frozen/thawed semen is less efficient than fresh semen, and its use requires a more precise timing of ovulation and, sometimes, more cycles of insemination.

Oocyte Cryopreservation. Standard criteria in assisted reproduction to obtain the maximum number of oocytes for immediate and future use often result in superovulation with multiple oocyte recovery, multiple embryo transfer and multiple pregnancies. All the statistics for multiple pregnancies indicate a greater than normal risk of obstetric pathology, prematurity, low birth weight, and uterine and perinatal mortality. In the light of this, accepted practice is to use no more than three ova in either GIFT or IVF-ET programs. This fuels the problem of what should be done with the remaining oocytes or pre-embryos. Almost all assisted reproduction centres have adopted cryopreservation (mainly embryo-cryopreservation).

A different problem is present in the case of frozen/thawed eggs, that is the lack of their development after insemination and the insufficient evidence that the resulting embryos will develop normally. This is probably due to the fact that the mature oocyte is arrested at metaphase II of meiosis, when chromosomes are arranged on the microtubular spindle. This cytoskeletal architecture is temperature sensitive and its disruption may cause loss of chromosomes. Possible results are aneuploidy (polyploidy digynic), polyspermic fertilisation or inhibition of fertilisation (as a result of changes in the zona sperm receptor surface or zona hardening). So, at the present time, the use of frozen eggs is limited and there are only a few reports of successful pregnancy resulting from cryopreserved oocytes.

However, as technology advances, the theoretical advantages of oocyte storage are evident. In particular, it could be of benefit to women with malignant tumours facing chemotherapy or women who require surgical removal of ovaries. It will also help all patients requiring ova donation. From a bioethical point of view, it can constitute an important incentive to perform oocyte cryopreservation instead of fertilising and freezing the developing pre-embryos. Such a procedure might reduce the need for storage of pre-embryos, which carries special bioethical and legal problems. Finally, another indication is oocyte cryopreservation for research purposes, in order to improve our knowledge of gamete physiology. At the present time, however fertilisation and transfer of cryopreserved oocytes should be considered still to be an experimental procedure.

3.3.3. *Embryo Cryopreservation*

Embryo cryopreservation has followed the adoption of IVF programmes and the creation of spare embryos. The rationale for the use of such a technique is the storage of pre-embryos exceeding the safe number (optimal pregnancy rate per cycle/increasing

risk of multiple pregnancy) for transfer to an individual patient. Other indications, from a theoretical point of view, are: to replace the thawed pre-embryos in subsequent spontaneous cycles (without endometrial asynchrony, which may be present in the stimulated cycle - though it is unclear to what extent this procedure could improve the pregnancy rate after a transfer of a fresh embryo has just failed); decrease the number of treatment cycles (stimulated cycle) and oocyte recovery to obtain a pregnancy; allow genetic screening before implantation in order to minimise pregnancy termination and use any pre-embryos in a donation programme.

In all cases it is necessary to obtain informed consent from the couple undergoing IVF for the storage of pre-embryos, and to define a time limit for that storage. This is because of the current ignorance of the possible damage of storage, cryo-injury (although pre-embryo viability after thawing, in some cases, may be related more to the quality of the embryo before freezing and to the viability of pre-embryos in an IVF procedure, than to cryopreservation) and the related cryo-protectant embryo toxicity.

The informed consent previously mentioned should include an exhaustive discussion of such risks and the pre-freeze dispositional directives of genetic progenitors of cryo-preserved embryos, because of the legal and ethical problems that may arise, in some circumstances, if the prospective parents (the gamete providers) have died, divorced, or been separated for some other reason. In making a directive (such as transfer, discarding, donation, research programme) one decision maker should be included (the couple, or one element of the couple) who can exercise decisional authority in such cases.   However, it is rational not to store more pre-embryos than the normal reproductive span of oocyte providers (although, to date, the upper limit of the reproductive range has been easy to modify, the 'menopausal mother' being an example) and when more than the primary objective of the storage - treatment of the providers of gametes - is in force. However, it is peculiar that, when such human lives begin they are placed in a suspended state so that, in a sense, individuals are born already old. This strengthens, furthermore, the question 'who are we and where do we come from?'.

3.4. EMBRYO DONATION

The argument for embryo donation is that it allows a couple to achieve a baby, and to experience pregnancy and childbirth. It may help the same group of women who benefit from egg donation and whose husband is also infertile. It constitutes a form of prenatal adoption and should be subject to the same controls and licencing as AID, IVF and egg donation.

In the case of embryo donation, the most important concerns are related to the possibility of genetic abnormality in the pre-embryo, and to the use of a third-party (the pre-embryo) for the couple, neither of whom have a lineal genetic relation to the offspring. Other problems that arise are about maternity (who should be considered the real mother: the genetic donor or the gestational mother?) and the social and legal status of the baby (is it the product of a form of incest? does it have the right to know

its biological parents? what are its legal rights?).

3.5. SURROGACY

3.5.1. *Surrogate Gestational Mother*

This is the practice whereby one woman carries a baby for another, who will become (because of a previous agreement in writing) the social and legal mother after birth.

The 'commissioning' mother may be a woman with a severe pelvic disease or who has no uterus or who has suffered repeated miscarriages, structural abnormalities, or suffers from pathological conditions that could be seriously worsened by pregnancy such as diabetes, or hypertension, or that may lead to an interuterine environment that could be potentially harmful to the child, as diabetes may.

Utilisation, for foetal gestation, of another woman's womb matches with the common practices of the 'baliatico' of the recent past. A mother who, for whatever reason could not or would not suckle a baby, engaged a wet-nurse to suckle both her own child and the mother's, or just the latter. *Mutatis mutandis*, a woman who cannot or 'does not want' to carry a pregnancy can contract (or simply utilise) some other woman's uterus to carry the pregnancy of her own genetic child, even though the use of a surrogate gestational mother for a non-medical reason might be difficult to justify.

This separation of gestational from genetic maternity is obviously a conceptual acquisition that is going to weigh on human aspects of maternity as the figure of the wet-nurse did in the past times. May be it will be resolved in time with the creation of an artificial biotechnological uterus (not yet at an advanced stage of design) as the wet-nurse was replaced by bottle-feeding, inconceivable in the first twenty years of this century.

However, the surrogacy procedure, although easy to perform from a clinical stand point, may produce some important effects on both contractors and offspring. These may, for instance, be psychological. Particular issues that may arise include the following.

1. Health screening, of an appropriate sort, of both recipient and couple. In the latter case the screening may be comprehensive, including genetic screening.

2. Concerns of the couple about the self-care and the habits of the surrogate during pregnancy - for instance, smoking, use of alcohol, and substance abuse (with its attendant risk of transmission of infections). In fact, the surrogate mother might be less concerned about the welfare of the child than a pregnant woman who will go on to rear her own child.

3. Concerns about the surrogate generally, as a pregnant woman, and particularly, as the recipient of a pre-embryo (making it necessary to test the gamete providers for infections that could be transmittable to the gestational mother through the pre-embryo).

4. The nature of the consent obtained, which must be voluntary and informed.

5. The involvement of the gestational mother in the family relationship (the couple's

relationship) when she is a friend or relative.

6. The fear of any bonding between the gestational mother and the foetus, and concerns about any decision to keep the child.

7. The child's right to know the identity of the gestational mother, which raises the issue of the child's own identity.

8. The nature of the contract and the question of payment.

3.5.2. Surrogate Mother

A different situation is found where the recipient (the gestational mother) also provides the female gametes. In such a case, a functional need (for a substitute womb) is conjoined to genetic need (for an oocyte). The purpose is to bear a child with a genetic link only to one partner (the husband). However, it is very difficult to think of the biological (genetic and gestating) mother as a 'surrogate' mother. Even so, the term has received widespread public recognition. The procedure is easy to perform, being artificial insemination (in contrast to surrogate gestational motherhood, which involves an embryo transfer).

After birth, the rearing role is given to the couple (the woman adopts the child). There are few indications for a biological surrogacy. The case of a woman who has had an hystero-salpingectomy is the only undoubted one, but in such a case it may be asked why a pregnancy is being considered. Hystero-salpingectomy, if it is carried out on a young woman, is usually done because she has a malignant tumour; and if the tumour is benign, the woman is usually peri-menopausal.

It is noteworthy that the biological surrogate mother essentially eliminates the need for a social mother to play any biologic role in reproduction. So, in borderline cases, surrogate motherhood could constitute a mere convenience (especially where it is a payed for service) or an opportunity to adopt a child more rapidly than in a traditional adoption.

4. Research on Pre-Embryos

Fertilisation is not an event, but a complex biochemical process requiring a minimum of 24 hours to complete syngamy, that is the formation of a diploid set of chromosomes. During this process there is no commingling of maternal and paternal chromosomes within a single nuclear membrane; after this process the parental chromosomal material is commingled.

The pre-embryo is the structure that exists from the end of the process of fertilisation until the appearance of a single primitive streak. At this time some authorities believe that the completely started life is not fully formed, and it is not a genetically unique human being because of the possibility that several processes may occur.

a) The loss of concepti during the pre-embryo phase is enormous. In fact, up to two-thirds of the products of sperm-egg fusions are in some way defective.

b) In this early phase, most of the developing structure will be devoted to nourishing the subsequent embryo.

c) Any cell, up to the 4 cell state (8 cell/mouse), has the potential to become a complete entity.

d) The pre-embryo genome is activated after the 4-8 cell stage.

e) The product of fertilisation may be a tumor - a hydatidiform mole or a chorioepitelioma.

f) Twinning or chimeras may occur.

Only the appearance of a single primitive streak guarantees that an anatomical differentiation has begun, and a biological individual is in the process of formation from the pre-embryo. So, some authorities believe that, during the pre-embryonic period, it has not been determined with certainty yet that a biological individual will result. For this reason the pre-embryo having the full rights of a human person is inconsistent with biological reality. (Obviously, this is only one side of the coin, since others believe that a zygote can already constitute a human being.)

In any case, the living human pre-embryo may be said to deserve special respect, because it possesses the potential to become a human being. Hence, obvious limitations and justifications can follow. However, the purpose of this chapter is not to deal with pre-embryo research, but just to summarise some research approaches of clinical significance, such as gamete micromanipulation and preimplantation diagnosis, that is, procedures that are consistent with a subsequent transfer of a viable pre-embryo.

Concerning micromanipulation, it aims to by-pass the last steps in the process of fertilisation, that is breaking through the zona pellucida and/or the oocyte membrane. It is used where the number of spermatozoa or their penetrative capacity is limited as in the cases of oligospermia, asthenozoospermia, and cyliary dyskinesis. However, where these barriers are by-passed, so too is the last natural selection process, which may lead to increased genetic risk. Partial Zona Dissection (PZD) and Zona Drilling are selective zona disruptions, producing small holes in the zona pellucida, by mechanical and chemical agents, respectively. Probably, PZD is a more suitable method, since it doesn't harm the oocyte, while after zona drilling pre-embryo development might be impaired, although the fertilisation process itself may not be influenced. Subzona Insertion (SUZI) is the insertion of multiple sperms (usually up to ten) into the perivitelline space. Microinjection is direct injection of a sperm into the ooplasm.

The difference between the above procedures lies in the extent of the by-pass (zona and/or membrane) and hence in the level of residual selection mechanisms. Concerns about micromanipulation refer to: the consequences of trauma for the gametes or resulting concepti; a possible increased risk of pre-embryo or offspring abnormalities; the possible occurence of polispermy (although, successful microsurgical removal of the pronucleus from an polyspermic human zygote has been reported); and the likely success rate of such interventions.

Preimplantation genetic diagnosis allows for identifications of unaffected pre-embryos before transfer. It carries the same aims as later prenatal genetic diagnosis, but at an

earlier period, in order to avoid pregnancy termination and its related consequences.

There are two possible ways of performing preimplantation genetic diagnosis: one is oocyte polar body biopsy; the other is pre-embryo biopsy. The former is the only method of performing gamete analysis, although it gives information only about the maternal side. So, in this technique, the pre-embryo genotype cannot be predicted. The latter technique consists in the removal of one or more pre-embryo cells at the cleavage or blastocyst stage, which can be done without detriment to normal development, to allow genetic analysis.

The methods currently used are fluorescent in situ hybridation (FISH) to detect chromosomal structural abnormalities, and polymerase chain reaction (PCR) to detect single gene defects. However, there are X-linked pathologies where a specific gene defect has not been determined, so the only screening approach is the idenfication of sex, by PCR or FISH methods, and the exclusive transfer of female pre-embryos (although, in this way 50% of male normal-unaffected pre-embryos are lost or eliminated). It is reasonable to offer the methods of sex selecting a child before fertilisation to couples who have good medical reasons for making such a selection, but it would be unethical if such methods were to be made available for any couple and selection were made on purely social grounds.

5. Selective Reduction of Multiple Pregnancies

Selective termination has been considered in multi-foetal gestations with more than four or five foetuses and in multiple pregnancies bearing one anomalous foetus. (A quadruplet pregnancy could be deemed an ART failure and it has been recommended that no more than three oocytes or pre-embryos be transferred per cycle.)

6. Counselling

All infertility problems require genetic counselling.

The very existence of genetic screeening and counselling encourages a culture which puts pressure on individuals to make particular reproductive decisions. Within such a culture, a number of issues and questions come to be of significance.

What counts as a genetic disorder.

The extent to which counsellors should be non-directive.

Whether abortion counts as a treatment.

To what extent an informed choice is possible for clients, taking into account the problems associated with perception of risk.

Whether there is a right to genetic information when no useful results can be achieved by imparting it, in relation to either unifactorial or multifactorial conditions.

Whether there is a right to remain ignorant.

Whether there is an obligation to tell someone that he or she has a genettic

predisposition to developing a late onset disease such as Huntington's chorea, or a
disease which has some environmental cause which may be avoidable.

At what point in time information should be conveyed e.g. childhood, adolescence.

Whether confidentiality should be respected with regard to, for example, non-paternity.

Whether there should be limits on reproductive autonomy, and if so on what grounds.

Possibly relevant issues also include the following. First, the consideration of the
welfare of future children and the economic and social costs of caring for individuals
suffering from genetic disease. Second, the extent to which it is possible to be
concerned for genetic public health without adopting discredited eugenic policies.
Third, the question whether people own their own genes, and if so, in what sense.

Ethical issues that arise here include:

a) for whose benefit such programmes would be carried out;

b) whether the potential benefits would outweigh the potential harms and how these
should be assessed. In particular, it may not be possible for the same criteria to be
used to evaluate prenatal screening, screening of newborns, and screening of adults.
In the case of prenatal populations, for example, it is not clear who is being served;

c) whether widespread genetic screening would lead to genetic reductionism and
genetic determinism;

d) to what extent there is potential for discrimination against groups on the grounds
of their genetic make-up.

7. Some Problems Arising From Control of Human Reproduction

People may be astonished that, on the one hand, doctors and couples are fighting to
force ovulation and/or the meeting between oocyte and sperm when, on the other, they
try to do their best to avoid or to stop it.

On this line lies the problem of abortion. The possibility given by amniocentesis of
making preterm analysis of diseases leading to severe handicaps, has opened the way
to abortion as an intervention legally accepted for eugenic purposes.

The situations in which voluntary termination of pregnancy is provided by law are
three. First, to save the mother's life and physical and psychic health (therapeutic
abortion). Second, to avoid the birth of an abnormal child (eugenic abortion). And
third, to avoid negative socio-economic and emotional consequences for the woman
arising from the birth of an unwanted child (abortion for social reasons). In this last
field, one can include: situations in which the pregnancy comes from rape or incest;
situations of illegitimacy, mainly among teenagers; conditions of deprivation or mental,
moral or cultural incapacity to rear children; conditions of psychological rejection of the
pregnancy, at the basis of which lie very different emotional reactions, that should be
evaluated and discussed very carefully with the woman in question.

In this case, the physician should evaluate, in addition to any physical damage coming
from an unwanted pregnancy, even the psychological damage resulting for the woman
to whom abortion is denied, and for the child who will be born unwanted. It is

necessary to think about the interpersonal relationships between the parents and their attitude towards an unwanted child.

Abortion has been for a long time the most widespread and frequent method of birth regulation in history, and is certainly less traumatic than the exposure or abandoning of the newborn, still practised in some so-called civilised populations. Today, more than 70% of the world population lives in countries in which abortion for reasons connected to health is allowed. It is necessary, however, to think about the fact that this procedure often represents a solution to the failure of public promotional campaigns for the use of anticonceptional drugs. Given this, women that come to want these services should not condemn themselves. It is even possible to foresee many selective or fashionable selective interventions wanted both by parents and society. It is obviously important to ask oneself how far it is ethically correct and to what extent these choices will affect the forthcoming generations' characteristics.

Moreover, inserting new genes, done experimentally even on terminally ill human patients, has opened the way to potentials never thought of before, to control or transform in an unlimited way the physical characteristics of our descendants.

Notes

1. These definitions are taken from *Stedman's Medical Dictionary* Baltimore, Wellmans and Wilkins, 1972.

2. Ethics Committee of the American Fertility Society 'Ethical considerations of assisted reproductive technologies' *Fertility and Sterility* 62 (5), Supplement 1, 1994, pp.67-69.

References

Braude, P., Bolton, V. and Moore, S., 'Human gene expression first occurs between the four and eight-cell states of preimplantation development' *Nature* 33, 1988, pp.459-461.

Cosmi, E.V., 'Assisted procreation: general data and ethical problems' *International Conference on Bioethics* Francia, Rambouillet Cesta, 1985, pp.231-233.

Dawson, K., 'Fertilization and moral status: a scientific perspective' *Journal of Medical Ethics* 13, 1987, pp.10-15.

Djerassi, C., 'Fertility awareness: jet-age rhythm method?' *Science* 48, 1990, pp.1061-2.

Edwards, R. and Steptoe, P., *A Matter of Life* London, Sphere, 1981.

Evans, M.I. and Dixler, A.O., 'Human *in vitro* fertilization. Some legal issues' *Journal of the American Medical Association* 245, 1981, pp.23-24.

Ford, N., *When Did I Begin?* Cambridge University Press, Cambridge, 1988.

Genazzani, A.R., Artini, P.G. and Droghini, F., 'Ethical considerations of assisted reproductive technologies' in Cosmi, E.V., and Di Renzo, G.C. (eds), *Bioethics in Research and Society* Pisa, Giardini Pbl, 1994, pp.63-70.

Haderka, J.F., 'Medical assisted procreation and legal questions of parenthood' *Global Bioethics* 5, 1992, pp.1-14.

Hammond, M.G. and Talbert, L.M., *Infertility: A Practical Guide for the Physician* second edition, Oradell N.J., Medical Economics Books, 1985.

Harvey, J.C., 'Ethical issues and controversies in assisted reproductive technologies' *Current Opinions in Obstetrics and Gynecology* 41, 1992, pp.5-12.

Hull, M.G.R., Glazener, C.M.A., Kelly, N.J., *et al.*, 'Population study of causes treatment and outcome of infertility' *British Medical Journal* 291, 1985, pp.1693-1695.

Iglesias, T., '*In vitro* fertilization. The major issues' *Journal of Medical Ethics* 10, 1984, pp.36-40.

Jones, H.W., 'The ethics of *in vitro* fertilization' *Fertility and Sterility* 37, 1982, pp.146-155.

Jones, H.W., 'Ethical and moral issues of assisted reproduction' *Annals of the New York Academy of Science* 626, 1991, pp.605-611.

Laufer, N., Tarlatzis, B.C. and Naftolin F., '*In vitro* fertilization: State of the art' *Seminars in Reproductive Endocrinology* 2, 1984, pp.197-210.

McLaren, A., 'Research on early human embryos from *in vitro* fertilization (IVF): The Warnock recommendations' *British Journal of Obstetrics and Gynaecology* 92, 1985, pp.305-307.

Menken, J. and Larsen, U., 'Fertility rates and aging' in Mastroianni L. and Paulsen C.A. (eds), *Ageing, Reproduction and the Climacteric* New York, Plenum, 1986, pp.147-162.

Olive, D.L. and Haney, A.F., 'Endometriosis-associated infertility: a critical review of therapeutic approaches' *Obstetrics and Gynecological Survey* 41, 1986, pp.538-541.

Quigley, M.M. and Andrews, L.B., 'Human *in vitro* fertilization and the law' *Fertility and Sterility* 42, 1984, pp.348-359.

Robertson, J.A., 'Ethical and legal issues in preimplantation genetic screening' *Fertility and Sterility* 57, 1992, pp.1-11.

Rosenwaks, Z., 'Donor eggs: their application in modern reproductive technologies' *Fertility and Sterility* 47, 1987, pp.895-909.

Rosenwaks, Z., Veeck, L.L. and Liu, H.C., 'Pregnancy following transfer of *in vitro* fertilized donated oocytes' *Fertility and Sterility* 45, 1986, pp.417-420.

Serr, D.M., 'The moral and ethical challenge of *in vitro* fertilization' in Papadia, G., Dodero, D. and Campana, A. (eds), *Bimbi del Futuro* Bologna, Monduzzi Pbl, 1985, pp.99-107.

Shushan, A. and Schenker, J.G., 'The use of oocytes obtained from aborted fetuses in egg donation programs' *Fertility and Sterility* 62, 1994, pp.449-451.

Singer, P. and Dawson, K., 'IVF technology and the argument from potential' *Philosophy and Public Affairs* 17, 1988, pp.87-104.

Singer, P., *Practical Ethics* Cambridge University Press, Cambridge, 1979

Trounson, A., 'Preservation of human eggs and embryos' *Fertility and Sterility* 46, 1986, pp.1-12.

Warnock, M., *A Question of Life* Oxford, Basil Blackwell Ltd., 1984.

Winston, R.M.L. and Handyside A.H., 'New challenges in human *in vitro* fertilization' *Science* 260, 1993, pp.932-936.

4. THE CLINICAL CLASSIFICATION OF INFERTILITY

Donald Evans
Centre for Philosophy and Health Care
University of Wales, Swansea
Singleton Park
Swansea
Wales

1. The Dangers of Generalising

'Every lion is different', explained an acknowledged expert in assisting the reproduction of lions. Mr. Flood, a keeper of lions at Dublin zoo was said never to have lost a cub. He was accounting for his secret of success which he had summed up in two words only, 'understanding lions'. One might venture to suggest that those asked to provide assisted conception services to people would do well to remember his words, for what is perhaps surprisingly true of lions is more manifestly true of persons.

John Wisdom has used the example of Mr. Flood to illustrate the way in which philosophical activity can turn out to restrict understanding:[1]

> … The trouble is that the concepts, without which we do not connect one thing with another, are apt to become a network which confines our minds. We need to be at once like someone who has seen much and forgotten nothing, and also like one who is seeing everything for the first time.

So, he points out, the Dublin zoo-keeper brought his great experience with many lions to bear on his understanding of any particular lion but always remained free to see that lion for itself.

With respect to the philosophical literature devoted to a clarification of the concept of human need it is most certainly true that comparisons made between one thing and another have led many writers to talk in general terms about what it is that people as people need. Insofar as this is true I shall contend that our understanding of health care needs may well be restricted by such considerations. Infertility in particular may be a condition which either ranks low on lists of health care needs or even drops off such lists altogether where such philosophical analysis informs resource allocation models.

In posing the question 'Is infertility a health need?' I am seeking further clarification. It is not my intention to ignore general accounts of human need that have been promulgated. However I shall be concerned to emphasise the dangers of seeking an answer in a general theory and to preserve a respect for particulars.

47

D. Evans (ed.), Creating the Child, 47–63.

Of course, the generality of the question invites a general answer. Moreover, the pressures on health care providers to prioritise services encourage blanket-type responses to such queries. How much more attractive to managers is an ostensibly objective matrix in which conditions can be categorised, ranked and evaluated, than an untidy and apparently *ad hoc* approach to determining what shall or shall not be offered to individual patients. However, the uncritical deployment of general theoretical models of allocation does violence to the needs of patients and is morally questionable.

2. The Peculiar Candidature of Infertility

Before proceeding to the question I have posed it is worth pointing out that there are some peculiarities attaching to the condition of infertility as a candidate for treatment as a health need. For example, together with a limited range of recognised health needs, the majority of treatments offered for the condition do not in fact treat the condition at all but rather circumvent it. The infertile person is enabled biologically to parent a child but remains as infertile after the procedure as before. For example, though tubal surgery may resolve a woman's infertility, in that she will be enabled to conceive naturally thereafter, the procedure of IVF does nothing to alter the ability of the woman to conceive naturally. For the vast majority of women treated this is not a very important consideration as their concern in seeking treatment is usually to be enabled to bear a child rather than to restore normal reproductive functioning. It would be rare indeed for a woman to simply wish to become fertile and not wish to conceive a child, though one can imagine situations where this would be so. Then again methods of resolving infertility or sub-fertility in men would also rarely be designed to restore fertility. Indeed most procedures which fall under the umbrella of infertility therapies are designed to resolve the problem of childlessness rather than infertility. This has extremely important implications which we shall examine later.

Further, in the case of infertility we are faced with a unique possibility. Neither partner of a given relationship may be technically infertile. Yet together they may be incapable of achieving a pregnancy. In other words, whilst neither can be said to 'suffer' from the condition, neither is biologically dysfunctional in this sense, taken together they are reproductively dysfunctional. Thus they may be said to have a fertility problem though neither, individually, can be said to have the problem. Whilst I can think of possible scenarios in psychological therapy where such paradoxes arise I cannot think of any other biological example. This kind of situation highlights the issue of consent of both partners in a relationship to seek therapy though that issue is, of course, also very important in the execution of assisted conception procedures in cases where one partner is infertile.

A further related oddity in infertility treatments is found where the alleged treatments involve the use of donor gametes. The biological problems of the couple are circumvented by compromising the biological contribution of one, or both, of the partners. In the case of uses of donor oocytes the mother's biological role is reduced.

In the case of use of donor sperm the 'father's' biological role is dispensed with. It is rather odd then to regard such treatments as treatments of his infertility.

We may make one final observation about the oddity of infertility as a candidate for health need status. Whilst for many the condition is a source of much grief and is properly said to be suffered, for others it is a blessing. Indeed fertility is regarded as a health problem by many. This is generally recognised in health services throughout the world where sterilisation procedures are commonly offered. It is not easy to think of other biological conditions which are open to such rival perceptions. I suppose some, like sickle cell anaemia, which may be advantageous, on balance, in some geographical settings whilst simply a disadvantage in others, may bear some resemblance. However there are crucial differences which we shall see are important. In short, in the case of fertility and infertility there is no common measure which can help us determine when it is proper to regard one or other condition as an advantage or a disadvantage.

3. Theories of Human Need

Let us now turn to the question of whether or not infertility should be classified as a health need. The character of attention we pay to other human beings is a matter of moral import. This attention is manifested in the kinds of judgements we make of them and in our responses to them. It is not something which we may ever make explicit to ourselves but it is, nonetheless, something for which we are morally responsible.

Such attitudes may surface in philosophical theorising even when we are ostensibly seeking or promulgating a neutral account of human nature. They most certainly appear in health planning policies which embody assessments of peoples' needs. Perhaps the most general features of such accounts are the most difficult to acknowledge as betraying moral views and as undermining their purported claim to neutrality. The feature I have in mind is, perhaps, the most ubiquitous of all, namely, the generality of such accounts. Theories or allocation models which talk of man as man show a disrespect for the particularity of persons which tends to do violence to the assessment of needs of those who fall within their scope. Some writers of this kind wear their hearts on their sleeves - perhaps none more so than Jacques Maritain[2] who writes:

...I am taking it for granted that you admit that there is a human nature, and that this human nature is the same in all men. I am taking it for granted that you also admit that man is a being gifted with intelligence, and who, as such, acts with understanding of what he is doing, and therefore with the power to determine for himself the ends which he pursues. On the other hand, possessed of a nature, being constituted in a given, determinate fashion, man obviously possesses ends which correspond to his natural constitution and which are the same for all - as all pianos, for instance, whatever their particular type and in whatever spot they may be, have as their end the production of certain attuned sounds. If they do not

produce these sounds they must be tuned, or discarded as worthless.

But who is to determine what is or is not the function or end of man? And who could claim plausibly that such a determination is value neutral? A brief reflection will show that the analogy he employs is morally offensive to many, if not most. An artifact made to fulfil an identifiable function is judged according to its effectiveness. A piano which cannot be tuned cannot fulfil its function. It is not a good piano unless the fault can be rectified. Of course it may not be discarded because other functions are found for it, or because it is aesthetically pleasing as a visual object, or it is of historical or sentimental value and so on. But as a piano it is no good and merits no consideration. The space it occupies, the expense it may incur, the worries it may bring cannot be justified. It is fit for the breaker's yard. From time to time people have been similarly assessed but such episodes of our history are not sources of pride or even matters of mere note. The employment of such an analogy as a means of identifying the needs people have is clearly not morally indifferent.

We find the temptation to generalise in this way in theories of ethics, some of which have been influential in the formulation of resource allocation policy. They have been neatly described as theories which assert that our moral views and judgements are of types rather than of particulars.[3] Diamond emphasises the importance of the imaginative life in making moral judgements which involves an openness of response to the human world:

Moral judgements are not here seen as abstractly true or false, true or false out of connection with their life on their occasions of use, their rootedness then in the heart, the imaginative life, of the person who thinks the thought or makes the moral judgement.[4]

She illustrates such imaginative activity by reference to Wordsworth's description of the tender scene in which he saw a labourer cradle his sickly child in his brawny arms:

He held the child, and, bending over it
As if he were afraid both of the sun
And of the air which he had come to seek,
He eyed it with unutterable love.

Experiences of this sort, not the framing of general rules, in other words the moral psychology of the perceiver, is bound up with his conception of the dignity and fulness of human life. What the framing of general rules tends to do is blunt the edge of moral sensitivity; it presses the particular into the general mould and blinds us to important possibilities. This is certainly true of Utilitarian views which have probably been most influential as an intellectual background to current resource allocation theories.

I can best emphasise the importance of sensitivity to the individual life in the making of moral judgements by means of a final reference to Diamond's paper which links with

Wisdom's observation with which I began.[5] She quotes the poem of Walter de la Mare entitled 'Ducks'. Having delineated various types of duck such as the Tufted, the Labrador and the Goldeneye, he writes:

All these are kinds. But every Duck
Himself is, and himself alone:
Fleetwing, arched neck, webbed foot, round eye,
  And marvellous cage of bone.
Clad in this beauty a creature dwells
Of sovran instinct, sense and skill;
Yet secret as the hidden wells
  Whence Life itself doth rill.

The child, for whom the poem is written, is taught to respond to an individual life - the particular duck which is himself. This is very different from a response to a type of creature, and more demanding of the perceiver. How much more demanding are such responses to individual human lives, the kind of response we have to people we know, our lovers, our children, our friends. Yet, Diamond points out, it is such response to particularity which informs the urgency we see in the rescue of a stranger:

The urgency we see in the rescue may be tied to a sense of each person being who he is, with his one life. There are situations in which we keep from ourselves this awareness of the individual life of people whom we do not know, precisely because of the kind of difficulties such realization can create for us, for example in official roles.

How revealing this is in the context of health policies where decision making is moved away from the clinician to the manager, a move from the particular to the abstract, from knowledge of the patient as a person to the processing of the patient as a type.

In identifying human needs philosophers have succumbed to just this temptation and this has shaped proposals of how priorities should be set in health care. This, as we shall see, has an important bearing on how infertility is regarded. As we have already noted, in Maritain's assertion, one way of identifying the needs of something is to identify a function that something has. A knife will need to be sharp if it is to cut well; a motor will need fuel if it is to drive a machine, and so on. One short route then, it may be thought, to identifying human need would be to elicit some end of man as man.

4. A Biological Model

Nowhere in the context of the Philosophy of Medicine has the identification of a goal of man as man been attempted more heroically than by Christopher Boorse.[6] His position promises to tell us much about a possible answer to our question regarding the

status of infertility. He argues that health is not an evaluative notion and that a value-free science of health is possible. In the course of his thesis he conceives of man, fundamentally, as a biological organism. The goals of any organism are not difficult to identify from its biological design. Indeed the higher level goals of survival and reproduction turn out to be those goals in terms of which the functioning of each component part of the organism are assessed. These he calls the apical goals of an organism. Theoretical health, therefore, becomes functional normality which is "strictly analogous to the mechanical condition of an artifact".[7] Disease then is an objective biological term with no ethical import constituted by an unnatural deficiency in the functional efficiency of the body. Illnesses, on the other hand, are a sub-class of diseases having normative features - they are conditions disvalued by the sufferer and thus the term illness is inapplicable to non-humans. Importantly, then, both the theoretical and the practical concepts of health are disease orientated and are rooted in the nature of the species - in the nature of man as man.

However, Boorse is reluctant to talk of health needs. In fact the assertion that his concept of health is value free prevents us reading any implication of need into disease conditions, for it prevents us assuming that health is desirable *per se*. The value of health is nothing but the conformity to an excellent species design, and biological normality is, for Boorse, an instrumental rather than an intrinsic good.[8] Thus it is only in the context of the desires of individuals that their needs can be determined - they do not, after all, belong to man as man. Thus, despite its promise for those who wish to regard infertility as a health need, Boorse's account of human nature establishes no such thing.

Yet even he acknowledges that man is a social being. "It must be conceded that *Homo Sapiens* is a social species", he writes.[9] He does not attempt a universal account of human nature in these terms but where he wisely demurs others have been more ambitious. They have attempted to identify certain basic needs which are contrasted with needs created by the adoption of certain ends. This distinction between basic and instrumental needs is supposed to make the important separation between needs and demands or desires, and also between objective and subjective needs - whatever that distinction is supposed to come to. Let us look at some examples and see whether this quest for the holy grail of basic needs holds out any promise of an acceptable universal account of human nature in terms of which we can categorise the condition of infertility.

5. Human Good and Harm

Philippa Foot has attempted to underpin the whole of morality by an account of human needs, that is, by an account of what all men want, which in turn depends on what they need.[10] She has performed a valuable service to moral philosophy by showing that there are logical limits to what can be regarded as a moral principle or a moral concern. As there are internal relations between an emotion like pride and possible objects of that emotion, between descriptions like dangerous and possible subjects of such descriptions,

so there is an internal relation between moral commendation and its objects. Unless a principle is somehow related to a family of concepts, including concepts such as honesty, murder, stealing, ostentation and treachery, then we are justified in asking why such a principle is to be regarded as a moral principle at all. Similarly if we are interested in whether something is a legitimate object of moral concern and we cannot relate it in any way to the concepts of human good and harm we can make no sense of it as a moral concern. The concept of need is clearly a matter of moral concern as it can be so related without difficulty. Thus it might be sufficient justification of my action towards others to point out that they needed the assistance I rendered to them.

All of this is very helpful as it rules out the possibility of principles being adopted, or objects or states being desired, as a matter of whim standing as candidates for moral status. There are limits to what it makes sense to say in morality and they are objective insofar as they reside not in the individual but in the form of life, the social environment of the persons concerned. Thus she asserts:

> It is surely clear that moral virtues must be connected with human good and harm, and that it is quite impossible to call anything you like good or harm. ... It would be ... odd if someone were supposed to say that harm had been done to him because the hairs of his head had been reduced to an even number.[11]

Clearly then, on her account, no one could claim plausibly that he has a need to have an even number of hairs upon his head. And surely she is right.

However Foot is concerned to do more than point out the general limits of moral discourse. She wishes to harden them into a positive theory of ethics and tries to do so by positing a positive theory of human nature. Might not there be features of our experience which carry the same inescapable significance for us all? Might there not be needs which we all share by virtue of our being human? Her answer to these questions is a firm yes. The fact of human nature she develops most interestingly, from our point of view, is the need to avoid injury.[12] What counts as physical injury is clear to everyone who uses the word. It involves the impairment of some or other function. So there are pretty narrow limits to the notion of injury which enable us to empirically identify cases without dispute. Further, injury is necessarily a bad thing, and this can be shown by reference to what all men want which, in turn, can be shown by reference to what all men need. Thus to show that some course of action will lead to injury is necessarily to give a reason for not pursuing such a course. Freedom from injury is part of what constitutes human good and harm. If the whole body of elements making up such features of human life was formulated it would show us what all men *qua* men really needed.

Such an enterprise is destined to fail. As far as injury **always** counting as a reason against an action goes, it has been shown that this thesis is false.[13] There may be cases where considerations of injury may be thought to be quite irrelevant to whether or not one should pursue a course of action. Maybe the action is far too important for such considerations to come into play. Here we are not simply considering situations where

there is an incidental gain derived out of injury. Rather they are cases where the business of injury carries absolutely no weight whatever in the deliberations. It does not constitute a negative element to be weighed against advantages produced by the action. This suggests that there are rival notions of human good and harm and that far from it being true that human good and harm, determined by what all men need, determine what moral beliefs they will espouse, it is rather the case that what moral beliefs men espouse determine what they regard as really good and really harmful, and thus what they really need.[14]

The concept of factuality then is more complex than Foot allows. Various data may be given various weightings by observers according to what they think is important. This will have the result of producing different descriptions of situations, including descriptions of need. These are not factual in a non-evaluative sense of course. The social context of this relation between description and evaluation has been well expressed by Stuart Hampshire as follows:

> Every reflective person has had the experience of oscillating between two possible descriptions of his own conduct, whether it is actual conduct or only envisaged conduct; one *correct* description makes the conduct acceptable and not to be despised, and the other *correct* description mentions features of the conduct which make it morally questionable and regrettable. Two competing ways of life, between which a man chooses, explicitly or implicitly, may impose different descriptions on the same envisaged conduct, which may emerge as prohibited in virtue of the descriptions relevant to one way of life and as positively required within another way of life.[15]

The context of the way of life of a person, a social context, may similarly produce rival identifications of what a person needs. It is not surprising, therefore, that what Hampshire calls "correct descriptions" may well conflict.

Foot herself is somewhat drawn to such a position in some of her writings. Indeed we shall notice that other writers who espouse talk of human needs *per se* are similarly drawn though, together with Foot, they do not give full weight to what they concede is an important aspect of man's being, namely his social identity. Foot, indeed, comes near to finding a role for the imagination in identifying moral concerns reminiscent of Diamond's position mentioned earlier when she writes:

> In conclusion it is worth remarking that moral arguments break down far more often than philosophers tend to think, but that the breakdown is of a different kind. When people argue about what is right, good, or obligatory, or whether a certain character trait is or is not a virtue, they do not confine their remarks to the adducing of facts which can be established by simple observation, or by some clear-cut technique. What is said may well be subtle or profound, and in this sort of discussion of character, much depends on experience and imagination. It is quite common for one man to be unable to see what the other is getting at, and

this sort of misunderstanding will not be resolvable by anything which could be called argument in the ordinary sense.[16]

Now what are we to make of this somewhat startling admission? Is she saying simply that actual moral assessments are more intricate than the model she has been considering? This is rather doubtful for argument in the ordinary sense is sufficient to clarify subtleties and complexities. Rather, the difficulties are seen to lie somehow in the role of the facts which are thought to be relevant to moral conclusions. What straightforwardly establishable facts add up to for one person may not correspond to what they come to for another, and one person may not understand another's construction upon the data. This may be true of whether infertility, for example, is regarded as an important need or even a need at all by a given individual.

6. Basic Needs

But may there not be *some* needs which all men have *qua* men, though others may vary from person to person and be relative to various times and places? This is a recurring theme in the literature. For example Braybrooke[17] identifies what he thinks is a class of needs which if experienced by any individual endanger the normal functioning of that person considered as a member of a natural species. These needs are contrasted with needs created by adopted projects of individuals. Significantly, however, he allows for needs which individuals may have by virtue of their temperament. But can such a distinction between *course-of-life* needs and *adventitious* needs bear the weight it is meant to do? I think not.

We have already observed in a critique of Foot that an impairment of normal functioning need not be a matter of importance to an individual. Additionally, we should note that it is impossible to draw a clear line between *course-of-life* and *adventitious* needs. Would infertility rank as one of the former or one of the latter group? For those whose temperament identifies as a key feature of human existence the reproduction of their own kind infertility would rank as a *course-of-life* need. We shall see in a moment that such a view is intelligible in terms of the social milieu of the subject. However, for those who regard biological parenthood as an option infertility will constitute an *adventitious* need. Such a distinction may make a great deal of difference in prioritising the needs of individuals. It would certainly be potentially harmful to the former group to assume that because such a need was not universally perceived it was therefore not one which should rank highly in a health policy. For those for whom few other considerations were more important such a policy would be morally deficient.

MacCloskey[18] is even more ambivalent in his treatment of basic needs. Whilst, on the one hand, he wants to hold on to the idea of basic human needs, i.e. "the needs of men as men, and the individual needs of particular persons as the unique persons they are (and not as holders of roles or stations)", specific needs which he ranks as secondary

arise out of the fact that "certain social, quasi-natural roles such as those of mother, father, parent become basic to the fabric of most human social organisations, as well as some which are basic only to certain social organisations".[19]

It is not at all clear what the claim to 'natural' status comes to. Certainly the social institutions in terms of which individual perceptions, emotions, desires and identities are created - i.e. persons as opposed to organisms - have a history which predates the individuals concerned and which, in this sense, may be said to have a reality beyond that of the person whose reality is, in turn, realised in terms of them. If this is accepted then the impossibility of biological parenthood may well be seen as a need of individual persons as the unique persons they are. MacCloskey is partially aware of this tension in his account for whilst, on the one hand, he rejects what he calls "social and cultural relativity", he acknowledges, on the other, that "the natural development of man, like that of the oaks, is determined in part by their environment which is both physical and social. This affects what is natural and hence what constitutes a need".[20]

So here we see more than one possible source of variation in the identity of infertility as a need. First, some societies may have developed an institution of the family making infertility or barrenness a source of grief and even shame, a failure of an important kind. Others may have quite different familial concepts. Thus to imagine, for example, that for Sara, the wife of Abram, and for a 'liberated' woman of a twentieth century western society the status of infertility as a need must be common to them *qua* women is to strain the boundaries of intelligibility. Second, some societies are less homogeneous than others. They contain a large variety of social movements and institutions to which individuals have varied allegiances. Moreover some of those institutions may be undergoing quite rapid change - as is the institution of the family in many European countries. Thus the perceptions and awarenesses of individuals vary greatly within such societies, given the mix of social movements passing through them and the flux each of these movements may be subject to between individuals. Thus, as Foot rightly suspected, individuals see and understand different worlds. This reversal of the relationship between the identity of human needs and the concept of human nature from that at the heart of the enterprises of the 'basic needs' theorists is well expressed by Peter Winch in his paper on human nature:

A child is born within, and grows up into the life of, a particular human society. He learns to speak and to engage in various kinds of activity in relation to other people. In the course of these activities he encounters problems of extremely diverse kinds, problems which change in character as he matures, and problems that bring him into new kinds of relations with other people. Along with this development there comes a growth in his understanding of what constitute problems and difficulties for them. This growing understanding manifests itself in the way he comes to treat people in the course of his daily life, which will include a development in his ideas of what is permissible in his treatment of them and what is ruled out. This growth in his understanding of other people through his dealings with them is at the same time a growth in his understanding of

himself, which is in its turn a development of the kind of person he is.[21]

Hence the imposition of one world view on a population in the form of a uniform and inflexible set of health care provisions which are based on some majority view or some ideological theory of needs is morally insensitive. Yet this we see constantly occurring in various kinds of 'maximisation of benefit' models of resource allocation in health care.

It is for reasons such as those outlined above that I have elsewhere resisted the proposal to reject the need for products of assisted conception procedures to know the identity of their biological progenitors on the grounds that the 'need' is socially induced.[22] Katherine O'Donovan had proposed that as this 'need to know' was socially induced we ought rather to be concentrating our efforts on changing society's attitude to the importance of the blood relationship and so preserve the anonymity of donors.[23] This prescribed activity is presumably designed to induce the establishment of a different need as the needs of the infertile, for treatment or for secrecy, may equally well be conceived of as being socially constructed. That a need is socially constructed, however, does nothing to disvalue it. One might well ask, in view of my earlier discussion, what human need is not socially constructed. If the importance of socially induced needs for the provision of medical treatment are to be denied then we shall have to deny treatments designed to produce longevity, physical grace and even the avoidance or palliation of pain.

I hope then to have established that no general theory of human needs entitles us to reject, or indeed establish, the status of infertility as a health need. I have, in the course of my argument, shown how, for some, the condition of infertility can certainly be conceived of as a need, and indeed a need of a fundamental kind.

7. Health Planning Policies

I have also warned against health policies which trade on assumptions of a general nature in not offering fertility therapies. I realise, of course, that in health planning general policies have to be adopted. Certain matters are properly taken into account in this context such as the incidence of a condition and the demand for treatment, though in the latter case care needs to be taken to ensure that low levels of demand are not themselves due to the failure of provision or of education of the public about what is possible in medicine.

However we find that other, less desirable, features sometimes determine the levels of service to be provided, and even whether assisted conception services be provided at all. Some of these have figured in the foregoing theories as assumptions which we have called into question. Consider one example. In an interesting paper[24] on the rationing of *in vitro* fertilisation the authors compare the reasons given by three purchasing authorities in the United Kingdom for refusing to purchase the service with the reasons given by three authorities for their decision to purchase the service. One

authority refused to purchase the service on the basis that the people demanding the service were not ill. Those who opposed the decision argued that the mental stress of being infertile should be taken into account. Both sides of the dispute therefore accepted a model of health needs which was illness orientated. But why should infertility not be regarded as a serious health need on other grounds? This question was answered unequivocally by two of the authorities who decided to purchase the service. One noted that in addition to psychological harm that may be caused by the condition marital difficulties often result. This authority attached great significance to the role of the family. A further authority recognised subfertility as a health problem with very definite physiological, psychological, and social implications.

8. Infertility as a Clinical Need

Having established the possibility of regarding infertility as a human need we still have some difficulties to address in its classification as a condition which is the concern of health care providers. First, why should such a need be regarded as a clinical need at all?

In order to answer this question let us consider the difference between two senses of having a need. All human beings have need of oxygen in the sense that without it they cannot survive. Yet few human beings have the need to be supplied with oxygen by others, or indeed to make extraordinary provision of it for themselves. It is as free and available as the air they breathe. Others may be said to need oxygen in the more urgent sense of needing to be provided with it either because their situation threatens the supply of it, as when they are buried in an avalanche for example, or when their physical or mental condition is such that they are unable to inhale adequate supplies though it may be freely available in the air about them. It is only those having a need in the latter sense who may be said to have a need which calls for a remedy.

However the classification of clinical needs cannot be drawn quite as widely as this, because the remedy of the need might not lie in any kind of treatment of the person. It may, for example, lie in education or in environmental measures. For instance, a lack of oxygen may be produced by pollution which in the long term damages people's lungs. Their health may therefore be preserved or improved by treating their environment rather than by treating them. Thus a possible lack of oxygen might denote, in such a case, a health need rather than a clinical need. The well-being of the person is ensured by such a measure or, alternatively, for example, by education about the hazards of smoking. A similar point can be made about childlessness. A husband who resolves his wife's childlessness by impregnating her in the normal way cannot be said to be offering clinical treatment. Where the need cannot be so met however the use of clinical means comes into the picture. The woman in question might not be infertile but might wish to conceive a child by other than normal means for various reasons. Or she, or her partner might be infertile, or they might together be infertile and desire help to produce a child of their own. It is hard to see why, where treatments

are possible, we can decline to identify the need as a clinical need. This is not to say that we rank the various conditions cited in any particular way. Neither is it to say anything about the priority which should be given to such clinical needs. It is simply to point out that the description is a proper one.

This leads to an interesting practical problem. Where such a need can be met by a variety of clinical means there may be various classifications. These will be determined by the character of the treatment called for: surgical, medical, psychological or whatever. When the need can be met by more than one of these modes of care, or by a combination of them only, can the patient be said to have both psychological, medical and surgical needs? And how should any priority, if any, be established in the classification? Should it be according to the most cost-effective, the least intrusive or painful, the least risky, the least expensive or the most readily available therapy? These are questions which purchasing authorities are asking. In the paper cited earlier some of the authorities examined ruled out provision of *in vitro* fertilisation services on the basis of poor cost-effectiveness, and others on the basis of clinical effectiveness. There was disagreement between authorities on the latter point where one authority purchased *in vitro* services because they had the advantage of detecting poor fertilisation and bypassing tubal damage. Clearly, however, this is one sensible way to determine which treatment a person may best benefit by and thus be said to need most.

In the absence of such clinical means of distinguishing the treatments who should decide which kind of need the infertile person has? What role should the patient play in this? Might not a strong preference for IVF prevail over tubal surgery if the woman feels strongly about it? Might this not be good reason for saying that her need is not surgical in the full-blown sense? She might so fear surgery that she would not consider it as a possible solution to her problem. This poses the question of how much room there should be for patient choice in the provision of infertility services.

9. Criteria of Access to Services

Before leaving the question of perception of need we must consider the issue of the perceptions of the professional carer. In the United Kingdom the carers' perceptions of need in this area are uniquely safeguarded, save for the connected area of abortion. There exist only two conscience clauses in English medical law which allow a health care professional to refuse to treat a patient on other than clinical grounds. No carer can be obliged to assist in the procurement of an abortion nor in the provision of assisted conception services where such involvement would be against his or her conscience. In the case of abortion it is fairly clear that a clinician who held that aborting the foetus amounted to murder, or at least the killing of a person, could hold that no-one could need that such a procedure be carried out. The moral grounds upon which a conscientious objection could be made under the Human Fertilisation and Embryology Act 1990 have been tested only once. That judgement is crucially ambiguous in an important respect, as we shall see in a moment. However it does not

preclude the case where considerations of unnatural interference constituting a destruction of the unity of the act of procreation will rule out such assistance as an option. A clinician who held such a view would then find it impossible to accept that any patient could need such a procedure, just as no transplant surgeon could believe that his patient needed the heart of any particular healthy man, even though he does need a healthy heart. A difficulty then arises as to how far such a clinician should go in making such provision possible by counselling and referral to other practitioners. A much more difficult set of problems arise where the conscientious objection issues from different non-clinical considerations and it is here that the court judgement is crucially ambiguous. These would be cases where considerations about the suitability of the patient to receive such services arise. I have canvassed these problems elsewhere[25] but will pursue them here for a moment as they raise important questions about the application of criteria of access to assisted conception programmes, questions which apply uniquely to these programmes but which have profound implications for the practice of medicine.

What if the moral objection took the form of objecting to the suitability of the patient on the grounds of her lifestyle. Maybe the clinician would not consider that it would be proper for him to assist a lesbian, or a mentally handicapped woman or a single woman to conceive a child. This objection might be cashed in terms of his refusal to concede that they need such services. For the first time, as far as I can determine, non-clinical criteria of suitability for treatment would be introduced into the ethos of medicine. (As opposed to *de facto* application of non-clinical criteria due to modes of rationing.) This change in medical practice would be one to fear, especially in times of scarce resources when patients are expected to take responsibility for their health and where it looks possible that they may, in the not-too-distant future, be refused treatments for conditions they have brought upon themselves. Such restrictions already apply in infertility therapy where reversal of vasectomy and reversal of female sterilisation services are either not provided, or figure low on the priority scale of infertility services. There is one case in the law in the UK where this principle has been tested.[26] Here a woman was refused access to services on the basis of her "lack of understanding of the role of foster parent". She had a history of prostitution but was now in a stable relationship. No information in addition to her life as a prostitute was given in the judgement. As surely as this history had barred her from fostering children so it was to bar her from access to assisted procreation services. The court upheld the rights of the consultant to refuse her IVF treatment. It also made it clear that if the reason had been because the woman was a jew or coloured then the policy of the clinic might have been illegal. The refusal in question was not seen in this light. The important question remains unanswered, however, *viz.* can the interests of the child be assessed independently of moral evaluations of the lifestyle of prospective parents?

The employment of criteria of access to assisted conception services serves another function than facilitating rationing, or protecting the moral sensibilities of the clinician. They draw our attention to the interests of the product of the services offered, *viz.* the child. For many this is the most disconcerting feature of assisted conception provision.

The bringing into the world of another human being, which is the whole point of assisted conception procedures, creates a further set of needs which may be in tension with the needs of the infertile. They are the needs of the new life. Where these needs are located in the need for good parenting especial care will have to be exercised. There is evidence that some of the groups of women mentioned a moment ago might be deemed by providers to be unsuitable as parents by virtue of their lifestyle or domestic situation. Very firm evidence would be needed to establish such unsuitability, indeed much more than is currently available. Where such criteria were then applied it is important that they be made explicit so that no covert moral prejudices are allowed to intrude into the clinical encounter.

10. A Problematic Caveat

It is a peculiar feature of assisted conception services that the need which is met is not primarily met by the treatment, though this is a necessary means to its resolution. In fact it is met by the child who results from the procedure. Achieving a pregnancy is not a supplying of the need but birthing a baby is. This is why I earlier talked of the condition of childlessness as constituting the need to be met by means of assisted conception services rather than the condition of infertility. Certainly then the interests of the child are not properly ignored. This poses the final puzzle which I wish to canvass as arising from the identification of infertility as a health need. One of the most prominent grounds employed by the three purchasing authorities referred to earlier[27] who decided to provide *in vitro* services was clinical. That is they recognised that the condition of infertility could give rise to psychological and physiological harms. The provision of assisted conception services was then a means of preventing or ameliorating these harms. In other words, the prime motive for providing the service was to provide a unique prophylactic - the child. But now the question arises as to whether this instrumental use of another person, the child, is morally justified. Maybe this note of caution is a suitable one on which to end a paper which has sought to establish the importance of maintaining moral sensitivity in recognising the possibility of regarding infertility as a health need. In so doing we need to take care that sensitivity to other moral questions is not dulled by sheer enthusiasm for the application of the new and exciting technologies of assisted reproduction.

Notes

1. Wisdom, John, *Paradox and Discovery* Oxford, Basil Blackwell, 1965, pp.137-138.

2. Maritain, Jacques, *The Rights of Man* London, Geoffrey Bles, 1958, pp.34-35.

3. See, Diamond, Cora, 'Martha Nussbaum and the need for novels' *Philosophical Investigations* Vol. 16, No. 2, April 1993, pp.128-153.

4. *Ibid.*, p.133.

5. *Ibid.*, pp.146-147.

6. Boorse, Christopher, 'On the distinction between disease and illness' *Philosophy and Public Affairs* Vol. 5, No. 1, Fall 1975, pp.49-68.

7. *Ibid.*, p.59.

8. *Ibid.*, p.68 and p.63.

9. *Ibid.*, p.64.

10. Foot, Philippa, 'Moral Beliefs' reprinted in *Virtues and Vices* Oxford, Basil Blackwell, 1978, pp.110-131. Reference to other papers of Foot will be to their page numbers in this collection.

11. *Ibid.*, p.120.

12. *Ibid.*, pp.121-123.

13. See, Beardsmore, R., *Moral Reasoning* London, Routledge and Kegan Paul, 1969, pp.22-23 and Phillips, D.Z. and Mounce, H.O., *Moral Practices* London, Routledge and Kegan Paul, 1969, pp.56-58.

14. See, Winch, Peter, 'Can a good man be harmed?' *Proceedings of the Aristotelian Society* Vol. LXVI, 1965-66, pp.55-70.

15. Hampshire, Stuart, *Public and Private Morality* Cambridge, Cambridge University Press, 1978, p.48 (emphasis added).

16. Foot, Philippa, 'Moral Arguments' in *Virtues and Vices op.cit.* pp.96-109, p.109.

17. Braybrooke, David, 'Let needs diminish that preferences may prosper' in Rescher, N. (ed.), *Studies in Moral Philosophy* American Philosophical Quarterly Monograph Series No. 1, Oxford, Basil Blackwell, 1968, pp.86-107.

18. MacCloskey, H.J., 'Human needs, rights and political values' *American Philosophical Quarterly* 13 (1), 1976, pp.1-11.

19. *Ibid.*, pp.3-4.

20. *Ibid.*, p.5 and p.8.

21. Winch, Peter, 'Human Nature' reprinted in *Ethics and Action* London, Routledge and Kegan Paul, 1972, p.84.

22. Evans, Donald, 'Legislative control of medical practice' *Bulletin of Medical Ethics* No. 55, 1990, pp.13-17.

23. O'Donovan, Katherine, 'What shall we tell the children? Reflections on children's perspectives and the reproduction revolution' in Lee, Robert, and Morgan, Derek (eds), *Birthrights: Law and Ethics at the Beginnings of Life* London, Routledge, 1989, pp.96-114.

24. Redmayne, Sharon, and Klein, Rudolf, 'Rationing in practice: the case of *in vitro* fertilisation' *British Medical Journal* Vol. 306, June 1993, pp.1521-1524.

25. Evans, *op.cit.*, pp.15-16.

26. *R. v. Ethical Advisory Committee of St Mary's Hospital ex p. Harriott* [1988] 1 Family Law Review 512.

27. See Redmayne and Klein, *op.cit.*, pp.1521-1523.

5. INFERTILITY, CHILDLESSNESS AND THE NEED FOR TREATMENT

Is Childlessness a Social or a Medical Problem?

Søren Holm
Department of Medical Philosophy and Clinical Theory
University of Copenhagen
Blegdamsvej 3
DK-2200 N
Copenhagen
Denmark

1. Introduction

In the last 20 years the rapid development of new techniques for the alleviation of infertility has forced us to reconsider our attitudes towards and understanding of the widespread social problem of infertility.

If we accept the medical definition of infertility (i.e. infertility is the failure to conceive after 12 months of regular unprotected intercourse or the occurrence of more than 2 consecutive natural miscarriages or stillbirths[1]) then up to 25 % of all women will experience infertility some time during their reproductive years and 6-10% of these will be 'permanently' infertile (i.e. will not be able to conceive without technological intervention or will not be able to conceive at all).[2] The prevalence of infertility seems to be fairly stable, but with the advent of new techniques for the alleviation of the problem, demand for treatment has risen.[3]

Treatment for infertility now involves many different techniques, of which only a few are curative in the sense that they permanently remove the specific cause of infertility. Most of the newly developed methods including *in vitro* fertilisation (IVF), gamete intrafallopian transfer (GIFT), zygote intrafallopian transfer (ZIFT) and all of the methods based on gamete donation are 'one-shot' procedures which do not affect the underlying causes of infertility but only circumvent these causal structures temporarily. Blocked tubes are not opened by IVF and azoospermia is not removed by donor insemination.

In the popular media the two words 'infertility' and 'childlessness' are frequently used as if they were interchangeable, but it is important to keep them separate. It is possible to be fertile and childless (e.g. if one has chosen not to have children and acted accordingly), as well as to be infertile and not childless (e.g. if one has adopted a child). Infertility is therefore best used exclusively for the biological condition of being unable to conceive or bear children, whereas childlessness should be used for the

D. Evans (ed.), Creating the Child, 65–78.
© 1996 *Kluwer Law International. Printed in the Netherlands.*

psycho-social condition of not having any child which one would call ones own. It is therefore possible to be childless in a household where all the children have been brought into the relationship by one's spouse. As mentioned above most infertility treatments only circumvent infertility, but they 'cure' childlessness if they are successful.

Modern anticonception makes it possible for a couple to choose to be infertile for a period of time, but in these cases infertility is not chosen as an end in itself, but as a means toward, at least temporary, childlessness. Although it is thus now possible to choose to be infertile, the choice to be temporarily or permanently childless is logically prior. For different reasons some people choose to be permanently childless, and it is therefore important to distinguish between unwanted and intentional childlessness.

2. Infertility and the Concept of Disease

The new possibilities of treating infertility have made it necessary to discuss who should pay for this treatment. Should the couple themselves pay, or should society at large? This question can be answered only through an ethical analysis of the principles of justice operating within the health care field.

One approach to the assessment of the ethical status of the new reproductive techniques and to the question of whether infertility generates a claim against society has been to ask whether infertility is a disease.

In most countries in the developed world labelling a condition as a disease or a handicap has important performative aspects. A person whose condition is labelled in this way can legitimately enter the sick role with its various exemptions from normal duties.[4] At the same time the labelling of someone as having a disease or handicap generates a legitimate *prima facie* claim against society for help.

Deciding whether something should be called a disease is therefore no trivial matter. In many countries infertile couples have formed organisations with the explicit purpose of lobbying for the recognition of infertility as a disease, and such efforts have met with considerable success.

On the other hand, among those who are sceptical about the new techniques, efforts have been made to show that infertility is not a disease, and that no claim is therefore generated against society.[5]

In many countries the health care system (not the 'sick care system') provides assistance in other areas than the alleviation of disease, and this is especially prominent within the area of reproductive medicine in general. Most countries provide some form of antenatal and postnatal care to all pregnant women even though pregnancy can hardly be construed as a disease. This shows, that at least in some areas, disease is not a necessary condition to obtain public health care.

To be able to decide whether or not infertility is a disease we need a concept of disease against which we can compare infertility in order to decide whether infertility falls within the boundaries of this disease concept.

Unfortunately there is no general agreement among medical philosophers on what constitutes a disease. We have several well-argued disease concepts that each seem to capture some core elements of a broader concept of disease. Each of the proposed disease concepts manages to include many of the conditions or states which we normally call disease, but at the same time, they all seem to exclude some other conditions or states which are also normally seen as diseases, as well as including states which are not normally taken as disease states. Or, to put it shortly, none of the proposed concepts of disease are just approximately co-extensional with our commonly held 'disease intuitions'.

When Christopher Boorse defines disease as the absence of health and health as "species typical functioning"[6] he clearly captures important elements of our common understanding of the concept, and he comes a long way towards achieving a value free definition, but his definition of the reference group used in establishing species typicality at the same time saddles him with two problems, the first being that the disease concept becomes partially relative and dependent on the exact choice of reference group. If we choose a late twentieth century reference group, almost all people in the Middle Ages were diseased, whereas if we choose a historical reference group they were all much more healthy. The second problem is that the definition becomes rather narrowly biological. In the psychological area our abilities to make value-free decisions on what to take as normal function, and our abilities to design instruments with which to measure such function is much more limited. We clearly want to be able to say that some people have mental diseases (e.g. persons with schizophrenia)[7], but we have great problems in reaching a definition of rationality that enables us to do so on a Boorsean definition of disease, without at the same time labelling ordinary magical beliefs and superstition as disease.

Approaching the problem from the other side, from a concept of health, does not meet with greater success. Definitions of health have played a large role in medical sociology, but most of these are in even greater disagreement with common intuitions than the definitions of disease put forward by medical philosophers (see Aggleton's excellent introduction to the sociology of health[8]).

The medical philosopher David Seedhouse argues that health and not disease is the core notion and defines health in the following way:

A person's optimum state of health is equivalent to the state of the set of conditions which fulfil or enable a person to work to fulfil his or her realistic chosen and biological potentials. Some of these conditions are of the highest importance for all people. Others are variable dependent upon individual abilities and circumstances.[9]

Seedhouse's concept of health is partially congruent with our ordinary notions of health and healthiness, but at the same time it includes much more in the concept than we would normally include. His conception of health is not as broad as the much maligned WHO definition (complete physical, psychological, and social wellbeing[10]), but it is still

very broad, and it makes it almost impossible to establish a useful demarcation between what is 'work for health' on the one hand and what is 'work for the general benefit of humanity' on the other.

Is there no middle way between a (too) narrow biological concept of disease and a (too) broad psycho/social concept of health?

Based on historical studies H. Tristram Engelhardt has shown, how the label of disease has been misused and exploited. His meticulous analyses of the draconian treatments for female masturbation and his discovery of some old papers on the 'diseases' of black slaves, e.g. *Drapetomania* (the disease which causes slaves to run away from their masters) are classics in the field.[11] Based on these analyses and similar analyses of the states included as diseases within the disease concepts proposed by contemporary medical philosophers, one is easily led to the conclusion, that the concept of disease is necessarily and inextricably bound to certain ideological interests, and therefore of no use in ethical debates. But has Engelhardt really accomplished a *reductio* of the concept of disease?

Not necessarily!

The great French philosopher Henri Bergson is said to have uttered the following memorable quote: "Every great philosopher has one core insight which he spends his whole life explaining". This observation can probably explain one part of the present state of the philosophy of the concept of disease, and also point to a way in which the project of thinking about such a concept can be salvaged.

If medical philosophers believe that all disease can be captured by one concept, and further believe that they themselves have reached the proper definition of this concept through their extensive philosophical analysis, then it is not difficult to explain why so much time and effort is spent on attacking the concepts proposed by other medical philosophers. It is a common experience in reading philosophical literature, that it is much easier to criticise others than to produce convincing, positive, and constructive ideas oneself; and it is a lot easier to hold on to one's core idea, than to admit that one is in error. In conversation some philosophers pride themselves on being ready at any time to examine even the deepest presuppositions of their philosophical views. Given this 'fact' it is surprising how few actually change their views in any substantial way. There is probably a natural tendency to overestimate the importance of one's own core idea, and such a tendency could easily lead to the establishment of several schools each adamantly defending their disease concept as the only true one.

It is perhaps worth considering why we believe that there should be a unitary concept of disease. Is there for instance any good reason to believe that there is one definable disease concept within which we can accommodate both schizophrenia and a fractured first toe as diseases? I cannot find one, and I don't think that this is an example of the 'argument from myopia'. Instead of trying to extend my concept of disease to cover all diseases, it may be more prudent to seek the limits for the different disease concepts, and accept that although my insight does shed light on some aspects of the concept of disease, its scope is still limited.

If infertility is a disease, then it must be a somatic and not a psychiatric disease.

There are therefore three problems which we will have to address when considering infertility as a disease, no matter which concept of disease we finally adopt[12]:

1. Is it reasonable to conceptualise infertility as one disease or is it many diseases?
2. Is it reasonable to talk of infertility as a disease or is it more reasonable to see it as a disability?
3. If infertility is a disease, who is then affected by this disease?

We know today that there are many causes for infertility, and it is therefore necessary initially to try to decide whether it is sensible still to regard infertility as one entity or whether we ought to perform separate analyses for each different kind of infertility (defined after putative cause). As disease classifications have developed there has been a progressive move towards more specific diagnoses. Consumption has been removed from the list of diagnoses and replaced by lung cancer, tuberculosis, sarcoidosis and other more specific diagnoses; but in other cases basic anatomical diagnoses have been retained e.g. duodenal ulcer. Development of new disease classifications is to a great extent driven by pragmatic considerations and not so much by a desire for a perfect taxonomy. That is, the question asked when a new diagnosis is proposed is not so much 'Is this really a different natural kind from disease X?' but 'Would the recognition of this as a separate diagnosis be able to lead to better diagnosis, prognostication, or treatment?'. Seen from this perspective it is probably still reasonable to consider infertility as one disease and not as many different but related diseases. After the introduction of the new reproductive techniques old surgical techniques for the opening of blocked tubes have fallen into disuse, and most infertility problems are now handled within a closely related family of treatments all based on hormone treatment and some form of ex-vivo manipulation of gametes. At present there is therefore no pragmatic need for a further specification of infertility diagnoses, but whether such a need will occur in the future cannot be predicted. There are thus presently no serious objections to viewing infertility as one disease.

Not all conditions that impair our biological functions are diseases. The person who has lost a leg after a traffic accident is biologically impaired, but he is not ill, and he does not have a disease. He is permanently disabled or handicapped. Likewise the person who has had a colectomy because of *Colitis ulcerosa*, is no longer ill, and no longer has a disease, but he is permanently disabled. Calling something a disease ordinarily implies some ongoing biological process and not just the reversible or irreversible but essentially stable outcome of such a process. However, this requirement for an ongoing disease process is not absolute. We accept that the person who has an intestinal obstruction has a disease and should be operated upon, even though there may be no current disease process. In the same way it could be argued that the women with blocked tubes have a disease, since the obstructed tubes interfere with the normal process bringing the egg from the ovaries to the uterus once a month. This is true but it is clear that this use of process falls on or beyond the absolute edge of the process concept normally used in talking about disease processes. And for other forms of infertility we cannot even find this kind of process. A man with azoospermia is neither ill, nor diseased, but he is clearly disabled. If we want to talk about infertility

as such, as one condition, it therefore seems more natural to talk about infertility as a permanent disability or a handicap and not as a disease.

The third core problem for any analysis of infertility as a disease is the question of who we should attribute infertility to. Is it a one-person condition or is it a two-person condition? In some cases the cause of infertility can be clearly established, e.g. blocked fallopian tubes in the woman or azoospermia in the man, but although the cause of infertility can be attributed to one partner in these cases, the treatment often involves both of them. In other cases the cause cannot be established or the infertility is caused by a combination of several additive causes of subfertility in the two partners. Many-person diseases are distinctly uncommon in medicine outside of psychiatry where we have both *folies a deux* which is a true two-person disease and family therapy which is a many-person treatment.

Consequent on the realisation that male infertility is a major factor in infertility some feminist philosophers have argued for the importance of attributing infertility to one of the partners and not to the couple as such. The main reason for this insistence on attribution of cause (and blame?) seems to be that it is necessary in order to be able to criticise infertility treatments as extensions of the oppression of women and the male usurpation of the control over women's bodies in patriarchal society.[13]

We are, however, still at a point where cause cannot always be attributed to one partner, and it is very likely that this situation will not be remedied in the future. We will probably always have a class of cases of infertility which are caused by a combination of factors specific to the couple in question.

So, feminism notwithstanding, we still have to decide whether these instances of infertility should be seen as a two-person disease or not. Because of the rarity of two-person diseases they have been relatively neglected in medical philosophy, and it is tempting to discount them, and deny that they are 'real' diseases. But this leaves us with a problem. How should we then describe such an infertile couple? Let us imagine a couple in which the wife has developed anti-bodies against specific antigens on her husbands spermatozoa. This couple is infertile when seen as a couple, but taken separately they are in perfect health. With a change of partner each of them would be as fertile as anybody else. We could say that such a couple had a (two-person) disease, without stretching the disease concept too far, but given the arguments above, it is probably more correct to say that the couple is disabled. This is further supported if we consider that whether or not the cause can be attributed to one partner, the common consequence for the couple will be unwanted childlessness.

The failure to reach clarity and closure when considering infertility as a disease state, could tempt one to ask whether the fault is in the question and not in the analysis. Is it at all sensible to expect a definite answer to the question of whether infertility is a disease? Probably not. Considered as a disease infertility lies somewhere near the fuzzy borders of most disease concepts and it will therefore always be a matter for serious argument whether it 'really is a disease'. This result is however useful in itself, because it enables us to defuse the rhetorical and performative force of statements claiming that infertility is or is not a disease. When we talk about infertility, disease

statements simply do not function as 'trumps' in the discussion in the way they may do in other areas.

Given the arguments presented above it is probably most sensible to conceptualise infertility as such as a permanent disability, functional impairment, or handicap[14], but some specific types of infertility could as well be seen as *bona fide* disease states.

3. Human Needs and Human Illness

Large parts of the rhetorical force in labelling something as a disease is acquired because disease is closely connected to two of the most important and basic concepts in ethics, human suffering and human need. We do not treat disease just because it is disease, we treat it because it causes suffering and creates need. Although suffering and need are connected in several ways there are situations where we have need without suffering and other situations where we have suffering without need. The most common of these situations is when suffering is caused solely by the frustration of desires or wants.

We therefore need some principle with which to separate needs from wants and desires. To claim that somebody needs something is clearly different from saying that he wants it or that he desires it. Third personal need statements refer to some thing which the person in question lacks[15], whereas want or desire statements are descriptions of his state of mind. Many of the things I want I do not need, and the fact that I want something does not produce even the weakest *prima facie* claim against others that they should provide me with the thing I want.

Garrett Thomson points to the fact that there are two different kinds of need statements, statements referring to instrumental needs, and statements referring to fundamental needs.[16] Instrumental need statements follow the normal analysis of need statements, i.e. to say that 'X needs A' is an elliptical form of expression which should be understood as 'X needs A in order to F' where F is some goal, state, or function that the person X wishes to obtain. Many philosophers have maintained that this is the only form of need statement. Thomson argues that fundamental need statements are different in that the antecedent is something which X *inescapably* must have in order to avoid serious harm or in order to be X. Fundamental needs statements are therefore independent of the agent's wishes or desires, and it is possible to need something that one does not consciously or unconsciously desire. Because such fundamental needs are desire independent it follows that if X needs A, and A = B in a functional sense, then X needs B, whereas the same is not true of desire statements.

It is this concept of fundamental need which is at the core of ethics, and which generates a claim against others. It is important to note that the notion of inescapability or necessity that is used here is neither logical necessity nor natural necessity if natural is taken in a very biological sense. That A is an inescapable need for a person X simply means that, given the present state of X, including the effects of his upbringing and social environment, X will be seriously harmed if he lacks A. Fundamental need

statements utilise a notion of practical necessity. It could therefore be true that a drug addict needs heroin and at the same time be true that he needs to be weaned off the drug.

This conception of fundamental needs puts no limits on the content of a given fundamental need statement as long as it is possible to make some sense of the item or state claimed to be needed (cf. Philippa Foot's treatment of the claim that someone needs an even number of hairs on his head).[17]

The physical conditions involved in infertility do not normally cause any suffering in themselves. They are not painful[18], and they do not interfere with normal life, except through the rather stringent requirements for a well ordered life that may be imposed during treatment periods. What is at stake here is therefore the psychological and social suffering and harm that can be caused by infertility and childlessness, and the attention therefore turns from infertility towards childlessness. That childlessness is really the primary issue can perhaps best be illustrated if we imagine the invention of a new wonder treatment that could restore normal fertility to infertile couples. In this case we would see masses of previously infertile couples voluntarily rendering themselves infertile once again (through the use of more or less permanent means of anticonception), as soon as their problem of childlessness had been solved by the conception and birth of a suitable number of children.

There can be little doubt that people often need children in the requisite fundamental sense. In many societies children are the only available old-age insurance, and even in societies with extensive social security children still play an important practical and psychological role. Children are also important earlier in life. Young couples are expected to have children, and this expectation is backed up by significant social pressures. Having children will attract increased parental attention, and it is the 'access card' to important social events from which a childless couple is excluded, or from which it excludes itself.[19] The suffering created by childlessness is therefore not only a function of the frustrated desire to have a child, but also a function of inescapable social structures.

But there are many ways to have children, and an argument for the societal provision of new reproductive techniques will have to show that these techniques meet fundamental needs that are not met by for instance adoption.

Before proceeding to this task it is necessary to say a few words about adoption. The decision to adopt will in many cases require some recognition of loss and a grieving process for the couple. At the same time there are several practical obstacles to be overcome. Adoption is expensive and in most countries one furthermore has to submit to detailed scrutiny by the social services. To adopt a child from a different ethnic background[20] also requires greater psychological resources on the part of the parents, since racism in some form is prevalent in all European countries. Adoption is no 'easy' solution to the problem of childlessness, but it is a solution which at the same time gives parents to an already existing child and gives a child to a childless couple. There may therefore be good arguments for a societal obligation to help couples who adopt economically and in other ways, but given the main topic of this paper I will allow

myself not to pursue these arguments.

Ruth Chadwick distinguishes three different desires which may be at play in the composite desire 'to have a child', that is (a) the desire to beget, (b) the desire to bear, and (c) the desire to rear. The desire to bear and the desire to rear can then be further subdivided depending on whether the desire can be fulfilled by any child or whether it can be fulfilled only by a child that is genetically related to one or both parents.[21] The frustration of these desires can lead to human suffering, but if need is ethically prior to suffering, as argued above, we have to decide whether any of these desires correspond to fundamental human needs.

There is no doubt that the desire to beget, bear, and rear a child that is genetically related to oneself can be a strong desire, but it is difficult to see how it could be a rational preference or a fundamental need, all things considered.

On the standard analysis of need statements i.e. 'X needs A in order to F', the need for some object or state A is explained by the function F, which A can fulfil for the person X; but what function can be fulfilled only by a genetically related child and not by a genetically unrelated child?

One suggestion could be that only a genetically related child can propagate the genes of its parents. Genetics and genetic relationships have been introduced in ethics through sociobiology and the different 'selfish gene' theories. This is not the place for an extended critique of these views, but it is important to note that even if we grant our genes the semi-autonomous status postulated by the 'selfish gene' theory this could not make it in *my* interest to spread my genes. I would not automatically have an interest in having genetically related children. My genes may have this interest[22], and my biology may be adapted to further this interest; but this does not make it *my* interest in any important sense. It may be inbuilt in my brain, but I can always override it in preference for something which I value more and make *my* interest. Furthermore, even if we granted that I had an interest in spreading my genes through having genetically related children, we would at the same time have to grant that other people and their genes would have diametrically opposed interests. It would not be to the advantage of other people's genes to help me to spread mine, unless these others were closely related to me. Even if we accept sociobiology, which we should not[23], this approach cannot generate a claim against society for help with infertility problems except in very small societies with a significant degree of genetic similarity.

Apart from sociobiology some other reasons for preferring a genetically related child come to mind.

It could be imagined that genetically related children bond differently/better with their parents, but to my knowledge there is no evidence even pointing in this direction, so there is probably no objective advantage in this sense.

Social conventions may of course play a role and make it socially more desirable to have genetically related children. This could be a real problem in some societies or in some specific social groups within a society, and if the social conventions are strong and immovable it can create a situation in which childlessness would give rise to a valid claim against society for reproductive assistance.

Finally legal constraints on inheritance rights, especially within the nobility, may produce a situation in which only a genetically related child will be able to fulfil the required role, but these are very special cases, and we cannot build social policy on the requirements of the Scottish Lairds and their noble blood lines.

If we then turn to the generic desire to have a child (i.e. the form of this desire that can be fulfilled without the child being genetically related to oneself) it is, in the context of the new reproductive techniques, necessary to look closely only at the desire to bear a child. I cannot beget a genetically unrelated child[24], and the desire to rear a child can, if no genetic relationship is required, be fulfilled through adoption. The question is therefore: does the generic desire to bear a child constitute a need?

To be able to answer this question we need to look closer at the desire to bear a child. On one interpretation this desire is no more than a desire for a certain set of experiences through a nine month period, ended by the unique, rather painful, but generally elating[25] experience of giving birth to a new human being.[26] It is difficult to argue for a need to bear based solely on this rather ungenerous interpretation of the desire to bear, since a mere desire for a certain set of experiences normally does not generate a need.[27] It is, however, obvious that apart from the experiences of the mother during pregnancy and birth, pregnancy also fulfils other important societal functions. Pregnancy can be seen as a protracted rite of passage, marking the change from an early, relatively independent, phase of adulthood to a later more mature phase in which one assumes greater responsibility for others. This function has no equivalent in the case of adoption, and depending on how one assesses its importance it may form the basis for a valid need statement. If this gradual transition is either psychologically or socially necessary, then there may be a real need to bear children, and not just a need to have and rear them. Whether such a need exists cannot be decided by philosophical analysis, but only by the empirical facts uncovered by sociologists and psychologists.

Finally and paradoxically the mere existence of a societal provision of reproductive techniques may in itself create a fundamental need for their continued provision. It is a consistent feature in the literature describing the experiences of women seeking treatment for infertility that the treatment process seems to reinforce the desire to become pregnant, and that it becomes more and more difficult to withdraw from the treatment programme[28] despite repeated treatment failures. More and more emotional energy becomes invested in the product, and the small extra amount to be 'expended' on each new treatment cycle seems to disappear compared to what is already invested. The treatment in itself therefore generates a situation in which the final frustration of the desire to conceive a child may cause serious psychological harm. This does seem to create a valid claim for further assistance, but such a claim is not extendable to new couples seeking treatment.

4. Infertility and the Medical Profession

In the preceding paragraphs I have argued that we should not conceptualise infertility

and childlessness as diseases, but from this it does not immediately follow that these problems fall outside of the scope of medicine.

The medical profession holds an almost absolute monopoly on legitimate bodily invasion. This is not because it is a more noble and responsible profession than others, but because its members possesses the requisite knowledge and skills to perform such invasions in a safe manner.

Many of the treatments for infertility require knowledge of this sort ('medical knowledge'), and it is tempting to argue that this in itself should place infertility within the scope of medicine proper. This temptation should be resisted!

It may well be prudent or expedient to require that treatment for infertility should be performed by duly qualified medical practitioners, but this does not make such treatment 'medical treatment' in more than a nominal sense. The fact that circumcision of male newborns is performed by medical doctors in some countries doesn't transform this circumcision into a medical procedure or treatment[29], and other purely cosmetic surgery is not made medical by being performed by doctors.

Developments in society have gradually increased the area which is seen as the proper purview of medical doctors, and it now encompasses many conditions, states, and processes which are completely normal (e.g. pregnancy and birth) and it is important to remember that this should not in itself change the status of these conditions or states. Being pregnant and giving birth should be considered as just as normal and non-pathological as they were before the control of pregnant women became a medical specialty.

All in all this means that no normative conclusions can be drawn from the fact that the new techniques for the treatment of infertility are normally performed by doctors.

5. Conclusion

This paper has argued for three main conclusions:

1. Infertility is best viewed as a disability or handicap and not as a disease, but nothing much turns on this distinction.

2. Although there may be a desire to beget, bear, and rear a child which is genetically related to oneself, there is no fundamental need to do so and therefore no strong claim to help from society in this context.

3. Because childlessness can cause significant psychological distress society should help to alleviate this problem. Given the number of orphans in the world, this is best done through adoption.

Acknowledgements

I gratefully acknowledge the helpful comments of Lone Schmidt

Notes

1. Greenhall, E. and Vessey, M., 'The prevalence of subfertility: a review of the current confusion and a report of two new studies' *Fertility and Sterility* 54 (6), 1990, pp.978-983.

2. There is no universal agreement on the medical definition of infertility, and figures for the number of 'permanently' infertile couples are difficult to find. Cf. Marchbanks, P.A., Peterson, H.B., Rubin, G.L., Wingo, P.A., *et al.*, 'Research on infertility: definition makes a difference' *American Journal of Epidemiology* 130 (2), 1989, pp.259-267, and Belsey, M.A., 'Infertility: Prevalence, etiology, and natural history' in Bracken, M.B. (ed.), *Perinatal Epidemiology* New York, Oxford University Press, 1984, (ch. 10) pp.255-282.

3. Templeton, A., Fraser, C. and Thompson, B., 'Infertility - epidemiology and referral practice' *Reproduction* 6(10), 1991, pp.1391-1394.

4. Parsons, T., 'Definitions of health and illness in the light of American values and social structures' in Jaco, E.G. (ed.), *Patients, Physicians, and Illness* New York, Free Press, 1958, pp.165-187.

5. See for instance: Kass, L.R., 'Babies by means of *in vitro* fertilization: unethical experiments on the unborn?' *New England Journal of Medicine* 285 (21), 1971, pp.1174-1179; Ramsey, P., 'Shall we "reproduce"? - II. Rejoinders and future forecast' *Journal of the American Medical Association* 220 (11), 1972, pp.1480-1485.

6.. The full definition is as follows:
- The reference class is a natural class of organisms of uniform functional design; specifically, an age group of a sex of a species.
- A normal function of a part or a process within members of the reference class is a statistically typical contribution by it to their individual survival and reproduction.
- Health in a member of the reference class is normal functional ability; the readiness of each internal part to perform all its normal functions on typical occasions with at least typical efficiency.
- A disease is a type of internal state which impairs health, i.e. reduces one or more functional abilities below typical efficiency. Boorse, C., 'Health as a theoretical concept' *Philosophy of Science* 44, 1977, pp.542-573, p.555.

7. Having worked in a department of psychiatry I am absolutely certain that persons with schizophrenia are ill in a very real sense.

8. Aggleton, P., *Health* London, Routledge, 1990.

9. Seedhouse, D., *Health: The Foundations for Achievement* Chichester, John Wiley and Sons, 1986, p.61.

10. Cited in Aggleton, *op.cit.*, p.8.

11. Engelhardt, H.T., 'The disease of masturbation: values and the concept of disease' *Bulletin of the History of Medicine* 48, 1974, pp.234-248; Engelhardt, H.T., 'The concepts of health and disease' in Engelhardt, H.T. and Spicker, S.F. (eds), *Evaluation and Explanation in the Biomedical Sciences* Dordrecht, D. Reidel Publishing Company, 1975, pp.125-141. The 'disease' of *Drapetomania* appears in Cartwright, S.A., 'Report on the diseases and physical peculiarities of the negro race' *The New Orleans Medical and Surgical Journal* May 1851, pp.691-715.

12. This is of course not strictly true. If one defines disease as 'the things doctors treat', then only the last of the three problems will be of interest.

13. Lorber, J., 'Choice, gift, or patriarchal bargain? Women's consent to *in vitro* fertilization in male infertility' in Holmes, H.B. and Purdy, L.M. (eds), *Feminist Perspectives in Medical Ethics* Bloomington, Indiana University Press, 1992, pp.169-180.

14. The use of the term 'handicap' could imply a negative evaluation of the person or couple and I will therefore suggest that the more neutral 'disability' is used.

15. We may be said to need things that we don't presently lack (food, water, clean air to breathe). Such need statements refer to the harm which would be caused if we lacked these things.

16. Thomson, G., *Needs* London, Routledge and Kegan Paul, 1987.

17. For a more detailed discussion of this point and Foot's example see Evans, Donald, 'The clinical classification of infertility' in this volume.

18. Certain aspects of treatment are painful and/or humiliating.

19. Lone Schmidt, personal communication.

20. In many European countries there are only a few 'domestic' children for adoption and most adopted children are therefore 'imported' from abroad.

21. Chadwick, R.F., 'Having children' in Chadwick, R.F. (ed.), *Ethics, Reproduction and Genetic Control* revised edition, London, Routledge, 1992, pp.3-43.

22. If genes can have any interests at all.

23. In the limited space of this paper I cannot present a full argument against all aspects of sociobiology, but others have already done most of this work.

24. If gametes from other people are available I can desire to have an embryo produced for me to bear, but this is a desire to have an embryo made and not a desire to beget.

25. Or so it is said by some. On the other hand the feminist writer Shulamit Firestone refers to this experience as "Like shitting a pumpkin" (Firestone, S., *The Dialectic of Sex* London, The Womens Press Ltd., 1979, p.189).

26. Some men also wish to see their wife pregnant.

27. If the desire to have the set of experiences during pregnancy was sufficiently important to justify societal assistance with infertility treatment, then it would presumably also be sufficiently important to justify funding research aiming at the production of male pregnancy, so that men could share this wonderful set of experiences.

28. For examples of this, see the stories in Klein, R.D. (ed.), *Infertility - Women Speak Out About Their Experiences of Reproductive Medicine* London, Pandora Press, 1989, and Arditti, R., Klein, R.D. and Minden, S. (eds), *Test-Tube Women - What Future for Motherhood?* London, Pandora Press, 1984.

29. It would be even more outrageous to suggest that female circumcision became a medical procedure if performed by a medical doctor.

6. *AD HOMINEM*

A Consideration of a Feminist Critique of the Moral Discourse of Embryologists and Others

Neil Pickering
Centre for Philosophy and Health Care
University of Wales, Swansea
Singleton Park
Swansea
Wales

Introduction

In this paper, I am interested in exploring an argument based upon points made by a number of women writers on medical technologies and their relation to women's interests and issues. But I do not wish to claim that any of the women writers would take (nor would have to take) the line pursued here; for this reason I refer often to what they might say given certain arguments against or questions about their position.

1. Scientific Discourse and Values

> Antonia kicking her bare legs against the sides of my pony when we came home in triumph with our snake; Antonia in her black shawl and fur cap, as she stood by her father's grave in the snowstorm; Antonia coming in with her work-team along the evening sky-line. She lent herself to immemorial human attitudes which we recognise by instinct as universal and true. ... She was a battered woman now, not a lovely girl; but she still had that something which fires the imagination, could still stop one's breath for a moment by a look or gesture that somehow revealed the meaning in common things. She has only to stand in the orchard, to put her hand on a little crab tree and look up at the apples, to make you feel the goodness of planting and tending and harvesting at last. All the strong things of her heart came out in her body, that had been so tireless in serving generous emotions. It was no wonder her sons stood tall and straight. She was a rich mine of life, like the founders of early races.[1]

The American writer Gena Corea drew the attention of a committee concerned with the scientific future of Depo-Provera (a contraceptive) to these images. She might be

79

e
D. Evans (ed.), Creating the Child, 79–95.
© 1996 *Kluwer Law International. Printed in the Netherlands.*

characterised as deliberately using a literary quotation as a contrast to the kind of language used in other submissions to the scientific committee. In this way she may be seen as setting up one kind of discourse (the value laden discourse of literary description) against another (the value free discourse of science); but she gives reasons for thinking this 'contrast' between them illusory.

Corea justifies quoting from *My Antonia* with the words: "This is indeed a scientific hearing of the technical evidence of Depo-Provera, but those who produced that technical evidence took their values to work with them every morning". These values, she says include "the vested interests of [their] gender and race in a society stratified into these categories", so that "an examination of the science they make must include an acknowledgement of their gender and race". She argues that this means that they cannot be seen as producing "pure science".[2] Even putting aside the vested source of their values, the claim is their discourse is value-laden like that of Cather's novel.

These vested interests may appear in the use made of science to further its own interests[3] which is a significant point; but here I wish to pursue another (though not unconnected) point. Corea foregrounds the scientists - humans perhaps necessarily[4] of some race and gender, and tending as a group to be of a particular race (white Anglo-Saxon[5]) and gender (male). 'Pure' science, on Corea's account, would *per impossibile* be a science carried out by humans detached entirely from their gender and race (and other such characteristics). As such, it would be a science working from assumptions and towards goals which people of different races and genders could share; but science she believes - in reality - falls short of this.

In response, someone may ask why individual white males should not take on such a detachment *qua* scientists. Gilbert and Mulkay ask:

> ... does a given set of activities constitute an experiment, an attempt indirectly to raise more research funds, an effort to secure professional credibility, a bid for more students; or can it be any or all of these, depending on the context in which the actor is talking or writing about his actions?[6]

Taking 'experiment' to include experimentation in embryology, and taking the last part of the question to be answered affirmatively, the suggestion seems to be that, in certain contexts, it can plausibly be claimed that a "given set of activities" within embryology is an "experiment" - that is to say, rightly described in purely scientific terms.

Now, Gilbert and Mulkay are asking only whether or not speaking of a "set of activities" as an "experiment" is itself a matter of the context in which the describer finds herself. If it is, such a description is appropriate (in some sense) for or in certain situations. It does not immediately follow from this that the set of activities is at core merely an experiment, for it may be argued that what someone will identify as 'the core' of some activity is itself dependent on context. Moreover, as will emerge later, one element of a feminist criticism is that the nature of 'the context' or 'the situation' requires exploration.

Some of the foregoing seems to rely on the idea that 'experiment' is a merely

descriptive notion, such that to whatever extent a set of activities carried out by white males can rightly be described as an experiment, it is to that extent free of any values, and *a fortiori* of their values. But, even if the concept 'experiment' is value free in this way, human interests may enter in its deployment, for instance where it is claimed to be the (or a) correct description of some activity. This point will be taken up again later. Here it may be argued that (in any case) other terms within embryology are clearly not descriptive. This point will emerge again when the use by embryologists of moral terms such as 'need' is discussed later; here much less obviously evaluative terms may be mentioned. For instance, the apparent 'finding' that someone has 'infertility'. 'Infertility' (it may be argued) suggests a problem of a certain kind. But if 'infertility' is a problem and moreover a problem of a certain kind, it cannot then be merely a 'finding' of any kind. Two points may be raised in support of this contention. First, the kind of problem identified has to be decided between rival conceptions of 'the problem', for instance, as a social problem ('childlessness') or a medical problem ('infertility').[7] Second, for there even to be a problem (as opposed to a mere puzzle, say) infertility must strike at human interests, wishes or desires.[8] It would follow - if this were all true - that to deploy the description of some state of affairs as 'infertility' is implicitly to evaluate and categorise it; and that, it may then be claimed, is implicitly to invoke features of the source of the evaluation, *viz.*, of the human evaluator and categoriser and the values that he (*sic*) carries with him and by which he evaluates and categorises, and the contexts other than 'science' in which such evaluations may be carried out - the ethics committee room, the funding council's offices, the assisted reproduction unit, and so on, which he dominates.

One counter argument which may be put against both points is to the effect that what is referred to by 'infertility' is a certain causal explanation of an (admittedly) value-laden state of affairs. Alternatively it could be argued that we may refer to chosen medical sterilisation as 'infertility', even though this may be viewed as a positive advantage; the presumption being that any state of affairs capable of being either valued or disvalued must, in itself, be value-free. These two arguments use 'infertility' in two different ways: in the first case to label the (factual) cause of some (value-laden) state of affairs, in the second to label the state of affairs itself. But in both cases a freedom from evaluation is argued for.

Corea's response might be that these are abstract points about the word at issue, which she is not disposed to deny; but that she is not in any case interested in such abstractions. In the mouths of the medical community, the word 'infertility', like the words 'cancer' or 'heart condition', can be seen most often being used to draw attention to medical problems, to things needing to be done, to medical advances, and so on, all of them clearly evaluative uses and in contexts in which such evaluation is typical.[9] It has already been suggested that a further move may then follow. Features of the evaluator himself may be highlighted in order to cash out some part of the nature of the context in which a term is used.

Corea's highlighted human features are gender and race conceived of as implying certain race and gender specific interests. But another feature of humans may be

conceived of quite differently, indeed, in contrast to such interested biases, that is, their moral attitudes. It may be claimed that humans (generally speaking)[10] are moral beings, who speak a moral discourse and live through moral understandings, institutions, and practices. Morality, in turn, is (whatever else it is) an attitude within which group interests may appear selfish (it may indeed be argued that selfishness is a basic moral characteristic, to be set against non-self-regarding altruism). Though science in its discourse may reveal certain gendered and racially specific outlooks, surely morality, in its discourse, in which such outlooks might be criticised (as sexist or racist, for example) must itself be beyond such criticisms. And, of course, if embryologists can speak moral language, they can apply such criticisms to their own practice; they may then come within the moral 'fold', and this seems to undermine a general attack on them as necessarily self-serving.

2. Embryologists' and Others' Moral Discourse

The last point may be supposed capable of being taken forward to two slightly different conclusions. The first is logical and centres on the use of moral discourse, *viz.*, all moral criticism takes place within moral discourse, any moral criticism of a particular use of moral discourse will by definition take place within the moral discourse. The idea of *morally* criticising the use of moral discourse *as a whole* would then be incoherent.[11] In this way, the use of moral discourse as a whole is beyond moral criticism.

   Corea must accept this, as will emerge shortly; but she has a slightly different point to make, I think.

> The technodocs' new emphases on "ethics" not only give them a high-minded language in which to wage battle for their self interest. It also gives them the appearance of being responsible, restrained and morally concerned.[12]

Corea is here characterising the role moral justification (and to that degree, moral discourse) plays in the context of artificial procreation and allied science as she sees it. It is, she says, designed to give a certain impression. But what follows from this? A potentially crippling scepticism will arise if this fact about some use of moral language is taken to characterise the use of moral discourse. Corea does not want (and does not have) to take this route, for she is implicitly able to distinguish (as in the quotation just cited) between the "appearance" of moral concern, and (presumably) genuine moral concern. Hence she implicitly accepts the logical conclusion that use of moral discourse cannot as a whole be morally criticised. But there will remain to her only a weak criticism of embryologists use of moral discourse if it rests upon suggestions of individual or collective bad faith alone. At the very least, persuasive reasons are required for thinking in this way of embryologists and clinicians involved in artificial procreation generally.

7. IS A 'HANDS OFF' POLICY TO REPRODUCTION PREFERABLE TO ARTIFICIAL INTERVENTION?

Maurizio Mori
Politeia. Centro per la formazione in politica ed etica
Milano, Italy
Editor *Bioetica. Rivista Interdisciplinare*

> *Just because the rule of sexual conduct by authority is dissolving, the need of conventions which will guide conduct is increasing. That, in fact, is the reason for the immense and urgent discussion of sex throughout the modern world. It is an attempt to attain an understanding of the bewilderingly new experiences to which few men or women know how to adjust themselves. The true business of the moralist in the midst of all this is not to denounce this and to advocate that, but to see as clearly as he can into the meaning of it, so that out of the chaos of pain and happiness and worry he may help to deliver a usable insight.*

Walter Lippmann

1. Introduction: Preliminary Distinctions and the Purpose of this Paper

Since the late '70s there has been a tremendous increase in our capacity to intervene in the human reproductive process. Contraception has become widely accepted and effective, abortion much safer and many new reproductive technologies have been introduced, such as IVF and prenatal diagnosis, to name but two. All together these new interventions, and particularly those concerning artificial reproduction which are our main concern in this paper, are likely to change not only our way of reproducing but also our view of what human reproduction is (or should be). For this reason there is a great deal of discussion over the ethical aspects of the new reproductive technologies. I think that this new concern is very important, but I think also that too much attention is currently devoted to the examination of each separate technical intervention and that too little interest is paid to the more general problem of the ethical frame involved. In this paper I want to try to redress this situation by focusing my attention on the general problem concerning the ethical permissibility of artificial interventions in human reproduction, though this means a risk of some generalisation and imprecision in details. And for this reason, too, I have chosen a general topic area, i.e. whether a 'hands off'

99

D. Evans (ed.), Creating the Child, 99–110.
© 1996 *Kluwer Law International. Printed in the Netherlands.*

policy in the human reproductive process is more neutral and more justifiable than artificial intervention.

Before examining this general question it may be convenient to make the thesis more precise by explaining some of its terms and presuppositions. By '"hands off" policy' I mean a policy recommending or advising no interference with the natural biological process of reproduction.[1] The ground for such a policy is that it is supposed to be 'more neutral' in the sense that it has at least 'fewer negative consequences' for people affected than the alternative provided by artificial intervention. Negative consequences may cover biological, social, psychological, and other consequences, and I leave their exact specification indeterminate, but it is assumed that there is a basis for comparison between the effects following an artificial intervention policy and a 'hands off' one, and that the latter is 'better' (or at least 'less bad') than the former, and for this reason is more justifiable. Finally, the assumption is that such a policy is justifiable from an *ethical* (or moral) point of view. In fact there are many possible viewpoints (legal, social, etc.). Nevertheless, here I presuppose that the understanding is that what is relevant is the *moral* point of view. As a matter of fact, at this level of discussion we want to know whether a 'hands off' policy is to be recommended or preferred (as more 'rational') and not whether it should be enforced, for instance by laws.

However, even these clarifications are not sufficient to define our task, and this is mainly because it is not at all clear what we mean by 'ethical' (or moral). As a matter of fact I think that there are two very different (and perhaps incommensurable) notions of ethics that sometimes are confused, and unless we are clear on this point, we cannot give an answer to our question. According to the first (and more traditional) notion, an ethics prescribes at least an *absolute* duty, i.e. a duty which does not admit of any exceptions and binds without qualifications. On the other hand, according to the second (and more recent) view, there are no absolute duties, but all duties are *prima facie*, that is, they bind only if there is no other stronger duty which takes precedence. These two notions of ethics are similar in that both use the notion of duty, but are also very different, since the reasons which justify compliance with the duty in each case are different, and so too is the hierarchy of different duties. These differences are so deep that sometimes holders of the absolute view think that holders of the *prima facie* view are not only immoral (because a certain duty wrongly overrides another one), but are also amoral (because they have a mistaken conception of what morality is).[2]

This distinction between the two notions of ethics is crucial for at least two reasons. First, because it makes clear that our received opinions derive from the absolute view, and in this view the 'hands off' policy is *a priori* better than artificial intervention for reasons which will become clear later on; and second, because even if conceptually the distinction between the two ethics is very clear, in practical life it is not easy to sort out the distinction and very often we are not fully aware of the consequences produced by a change departing from nature. In this sense, following what Lippmann says in the opening quotation, my task in this paper is not to advocate a particular position, but to try a logical analysis of the different positions. For these reasons, I think it is convenient to start with a short outline of the absolute view, which in a sense constitutes the

background of the whole story.

2. Outline of the Absolute View

Our common sense morality presupposes a grand world view according to which there is a design in the universe which sets the ground for the moral government of the world. Granted that, moral law prescribes obedience to this rational plan. The plan is independent of human volitions and decisions[3], and it is something towards the accomplishment of which our volitions should work. In particular, morality concerns absolutes. Such absolute prohibitions are not related (as commonly believed) to the fifth commandment "Thou shalt not kill", which has many exceptions, but to respect for the human body's (presupposed) teleology. There are two main finalistic processes in the human body. The first is self-preservation, and the absolute duty not to violate such a teleological process justifies the absolute prohibition of suicide. In this sense, suicide is not homicide, and it is not a violation of the fifth commandment[4]; but the idea of 'natural' death requires the prohibition of suicide. The other finalistic process of the human body is reproduction, and the absolute duty concerning it justifies the absolute prohibition of any 'interference' with such a process, such as contraception, permanent sterilisation, abortion, homosexuality, etc.

Such prohibitions are concerned to protect the 'transmission of life' and guarantee 'natural' birth, and the expression of sexuality is permitted only within marriage, which is conceived as indissoluble. Here we reach the third point of the picture. Marriage is the (moral and legal) institution devoted to procreation, and the absoluteness of moral obligation regarding the biological process is reflected in marriage's indissolubility. In other words, indissolubility is the other side of the coin of the absolute moral duty to respect the natural teleology of the reproductive process. So marriage is a very peculiar contract, because it is subscribed to and accepted by the interested parties, but they cannot choose the nature of the agreement, which is defined according to 'nature'.

This general moral view, according to which sex is allowed only within an indissoluble marriage, has specific consequences at a legal level. Law is concerned mainly with public effects, and not with private and intimate facts. So, apart from the fact that females having adulterous relationships were punished, legal control was usually effected through the consequences of sexually unlawful relations. As a matter of fact, children born outside marriage were not recognised as 'legitimate children'. This is a point of the utmost importance, because it shows that according to the traditional view 'children' can be born only within a (valid) marriage. They are not the biological product of two individuals but the result of marriage by means of the cooperation of the husband and the wife.[5] This point is even clearer if we look at regulations concerning the children of adulterous relationships. In fact there is always a presumption that the husband is the father, unless he wants to disown a child. In this case, the Italian law, for instance, admits a procedure according to which within a given time the husband may show that his wife was unfaithul and that such a child is not his. But, this action is a husband's faculty (or choice), because if for whatever reason he

may prefer to do nothing, then automatically such a child is his own son (or daughter). This might occur even if many people knew that biologically the child was not the offspring of the husband. On the other hand, if the husband was successful in disowning his child, such a child had 'no father' in the technical sense.[6]

According to the traditional view briefly outlined here, it is clear that parenthood is a *social* relation, and not a *biological* one; being a son depends on a valid marriage (and if there is no marriage the off-spring is not legally speaking a 'son' or a 'daughter'). But since the institution of marriage is regulated (and protected) according to the absolute duty regarding licit sex, usually there is a coincidence between the two sorts of relationships (social and biological). From this viewpoint, the 'hands off' policy concerning reproduction is certainly the best policy, because human beings should not interfere with the natural teleological process of procreation.

It should be noticed that this point is justified because, according to the traditional worldview, teleology in nature is evidence for the grand design intrinsic to the universe, so that if we recognise biological teleology and the absolute duty to respect it, we implicitly recognise the divine plan intrinsic to reality and the moral government of the world underlying it. And here we have a connection between morality (and law) and theology: as a matter of fact, from the Catholic perspective, marriage is not only a special contract, it is also a sacrament and, more precisely, a *sacramentum magnum*. So the natural process is elevated to a new dimension, and what is natural joins with the super-natural, nature with grace.

I have outlined the ethical, legal and theological presupposition of what I call the 'traditional view' not only because it is still strongly supported by Catholics, but also because I think it is a major (possibly still the main) source of received opinions and still provides a sort of general framework within which to interpret reality. However, in recent centuries it has been challenged, and now I want to begin an examination of the points over which it is criticised.

3. Criticisms of the Absolute View of Family Ethics in the Past

It would be surprising if today someone in an ethical argument considered even some purely dogmatic-theological aspects with regards to marriage, but I think consideration of such aspects is important because these remarks allow us an historical perspective. As a matter of fact, the theological aspect of the traditional view of family ethics was the first one to be challenged in the Western world, and in particular during the Reformation. As is well known, reformers denied that marriage was a sacrament, and therefore admitted its solubility, at least for non-believers. While Catholics still hold that indissolubility is 'rational' and 'natural', so that each righteous man (independently of his faith) should accept it, for most reformed denominations this view is nonsense, because after the Fall the whole relationship between 'nature' and 'grace' was changed, and it is not any more possible to perceive the moral government of the world. I stress this point because in one sense the origins of the crisis of what I call the 'traditional

view' are to be found in the Reformation, that is, they are to be found at a purely theological level.

However, for about three centuries no significant consequence was perceived at the practical, normative level, because the first serious arguments in favour of divorce had to await French Revolutionary times. Even J.-J. Rousseau held that the family is a 'natural society' different from the larger society based on the 'social contract', and that such a natural society has its own peculiar rules which are not freely decided by the contracting parties. Taking this into account, and even though some Revolutionaries advocated a legalisation of divorce, we have to wait up to the end of the 19th century and our century before finding a widespread movement for the legalisation of divorce. And even though in our century new laws have been passed concerning divorce, defenders of reform often argued only on legal grounds, admitting its immorality. Once divorce is allowed on normative grounds, the absolute view begins to fail, and marriage looses the peculiarity of being a very 'special contract', and this constitutes an important step in a practical change of mentality.

However, divorce affects what we can call the *social* aspect of marriage, i.e. the cohabitation level, it does not influence moral and legal views on other aspects of family life, in particular those connected with biological processes. As a matter of fact, in this area the traditional view has maintained its influence, and probably for good historical reasons. On the one hand, we should not forget that only at the very end of the 18th century - with Malthus' celebrated book[7] - did the 'population problem' begin to be an issue. Up to then, the general idea was that stated by Adam Smith (and many others) according to which the most decisive mark of the prosperity of any country is the increase of the number of its inhabitants. This view continued to be common for long after Smith's time, and I dare to say that it is even now upheld by some. On the other hand, we have to wait until late 19th century for technically effective means of contraception to become available. A brief look at history shows that Christian churches in general, and the Roman Catholic church in particular, vigorously opposed contraception because - as Lippmann reports - they immediately recognised "that whether or not birth control is eugenic, hygienic, and economic, it is the most revolutionary practice in the history of sexual morals".[8] While the Catholic church rejected (and still does) contraception *on principle*, being an act contrary to natural moral law, many others, like Lippmann himself, opposed contraception on different grounds. He thought that ultimately the practice of birth control would be self-defeating in terms of human happiness and fulfilment.

Lippmann's argument deserves some attention. He admits that divorce and birth control sometimes are "remedies for manifest evils"[9], but even if remedies for failure are important, they are not enough to constitute an ideal by which one expects to live successfully. And at this point Lippmann remarks that birth control will not produce human happiness because those who support it wrongly assume that the primary function (procreative) and the secondary function (compagnate) of sex can be set "in separate compartments of the soul".[10] But

since human nature is organic and experience cumulative, our activities must, so to speak, engage and imply each other. Mates who are not lovers will not really cooperate, as Mr. Bertrand Russell thinks they should, in bearing children; they will be distracted, insufficient, and worst of all they will be merely dutiful. Lovers who have nothing to do but love each other are not really to be envied; love and nothing else very soon is nothing else. The emotion of love, in spite of the romantics, is not self-sustaining; it endures only when the lovers love many things together, and not merely each other. It is this understanding that love cannot successfully be isolated from the business of living which is the enduring wisdom of the institution of marriage.[11]

The deep fallacy of romantic theory is that it rests on an immature theory of desire which fails "to realize that compatibility is a process and not an accident, that depends upon the maturing of instinctive desire by adaptation to the whole nature of the other person and to the common concerns of the pair of lovers".[12] Lippmann suggests "the schooling of desire" instead of the logic of birth control as a more reliable way "to transcend naive desire and to reach out towards a mature and disinterested partnership with their world".[13]

I have devoted some attention to the history of these criticisms of the 'traditional view', because I think that we can learn at least two things from them. We can learn, first, that it takes time and the appropriate historical conditions before a change of moral principle can show its effects in practical life. So, for example, theologically the absolute principle of indissolubility of marriage was abandoned in the 16th century, but it was not until a few centuries later that this abstract move produced some palpable consequences for social life; and it took about another hundred years before the moral acceptability of contraception was admitted by large fractions of the population, after the '60s with the 'pill-revolution'. Second, we can learn that a superficially similar position can be justified for different reasons, and sometimes it is not easy to distinguish and to evaluate them, particularly in the heat of the discussion.

The situation becomes simpler after some time, because then the first task (concerning a clear individuation of the different arguments) is easier, even if the evaluative task still presents some problems. As a matter of fact it is difficult either to say or to deny that birth control is contrary to our (psychological) nature because according to our organic nature and the cumulativenss of our experience we should keep united the two functions of biological life, unless we espouse the wrong assumption that our soul is separated into different compartments. Certainly it is still possible to say that a person is happier if he or she can school his or her desires so as to keep the primary and secondary functions united, but it seems to me that this is not true, or at least it needs further arguments to show it is. But a supporter of Lippmann's view can hold that if one can achieve this, his happiness will be much greater, and it is difficult to argue against this view. On the other hand it is even more difficult to criticise the opposing view. In fact we would have to prove that there is no teleology in biological nature or that there is no alleged absolute duty to respect such a teleology, and this is a metaphysical task

which is outside the scope of our inquiry. There are strong reasons in favour of the appearance that there is an intrinsic teleology in the reproductive process, and in this sense sterility is an illness which can be cured by reinstating the proper function. But for the same reason, sterilisation (temporary or permanent) is contrary to the goals of medicine, because it is analogous to the inducement of an illness. On the other hand, this view is strongly counter-intuitive, because we are inclined to hold that divorce and contraception are allowed, and therefore we have to give up the whole logical construction. But of course someone can argue that our current intuitions are misleading and we have to change them.

I am fully aware that it is not easy to criticise these views, but I do not need to do so here. As I indicated at the beginning, my argument aims to show the logical differences between different perspectives. So far I have shown that historically we have had three perspectives: the traditional one based on absolute principles; a moderate one holding a similar position but for different reasons; and a radical one. I think we have to realise that the pre-eminent one was the most radical, and that we have given up the idea of an absolute ethics. I think that people like Lippmann have a lot to say concerning love as a process of self-education, but they are mistaken because they do not understand that they have completely to change our current perspective. In any case, now that we have examined the past, we can procede to consider problems of the present and near future.

4. Current Problems of Family Ethics Concerning Artificial Interventions in the Human Reproductive Process

I remarked that when we are involved in a controversy it is difficult even to individuate the problem at issue with clarity, and this is not only because it takes time and appropriate socio-historical conditions before we can discover all the consequences of the abandonment of a moral principle, but also because it may happen that even if we explicitly abandon a principle, it may remain in the back of our minds, so we still continue to think as if it were there. In other words, the abandonment of a principle requires a sort of *Gestalt* switch, but in some cases we still continue to think in terms of the old view. This happens more often when it is possible to maintain similar (or even equivalent) practical conclusions by means of different kinds of justification, because in these cases we are led to a peculiar sort of mis-description of the general situation in order to continue to hold the received intuitions. I think that this is one of the main problems concerning our doubts about the morality of artificial intervention in human reproduction and the 'hands off' policy.

There are several instances of this sort of mistake, and probably the most controversial and highly debated is the one concerning abortion. Nowadays abortion is opposed as a kind of homicide and not as a kind of contraception. This probably depends on the widespread acceptance of contraception which would make any alleged prohibition of abortion on those grounds totally ineffective, so that in order to maintain the prohibition it has shifted to a different justification. This topic, however, does not concern us here,

but I have discussed it elsewhere.[14] At this stage, I think it more important to examine another mistake concerning the notion of parenthood, because it is more connected with our topic of the 'hands off' policy. As we have seen, in the traditional view it was clear that parenthood was a social relationship (and not a biological one), depending on the existence of marriage. But since marriage was itself seen as regulated according to natural law, usually there was a coincidence between social and genetic parenthood.[15]

We have abandoned natural law in so far as it concerns divorce and contraception, but the newness of the separation of sex and reproduction leads us to be astonished by the new possibilities open to us, so that some people think that the new interventions are an 'assault on parenthood'.[16] Of course, so goes the argument, this is not true in all cases, as sometimes the new technologies may be helpful in overcoming the infertility of a couple, but this happens only in the 'simple' case, i.e. when all the genetic material comes from the couple while both partners are alive. In such cases, technology is only a help to overcome natural misfortune. But all the other interventions are problematic and controversial as they separate the biological aspect from the social one. So, even without going into more complex cases which nowadays are possible, something as technically straightforward as artificial insemination by donor (AID) is strongly criticised because in it the biological aspect does not correspond to the social one. From the viewpoint being considered, it is held that even in the relatively simple case a 'hands off' policy concerning reproduction is more neutral or more justifiable than artificial intervention.

But it is exactly at this point that we have to consider the justification given to such an opposition to artificial intervention in the reproductive process. And here we find different options. We can continue to say that there is an absolute duty not to intervene, and in this case we abandon even the most simple case of AIH (i.e. insemination within the couple), as, with due coherence the magisterium of the Catholic church does. On this view, once again, it is certainly possible to maintain that a 'hands off' policy is more justifiable than artificial intervention. Indeed, artificial intervention is *a priori* mistaken simply because it violates the principle. But it is exactly at this point that such a view shows difficulties: in fact the appearance is that sometimes such an intervention is beneficial, and that we have to abandon the *a priori* prohibition.

But when we come to empirical argument, the case against artificial intervention rests either on a confusion arising from the fact already noticed that the *Gestalt* switch has not been completed or from debatable assumptions concerning human nature. Let's examine both cases separately.

The incompleteness of the *Gestalt* switch, I think, depends on a mistake produced by the fact that having once abandoned the absolute principle we nevertheless still continue to maintain some traditional insights by means of a re-description. This becomes clear in the case of AID. We have seen that in the traditional view it was clear that parenthood was a social relation depending on a valid marriage, and it was a problem of marriage to ensure the biological relation. Currently, the absolute view on marriage has vanished, but the common sense idea of 'biological' parenthood is still maintained through a re-description. Because of the regular coincidence of the 'social' father with

the 'biological' one, someone is led to think that parenthood depends on the genetic (or biological or physiological) relationship, and AID would really be disruptive of parenthood taken in this way. In support of this view, authors sometimes admit that the older legislation forbade legal recognition of children born outside marriage, but remark that changes occurring in this century show that more recently parenthood is related to the genetic aspect. According to these authors this is confirmed by the fact that in recent legislation even babies born outside marriage are children (natural children) exactly as are those born within a marriage, and the same applies even in case of adulterous off-spring, who are children of the biological father. On this view the fact that blood and DNA analysis are nowadays permitted (and sometimes required) in order to find out who the biological father is shows that more recent legal systems have abandoned the older traditional view in order to accept a newer one, according to which the biological relationship is the essential one. In this sense some disagreeable (or disgusting) results of the older legislation are avoided (for instance the impossibility of recognition of some natural off-spring). However, the main point is maintained since AID would be against the spirit of current Italian legislation.

However, even if it is true that most current legislation (like the Italian one) allows a much larger possibility for research into who the biological father is, this happens not because 'fatherhood' is supposed to be primarily a biological concept, but because the biological aspect is evidence of a certain act the consequences of which the man is held to be responsible for. That is to say the *ratio* underlying more recent legislation on parenthood is based on the concept of 'social responsibility' for certain acts, responsibility that in the traditional view was ascribed directly to the marriage contract (regulated by natural law), and now is ascribed directly to individuals. But in any case, even on this account, fatherhood (and parenthood in general) is a *social* concept and not a biological one, and therefore, having once abandoned the traditional absolute view prescribing a full respect for biological teleology, we can choose to ascribe responsibility in the way most convenient to social life. So more recent legislation has ascribed responsibility to the sexual act as such in order to avoid 'fatherless children' or even 'no man's children'. On this view, in the case of natural off-spring it is allowed (and even compulsory) to search out the man whose genetic material is the cause of such an off-spring, and this man is held responsible for the birth of the child and cannot avoid becoming (legally) the father. Nevertheless, there is no special problem in saying that in the case of AID the donor is not the father, and this is because he donated his sperm to another man, and therefore he is not responsible for the consequences deriving from the use made of his donation. Of course, it is debatable whether such a policy is socially beneficial, but this is a socio-psychological problem to be solved at the appropriate level. Certainly, sometimes AID produces some difficulties, but the appearance is that in general with a proper regulation it is beneficial, and that, this being so, the 'hands off' policy is not justified. Of course such a policy may be more neutral or justifiable in the case of other artificial interventions, but this cannot be shown through generalisation and must be proved in any individual case according to empirical evidence.

Having cleared up the confusion concerning the alleged 'empirical' argument in favour of the 'hands off' policy, I can now focus my attention on the second one, which I want to examine in the version advanced by Oliver O'Donovan.[17] According to O'Donovan, it is possible to show that a 'hands off' policy in reproduction is better than artificial intervention because "the relation of human beings to their own bodies ... is the last frontier of nature. ... When we take off our clothes to have a bath, we confront something as natural, as given, as completely nonartifactual as anything in this universe".[18] In this light, to say - as has been said - that "to do nothing is just as much an ethical decision to be defended as to introduce new methods of therapy"[19] is to shift the tradition of medicine according to which there was a presumption in favour of the natural process. But this shifting of the burden of the proof results in a real revolution which ends up being unfavourable and negative for human beings. In fact:

> human freedom has a natural substrate, a presupposition. Before we can evoke and create new beings which conform to the laws we lay down for them by our making, we have to accept this being according to its own laws which we have not laid down. If, by refusing its laws and imposing our freedom wantonly upon it, we cause it to break down, our freedom breaks down with it. This is in fact the law of our relations with all nature, with the climate, the soil, the animal world.[20]

And particularly, it is the law of relations with our own bodies. If we try to abolish the limits implicit in our bodies, we have a self-defeating result, because we think we reach real freedom when in fact we become slaves.

Mutatis mutandis, O'Donovan's attempt is reminiscent of Lippmann's one to prove that contraception is against human interests. If it was difficult to criticise Lippmann's argument, it is even more difficult to criticise O'Donovan. However, I do suggest the analogy because I think that if the limits of human freedom have their last frontier in human bodily constitution, then this frontier was already violated with the acceptance of contraception and the rejection of the natural moral law. Certainly the new reproductive technologies are more powerful, but this quantitative difference does not affect the *conceptual* problem which is at stake. Nor is the psychological shock that these new artificial interventions have on people significant, because very likely it depends on the novelty of the facts, and we have already forgotten how astonishing was the idea of allowing contraception in the first half of our century. Given this, once again, either we do accept the absolute view, or we give it up, and then we have no general empirical argument to prove that the 'hands off' policy is more neutral or more justifiable than artificial intervention. In order to achieve such a proof, we would have to examine empirical data as to what happens in real societies so as to see whether or not a specific intervention is disruptive of individual or social life.

Notes

1. *Webster's Dictionary* defines 'hands off' as "don't touch! don't interfere!" and the *American Heritage Dictionary* defines it as "Do not touch. Keep away".

2. For a difference between these two notions of ethics, see Mori, M. 'Etica' in *Appendice 1991 Grande Dizionario Enciclopedico* (terza edizione), Torino, UTET, 1991, pp.276-285. The two notions are based on similar distinctions made by Frankena, W.K., in the 'Postscript' to the Italian edition of his *Ethics*.

3. Certainly it is not independent of our knowledge, but we know something that is independent of our existence.

4. I do not want to argue for this point here. But see Mori, M., 'Sulla distinzione tra eutanasia e sospensione delle cure' in Salvoldi, Valentino (ed.), *Oltre l'eutanasia e l'accanimento terapeutico. Politica, scienza e morale* Bologna, Edizioni Dehoniane, 1991, pp.125-180.

5. So according to the traditional view 'illegitimate off-spring' could not receive any inheritance, and this shows that they had no 'real' family.

6. For more information on this point, see Mori, M. *La fecondazione artificiale: questioni morali nell'esperienza giuridica* Giuffrè, Milano, 1988, and Mori, M. 'Nuove tecnologie riproduttive ed etica della qualità della vita. Per un chiarimento dei problemi morali posti dalla 'rivoluzione riproduttiva'', in Ferrando, Gilda (ed.), *La procreazione artificiale tra etica e diritto* Padova, Cedam, 1989, pp.246-317.

7. Malthus, Thomas, *An Essay on the Principle of Population as it Affects the Future Improvement of Society* London, 1798.

8. Lippmann, W., *A Preface to Morals* London, George Allen, 1929, p.291.

9. *Ibid.*, p.308.

10. *Ibid.*

11. *Ibid.*, pp.308-9.

12. *Ibid.*, p.310.

13. *Ibid.*, p.313.

14. For an analysis of these topics, cf. Mori, M. 'Abortion and health care ethics I: a critical analysis of the main arguments' in Gillon, R. and Lloyd, A. (eds), *Principles of Health Care Ethics* Chichester, John Wiley and sons, 1994, pp.531-546, and Mori, M. (two part article), 'Do we have a moral duty not to cause human embryos' death?' *Forum. Trends in Experimental and Clinical Medicine* Vol. 3, No. 2, March/April 1993, pp.5-12, 'An analysis of the problems concerning ethical treatment of embryos' *Forum. Trends in Experimental and Clinical Medicine* Vol. 3, No. 3, May/June 1993, pp.13-18.

15. I should remark that strictly speaking there is no 'genetic' *parenthood*, since the notion of parenthood is only *social*. We should speak of genetic *ascendents*.

16. This is the title of a very disappointing book, by DeMarco, D., *Biotechnology and the Assault on Parenthood* San Francisco, Ignatius Press, 1991.

17. O'Donovan, O., *Begotten or Made?* Oxford, Oxford University Press, 1984.

18. *Ibid.*, p.5.

19. *Ibid.*, p.4.

20. *Ibid.*, p.5.

8. NATURALLY CONCEIVED

The Idea of the Natural in Moral Arguments About Assisted Conception

Neil Pickering
Centre for Philosophy and Health Care
University of Wales, Swansea
Singleton Park
Swansea
Wales

This paper will attempt to explore the idea of the natural, and the significance of that idea, in the context of reproductive medicine. IVF and AID, and moral disagreements about these procedures, will form its background. The intention of this paper is to attempt to see how the notion of natural procreation is used by the disputants. How may we characterise these moral disputes, given the use of the idea of natural human procreation?

The paper will, first, present two positions which may both be opposed to, or at least doubtful about the appropriateness of, IVF or AID or both. Second, it will look at some of the below-the-surface agreements and disagreements which may be found in the two initially identified moral attitudes to assisted procreation, and at how these are associated with 'natural procreation'. Third, the paper will look at the logical features of one of these conceptualisations, particularly as it involves three 'realms' (as I shall call them for the time being); these being the realms of the human, of the natural, and of the divine.

1. Two Possible Positions Concerning the Appropriateness of Assisted Conception

Both the positions put forward in this section may be seen as opposed to assisted conception. The first position I shall call natural procreation and humanness.[1] In this, humanness is perceived as contrary to and threatened by reproductive technologies.

> ... technological power does not guarantee truly human solutions to the deepest human problems. ... technology is there to give us what we want. But we ought to ask questions of value. We ought to ask what constitutes 'the good life', what it is that fulfils people's deep humanity.[2]

An important proponent of these ideas, O'Donovan, adds that if these questions are not

D. Evans (ed.), Creating the Child, 111–125.
© 1996 *Kluwer Law International. Printed in the Netherlands.*

asked we may have " ... a society ... incapable of acknowledging the inappropriateness of technical intervention in certain types of activity".[3] He makes a specific link to the 'natural' and to 'natural procreation' in particular:

> The great intellectual challenge that faces our age in view of these innovations [perhaps IVF and AID] is not to understand *that* this or that may or may not be done, but to understand *what* it is that would be done, if it were done. And it would be mere intellectual evasiveness to pretend that the human mode of reproduction was a contingency that chanced upon our human race, and might as well not have done.[4]

The second sentence seems to be a *non-sequitur*. O'Donovan's point is that the proper evaluation of IVF (an understanding of what is done when IVF is carried out) requires an understanding that the human mode of procreation is not a contingency of humanness. An earlier writer to whom O'Donovan is indebted, Paul Ramsey, argues:

> ... [I]f, and only if, we highly respect the God-given nature of human parenthood are we apt to resist the powerful pressures in our technological civilization toward breaking apart and recombining in a multitude of possible ways, the personal and the biological dimensions in human procreation.[5]

The breaking apart and recombination of these dimensions of human procreation is, in effect, to act as if the natural human mode of procreation were just one, and hence, contingent, possibility. But, for O'Donovan and Ramsey, it is not. Moreover, there is a natural unity among the elements of natural human procreation. About this unity, more will be said later. The unity has a moral authority in being the gift of God, and more will be said about this too in what follows.

This unity and the naturalness of human procreation is essential, in the view of O'Donovan, to our humanity. The principle feature of technological procreation is that what results from it cannot be human. This seems a stark claim, and it is one which O'Donovan himself has some difficulty in holding on to. Nevertheless, he sees he is in some sense committed to it:

> That which we beget is *like* ourselves. ... But that which we make is *unlike* ourselves. ... That which we 'make', then, is alien from our humanity. In that it has a human maker, it has come to existence as a human project, its being at the disposal of mankind. ... [M]an's will is the law of its being.[6]

(The word 'beget' stands for natural human procreation.) Something of the implication of this analysis can be grasped if the impersonal pronouns here are replaced by third person personal pronouns. '*She* has come to existence as a human project, *her* being at the disposal of mankind'. O'Donovan seems to present this as a view likely to dominate if attitudes shown by some medical techniques in reproductive medicine

interests then that is the wrong sort.

What is to count for (or against) that in any particular case? A problem may be perceived as arising here. The relation of discourse to speaker may be said generally to have an ambiguous character; and this particularly where the individuals' self interest may be involved. Certain branches of psychology, for instance, seem to start from this possibility.

> The focus of discursive psychology is the action orientation of talk and writing. ... Rather than seeing such discursive constructions as expressions of speakers' underlying cognitive states, they are examined in the context of their occurrence as situated and occasioned constructions whose precise nature makes sense ... in terms of the social actions those descriptions accomplish.[30]

Thus, someone who produces a scientific, a moral, or any other, description of some state of affairs is not, as it might appear (to other branches of psychology, such as 'perceptual cognitivism' for instance[31]), revealing an underlying 'objectivity' in her mind, and is not taking on a non-subjective stance (though she may claim to be doing so). Rather, when one looks one sees that "in everyday discourse, descriptions and reports are often drawn on precisely when there is a sensitive or controversial issue at stake".[32] Potter and Edwards continue:

> Indeed, we suggest that reports and descriptions may be used to manage what, for participants in natural settings, is often a crucial dilemma: the dilemma of presenting factual reports while being treated as having a stake in some specific version of events or some practical outcome.[33]

The dilemma, in moral cases, may be stated in terms of the extent to which the choice of or commitment to particular practices is conditioned (on the one hand) by something intrinsically good in them which makes them worthy of commitment, and (on the other hand) by someone's interests (and so forth) in the service of which she find's them useful.[34]

There may be a temptation to dissolve this dilemma. The mixture of the self-interested and the moral seems on one reading of Corea's account fatal to the latter. This is not because the embryologists have no genuine moral commitments to the meeting of needs and so forth. Rather, on this account, embryologists have no genuine moral commitments to these because they have (selfish) interests in acting as if there were genuine need here. On this account, an act can have moral value at all only where it is wholly appropriately motivated. A position like this is reminiscent of parts of Kant's *Groundwork*.[35]

This seems to set too stiff a test. One reason for thinking this is that it is not clear that the mere presence of self-interested motives in a particular person's acts must nullify the act in moral terms (at least in the sense that the moral reason - the authentic commitment to what is worthy in the act - cannot have carried any weight in the

person's motivation). Even the murderous Bill Sykes, who has the blood of Nancy on his hands, and who, when on the run, acts with great bravery at a fire, may be admired for his acts there, though it may be said that, at the same time, he has the deepest self interest in doing something good. However, the interest is not just in *appearing* to do something good, but actually in doing good.[36] The distinction between appearing to do something good and actually doing something good may be said to rest upon the appeal to what is intrinsically good in the act. If it is argued that Sykes did what he did to make himself feel better, we may still ask what it is in acting bravely at the fire which did make him feel better? I would suggest we cannot rule out that it was the sense of having done something fine, good, right.

Corea's own position, when taken as a whole is, in any case, a corrective to *a priori* ruling out the possibility of goodness among those who also have race and gender bias. The description of Antonia - to which this paper is about to return - invites a particularity of attention to the human individual within the numerous contexts in which individuals find themselves.

4. Shared Discourses. Shared Values?

At the risk of repetition, Gena Corea, appearing at the committee hearings into Depo-Provera, quoted the extract from *My Antonia* and then said:

> When a woman is real to you as Antonia was real to Willa Cather and to her character Jim Burden, you cannot say: Let's give her this powerful drug, Depo-Provera, which causes cancer in animals and may or may not cause cancer in human beings, and then let us do a prospective study and see if Antonia does indeed become cancerous. You could not do it. ... such thoughts would be unendurable because you would know what a great loss would be the defeat of Antonia'a body and spirit.[37]

This is a summing up of Corea's sense of the moral potency of the image of Antonia which Willa Cather has created. What is appealed to here? The original writing, as Corea indicates, is particular - if, that is, we may interpret Corea's use of the word 'real' here as meaning something like 'individually present'. The individuality is signified by Corea's (and Cather's) use of a personal name, and by the reference to Jim Burden's memories of Antonia: she has a story of her own. Cather's writing is also positive, perhaps celebratory in its tone, which may be implied in Corea's words by the reference to Antonia's spirit.

With her individuality and the celebration comes also the value - that is the moral value - which, it might be said, is *inter alia* what has been individualised and celebrated. Perhaps the value may be cashed out in terms of Antonia's rights, needs, and so on. Cather speaks in different terms:

She lent herself to immemorial human attitudes which we recognise by instinct as universal and true. ... [S]he still had that something which fires the imagination, could still stop one's breath for a moment by a look or gesture that somehow revealed the meaning in common things. She has only to stand in the orchard, to put her hand on a little crab tree and look up at the apples, to make you feel the goodness of planting and tending and harvesting at last.

It has been the intention of this paper to consider the way in which moral discourse has been presented by its speakers, among other things, and it is interesting to do that here (with Corea's use of this passage) too. First, in Corea's drawing attention to Antonia, there is an appeal to that which is given, in some sense. Antonia's body and spirit are there to be seen, to be found, if one will only look. The impossibility of experimenting on Antonia arises from her reality, and that is all one needs to know that it would be 'unendurable' to do anything to defeat that by experimentation: knowing this one could not but be blind to other points (for example, the 'benefits' of carrying out the experiments - and such a blindness would not be culpable). And there is a sense in which the considerations which Corea invokes seem not to be chosen by her. She has not elected to speak like this of Antonia: she is controlled, if you like, by these considerations herself.

In making implicit claims about this discourse and about its relation to her own life, Corea may be seeking to draw attention to something which may be shared by both listener and speaker. The sharedness is expressed, perhaps, in these ideas: That what may be found, may be found by more than one; that what may 'blind' one may 'blind' others too; and that what may be a binding or controlling value, and is (as it may be) a binding value for the speaker and for the listener, suggests, and indeed is, part of the substance of a shared way of living.

An appeal to these controlling and fundamental values cannot make them shared. Corea may suggest in speaking this discourse the hope of being understood. But, at the same time, she may well be aware that the actual and particular view point of those who share this discourse, and use it to make and express their judgements, may be deeply different from her own. Her analysis has traced a source of such differences in race and gender interests; yet in reaching across the divide between her and the technodocs with this passage she expresses the hope that these interests may be put aside.

The question then arises as to whether moral differences of that sort can always be traced to interests (such as gender or race). In response, someone may say that the more profound disagreements are not those merely between interest groups, but exactly those which arise within and are made possible by having a moral life and speaking a moral discourse.

Notes

1. Cather, W., *My Antonia* 1987, p.926 quoted in Corea, G., 'Depo Provera and the politics of knowledge' in Hynes, H. Patricia (ed.), *Reconstructing Babylon. Essays on Women and Technology* London, Earthscan Publications Ltd., 1990, pp.188-214, p.206.

2. Corea, *ibid.*, pp.207-208.

3. For example, the human reality of the scientist lies behind his words. Robert Edwards, speaking of his early work, points out "that it was more than ten years before any other clinic produced human embryos of comparable quality, indicating how far ahead we were in our concepts of treating infertility during those early years" (Edwards, Robert, 'Ethics and embryology: the case for experimentation' in Dyson, Anthony and Harris, John (eds), *Experiments on Embryos* London, Routledge, 1989, pp.42-54, p.44). From this may be inferred the presence of ordinary human competitiveness within the practice of embryology. More broadly, it may be asked why scientists choose the particular fields they do, or pursue certain lines within them, and whether such choices could be made independently of a desire for academic cudos or (less cynically) of moral concern. Janice Raymond speaks of the new reproductive technologies as "more of an ideological than a technical feat - more of a medical and media production" (Raymond, Janice G., 'Of eggs, embryos and altruism' in Hynes (ed.), *op.cit.*, pp.83-91, p.87). Raymond's point here is that embryology is inherently self-serving; that its aim is to expand its own area of operations, its own cudos, and so forth. But such an aim is conceivable only where science is interested in such human things.

4. It might be argued that it is not logically impossible for race and gender to become forgotten categories.

5. I shall use the term 'white' hereafter to refer to this racial group, though it should be noted that it may be said to cover a wide range of races on some accounts.

6. Gilbert, G. Nigel and Mulkay, Michael, *Opening Pandora's Box* Cambridge, Cambridge University Press, 1984, p.9.

7. Cf. Holm, Søren, 'Infertility, childlessness and the need for treatment' in this volume, and Evans, Donald, 'The clinical classification of infertility' also in this volume.

8. Someone may say that it is no less a discoverable fact about infertility that it strikes at such human concerns, than that it may be caused by a low sperm count. Nevertheless, it might be argued the former fact cannot be a fact within embryology.

9. "We believed the most urgent [study] was the alleviation of infertility" (Edwards, *op.cit.*, p.44); "We felt that the urgency of treatment for patients with infertility, which has far more serious implications to health than is usually accepted was sufficient justification to continue the work" (*ibid.*, p.45).

10. I believe some socio- or psycho-paths are described as lacking what is widely regarded as a genuine grasp of moral notions.

11. This might be because the notion of 'the use of moral discourse as a whole' is itself incoherent. Perhaps a better, though necessarily slightly longer winded way of putting the point is this: that if we regarded each particular moral statement, assertion, judgement, claim, etc, as morally untrustworthy (a form perhaps of self interest thinly disguised) then the way of life in which we tend to take these at face value would collapse. This is not of course to claim that there could not be a society in which 'moral' language played only the role

of advancing self-interest; it is to claim only that it would be a vastly different society from the one we might be said to live in, and which Corea presumes (and indeed has to presume) in much of what she says.

12. Corea 'Who may have children and who may not' in Hynes (ed.), *op. cit.*, pp.92-102, p.101.

13. "Speaking in favour of embryo research and experimentation, doctors constantly reiterate that it is unethical not to help people in need" (Raymond, *op. cit.*, p.89; "For the husband of an infertile woman, the use of a surrogate may be the only way in which he can conceive and rear a child with a biologic tie to himself ... " (Corea, 'Who may have children and who may not', *op. cit.*, p.95). Edwards notes at one point that "For me, the ethics of such work is fundamentally utilitarian ..." (Edwards, *op. cit.*, p.48) and at another that "I have obviously taken a consequentialist viewpoint to justify research on embryos ..." (*ibid.*, p.51).

14. "Mr Powell's Bill [the Unborn Children's Protection Bill] tried to insist on the need for infertile couples to gain the Secretary of State's permission to undergo in vitro fertilisation, and this attempt to impose a political decision on couples seeking to have a child must surely be one of the most serious infringements of individual rights ever to be placed before the Mother of Parliaments" (Edwards, *op. cit.*, p.54).

15. "These kindly looking physicians may even speak with a feminist or liberal rhetoric, passionately defending a woman's right to choose these technologies and 'control her own body'" (Corea ('How the new reproductive technologies ... '), *op. cit.*, p.78). Corea also quotes a report of the AFS "A strong legal argument can also be made that a married couple's procreative liberty would include the right to enlist the assistance of a third-party donor or surrogate to provide the gametes or uterine function necessary for the couple to beget, bear, or otherwise acquire for rearing a child genetically related to one of the partners" (in Corea, 'Who may have children and who may not', *op. cit.*, p.101 quoting The Ethics Committee of the American Fertility Society, 'Ethical considerations of the new reproductive technologies' *Fertility and Sterility* Vol. 46, No. 3, suppl. 1, September 1986, p.4).

16. Raymond, *op. cit.*, p.86.

17. Corea ('How the new reproductive technologies will affect all women'), *op. cit.*, p.76.

18. This is, of course, philosophically rather deep and treacherous water. For accounts of debates relating to the independence of the moral realm, see Mackie, J.L. *Ethics. Inventing Right and Wrong* Harmondsworth, Penguin, 1977, especially chapter 1, and Singer, P. (ed.), *A Companion to Ethics* Oxford, Basil Blackwell, 1991, chapters 35-39. If the reader disagrees with what is said here, I hope they will take it that this forms a fundamental assumption of whole paper, one which might be questioned in a different context.

19. Hynes, *op. cit.*, pp.15-16.

20. *Ibid.*, p.14.

21. Dudden, Barbara, (trans. Hoinacki, Lee), *Disembodying Women. Perspectives on Pregnancy and the Unborn* (*Der Frauenleib als Öffentlicher Ort: Vom Missbrauch des Begriffs Leben*) Cambridge, Mass., Harvard University Press, 1993 (in German 1991). She asks: "How did the unborn turn into a billboard image and how did that isolated goblin get into the limelight? How did the female peritoneum acquire transparency? What set of circumstances made the skinning of woman acceptable and inspired public concern for what happens in her innards? And, finally, the embarrassing question: how was it possible to mobilize so many women as uncomplaining agents of this skinning and as willing witnesses to the creation of this haunting symbol of loneliness?" (p.7). She earlier describes her purpose in the book as follows: "I want to

examine the conditions under which, in the course of one generation, technology along with a new discourse has transformed pregnancy into a process to be managed, the expected child into a fetus, the mother into an ecosystem, and the unborn into a life, and life into a supreme value" (p.2).

22. Corea, 'Who may have children and who may not', *op.cit.*, p.101.

23. *Ibid.*, pp.89-90.

24. Literally, autonomy means 'self government'.

25. Corea ('Depo-provera and the politics of knowledge'), *op.cit.*, p.207.

26. Edwards, *op.cit.*, p.47, emphasis added. There are a number of references, too, to the urgency of the problems: "We decided there was an urgent need to carry out studies on human embryology in order to introduce the replacement of embryos for the alleviation of infertility ... Many other studies were also possible besides the alleviation of infertility ... but we believed the most urgent was the alleviation of infertility" (*ibid.*, pp.43-44) and "We felt that clinical urgency justified the work ... " (*ibid.*, p.44).

27. Nietzsche, F. (trans. Kaufmann, Walter and Hollingdale, R.J.), *On The Genealogy of Morals* in Nietzsche, F. (ed. Kaufmann, Walter), *On The Genealogy of Morals and Ecce Homo* New York, Vintage Books, 1967.

28. For a very interesting discussion of Nietzsche's position see Foot, Philippa, 'Nietzsche: the revaluation of values' in Foot, Philippa, *Virtues and Vices and Other Essays in Moral Philosophy* Oxford, Basil Blackwell, 1978, pp.81-95.

29. Corea has in mind the American Fertility Society (AFS) report *Ethical Considerations of the New Reproductive Technologies* (Ethics Committee, 1986) which, she notes, concludes that "It may be our human right to produce test-tube babies and hire breeder-women. (The latter are sometimes termed "surrogate mothers" or "surrogate wives".)" Corea notes that the AFS is "a professional association of some 10,000 US physicians and scientists who work in reproductive biology". She asks "Where did this report come from? ... an ethics committee led by Dr Howard Jones. Jones is co-lab-parent of the USA's first test-tube baby and a leading practitioner and proponent of reproductive biology ..." (Corea ('Who may have children and who may not', *op.cit.*, pp.92-93). Corea goes on to tell us that the committee had eleven members (ten men and one woman) of whom seven were 'technodocs' among whom were "the chief of a California *in vitro* fertilization (IVF) team who is experimenting in human embryo freezing ... " (*ibid.*, p.93). She concludes: "Surprise: the technodocs determined, after 18 months serious deliberation, that what they do is ethical" (*ibid.*).

30. Edwards, Derek and Potter, Jonathon, *Discursive Psychology* London, Sage, 1992, p.2.

31. *Ibid.*, p.3.

32. *Ibid.*

33. *Ibid.*, p.3. Relating back to scientific discourse, they go on to suggest that "a novel analytical realm is brought to the fore. This is the realm of fact construction: the sorts of everyday procedures that are drawn on to make any particular version appear credible and difficult to undermine" (*ibid.*).

34. This is not to say that no one may speak of one practice being for her the chief, or even the only, really worthy one; but for others, the reality is perhaps that while many things they might do would be worthy of doing, far fewer (and perhaps more specific) things may happen to grasp their attention and interest. In such cases, where justification is concerned, the moral may seem always to be one among other matters, and it may not be clear which, ultimately, is the weightier consideration. In just this sense, then, where justification is sought, the person giving it may have moral reasons and a self-interested stake in the success of a moral justification.

35. Kant, I. (trans. Paton, H.J.), *Groundwork of the Metaphysic of Morals* New York, Harper Torchbooks, 1964. I have in mind the passage where he argues that an act has "genuine moral worth" (he uses phrases like this in two or three places) only where it is done out of duty (pp.65-67) which "includes ... a good will, exposed, however, to certain subjective limitations and obstacles" which "bring it out by contrast and make it shine forth more brightly" (p.65). The contrasting features are things like inclination, desire for happiness, and so forth.

36. Dickens, Charles, (ed. Tillotson, Kathleen), *Oliver Twist* Oxford, Oxford University Press, 1982, p.309.

37. Corea ('Depo-Provera and the politics of knowledge'), *op.cit.*, p.207.

PART TWO

Assisted Procreation: Rights and Duties

interested not in moral discourse *per se* but in particular uses of it, whereas Nietzsche can be seen as criticising morality altogether.[28] Nevertheless, they are not merely making arguments *ad hominem*; or, if so, something can be said to further characterise their so doing. For there is an important sense in which their arguments do apply to the users of moral discourse, and not to the discourse itself. Typically, where such 'personal' arguments are used, it can be responded: these comments may apply to specific people - Robert Edwards, Carl Wood, Howard Jones or the 'technodocs' for instance - but do not tend to undermine their arguments, in that these take up concepts existing independently in the moral discourse, and may give a perfectly plausible moral picture of events. However, this response misses the point. The points Corea makes must be aimed at individuals as they make their arguments. The argument that she takes an *ad hominem* line conceived as a criticism of what she does, repeats what is for Corea the fallacy that moral arguments and justifications (and to that extent, the moral discourse itself) must have the same moral impact on both listener and speaker (that is it must have the same relationship to each). She asks us, instead, to look and see if this is how it really is in this particular kind of case, which just does mean looking at the people giving the arguments. (Or, to put it in Raymond's terms, involves looking at the technodocs' appeal to altruism to see if it is in some way associated with self-serving interests furthered by constructing women as "givers".)

What, then, is to be looked for?

Where the moral discourse in the mouths of women is concerned, one account has already been given: this is, if a woman speaks of duty, she speaks of something which affects her, or controls her, in a non-pernicious sense. It is presumably at least this quality of self-affecting which is to be looked for in each individual case. But, embryologists will fall under this description if they too are 'controlled' by the moral obligations they refer to. Corea doubts, however, that they are, and makes her scepticism plain in her comments on the considerations of an ethical committee of the American Fertility Society (AFS).[29]

To sum up her scepticism, those who, like the members of the AFS have an investment in a certain set of practices and institutions, can be expected (she suggests) to find what they do through and within those practices and institutions ethically acceptable. The strong likelihood of this may be determined before they start their deliberations. This is to give a picture of the discourse of morality in which it is useful to those who have certain ends, but is, in a sense, independent of those ends, and of the practices and institutions which may be associated with them. This, however is not independence in the sense that the discourse may be (for them, as it is for others) critical of technodocs' interests and means of achieving them. Certainly that kind of independence would give some sense to the idea of genuine moral deliberation in the case of the AFS committee. But Corea's point is precisely that, in this sense, the committee did not engage in moral deliberation at all.

In short, some measure of critical independence of the resources of the discourse from its speaker, of the right sort, is necessary to genuine moral deliberation. If the self-affecting quality of the discourse arises because the discourse fits in with the person's

forms of inherited disease".[26] What may characterise this way of speaking is that the moral force, be it of need or necessity, is presented as felt by the scientists, quite outside their control. They are not unwilling to respond, of course; but moral considerations of this sort have a power over their wills independent of their wishes. In this, it may be claimed, they are no different from the women (though one could object upon the rather weak basis - mentioned before - that in these claims the scientists are simply lieing).

It might be argued that, if technodocs are also controlled, then they should take the same view of matters as their critics; but they do not take the same view, so they cannot be 'controlled'. And on this account, Corea and Raymond share with the scientists escape from the control. But the account requires an invalid jump from the idea that values control (in the way explicated above) to the idea that the same values control all who are controlled, and/or the idea that the same values will control to the same extent, in a given situation. I shall try to show in section 4, Corea might hope for such an agreement; it cannot be logically guaranteed.

It is possible that Raymond has in mind something other than the direct self control of moral commitment (which is broadly what is at issue here). The women's acts are both free and powerfully bound; and presumably they are free in the sense that these women choose their own acts according to their own values, and powerfully bound in the sense that they do not choose their own values. These are, instead, the result of socialisation, and of upbringing as women. Seen at this level, the women are not free.

However, this is still not quite the right way of putting it. The same could, after all, be said of technodocs. One response to this point is to accept it. These men are, indeed, also the 'victims' of upbringing, which blinds them to the interests of women as a group, and they are no more able to shake these mores off than are the women. But this seems not to be the line Corea and Raymond would wish to take; they refer to control to distinguish between women patients and men scientists in the context of medical technology.

Here it is important to refer again to Raymond's notion of the 'ideology of altruism', which may help locate the distinction. An implausible interpretation of this phrase is that all morality is in effect ideology. This would be to assume that the notion of altruism is synonymous either with all of morality or with some of its core notions. This is implausible in part because it seems to set Raymond on a collision course with good sense. Corea wants morally to criticise embryology for gender and race self-interestedness. She, then, judges it by the tenets of altruism (by which it is condemned): and on this account she too would be an ideologist of altruism. But Raymond would surely share her criticisms. A more plausible account of Raymond's notion is that altruism is (like need) a moral notion used in a particular way by those who have a self-interested ideological starting point. (Nevertheless, what has here been labelled the implausible account is not impossible, and something similar may be found in some of the analysis Nietzsche puts forward of Jewish-Christian notions of good and evil in *The Genealogy of Morals*.[27])

But I do not believe Corea or Raymond to be taking a Nietzschean line: they are

woman evinces time and again the value of giving. This is a picture in which, first, the practices and institutions of morality are what the (individual) woman's life is embedded in, and are what grant to her life many of its values and meanings; and in which, second, the discourse of morality just is much of her language for reasoning about, reflecting on, and judging her life and the ways of the world generally.

Someone may say that this does not cash out into any meaningful idea of control after all, or, if so, it cashes out as self-control (autonomy[24]), and that this, while it is a form of control, lacks the pernicious features of external control (by others) which Raymond and Corea fear. Corea, at least, argues herself that certain moral controls of this sort are good.

> When a woman is real to you as Antonia was real to Willa Cather and to her character Jim Burden, you cannot say: Let's give her this powerful drug ... which causes cancer in animals and may or may not cause cancer in human beings ... You could not do it ... such thoughts would be unendurable to you.[25]

This is an appeal to what may be the ultimate control or binding which morality may offer - the ability to make something unthinkable to the individual: thought control of a benign and morally (and socially) necessary sort.

It may here plausibly be objected that the discussion has slipped to the level of the individual, and that the group level - conceived of as a pattern within a specific kind of individual (women as women; men as men) - has been lost. It might be responded that the 'group level' is difficult to grasp or specify independently of the individuals taken to make up the group. And, indeed, when Corea wants to draw attention to the moral weight which women's concerns should carry, she does so (as in the quotation just cited) through an individual - Antonia (see also section 4 below). Rather than try directly to speak about this 'group level', I will bring in the notion of a controller, assuming that the control exercised may show in a pattern revealed in individuals considered as members of a group.

3.2. WHO IS CONTROLLED?

So far, however, the contention that there is control by 'technodocs' over women has not been adequately supported. It is not necessarily a feature of the picture, just discussed, of individual women and their moral lives. Control as so far discussed does not necessarily imply a controller independent of the mechanism of control or of the person herself. But in so far as reasons may be given by one person for why another should or should not do something, this brings much closer the notion of a controller, in this case the technodocs, acting, perhaps, for and on behalf of society, or some section of it.

But how could the so-called technodocs be immune from this same control? Edwards, speaking of (then) future embryo research, says: "A second piece of research, rapidly becoming *necessary* in my opinion, is to find out if embryos can be typed for specific

3. Discourses and Speakers

In the course of the last section, the word "ethics" has taken on a distinct meaning for Corea: she refers to a discourse which may be used to shape or control the human world in a particular way (or perhaps for particular ends). In this section something will be said to show how that might happen. But first a little more may be said about the logic of the claim Corea seems to be making.

As a broad claim about morality in human life, Corea's claim seems not necessarily to be true. It may be said that morality is one form of control within the world of human action and intention, but without thereby implying the question *why* morality controls, what its purpose in so doing is. Corea might be prepared to accept that morality *per se* has no purpose or end, however, for her main concerns are not, once more, with morality or moral language *per se*, but with particular uses of moral discourse; and by particular is not necessarily meant 'individual human', but rather something patterned (that is, something that can be perceived in a number of individuals people who share also features and who operate within particular contexts).

She wishes to speak of a very specific form of value (self-interest of race and gender) and of a very specific context of control: that of a woman's bodily processes by medical man in particular. What needs to be asked in these specific contexts is how the notion of control through 'ethics' may be cashed out; and it has yet to be shown that the control is applied *only* to women. Sections 3.1 and 3.2 take these points in turn.

3.1. CONTROL

> On an individual level, there are times when a person may feel obliged, morally, to make certain gifts. Many, for example, feel an obligation to donate bone marrow in response to a family member's need. This kind of limited individual situation gets expanded to a social level, however, when a giving population has been socialized to give as part of their role. Within such populations, givers who apparently give freely are also powerfully bound by social expectations and the regulation of gift behaviour. Women are the archetypal givers to whom all these expectations and regulations apply par excellence.[23]

This, then, is how the "ideology of altruism" functions. Raymond's point is perhaps that such social expectations evince a pattern of control over women as a group within society, to the extent people in that group are or perhaps tend to be 'powerfully bound' by these. One problem now may be to cash out the meaning of "powerfully bound".

A way of explaining it may be this: the value of giving is a value for the women themselves. Appealed to through this value, a woman may see her response in terms of personal morality ('I felt I had to') rather than in terms of her socially patterned and manufactured situation ('I needed the money' 'women seem always to be expected to …'). And, it may be mistaken to say that these are values she feels she ought to adhere to - as if they were somehow external to her. Rather, it may be said that in her life a

need (the one the Monash team can meet) is identified. The claim is like the claim that the chief deployment of the notion 'infertility' is to speak in a certain way of a situation (as a problem needing medical attention). The claim Corea and Raymond seem to be making is that particular applications of particular concepts (such as 'infertility', 'needs', 'rights', and so on) necessarily play a role within a wider context, and taken at an (as it were) very wide angle this context comprehends the context in which women are disempowered in a male dominated society.

To put the point very shortly: people's moral discourse constructs the (or a) world and does not (or not only) describe it. Now, again, this point may take a principally logical emphasis. Simply, it may be said, in so far as morality is constituted by human attitudes and judgements and so on, it is not an aspect of the world independent of humans, but is rather put in the world by humans, which is to say the world is constructed as partly a moral place by humanity.[18] But while Corea might accept this, it is too broad a claim for her specific purposes. Rather, she might want to argue that the ways in which different people see the world morally do not necessarily share any features of detail. 'Needs' and 'rights' talk may not be beside the point, but the embryologists' and others' use of these terms is restricted; and it is how it may be restricted that is crucial.

Patricia Hynes argues that "The foetus, the doctor and the father are the axes of ethical consideration, while the major health and welfare impacts of these technologies are on women ...".[19] The reason is that "that gender specific - that is, woman specific or woman-centred - questions are not asked ...".[20] Barbara Dudden has analysed some of the historical underpinnings of this point in great detail in a fascinating book which takes up, in particular, the emergence into sight of the embryo/foetus and the complimentary yet contrasting transparency of women. This, she argues, has had a dramatic impact upon the evolution of the debate about abortion; an impact which is particularly clear contemporarily, and can be seen in a wider context as being part of what has shaped the modern debate itself. The visualisation Dudden highlights is particularly important, in the light of the kind of failures which Corea and Raymond are interested in in the context of moral debates about the applications of the new medical technologies.[21]

Particular moral judgements and attitudes may be characterised as showing some form of blindness ('looking straight through' might be Dudden's preferred phrase). But, even if this is accepted as a correct description of the 'technodocs', it may still be felt there are kinds of moral blindness and that some are less culpable than others. Among the less (or, indeed, non-) culpable are those where one moral consideration outweighs another; or where one dominant consideration simply makes others of no consideration at all. (Such might be the claim of the Catholic Church concerning the sanctity of life of the foetus; the Church sees no other consideration.) But Corea has something much more conscious and manipulative in mind: " ... in contending that some women have a moral duty not to bring children into the world, 'ethics' helps technodocs to control women further".[22] It will be taken here that Corea means, by ethics, in part the moral discourse to which 'technodocs' may appeal.

That moral justification is a part of the embryologist's discourse, as Corea notes, is clear enough. Within the writings of Edwards and other apologists for IVF and embryology, can be found appeals to need[13] and to human liberty from state interference[14] and to human rights to methods of bearing children.[15] Janice Raymond, however, suggests that there may be a greater complexity (both in the giving of justifications and the criticism of them) than at first appears. Her remarks return this paper to the notions of the selfish and altruistic mentioned earlier.

> One of the new/old images generated by new reproductive technologies is that of the altruistic woman. The ideology of altruism makes a woman's inequality noble. For example, surrogate brokers enlist the services of women who most often need the money or are economically dead-ended, and portray them as women who have a "special gift" to bear another's child. Non-commercial surrogate arrangements are depicted even more as "the greatest gift a woman can give".[16]

(The most striking phrase here is 'the ideology of altruism'; and I will return to it later.) What picture of the role of moral discourse appears here? Two points may be highlighted. The first relates to needs, liberties and rights. Moral concepts such as these, part of the language of morality, applied indiscriminately to men and women in a world where women have secondary roles, may tend to maintain those roles. For instance, in a discourse in which women are said to 'need' babies, or 'have rights' to them, the role of women as principally mothers of children tends to be fostered.
  Corea seems to be making a point similar to Raymond's here:

> Professor Carl Wood, head of the Monash IVF team ... said that women in the IVF programme had been asking for donor eggs because they were not happy with some aspect of themselves and he specifically mentioned appearance and intellectual capacity.
>   Did he follow up this observation by saying: "We have a serious social problem here. These bright, capable women are feeling inadequate in so many ways. Why is this happening? What social forces are creating a climate in which women feel so badly about themselves? How can we eliminate these forces? We must do something about this because it is a horrible tragedy."
>   No, he did not say this. He acted as if it were perfectly appropriate to accept the women's perception of themselves as defective and to reinforce that perception by using the eggs of donors who, unlike the women themselves, are intelligent enough, are attractive enough.[17]

Corea here does not want to question the fact that some moral problem is identified (nor necessarily to assert that the words 'rights' 'needs' and so on must be entirely beside the point in expressing that problem). She is interested, rather, in the extent to which the economic, political and gender situation in which it is identified is ignored by the response, such that alternative conceptualisations of 'the problem' are ignored, and one

become generalised. He says that other, wiser, ideas may well continue, resisting this attitudinal shift. He is committed, intellectually at any rate, to the idea that such a shift is already present in some attitudes expressed by certain reproductive procedures.

It does not follow, necessarily, from what I have so far presented, that IVF or AID must be rejected. What does follow is that if either or both characteristically disrupt the unity of natural human procreation, then they would be rejected by O'Donovan and Ramsey.

A second attitude towards medical interventions in human procreation I shall label: natural procreation and dominant values. It deserves attention in its own right; but here I shall present it as a contrast to the ideas of O'Donovan and Ramsey.[7]

> With the implementation of the IVF procedure, the issue of the social construction and the social meaning of motherhood is not addressed. Instead, the concept of motherhood as the biological production of a baby is enhanced. ... The location of infertility and fertility solely within the discussion of biological relationships exemplifies dominant values around the nuclear family and sexuality. Marriage and the social structure of the nuclear family are based on heterosexist ideological presumptions about the relationship between sexuality and reproduction. IVF attempts to 'produce' a child through the bonding of heterosexually-linked partners. Hence it strengthens particular values by structuring marriage and heterosexuality into the scientific practices themselves. ... IVF not only reflects normative structures relating to reproduction in society, but reinforces such structures by specifically expressing a set of *social* [emphasis in original] conditions necessary for biological reproduction.[8]

The fundamental claim is that an account of reproduction as biological is fostered by society. IVF, for instance, is a technique which is based upon a biological understanding of reproduction. Now, in concentrating on the biological, complex social issues are ignored, and in being ignored, certain normative values enter unseen into this description of human reproduction and are legitimated by it. Society chooses a particular context and mode of procreation to constitute the natural, to wit, heterosexual, monogamous procreation. The idea of the natural, in actuality, is used to rule out certain threatening variations from this norm.

Both positions - natural procreation and humanness and natural procreation and dominant values - demonstrate a concern about what IVF and other reproductive medical technologies may mean in and for society. Both express doubts about the unthinking use and development of such technologies; both advance moral considerations potentially against, or restrictive of, their use. Proponents of these positions might find themselves at the same protest rally, though marching under different banners.

2. Agreements and Disagreements Over the Conceptualisation of Natural Procreation in the Two Positions

2.1. AGREEMENTS

There are four aspects of agreement between these two positions apart from the immediate consensus on caution regarding medical intervention in procreation. The first is a methodological agreement. Both assume that humans, by their actions and claims, reveal attitudes to procreation in which may be seen the real meanings of these actions and claims.

> ... [M]edical scientific technologies are never value free or neutral, devoid of historical specificity, context or the values of those who, in the first place, developed them and, in the second place, use them. ... Technologies are, in this sense, a language or discourse of values, a structural (materially structured) encoding and expression of the priorities and consciousness of those who invent and then utilise them.[9]

A similar analysis is implicit in O'Donovan, who goes on: "Human life, then, becomes mechanised because we cannot comprehend what it means that some human activity is 'natural'. ...   [B]egetting children becomes subject to ... medical and surgical interventions ...".[10] That is to say that our medical and surgical interventions in human procreation may express the failure to see that some activities have a certain standing; in that failure is seen the real meaning ('language or discourse of values') of the act of medical and surgical intervention.

This suggests a second level of agreement: the dominant meanings seen in medical technological interventions in procreation may be identified with establishment views held throughout society and with projects based upon those, and should be resisted. The resistance is necessary, because of the moral damage implicit in these meanings. For O'Donovan the damage is done in the failure of understanding cited above. For Steinberg (a proponent of the natural procreation and dominant values position) the damage is done to the oppressed groups in society, even in the wording 'in vitro fertilisation' which "names the one part of the process from which women are physically absent".[11]

A third aspect of agreement is this: the 'natural' in relation to procreation is seen as having a powerful moral standing which natural procreation brings with its (claimed) naturalness.

> The term "natural" ... is often taken as a standard by which moral rightness can be judged. Are reproductive technologies "natural", we ask, assuming that either they are or they are not. Those who purport the "unnaturalness" of IVF or cloning, for example, rely upon a tradition of heterosexual intercourse within marriage as a definition of "natural". On the other hand, those who purport that

IVF and cloning are indeed "natural" may choose as a standard of defense the observation that it is in man's nature to manipulate, restructure, and control his environment and his own evolution. Now what does a concerned, thoughtful *woman* [original emphasis] do when faced with the "either/or" sort of logic? Perhaps to escape this verbal dilemma of equivocation, we must expose it for what it is: whether you take the "either" or the "or" side, "natural" really means "what is in the best interest of those in control".[12]

Setting aside the moral judgement, here is the idea that the 'natural' is a marker for something regarded as good by who ever uses the word. The natural is a moral category, constituted by what is regarded as good. This is something O'Donovan or Ramsey might say. The natural, then, for both positions, identifies the morally acceptable - though one position notes this with approval, and the other with irony.

The fourth agreement takes this form: the natural in relation to procreation is associated by both positions with being (in some sense) beyond human understanding if properly approached.

Walters quotes Kass as a strong proponent of the first position ["Natural reproduction is inherently superior in a moral sense"]: "Is there possibly some wisdom in that mystery of nature which joins the pleasures of sex, the communication of love, and the desire for children in the very activity by which we continue the chain of human existence?" And, again, "the laboratory production of human beings is no longer *human* [italics in original] procreation ... making babies in laboratories - even "perfect" babies - means a degradation of parenthood."[13]

Kass would be a strong supporter of O'Donovan. He is said to say that the natural is rightly associated with moral wisdom, and that this is something to do with the mystery of the unity of procreative processes as found naturally in people. That unity guarantees the human dignity of the act of procreation, the sense of mystery diverts inappropriate curiosity, and the technologising of procreation by definition undermines both.

Those who take the natural procreation and dominant values position, as I have outlined it, would hardly find either the acceptance of this idea of mystery, or its use (typically, they would claim, against oppressed social groups) to be praiseworthy. They agree, however, that this is how the label is used, that this is what the notion of the natural characteristically comes to: the natural is 'appropriately' beyond certain kinds of human analysis, and 'rightly' insured against impertinent moral exploration by groups within society. To this extent, the two positions agree with one another. More will be said about the notion of mystery when this paper comes to consider the providential and the divine.

2.2. DISAGREEMENTS

The basic disagreement between the two positions is over the construction of the natural by personal or social forces. The argument from natural procreation and humanness resists such construction of the natural; the argument from natural procreation and dominant values insists upon its recognition. Here I explore the former point of view.

Ramsey asks with an ironic tone:

Is there not ... 'a personal dimension' which is 'something other' or 'beyond' the 'biological dimension'? From this small suggestion people are supposed to be convinced of quite another proposition, namely, that the biological 'dimension' of his existence as a man of flesh really is an 'other' entirely submissible to man's limitless 'dominion'.[14]

Ramsey's point is a moral and logical one; that is, he sees it as logically possible for the 'personal' to intrude into and disturb the natural dimension, when both dimensions are construed in a certain way. Ramsey's objection is to a construal of the personal and biological as 'other' *vis a vis* one another in which the personal is 'dominant'.

O'Donovan's view may be taken to be similar, though (rather than the 'personal') he has society in mind: he speaks of natural human procreation as an "aspect of human activity which is not a matter of construction ...".[15] For him, what is intruded upon may be changed by the intrusion. Thus, while it is logically possible for society to be interested in some senses in 'natural procreation', it is not logically possible for society to intrude into it, for the intrusion is only possible where the sense of the natural in a human activity has been lost. Hence, his insistence that we see *what* we do when we do intrude.

Now, clearly, not any human intrusion will count as the kind which by definition alters the object of the intrusion. For instance, medicine may intrude into the growth of cancer cells in a person's body, trying to prevent it. But this does not commit anyone to seeing cancer as non-natural or unnatural. O'Donovan refers to the proper role of medicine, in explanation of his view.[16] Cancer is a disease; medicine properly intervenes against it in an attempt to restore natural functioning to the human body. The natural procreation of a human child is not a disease, and it is not appropriate for medicine to intervene in it. It might be urged, in reply, that *in*fertility is a disease, and medicine properly intervenes to put it right. However, for O'Donovan, this is not decisive in the case of IVF and AID. Their aim is not to put right what has gone wrong. The aim of both is to circumvent a problem, by taking over a part of the process. Whether this is acceptable will be discovered only by seeing whether the act of IVF or AID may be characterised as part of a natural unity of the process of procreation.

For O'Donovan natural human procreation must logically be outwith a certain kind of human involvement.[17] This seems to commit O'Donovan, in this aspect of life at least, to a hard and fast distinction between the human realm and the natural realm.

This distinction appears, for instance, in his insistence on the differences between social scientific and biological descriptions. In the following, a certain account of sexual differentiation is at issue:

> The most significant moments in the 'natural' process of sex-differentiation ... are those in which society 'assigns' and 'reassigns' the patient, first to one sex and then to another. These are the only moments in the process that are conclusively determinative. ... Beneath the surface of this theory the epistemological autonomy of the natural sciences has been undermined and replaced by a sociological epistemology, which gives priority in the interpretation of events to the social construction which is placed upon them. ... The natural sciences lose confidence in their ability to offer a description of natural reality in itself, and turn to the social sciences to make good the lack. But this turn to the social sciences constitutes an admission that reality-descriptions cannot be based on pure observation, but depend upon a construal that society will impose upon what is observed. And what is the meaning of this social construal other than the imposition of society's projects and purposes upon the way reality is understood - which is to say, the conversion of 'science' into 'technique'?[18]

While biology and the natural sciences may give an observer's description of natural reality, nothing which can plausibly be called such a description can emerge from social sciences. From their interest emerges a social construal, one which is a vehicle for the purposes and projects of society. This, then, replicates Ramsey's fear that a separation of the personal/social, on the one hand, from the biological, on the other, threatens the notion of the natural in so far as that separation entails giving to the social and personal the decisive role in describing how things are. That it does not have to be, and should not be, like that, is their point in response.

The construal of society as dominant in how things are is entailed as surely by certain attitudes as by actual human intervention.

> It is the standard temptation of a technological culture ... to conceive even the natural as a special case of artifice, to argue for letting nature take its course simply as the best of all instrumental means to some humanly chosen end.[19]

The claim O'Donovan makes here is that to fail to see the natural for what it is, it is enough merely to conceive it as a possible route to a human end (a social project); one of several routes which may be chosen. It is not necessary to intervene in human procreation to demonstrate blindness to its naturalness; it is sufficient to construe the child as its primary goal and principle justification.

To illustrate some of the routes which social sciences appear to make available to the achievement of this goal, I reproduce a table from a sociological investigation of assisted conception.[20]

Possible Categories of Motherhood and Fatherhood as a Result of Artificial Reproduction

Genetic mother
Carrying mother
Nurturing mother
Complete mother (combining the genetic, carrying and nurturing roles)
Genetic/carrying mother
Genetic/nurturing mother
Carrying/nurturing mother
Genetic father
Nurturing father
Complete father (combining genetic and nurturing roles)

How is this analysis morally dangerous? For those who advance the natural procreation and humanness position the damage arises from an implicit redescription of natural procreation in terms dictated by human projects - particularly the use of the socio-biological notion of 'roles'. However, it might be asked what is wrong with that description and those terms? The wrongness, for O'Donovan, is that these human projects have a tendency to break down the process of procreation, and it is, for him, the very fact of this break down which shows and ensures that the naturalness of the process is lost to sight.

Consider the table in the light of this last point: any account of a natural procreative process now appears to be *made up of* other smaller units of the process. O'Donovan's question for this kind of analysis is well taken: why should we accept that the family of two parents, procreating and then nurturing their child or children, is a *combination* of bits? But asking 'why see any bits here' is not the same as showing why we need not see them. If O'Donovan thinks he sees a unity here, he still owes us explanations of how it is that he sees it, and how, if it is there to be seen in the observations of biological science, it is apparently not visible to everyone.

3. The Natural and Other Realms

3.1. THE NATURAL AND THE HUMAN

An epistemological point seems now to be at issue. Someone may try to show that the observations of biology cannot do the work O'Donovan seems to think they can do as follows:

> ... [S]hared biogenetic substance is the 'true' basis for kinship ties, but it must be legitimised by the institution of marriage. ... Thus the legal (social) and 'natural'

requirements of 'true' and legitimate parenthood should be sequenced as one, unified trajectory. Like all kinship beliefs, this sequence and trajectory are considered normal, 'obvious' and even 'natural' despite the fact that exceptions abound. ...

It is, of course, precisely the unity of the procreative and the conjugal function which is so profoundly disrupted by the new reproductive technologies. ... [T]he 'naturalness' of procreation and the 'biological' family are thrown into question by new reproductive technologies through which an unprecedented degree of 'artifice' has been introduced into the procreative process. ...   [I]t is this difficulty, of mediating the contradiction between the existing kinship system and the unprecedented 'artificial' procreative arrangements made possible by new reproductive technologies which, in part, explains the persistence of certain rigidly specific narrative and discursive mechanisms in the representation of infertility.[21]

Franklin's counter description is this.   She recognises (as does O'Donovan) the disruption to the unity of conjugal and procreative elements which the reproductive technologies have caused. She goes on to say that any attempt to reunite these must be a human project to maintain the link between the natural and moral intact (it is a moral project). For her, O'Donovan's is one of the rigidly specific narrative, and discursive mechanisms used to represent infertility and legitimate certain understandings of it. How can O'Donovan resist this characterisation of his argument?

He might do so in these terms. Franklin's unity (of the procreative and the conjugal, that is the 'natural' human form of procreation and the 'moral' social form of marriage) rests upon what he rejects. An analysis such as hers of his position shows in its own categories, and her construal of the relationship between them, the kind of combination of social and natural which O'Donovan wishes to resist. So far as natural human procreation is concerned, there is no combination of the biological and the social in which the former may be constructed by the latter. Rather, an appreciation of what is natural and right is expressed in certain social institutions, which see the naturalness of biological processes, and enshrine, in their institutional form, what is seen. On this account, then, a social institution, such as marriage, is not another part of the unity, and not a social idea imposed upon and organising a biological world. Rather, marriage is an expression of a social understanding that in natural procreation there is a moral unity.

This point may now be combined with O'Donovan's earlier point about the logic of the natural *vis a vis* the human. To see anything as natural entails a certain attitude towards it. To see natural human procreation as in reality it is is to see that its reality is properly expressed in social arrangements such as marriage. To see it in any other way is to fail to see it as it really is. The moral unity and logic of naturalness are commingled in natural human procreation.

But this is still to leave us short of an account of the unity which O'Donovan ought to claim is shown to us in the biological and expressed in some social institutions.

Franklin's initial point is that biology shows us nothing of the sort. Rather, she implies, it shows us a series of processes which suggest disparateness. So, for Franklin, if there is a unity it must come from somewhere else - from social norms.

O'Donovan cannot answer that we see natural human procreation as one process when we see it aright. For, to answer in this way would be to make the moral unity and naturalness a matter of how we saw the biological events, rather than given to us by the biological events; contingent to them and not integral, socially defined and not natural.

3.2. THE NATURAL AND THE DIVINE OR PROVIDENTIAL

To restate the current position: O'Donovan wants to say that we should seek to know the meaning of what we do. This meaning, however, is not necessarily given to what we do by society; rather, had we the wisdom to see it, it is visible or integral to the unity and nature of certain processes (natural human procreation, for example) that they are how they should be. However, a difficulty arises because, observed through the instruments of modern biology, there appear to be a number of discrete processes involved in human procreation - human attraction, sexual intercourse, ovulation, fertilisation, implantation, parenting and so on. At any rate, it seems merely arbitrary to see these processes as parts of a whole, rather than as individual events. It is not possible, on O'Donovan's account, to overcome this arbitrariness by reference to how social humanity happens to construe the biological.

He turns instead to the idea that in this biological realm may be seen another realm: that of the divine, as I shall call it. O'Donovan refers to providence. Natural procreation reveals the providential in certain facts about itself. These facts appear as they truly are when they are seen as a kind of limit to what Ramsey might label 'human dominion'. O'Donovan enlarges on this theme. He grants that IVF may aim at the treatment of pathology and not at reducing "contingency", but asks whether, in aiming at the former it may not also abolish the latter. For him, if this is the case, it is a ground for objection to IVF:

> For the element of chance is one of the factors which most distinguish the act of begetting from the act of technique. In allowing something to randomness, we confess that, though we might, from a purely technical point of view, direct events, it is beyond our competence to direct them well. ... To say 'randomness', of course, is not to say 'providence'. Randomness is the inscrutable face which providence turns to us when we cannot trace its ways or guess its purpose. ... There are, to be sure, ways in which we reduce the degree of unpredictability indirectly, by choosing the time of intercourse carefully, for example, to fit in with natural rhythms of fertility. Yet for all that we may encourage conception to take place, its occurrence is not the direct object of our technique. We do not, in natural begetting, bring sperm and ovum together, and, as it were, forcibly introduce them to each other. Thus we distinguish the act of begetting from those other acts in which we attempt to control the outcome directly ... .[22]

The remaining contingency - that of implantation - he claims is seen as an imperfection in the technique to be overcome.[23]

According to O'Donovan, what we have to see, in order to be wise, is that natural procreation leaves something to chance, and that this chance is not an imperfection of the natural, to be remedied, but the face which providence turns to us and which functions as a proper limit to our intervention. What determines that it shall be this fertilised egg which implants rather than these others is hidden from us: it is mysterious; but that there is a determining principle is in some sense clear.

In what sense clear? The location of providence in the biological chance of natural human procreation looks over simple. For how could the removal of the mystery O'Donovan has in mind be sufficient to remove also the element of divine providence? Suppose it was discovered exactly what it was that meant that some zygotes did and some others did not implant. Suppose also that we knew what genetically determined that a zygote would develop in such a way that it could implant, or in such a way that it could not. What would follow? Not that we would then have ruled out the providential. Even though we knew why a zygote had developed a biology which allowed it to implant, biology does not tell us why a particular zygote is chosen to have the genetic make-up such as to enable this to happen. And this is not because there is something biological we do not yet know, which we might find out, but because there is something which has now been asked which it is impossible to find out biologically. That is for what reason things happen as they do, or, if it were preferred, what it means for such and such to happen; what happens when X happens.

Now it looks as if there is still another point to be made here, which is this: why should I see this natural selectivity among zygotes as anything other than chance? Which is to say, in virtue of what is the question 'why this zygote?' intelligible? Surely, it may be objected, it is at least possible to say there is nothing actually to see here except that it was one and not the other which did develop in the right way. Hence, the idea that there is something other to be seen here rests upon an evaluation that there just is more to see in the natural biology of what happens in implantation; and this is to bring to the biological realm some other realm, a bringing which will be done by humanity.

This objection, which looks fundamental, loses much of its force, however, when it is recognised that it rests upon a fundamental assumption itself. The fundamental assumption it rests upon is that asking whether there is any intelligibility to the question 'why this zygote?' represents a further level of analysis, which anyone might perceive to be available. In fact, there is not necessarily such a further level. For it to be necessarily the case that there is such a further level, it must be assumed that the question 'why?' arises about the biological situation, or, to put it another way, stands outside it. However, it need not necessarily be like this, to the extent that someone may plausibly claim that, for her, such a question is an aspect of the situation. We might put it like this: in such a situation, when the future of a human individual is at issue, the obvious significance of the moment of implantation tends to find an explanation in terms of a divine plan.

Someone who asks 'why this zygote?' may show how she sees the situation. Asking the question may, for instance, express the moral significance she places upon the life of humans, which she does in seeing them as being the special concern of God. Now, there may be more to say. For, even where someone expresses in this way an idea that people are important, it may not be unintelligible to them to have that way of speaking questioned. But, from that fact, it does not follow that she will have to adduce further considerations than those already alluded to in response. It would not, for instance, follow that she has reasoned herself into this view of things, or (as would follow from that) that she might be shown to have reasoned invalidly, or that she could be reasoned out of it again. The objection against O'Donovan, then, rests upon an assumption about how far analysis goes, and may be rejected by O'Donovan on the grounds that it has gone far enough.

We still need to characterise this rejection. O'Donovan has claimed both a moral and a logical basis for his ideas. The logical basis is that natural human procreation *qua* natural is outwith a certain kind of human interest and involvement. I have cashed this out in the idea that certain kinds of question asked in a context express the attitudes of people. That is, the question 'why this zygote?' shows what the person takes to be intelligible. However, this, of course, does not go so far as to show that this question will always and everywhere be intelligible. Its intelligibility is a function of the culture and value system in which, and by which, the person for whom it is intelligible lives. Indeed, the question in so far as it is meaningful expresses or implies something of that value system.

It is not the case, either, that the question, and the values it shows, are necessarily detachable from and applicable to the observable world. Rather, it may be that observation, the natural, the world itself, are not describable independently of such basic attitudes. The 'way of life' (as Wittgenstein might have called it) has its own criteria of intelligibility. These criteria cannot intelligibly - that is to say meaningfully - be questioned from within the way of life itself. But the point which tells against O'Donovan's logical claims for his position, is that the intelligible and the moral have a necessary interdependence in this context.

For example, O'Donovan and Ramsey both appeal implicitly to divine authority in describing natural human procreation. The moral standing of natural human procreation is explained by both in terms of God's will that this is how human procreation should be. The word 'natural' then signals a recognition of this moral standing. This is as much as to say that the right form of human procreation is that given or willed by God. To put it like this is apparently to beg a question about the relationship between the will of the deity and the right. Socrates and Euthyphro agreed that the gods loved what was right in virtue of its rightness; they rejected the idea that what was loved by the gods was right in virtue of their loving it.[24] In contrast, Wittgenstein talks of a sense of awe in the face of 'absolute value' (moral rightness for instance) which he could explain only by reference to its being the will of God.[25] We might say that O'Donovan and Ramsey tend to speak in the same way.

Now, someone who does not tend to speak in this way of the rightness of natural

human procreation could not be shown to be confused. Of course, O'Donovan might persuade someone who tends not to speak in this way, to see things as he sees them. That would be a moral persuasion as much as a logical persuasion. We could say that when a person felt morally compelled to reject certain kinds of human procreation, then they might be seeing things as O'Donovan and Ramsey see them. At any rate, no clearer kind of proof could be found.

But now it is clear too, that O'Donovan's is not a position which should claim for itself a greater logical plausibility than all others. Integral to his position are moral attitudes, which claim for themselves greater wisdom. Beyond that claim no argument may go which is not equally committed to some version of wisdom of its own. But, there is no purely logical or ultimate reason why anyone should prefer one version of wisdom to another.

Notes

1. I construct this position from a number of sources, and in doing so I am aware I have done some damage to the arguments as a whole advanced by the various authors on whom I draw. This is because not all of those authors would necessarily support the conclusion I impute to these arguments.

2. Free Church Federal Council and The British Council of Churches *Choices in Childlessness* Report of a Working Party, 1981, quoted in Snowden, R., Mitchell, G.D. and Snowden, E.M., *Artificial Reproduction: A Social Investigation* London, Allen and Unwin, 1983, p.163.

3. O'Donovan, Oliver, *Begotten or Made?* Oxford, Oxford University Press, 1984, p.3.

4. *Ibid.*, p.16.

5. Ramsey, Paul, *Fabricated Man* New Haven and London, Yale University Press, 1970, p.136.

6. O'Donovan, *op.cit.*, p.1.

7. In the course of the paper, I shall present an argument which is a patchwork of ideas from various author's positions, but which form a single position. As with the previous argument from natural procreation and humanness, I will present this attitude as generally opposed to IVF and AID, though this may do some damage to the point of view of the authors from whose writings the argument is stitched together.

8. Crowe, Christine, 'Whose mind over whose matter? Women *in vitro* fertilisation and the development of scientific knowledge' in McNeil, Maureen, Varcoe, Ian and Yearley, Steven (eds), *The New Reproductive Technologies* Basingstoke and London, Macmillan, 1990, pp.38-39.

9. Steinberg, Deborah Lynn, 'The depersonalisation of women through the administration of '*in vitro* fertilisation'' in McNeil, Varcoe and Yearley (eds), *op.cit.*, pp.74-122, p.75.

10. O'Donovan, *op.cit.*, p.3.

11. The whole passage is worth quoting:

> While the process as a whole constitutes a recombination of women's bodies and reproductive processes, principally to extract women's body tissues (their eggs), the label '*in vitro* fertilisation' names only the act of fertilisation and the place, Petri dish (glass), where it occurs. ... The term conceals: (1) procedures, all of which, including surgeries and hormone treatments, are and can only be performed on women; and (2) that fertilisation in glass is *predicated* [original emphasis] on, (not possible without) prior, protracted and intensive intervention, manipulation and scrutiny of women. In fact, '*in vitro* fertilisation' names the one part of the process from which women are physically absent.

(All emphases as in original.) Steinberg, *op.cit.*, pp.77-78.

12. Salladay, Susan Anthony, 'Ethics and reproductive technology' in Holmes, B. Helen, Hoskins, B. Betty and Gross, Michael (eds), *The Custom Made Child? Women Centered Perspectives* Clifton, New Jersey, The Humana Press Inc., 1981, pp.241-248, p.246.

13. Grobstein, Clifford, *From Chance to Purpose An Appraisal of External Human Fertilization* Reading, Mass., Addison-Wesley Publishing Company, 1981, p.62.

14. Ramsey, *op.cit.*, p.132.

15. O'Donovan, *op.cit.*, p.3.

16. Cf. *ibid.*, p.6. O'Donovan's picture of the traditional role of medicine would seem to be an over-simplification in view of the very different attitudes towards health and the role of medicine in maintaining health which might be said to hold in the humeral account of illness.

17. The contrary position is that what constitutes natural procreation cannot ever logically be outwith all human involvement. An example of an argument which takes this as a basic tenet is this:

> Of particular importance is the relationship between the discourse of social loss and the discourse of biological destiny. As we have already seen, the 'desperateness' of infertility is explained in biological as well as social terms. The desire to biologically procreate is described as essential and innate. It is described as 'the natural product of pair-bonding', as 'deeply rooted in biological instinct' and as a 'natural expression of love'. Experts call it an 'inner drive', a 'biological need' and refer to it as instinctual. 'The desire for a family' is said to '[rise] unbidden from our genetic souls' as a result of 'human destiny' and the 'powerful urge to perpetuate [our] genes through a new generation'.
>
> [B]eliefs about the *naturalness* [original emphasis] of heterosexuality and the nuclear family (also known as the 'biological family') derive their authority from the biological sciences. Defining infertility in accordance with the dictates of science further locates it within the domain of the natural family.

Franklin, Sarah, 'Deconstructing 'desperateness': the social construction of infertility in popular representations of new reproductive technologies' in McNeill *et al* (eds), *op.cit.*, pp.200-229, pp.221-222. There is nothing much here which O'Donovan or Ramsey would disagree with, except the tone. For Sarah Franklin, the desperateness which some couples feel for a child is said to be natural, innate, instinctual. That is to say, the natural is said to be constituted by such desperation. Her point is, however, that this is what is said; it is not a fact about the desperation for children, nor about procreative desires. Science speaks with the tongue of modern male dominated western liberal society, and selects these things to put into the category

of the natural (thereby giving them certain apparent moral significances).

18. O'Donovan, *op.cit.*, pp.24-25.

19. *Ibid.*, p.19.

20. Snowden *et al*, *op.cit.*, p.34.

21. Franklin, *op.cit.*, pp.222-223.

22. O'Donovan, *op.cit.*, pp.70-72.

23. *Ibid.*, pp.72-73.

24. Plato, *Euthyphro* in Plato (trans. Tredennick, Hugh), *The Last Days of Socrates* Harmondsworth, Penguin, 1969, pp.31-33.

25. Commenting on Schlick's Ethics, Wittgenstein is reported to have said: "Schlick says that theological ethics contains two conceptions of the essence of the Good. According to the more superficial interpretation, the Good is good because God wills it; according to the deeper interpretation, God wills the Good because it is good. I think that the first conception is the deeper one: Good is what God orders. For this cuts off the path to any and every explanation "why" it is good, while the second conception is precisely the superficial, the rationalistic one, which proceeds as if what is good could still be given some foundation." ('Wittgenstein's Lecture on Ethics: II: Notes on Talks with Wittgenstein' taken by Friedrich Waismann, *The Philosophical Review* January 1965, pp.3-26, p.15.) Monk reports that in a note book contemporary with the Lecture on Ethics, Wittgenstein wrote: "What is good is also divine. Queer as it sounds, that sums up my ethics" (Monk, Ray, *Ludwig Wittgenstein: The Duty of Genius* London, Vintage, 1991, p.278).

9. A RIGHT TO PROCREATE?

Assisted Conception, Ordinary Procreation and Adoption

Martyn Evans
Centre for Philosophy and Health Care
University of Wales, Swansea
Singleton Park
Swansea
Wales

1. The Idea of a 'Natural Right' to Procreate

If there is a 'natural right' to procreate it might seem that those who wish to do so should at the very least not be prevented from procreating, and perhaps beyond this be positively helped to procreate. In either case, the 'right' in question would entail an obligation on the part of someone else, and the scope or extent of the 'right' would be partly a matter of who that someone else turns out to be. A right not to be prevented from procreating (were such a right to exist) might be understood very generally as being held against all the other members of the society in which the right-holder lived: none of us should prevent any of our fellows from procreating. By contrast anyone's enjoying a 'right' to be positively helped in procreation would seem to entail actual or imaginable obligations on the part of very few of her fellow-citizens; even marriage partners can scarcely be *required* to provide one another with procreational opportunities (although what is euphemistically called 'non-consummation of the marriage' is a traditional ground for divorce in English law).

I think we can see immediately where most of the difficulties with the idea of a 'natural right to procreate' will lie, and we shall shortly proceed to explore them. But first let us notice the importance of the question. If there really is such a 'right', then it may entail obligations of the most dramatic kinds in an age in which assisted conception is a medical reality: at the very least it would seem to entail *prima facie* equitable opportunities, for everyone who so wishes, to gain *access to the system* of providing assisted conception services. Yet questions of access to such services produce obvious and deep moral disagreements among practitioners and commentators alike, as instanced in the recent case of oocyte implantation in a British woman who is in her late fifties. Procreation, natural or otherwise, is not a morally neutral matter. On a stronger interpretation, such a 'right' would imply that all who wish such services must be given repeated access to them until they achieve what they regard as a satisfactory number of *successful outcomes* - a commitment probably unparalleled elsewhere in

D. Evans (ed.), Creating the Child, 127–143.
© *1996 Martyn Evans. Printed in the Netherlands.*

health care provision. The challenge of these implications is however wider even than this, for they appear to entail something which modern societies simply do not believe: that anyone who wants a child must be able to have one regardless of his or her competence, rationality, experience or conduct. A genuine 'natural right to procreate' would, if well-founded and regarded as absolute rather than merely provisional, be moral, social and legal dynamite. Thus the question of whether or not such a right obtains is of the first importance.

It has a distinct importance for my present purposes, moreover, because it bears centrally on the other question which I shall address, namely of whether the provision of assisted conception ought to be considered comparable to natural procreation ('ordinary parenting', as I shall term it) or comparable to the adoption of existing children. The view that there were some natural right to procreate would tend to undercut this question, since such a view would (a) be likely to assume that the biological and genetic dimensions of assisted conception - ultimately involving procreation after all - decisively aligned such procedures with ordinary parenting *as opposed to* adoption; and (b) be likely to make its primary appearance in any case in a claim to the provision of assisted conception services. It is, in general, those who feel that a claim of theirs is under threat who most readily resort to asserting a *right* to the object of their hopes. (Those who think such a right to be absolute would of course have to assert for it a status beyond that sometimes asserted on behalf of those who wish to have children in the ordinary way, for instance when facing the enforced separation of imprisonment or some restrictive social response to lack of mental competence. Those who think it merely a *prima facie* or provisional right of course face difficulties in showing why it imposes obligations on society beyond those of ordinary non-interference, as we shall see.)

Accordingly, if we could settle the question of whether there is indeed a natural 'right' to procreate, we would have gone some way towards establishing whether the comparison between assisted conception and adoption was a significant question and, depending on the outcome of our first enquiry, what force the comparison might have. (If there were no such right, then other considerations become pertinent and potentially decisive.) Let us therefore now return to a consideration of the claim that there is a 'natural right' to procreate.

2. Conceptual Limitations on a 'Natural Right' to Procreate

Generally, a natural right is held simply in virtue of one's being the kind of creature which one happens to be. Thus, those who appeal to a 'natural right' to procreate are assuming that certain biological features which are normally true of human beings, such as the desire to procreate, are so essentially true and characteristic of the human condition as to require at least provisional and perhaps absolute protection; they are further assuming that this protection can be secured or at any rate demanded and promoted by declaring that there is a right to it, and that the right attaches to human

beings by virtue of their humanity. In so doing, of course, they are making two elisions, neither of which seems supportable. First, they are translating biological norms into essentialist claims about the meaning of the human condition. No-one could doubt that the basis of procreation is biological, but the *desirability* of children is a social phenomenon, which allows for divergent views on the extent to which begetting children is valuable, among individuals within societies and indeed among different societies separated in environmental and economic circumstances. Unless we wish to hold that the childless (whether voluntarily so or otherwise) are necessarily deprived *as human beings*, we cannot seriously elevate statistically normal biological procreation into a prescription for the essentially human. Second, they are translating biological norms into moral norms. That is to say, they are asserting obligations (on the part of other people, or more likely society) to ensure that, in those individuals who are disadvantaged in the relevant biological respects, certain normal levels of functioning be restored and maintained. Of course such obligations could *come about*, but they cannot be asserted simply because they reflect biological norms. If, as seems more likely, they reflect dominant social expectations in those societies where the language of rights has an established tradition, then they are obligations held in virtue of what is widely agreed to be desirable - and not held in virtue simply of the *kind of creature* to whom they are owed. Whether there are any other more plausible candidates for 'natural rights' is not here my concern; I am however concerned to question whether procreation could plausibly be among them.

3. Other General Limitations on a 'Natural Right' to Procreate

As we noted at the outset, there is a distinction between believing we should not intervene to prevent procreation on the one hand, and believing we are obliged to intervene positively to facilitate it on the other. Whilst these two beliefs are obviously connected, the former does not entail the latter, and this divergence reflects the well-recognised distinction, in discussions of rights, between rights to freedom from interference, and rights requiring the fulfilment of positive claims. The former are generally agreed to have wider application, more general plausibility, and more extensive and straightforward enforceability: if ever we doubted that, the example of the 'natural right' to procreate should convince us. Thus for example the right (if there were one) not to be prevented by societal *restraint* from engaging in procreative acts could not entail the right to be provided from society's *resources* with a procreative partner. Now by extension, and in exactly the same way, it could not follow that there were any positive right obliging society to overcome, on behalf of the individual claiming the right, any other obstacles to procreation such as the infertility of that individual or of his/her partner. In short, a right not to be prevented from having a child would not entail the right to be provided with a child.

Now against this it might be argued that biological impairment constitutes a kind of interference with one's ability and opportunity to procreate. But the limitations of such

a reply are immediately evident: rights of non-interference are meant to prevent or overcome *wrongful* interference, and it is to some extent a matter of moral debate which interferences are, and which are not, wrongful. However it is not a matter for debate whether *natural impairments* are in themselves wrongful: they are not, since they lie outside the sphere of moral agency. That this is so can be recognised in the fact that the only exceptions to this exclusion involve impairments which are shown precisely to arise from culpable human agency or negligence. Thus, the impairments arising from the use of Thalidomide during pregnancy are wrongful in a way in which inherited impairments having no known root in human agency are not. But we can put this point much more simply: rights are held against other moral agents, and not against biological circumstances as such. Thus, were a given case of impaired fertility attributable to culpable human agency or neglect, then a plausible claim might be made to some compensatory right to have that impairment overcome; in such circumstances, a right might be established to having such assistance in conception as was necessary to overcome the impairment itself. But notice that even this does not entail being provided with the other necessary resources, such as a procreative partner.

Even in this case, we ought to notice one further general limitation: a right to being assisted to conceive is still not a right to have and to bring up a child free from social scrutiny. This should be apparent from considering ordinary parenting, for even those majority of parents who are justifiably and defensibly free from social interference in procreation have no entitlement to proceed from the *biological* to the *social* dimension of parenting without very general scrutiny. On the face of it, this limitation is beside the point: it is not freedom from scrutiny that is being claimed, but rather the opportunity to conceive a child. However the relevance of the limitation re-emerges when we recognise that having and bringing up children is the reason why people wish to conceive: there can be very few who would wish *simply to conceive* and, frankly, such a wish might in itself count strongly against the suitability of such a person to conceive at all, let alone to do so with the active assistance of society's resources. Thus to ask, of someone who wishes to have assistance to conceive, whether she is in a position to take on the responsibilities of bringing up the resulting child is not at all beside the point, and is scarcely an infringement of a plausible or defensible 'natural right'. Of course, whether or not we *ought* to make such enquiries is a substantial moral question, and it is not settled merely by noticing that no genuine rights are at stake. (We shall return to this question more fully below when we consider the analogy between assisted conception and adoption.)

4. Specific Limitations in Respect of Assisted Conception

It follows from what we have so far said that, to be convincing, any claim right to the provision of specific means of assisted conception, must be decisively more compelling than any supposed claim right to being provided with the ordinary specific means of natural procreation (*viz.* a sexual partner, for instance). In our discussion so far, no

such claim right has emerged. Now it might be objected that a sufficiently stronger claim right has indeed emerged, and that it has done so because society now for the first time *has available* the medical and technical means to understand clinical infertility and to facilitate assisted conception. In other words the novel technical environment reflects (or perhaps compels) a novel social and moral environment: now that we understand the biological origins of infertility and the routes to overcoming it, we attract new moral responsibilities to do so. There are after all (it might be said) many precedents for this in clinical medicine: where extraordinary treatments become ordinary, for instance, the obligation to provide them in appropriate circumstances becomes more real. In the present context, this line of argument relies on establishing (i) that being provided with assisted conception services is, fundamentally, simply being provided with a medical treatment; and (ii) that the provision of medical treatment is properly the subject of unusually compelling obligations. Thus in response we need do little more than observe that, if even the second of these assumptions is no longer beyond the reach of sceptical objection, the first assumption that assisted conception is nothing more than a medical treatment is precisely what is at issue in the present discussion and in a wider contemporary debate. So far from settling disagreement, the assumption ignites it.

However, if there is no plausible general right to freedom from the effects of biological impairment of fertility, there could in certain contexts be a claim right to the correction of specific biological impairment. We have already noted one such context above, namely that of infertility arising from culpable human agency or negligence. A quite separate claim right might arise as a result of a contract to provide certain services, always supposing that the provision of those services were something which society was willing to be regulated by contract alone. Although there are good reasons for doubting this, we should notice in any case that such a contractual right is clearly distinct from the idea of a *natural* right to such provision: indeed, it is hard to see that there could be a *natural* (claim) right to any *specific* medical procedure (as distinct from a putative natural right to a share in the generalised health care resources of one's society). Moreover, even where a contractual right exists in support of claims to the provision of certain specific medical treatments, we must distinguish between the idea of attempting to treat a medical condition, such as an organic dysfunction, and the idea of *overcoming the effects* of that dysfunction. Thus, for instance, even a contractual right to receive tubal surgery to correct biological dysfunction is not the same as a contractual right to be made pregnant.

Indeed, I think it is here that we will find at least a *formal* answer to the question raised by the unrestricted availability of assisted conception services. Those services which confine themselves to the correction of biological dysfunction could attract a claim parallel to ordinary claims to medical treatment - enjoying both the strengths and weaknesses of the latter. Plausibly such treatment restores a kind of *status quo ante*, in which the ordinary opportunities to procreate are themselves restored. Services which go beyond this to the actual furnishing of a pregnancy seem different in kind. Moreover, even were there to be in some circumstances a contractual right to be made pregnant (and it is not easy to see that there could be), this would clearly not be

equivalent to a contractual right to be furnished with a complete and successful gestation, a safe delivery, and a 'take-home baby' at the end of it. In other words, even were we to imagine circumstances which supported a contractual right to assisted conception, such a right does not entail or convert into a right to be *provided with children*.

The importance of this distinction lies in the fact that neither the (provisionally) medical need to have one's clinical infertility treated, nor the more ambiguous desire to receive assisted conception (i.e. be made pregnant) is what really concerns intending parents seeking infertility treatment. Their need or desire is to have a baby, and it is hard to see circumstances under which the *desire* for a baby plausibly becomes a *right*.

***

Social scrutiny of the provision of assisted conception services might have been 'trumped' by such a right under certain circumstances, although these are somewhat hard to imagine: the right would need to be socially acknowledged to be absolute or inviolable or otherwise immune from a consideration of circumstances. Such rights are vanishingly rare. But since no 'natural right' can in any case plausibly be established in the case of procreation generally, let alone in the case of assisted conception in particular, social scrutiny of assisted conception is not disposed of, and the desire for a baby falls subject to other kinds of consideration such as those to which we shall now turn.

***

5. The Natural and the Artificial

The obvious starting point for discussion of the ethics of assisted conception concerns one of its equally obvious moral characteristics: the express intervention in the procreative process by third parties. The familiar way of referring to this characteristic is that it is *artificial* by contrast with ordinary procreation which is by implication 'natural'. However in this discussion I propose to follow the terminology indicated in my title, which refers not to 'artificial procreation' but instead to 'assisted conception'. The reason for this is that the distinction between the 'natural' and the 'artificial' is neither simple nor uncontroversial, as I shall presently elaborate; to assume that the new clinical infertility treatments are in the relevant sense 'artificial' is to move too hastily to a position that appears to concede too many of the moral claims concerning social scrutiny of assisted conception services. Although we may indeed conclude in favour of that scrutiny, I do not believe that we can do so by means merely of a stipulation that the services in question are 'artificial' as distinct from 'natural', since *inter alia* there are many things which it is natural for us to do yet against which compelling social and moral

sanctions may be found. Indeed there is a sense in which much of our moral life consists in the reflective and conscious resistance of things which we would otherwise incline only too naturally to do.

As I have suggested, the distinction itself requires examination (probably a more searching examination than is possible in this paper). For instance, it is ordinarily true that the two categories, 'the natural' and 'the artificial' are readily distinguished in that we ordinarily know what it is people wish us to understand by them; the familiar distinction is that between what is essentially the product of human agency or intervention, and what is the product of forces and events independent of human agency. Each category has clear and paradigmatic cases: for instance the virgin rainforest is clearly natural in not being the product of human intervention, and the bulldozer is clearly artificial in being more or less exclusively the product of human design and fabrication - in this sense, human artifice. That said, it is equally obvious that particular things or phenomena need not fall entirely into one or the other category. For instance a landscaped garden is a natural phenomenon modified by human intervention, whereas a canvas-and-wood glider is an artifice using natural materials and inspired by the natural example of soaring birds. Indeed since Man himself is part of nature, there is an essential ambiguity about all his works: the interventions Man makes into the natural order also arise in this sense from *within* that order, and may express his social purposes which themselves cannot entirely be detached from Man's physical nature and biological needs.

Now distinctions such as that between the natural and the artificial are often appealed to in moral dispute, where what is 'unnatural' is almost always used as a term of moral disapprobation. An elision seems to be at work here between 'natural' in the sense of being independent of human agency, and 'natural' in the sense of being uncontaminated by *wrongful or inappropriate* human intervention. The importance of this for our present purposes lies *inter alia* in the fact that the idea of the 'unnatural' in this pejorative sense flourishes in discussions of sexual morality and in discussions of the morality of biotechnology above virtually all other contexts: our present concern, assisted conception, has the honour of combining both these disputed contexts in one arena. Perhaps we should therefore notice at once that, although it is fashionable to prefer 'the natural' over 'the artificial', particularly in terms of lifestyle, diet and - increasingly - medical care, there is something contrived about this preference, and indeed about the distinction itself in these very contexts. For instance organically grown food is full of chemicals; in preferring (if we do) these particular chemicals to their synthetic alternatives we express a certain kind of faith, but that given substances occur naturally is no proof of their desirability, as Socrates well knew when drinking hemlock. Equally whilst it might be true that most people would prefer to succeed in ordinary procreation rather than rely on assisted conception, this does not *in itself* show that assisted conception is of greater moral concern than is conceiving children under any other circumstances. Of course we might well think that assisted conception *does* prompt additional moral concern: my point is that we should not think this *simply* because most people would prefer not to have to rely on it.

If assisted conception does indeed prompt an especial and additional moral concern, this must nonetheless arise from its being to some degree artificial; but here I think we can see what the force of the artificiality is, and where the focus of the additional concern must lie. It is the *involvement of third parties* in the conception which places upon them a share in the moral burden ordinarily carried by the parents alone. When, as in publicly provided health care systems, assisted conception services are provided substantially at the public expense and in the public's name, the third parties who are involved in the conception effectively include society as a whole: and what society does, society may also ponder. Society's moral concern is legitimated by virtue of its being asked not merely to tolerate but also frequently to underwrite the new reproductive technologies: if society has a legitimate concern in the matter of ordinary human reproduction - and I know of no-one who seriously argues that it has not - then that concern is, legitimately, intensified when society finds itself required to be an *agent* in reproduction itself. It is in this context then that the question arises of how widely assisted conception services should be offered, which is to say, of who should qualify to receive those services, and who should not.

An obvious precedent exists for the scrutiny of prospective parents, namely the screening and selection of those who wish to foster or adopt the children of others. Here as in assisted conception, individuals who wish to take on the role of parents must do so through the agency of third parties acting in society's name. Adoption is not an opportunity afforded simply to anyone who wants it; as a party to the adoptive arrangements, society takes responsibility for the interests of the children involved, and assesses the suitability of the prospective adopting parents in terms of their competence, circumstances, motivation and character. It is therefore attractive to think that adoption might offer us a model on which we could base a social policy towards the availability of assisted conception services. This hope will largely stand or fall by the aptness of the analogy between adoption and assisted conception. A full consideration of that aptness is beyond my scope in this paper. Accordingly I shall confine myself to what I take to be its most important dimension, namely the involvement of social agency as a third party in parenting. If the social agency which is evident in adoption justifies societal scrutiny of prospective adopting parents, does the social agency involved in assisted conception similarly justify societal scrutiny of individuals and couples who wish thereby to become parents?

My approach will be this: I will attempt to show that there is both a 'natural' and an 'artificial' dimension to both adoption and assisted conception. In so doing, I shall distinguish between what we might call the *biological* and the *social* dimensions of ordinary parenting (a distinction which is thereby pertinent in considering extraordinary parenting as well), and I shall explore the idea that it is the social rather than the biological dimension which most legitimises societal scrutiny and intervention in parenthood. Following this I shall suggest that the naturalness or otherwise of any given form of procreation is after all secondary to the inevitably institutional character of parenting; the usefulness of the adoption analogy will thereby be seen to lie less in what it shows us about assisted conception *per se* than in what it reminds us about the

bringing up of children *howsoever conceived*. Finally I shall argue from this that sheer 'naturalness', even where it can plausibly be claimed, offers no exemption from legitimate societal scrutiny of the social and institutional dimension of parenthood. I hope thereby to show that the importance of the adoption analogy lies less in establishing the case for proper societal scrutiny - since that case is already established in ordinary parenting - than in establishing that scrutiny's proper *extent*. I cannot explore that extent in this paper, beyond suggesting three areas where the adoption analogy may help us.

6. Adoption as Both 'Natural' and 'Artificial'

The naturalness of ordinary parenting (which I take to be incontestable) seems to lie in two aspects: first, the physical aspect of ordinary human reproduction is natural in the sense of biologically normal, indeed, inevitable for the overwhelming majority of fertile adults (themselves the overwhelming majority of adults within a given age range); second the social aspect of ordinary human reproduction is natural in the sense of being an expression of an urge to procreate and to nurture which, though modified by societal variations, is in general terms common to all societies (as of course in some form it must be for any society to persist) and generally sensed as instinctual. Of these two aspects, the physical and the social, it is the social which is expressed in adoption. The point therefore is that, whilst lacking the straightforward physiological links between parent and child, adoption nonetheless expresses the nurturing instinct which is sensed as natural. Now since human reproduction has irreducibly *moral* dimensions as well, which are important in both ordinary parenting and adoption, it might seem that in the morally relevant sense the similarities between ordinary parenting and adoption are more significant than the differences: both express natural or instinctual urges; both expressions of those urges have societal aspects (both involve the *social* role of parenting), and both are properly subject to society's scrutiny.

The difference between children who are parented in the ordinary sense, and children who are adopted, is perhaps chiefly that ordinarily the biological parents and the social parents are one and the same. Adopted children, after all, are no less natural in this respect: they have biological parents, but these parents are not their social parents. However even this difference is one which might be exaggerated in the context of contemporary urban, industrial societies in which the nuclear family predominates. In traditional rural or nomadic societies where extended families are more usual, non-adopted children may nevertheless be socially reared by a collective of related adults and older children. To some extent an informal separation of biological and social parenting may be perfectly 'natural' in such contexts.

In short, the idea of 'the natural' is inevitably somewhat flexible, and includes necessarily social aspects in which adoptive parents must participate. It is 'natural' to foster children who would otherwise lack parents. To regard arrangements of this kind as essentially conventional or artificial is sheer stipulation; there seems no reason to

deny that the same protective urges are at work in fostering and adoption as are at work in ordinary parenting.

It is apparent however that some of these same arguments, which link together the pertinent dimensions of ordinary and adoptive parenting, can be used to opposite effect: that is to emphasise the importance of the distinction between the biological and the social aspects of parenting *per se*. In modern industrial societies - that after all are those societies which most readily furnish the context of assisted conception - it is the social aspects of parenting which most concern us from a moral point of view. Being the biological parent of a given child ordinarily indicates one as that child's social parent as well, but not necessarily or exclusively: and it is precisely here that adoptive parents take over that role. Any society which formalises and regulates stable parenting relationships (whether or not these be called marriages) has already conventionalised *all forms of* parenting to some degree, defining and perhaps enforcing social ideals and criteria for the bringing up of children. Thus the 'naturalness' of ordinary parenting is, for the purposes of societal regulation, seen as secondary in importance to the moral and institutional character of bringing children up - that is, *social* parenting.

Adoptive parents play only this role, lacking as they do the ordinary biological relationship with their adopted children. Whatever the biological relationship can support or excuse in the bringing up of children by their natural parents, it cannot support or excuse in the bringing up of adopted children. The social, moral and institutional elements in ordinary parenting completely dominate adoptive parenting. The presumptions that are made in favour of the competence and intentions of biological parents, with regard to the bringing-up of their children, are no more than presumptions; furthermore these cannot be made in connection with adoptive parents. On this view, adoption is an entirely artificial or institutional matter: the logically defensible contrast with ordinary parenting is however merely that ordinary parenting is only *partially artificial* or institutional, and not the more robust but insupportable contrast between adoptive parenting and a somehow 'purely' natural form of parent/child relationship in biological parenting.

Thus adoption is on this view an *institution* to be compared with the social rearing of children in any other context essentially regulated by society, for example residential care facilities provided by welfare and social services departments. As such, adoption is subject to the full range of safeguards, scrutinies and sanctions. Furthermore, whilst it is obviously the case that social scrutiny of the prospective adopting parents is driven by a concern for the interests of the child, precisely the same concerns are at work in, and underlie, the regulation of ordinary parenting in its social dimensions - which is to say, all of parenting beyond the original procreative acts. Once a child is born (and some would urge that this be extended to the child who has been merely *conceived*), her interests largely determine social regulation of parenting. The concern for the interests of the child is therefore not exclusive to adoptive parenting.

***

We are concerned with whether the provision of assisted conception services should be considered as more closely akin to the institutions concerned with ordinary parenting, or more closely akin to those concerned with adoption. The purpose of this, let us remind ourselves, is to consider the extent to which (and the circumstances in which) assisted conception services ought to be offered; or more specifically the degree to which societal scrutiny and discrimination is morally justified (or even mandated) in the matter of who should receive those services. It appears so far that this question cannot be settled by an appeal to a 'natural right' to procreate, since whilst there is *a fortiori* no such right to adopt the children of other biological parents, there is furthermore no absolute 'natural right' to undertake the upbringing of those children who are biologically one's own, nor even an absolute 'natural right' to the opportunity to procreate.

However since at any rate different *presumptions* operate as between biological and natural parents, concerning their bringing up of children, it might still be the case that whichever of these more closely resembles procreation by assisted conception will guide us as to the presumptions we should make in those cases. We have already noticed that what appears most to unite adoption and assisted conception is the artificiality of their circumstances, defined as *society's necessary role* in bringing them about. To see whether this appearance is reliable, we should now consider whether assisted conception really is better thought of as artificial, or better thought of as natural.

7. Assisted Conception as Both 'Natural' and 'Artificial'

The motivation for seeking assisted conception is ordinarily, and *prima facie*, presumed to be the natural biological urge to procreate which is felt by most adult humans in varying degrees. It is in all senses 'natural' for the infertile to seek assistance in overcoming their infertility. However we have already noted that the urge to adopt can be a natural urge, so showing the pursuit of assisted conception to be in response to a natural urge cannot be decisive in indicating the limits of justified social intervention and discrimination.

As against this, one could draw attention to other, and necessarily biological, features of assisted conception. Chiefly, babies cannot be synthesised; *in vitro* fertilisation is not yet accompanied by *in vitro* gestation. However much technology is involved, it is still true that assisted conception supports, promotes and utilises natural *biological* functions. In other words, our notions of what is natural in human procreation shall have to become flexible. After all, 'family planning' is a phenomenon whereby humans moderate and intervene in what would otherwise be essentially biologically-regulated processes in order to achieve a chosen outcome - a family of a given size, or no family at all. Even those who distinguish 'natural' from 'artificial' family planning would not claim that the children who result from 'artificial' (mechanical or chemical or other invasive) family planning methods are anything less than the *natural* children of their parents. Of course, we should in this context recall that society's resources are

implicated in the provision of family planning programmes, and are moreover the subject of moral disagreement. Thus to an extent the relevant sense of 'artificial' (the involvement of third parties) is again recalled as a moral justification for societal scrutiny. However, this does not of itself show that the biological connections between parent and child in the context of assisted conception are somehow beside the point; rather it shows that they may not be morally decisive.

The contrasting perspective would of course emphasise more than the somewhat narrow sense of 'artificial' with which we have mainly been concerned (the necessary involvement of third parties). Plainly, the intrusion of technology in assisted conception is self-evident, ranging from simple artificial insemination to laparoscopically-controlled GIFT/ZIFT. In assisted conception, procreation has *become* a technology, wielded by and on behalf of society. A thorough-going scepticism regarding such developments would protest that the natural dimensions of procreation have been usurped - indeed obliterated in the case of, for instance, those 'spare' embryos which result from superovulatory drugs and which proceed either to be (as it is euphemistically put) selectively reduced post-implantation, or to be frozen whilst awaiting either future implantation or lethal research. The difficulties with such a view arise when we recall that all of medicine represents a more-or-less technological intervention into natural processes: like hemlock, diseases are also accounted for by nature, having a natural history and a natural course if unopposed by artificial means.

Another aspect of the claim, that assisted conception is artificial, would pursue further the parallel with 'family planning' which we have already identified. Since ordinary 'family planning' at any rate *rationalises* (and to some extent conventionalises) what was hitherto a more obviously biological process, it is obvious that assisted conception greatly intensifies this tendency. The purposive and reflective deliberation underlying decisions to use assisted conceptions are likely to be in proportion to the extent and intrusion of the technology involved (as well as to its success/failure rates and its accompanying hazards). Again, whilst largely undeniable, this claim may not be *morally* decisive, since it too falls victim to the rejoinder that the morally appropriate is not identified by distinguishing the natural from the artificial.

A more obviously compelling moral objection would concern the interests of the child, and one such is the following. Although throughout history particularly male children have to an extent been objectified as desired heirs and successors, the use of extraordinary technical means to avoid biological infertility carries the risk that the children so produced be regarded as 'successful outcomes'. People can have many reasons for wanting children; resorting to extraordinary means for their production is liable to intensify the scrutiny which people's desires for children attract. The danger is that the child who is the object of technological last resort become the child as an object *simpliciter*. Here, the argument runs, we have a sense of 'artificial' which is quite unlike the narrow sense with which we have so far been interested: here is a sense of 'artificial' which is self-evidently pernicious, since the child whose interests we are most concerned to promote is now in danger of *becoming an artifice*.

I think the strength of this objection must depend on the extent to which it is invited

Notes

1. The denial of procreational opportunities might in this sense be no more than an contingent consequence of imprisonment.

2. It was precisely this intention, and the alleged likely failure of a contraceptive regime as a means to fulfilling that intention, that underpinned the arguments in favour of the compulsory sterilisation of F, a mentally handicapped adult.

3. I am grateful to Jean-Marie Thévoz for putting this point so vividly in discussion following an earlier draft of this paper.

4. See, Ruyter, Knut W., 'The example of adoption for medically assisted conception', and Thévoz, Jean-Marie, 'The rights of children to information following assisted conception' both in this volume.

10.   CHILD OR PARENT ORIENTED CONTROLS OF REPRODUCTIVE TECHNOLOGIES?

Demetrio Neri
Full Professor of History of Philosophy
University of Messina
Italy
Translated by Maurizio Mori

1. Two Conflicting Approaches

One of the central issues in recent debate concerning the new reproductive technologies (NRT)[1] is about legal regulation of access to the new techniques and about selection criteria of prospective parents.   Roughly speaking we can distinguish two major approaches to the problem.   One is 'child-oriented', and according to it, access to NRT is justified only on the grounds of possible benefits for the future child.   The other is 'parent-oriented', and according to it, parents are free to decide whether or not to resort to NRT facilities.   Of course there are various versions of these two general perspectives, but here I am concerned with a clarification of the basic significance of the two in relation to the problem of possible legal constraints on access to NRT.

The 'child-oriented' approach expresses fears stemming from the availability of NRT, particularly after 1978 with the advent of the new technique of *in vitro* fertilisation. As a result this perspective is rather conservative, in the sense that it aims, as far as possible, to view access to NRT within a traditional way of conceiving the family.   One tenet which different versions of the 'child-oriented' perspective hold is that NRT should be understood as a remedy for a couple's infertility, and not as an alternative method of reproduction available to everybody.   In order to ensure restricted availability, holders of this view claim that a fundamental requirement of legislation is to guarantee various interests and rights of newborns, e.g., the right to health, to welfare, to two parents of different sexes, to know the modalities of one's birth and one's genetic origin, etc.   The basic meaning of these constraints is well expressed by the following passage of the Report to the Secretary of the Council of Europe:

> CAHBI is unanimous in believing that artificial techniques of human reproduction should not be employed unless there exist conditions which guarantee the well-being of the new-born child, and allow it, in particular, the chance to develop in an environment permitting it the full flourishing of its physical, mental and spiritual capacities.   This condition must be met in the case of recourse to artificial techniques of human reproduction, in addition to the satisfaction of other

145

D. Evans (ed.), Creating the Child, 145–156.
© 1996 *Kluwer Law International. Printed in the Netherlands.*

conditions.[2]

The 'parent-oriented' approach is generally more liberal, in the sense that it tends to reduce as far as possible legal constraints on access to NRT in respect of both the range of different types of techniques and the selection criteria for prospective parents. The basic principle of the 'parent-oriented' approach is that it is wrong to set limits on people's procreative choices unless there are *sufficient reasons* (and not only vague fears or general feelings) for believing that such choices can really harm the interests or the rights of others. As Ruth Chadwick remarks, from this perspective it is usual to assume as a starting point the appeal to the so-called 'right to procreate'.[3] In the next section I will try to explain the meaning and the importance of such an appeal.

I want to make clear now that in speaking of a 'parent-oriented' approach I take for granted that there may be an argument for limiting access to NRT of heterosexual married or non-married but stable couples who, for various reasons, do not want to procreate through normal sexual intercourse even though they are not infertile. I know, too, that there is a controversy over the requirement that a couple be stable or married before such access is allowed, but I do not want to deal with it here. The problem I want to clarify stems from the following question: once we have granted the right to a parental couple, how should we understand the claim (central in the 'child-oriented' approach and largely accepted by current legislation) that the desire of two adult and responsible people to have a child must be submitted to further scrutiny in the light of the interests and rights of the future child?

I think that this claim reveals clearly that there is a suspicion of NRT as a means to becoming parents, which makes people want to prevent its use. As I will show, in Section 3, this suspicion is unjustified. Of course, I do not want to challenge the idea that it is right to pay attention to the well-being of future newborns - an attention which should be present in *any* and *every* procreative choice; but what worries me is the claim that the well-being of newborns sets special constraints (such as identification of a donor) in the case of NRT. This worries me because such constraints seem to be a way of preventing the fulfilment of people's desire to become parents.

2. The Appeal to the Right of Procreation

Since scientific progress gives us the opportunity to resort to methods of achieving parenthood different from both the 'natural' one and from adoption, even people who, before, could not have become parents because of the distribution in nature's lottery of fertility (or perhaps because of improper life styles) can now fulfil their desire to have children. Once we are able to fulfil a desire - if and insofar as the fulfilment of such a desire is morally licit - this may become a basis for the claim that its fulfilment is to be protected against constraints which are perceived as unjustified. This is because current natural limits by themselves have no special significance and cannot be taken as a legitimate source of moral claims: what has a moral value is what we do - the

nature of our actions and not the actions of nature taken by themselves are what matter. In this sense, when socio-economic development (as in the case of the 'rights of man') or technological development (as in our case) creates the conditions in which unfortunate events produced by the natural lottery may be 'repaired' or 'corrected'[4], there may arise a moral claim or a right against any person or institution trying to limit the availability of the new device.

This dynamic is well-known to historians of political ideas because it has often occurred since the great era of the 'rights of man' when the tendency to express desires, needs and interests in the language of rights became attractive for interested people and social groups. The term 'right' is connected with great and victorious fights for human claims and civil liberties and can certainly wield a strong persuasive power in our times, which has even been defined (by Norberto Bobbio) as 'The Age of Rights'.[5] To speak of something as a 'right' means to recommend it as a good thing.

So far this account has been concerned with the terminology of political struggles, but if we want to specify the meaning of the appeal to rights within a moral discourse, then the situation is more complicated. As R.M. Hare remarked, "it would be difficult to find any claim confidently asserted to a right which could not be as confidently countered by a claim to another right".[6] The conflict between the two approaches outlined earlier is a clear illustration of Hare's remark: the 'right to (have) a child' may be opposed to the 'rights of the child', and certainly where there is such a tension it is not easy to resolve.

I do not want to argue - as Hare does - about the theoretical inadequacy of an ethics based on 'rights'; I want to remark only that a moral claim is right not because it is a right, but that it is (or can become) a right where there are valid reasons which support the claim. This means that no claimant to a right is exempt from giving good reasons for holding that it is right to do what she claims she has a right to do. Given this, any expression beginning with the term 'a right to' is to be understood (within moral discourse) simply as short-hand for a complete ethical argument, and the claim expressed is valid just so far as the corresponding argument is. I do not think that any appeal to rights can have more value than this.

It would be useless to look for a 'right to procreate' among the so-called 'natural rights' or among the more recent 'basic rights' in order to see the implications of these for the limitation (or otherwise) of access to NRT. Similarly it would serve no purpose to look in the U.N. Declaration of the Rights of Man, or in the European Convention. As a matter of fact there are many rights and duties connected with procreation, but the the choice to do acts apt to lead to procreation is left to people to make in private and according to their own desires and at their own responsibility. Society constrains such activities only in very exceptional cases (for instance in the case of the sterilisation of handicapped people) or for very serious reasons (for example to cope with overpopulation). Granted this general rule, our problem is to examine whether or not, in our case, there are reasons so compelling that we may say that this normal liberty cannot be extended to the new techniques. In order to examine this, I propose to abandon the fuzzy and uncertain field of 'rights' and formulate the question in terms of

'preferences', 'needs' and 'interests' of persons. Our problem is then to know whether or not becoming parents by means of NRT is compatible with what is usually identified as the 'essence of parenthood'. If - as I think - the answer to this question is that it is, then the problems of limiting access to NRT is a specific issue within a more general one about the limitation of individual liberties in the context of a pluralistic society, that is to say that such limits can be applied only by means of an evaluation of the consequences of public policy choices on those involved.

3. Being Parents

The first question to be addressed is whether or not NRT are apt to ensure the existence of elements which are usually reckoned to constitute 'parenthood'.

Now I think that there is widespread agreement that 'parent' is a role depending on a complex cultural construction (and institution) which is socially and historically determined, that the focus of such a role is the assumption of responsibility for the consequences of one's acts, and has to do with caring for the child - loving, nurturing, educating (etc.) him or her. Usually, this assumption of responsibility is subsequent to a 'natural' process which presupposes sexual intercourse. However, it is important to emphasise that it is not the biological-natural process which is important for parenthood, but the responsible assumption of the functions of care which is in no way (other than in the obscure allusion implicit in the expression 'voice of the blood'[7]) necessarily connected to or produced by the biological-natural process.

Those who resort to NRT certainly accept a peculiar responsibility for the child, which is certainly desired and wanted perhaps 'at any cost'. NRT, then, can ensure this important aspect of parenthood just as well as the more traditional way of becoming parents through sexual intercourse. Moreover, according to one common sense opinion, natural procreation is not in itself a valuable thing unless there is a responsible parental project. In reality, then, what I called a 'preventive suspicion' against NRT does not depend on the fact that the new techniques diminish in some way the assumption of responsibility for a child, which could be called the 'natural basis' for parenthood. Taking on such responsibilities happens even in the case of adoption.

The suspicion seems rather to arise because the new techniques interfere in some way with the natural process of generation, and it is this fact which is reckoned to be an evil. Those who hold this thesis generally either assume that the traditional (sexual) method has also a normative value, or (and often at the same time) point to a series of negative consequences which can derive from conceiving human reproduction within a technological context (and even a commercial one).

Holders of the first position, who think that the natural procedure of becoming a parent has a normative value, must in some way affirm the existence of an intrinsic and necessary connection between being a parent and procreation through sexual intercourse. Richard A. McCormick summarised what those who hold this position think in the following words:

They maintain that a meaningful and reciprocal relationship between sexual love and the generation of human life exist and that it is no mere evolutionary accident that human beings come into existence through an act that is also capable of expressing love between man and woman.[8]

We can think of two different philosophically meaningful interpretations of the normative value of this connection between sexuality and parenthood. The first one ascribes normativity to the connection within a more general natural teleology which imposes an intrinsic respect (as Hans Jonas would say). This is equivalent to saying that 'nature wants it', opening the *vexata quaestio* of nature's normativity. As is often said, if one does not assume theological premises concerning a divine design intrinsic to the world's creation, it is very difficult to hold an account rationally acceptable from an ethical point of view. Jonas' thesis about an intuited self-evident teleology requires a fideistic acceptance as well as the appeal to a divine design.[9] For instance - and setting aside Hume in this connection - Kant did not agree that 'what nature wants' has any normative value *for us*; and concerning our topic he remarked that the goal of procreation and education of children can be the one aimed at by nature by means of the sexual drive among men and women, but that human beings are not obliged to accept such a goal, because if the shared life of a man and a woman were legitimated only by procreative goals, that shared life would be capable of dissolution once this goal had been reached.[10]

The other interpretation can be presented in this way: Independently of any controversial normativity of nature, the connection between being parents and sexual procreation is so important for the human species and implies so many affective meanings and values (generally we could say that 'it is not a mere evolutionary accident') that in any case it is better not to break it, even if as a matter of fact such a breaking is not infrequent. Now, in the case of the importance to the species of maintaining the connection, it is clear that here the wrongness of the breaking cannot depend on the fact that sexual procreation is 'natural' (this would be circular), but must depend on empirically testable negative consequences deriving from such a break. But empirical evidence of this kind does not seem available, and therefore the first part of the argument cannot be affirmed.

As for the other part concerning the affective meanings and values commonly ascribed to sexual procreation, there is no reason to deny its importance for the parental relationship. What I deny is that natural (sexual) procreation is the *only* way (i.e., a necessary and sufficient condition) of constituting such values and meanings. The importance of such values in people's lives is a good reason for allowing NRT when natural procreation is impossible; indeed I claim that fulfilment of the parenting need has a peculiar human value, particularly in the cases of infertile couples and of those who could procreate sexually but who, for various reasons (because they may transmit some genetic disease, for example) are recommended to resort to artifical procreation. As an Italian gynaecologist has remarked in this connection: "one of the most beautiful things I did in my life was to give 'healthy children' to paraplegics and to the deaf and

dumb!".[11] In conclusion, I think that both from the point of view of assumption of the responsibility to care and of the social and affective meanings linked to it NRTs are - all other things being equal - a good way of becoming a parent.

The phrase 'all other things being equal' indicates that there might be other reasons for saying that NRT is an improper means of becoming a parent, or for strictly controlling access to it. These reasons are about the consequences concerning, on the one hand, the subjects who are directly involved in the process, and, on the other hand, society in general. I will examine the first sort of consequence in the next section, focusing my attention on the consequences for the child who is born as a result of NRT. It is more difficult to identify exactly the other sort of consequences. Usually the claim is that admitting that generation of human life can happen in a technological and 'de-humanising' context can change (and that for the worse) our vision of life: what is at stake is our concept of humanity.[12] It is not the techniques in themselves, then, but the attitude that they can cause to develop, which worsen the situation, since they can produce the sort of commodification and commercialisation which leads to the exploitation of people.[13]

I think that these worries are certainly relevant, and they need more analysis than I can devote to them here. However, I note that it is difficult to point out the specific consequences on our attitudes deriving from a more widespread diffusion of NRT. Certainly, it will lead (and already has led[14]) to a change of our notion of the family: but should we say that such change is *necessarily* negative? Why not say that it is simply a *different* conception, without adding any particular evaluation? I think that unless we presuppose a static view, we should say that this general objection is very difficult to specify, and to hold.

However, the real moral problem concerning NRT seems to be that concerning the consequences for the child born by means of the new techniques. We should ask: is being born through NRT a good way of coming into the world?

4. Being Born Through NRT

When we focus our attention on the evaluation of consequences connected with specific modalities of being born, we have two basic question to ask. 1) Is a baby born through NRT disadvantaged in his/her pursuance of goods proper of human life because his/her procreation was artificially assisted? 2) Assuming that the child born through NRT is really disadvantaged because of the way he/she was born, can such a disadvantage be eliminated or not? I think that we should answer these two questions because often authors who rightly emphasise the need to protect the child's interests smuggle further premises into the discourse which should be clearly identified and rationally examined in a public analysis. This is what I will try to do now.

Let us take a case concerning the rights of the newborn. Up to a few years ago, the trend of legislation was for a guarantee of secrecy concerning the modality of someone's birth and anonymity for donors in cases where they gave help. Recently an opposite

trend has led to the application of what is common in adoption to cases of NRT births. So the principle of equality compels the giving of a guarantee to the newborn of a right to knowledge both of the modality of his/her birth, and of his/her genetic origins, as is common in adoption.

So far as the first right is concerned, the argument is that there are good moral, psychological and sociological reasons for abandoning secrecy: morally, it said to be important to comply with the principle of truth-telling; psychologically, it is believed in the long run a family-life based on secrecy could have a negative influence on a child's development; and sociologically, it is argued in a society which holds such secrets, even children born naturally could have doubts concerning their own birth. These are important arguments[15] on which future research can certainly provide further enlightenment and suggest possible policy solutions. For instance, we might think that even if secrecy were not to be strictly mandatory, it is not necessary to go to the opposite extreme, i.e., impose a strict obligation to tell the truth. Rather there is the possibility of leaving to parents a margin of discretion to tell the truth according to a careful analysis of a child's psychological growth. Why should we transform an issue of opportunity into an issue of rights? It is not difficult to imagine a case in which the real child's interests are not to know the circumstances of his/her conception or birth, and in such a case it would certainly be harmful to tell the truth. In brief: this presumptive right to know about the modality of one's birth is in the last analysis an 'abstract right', which, if always acted upon, would sometimes compel the sacrifice of one's own welfare.

Even more controversial is the trend to abolish the anonymity constraint in case of donor insemination, in the name of the so-called 'right to know one's genetic origins'. As a matter of fact, for those couples needing to resort to a donor and who do not desire that he/she has a role in their family-life, this constraint can be a real obstacle to having a child. As a consequence, for many possible children this right implies their non-existence. Apart from this odd consequence, which is worthy of reflection, it would be better to choose a straightforward prohibition of donor insemination (if we have sufficient reasons for it) as was accepted by a recent Austrian law.[16] But if we allow the meeting of two gametes which have no common history behind them, then why give the future child a right to trace a history which is non-existent? Unless we confuse 'personal history' with 'biological history', the alleged right is irrelevant to a child's personal identity, and therefore there are no supporting grounds for it.

We may now consider the argument concerning the protection of the psychological and material welfare of future children. I have already mentioned a passage of CAHBI which is a model of this new trend, and probably summarises the argument: putting the child's welfare at the centre of our attention implies a severe scrutiny of prospective couples wanting to become parents. Now, I think that it is trivial to say that we should care for future children's welfare; but this applies to *all* children, that is both those born through the 'natural' method and those born through NRT. Why, then, should we scrutinise only couples who seek assisted reproduction? I think that those who resort to NRT already present what we usually consider to be one feature of good parents:

they are wealthy enough to rear and educate the child, and they show a strong desire to have a child, proved by their willingness to undergo the stress of tests and the other medical procedures associated with NRT. Such desire is a good ground for thinking that they will be a loving and stable couple, which we think is ideal for a normal education. As a matter of fact, in the U.S. the divorce rate is about 48% in normal marriages, but it decreases to 1% in the case of couples resorting to NRT.

We must ask why we want to guarantee to children born through NRT optimal conditions which seem to be irrelevant in the case of children born through 'natural' methods. It could be remarked that, paradoxically, in seeking these extra guarantees only for children born as a result of NRT we discriminate against children born 'naturally'; if the parents of a child born through NRT are carefully chosen in order to ensure it better conditions of life, then this child (if ever born, given there are so many constraints) will be likely to be better off than a child born in the more usual way. Looking at the situation from the point of view of 'future children' in general, they may see that children born through NRT are better-off than others, and therefore, supposing they could choose by which method they would be born, they might well opt for NRT, or at least demand similar constraints also in the case of 'natural' procreation.[17]

This conclusion is certainly paradoxical, but it shows that very likely underlying the 'request for safeguards' there are other implicit premises which should be openly examined. One of these premises is the idea that being born through NRT does not, in any case, fulfil standards of human dignity, and so the child should be 'compensated' for that. But this shows that what is important is the 'dignity of being born' independent of any negative consequence. So we have to try to understand why it is sometimes claimed that NRT undermines 'human dignity'. A good suggestion is that of O'Donovan according to whom natural procreation guarantees the future person's dignity because there is no 'project' implicit in it, while intrinsic to NRT is a sort of 'programming'. To procreate a child is to share with him or her one's being, and does not involve making him/her the goal of a project of our will. What is valuable in natural procreation is randomness: allowing something to happen randomly even if we could control it technically is to leave it to God's providence, recognising that to control it wisely is beyond our power. Our participation in the event of procreation is a simple 'doing', rather than a case of 'instrumentally doing'.[18]

This sort of argument leads us to the problem of choice of moral styles of life, which I do not want to consider in this paper. I think that unless we presuppose some religious premises, it is very difficult to give a rational justification for positions such as O'Donovan's. In 1949 Pius XII held that people's desire to become parents could be fulfilled only through procreation according to God's will and His own plans (which are for us inscrutable). He held that only if one accepts such a perspective is it possible to assign a positive value to randomness and to the (alleged) absence of a project in natural procreation. But this perspective is unacceptable for those who reject its theological assumptions. As a matter of fact, many people seem to think that 'family planning' represents progress, permitting control *when* having children and as to their number. And the fact that this places procreation within an 'instrumental making' in

no way diminishes the 'value' of the children which result. On the contrary, there are good reasons for holding that such a value is increased.

Moreover, we may in any case ask why it is assumed that 'wanting a child' (in the strong sense of having a 'project' or a 'plan') should be so degrading and contrary to the child's human dignity as to require that we abolish any means to the realisation of such a 'project' and leave it only to divine providence. To hold that the 'intrinsic value' of something is diminished by being the object of an act of human volition is to confuse *attribution* of value with *recognition* of value. I can want something and thereby give it value or attribute value to it, and I can want something also for its intrinsic value. The alleged absence of any project in natural procreation does not seem always to be something good, and it does not guarantee by itself the intrinsic value of the future person, which is supposed inevitably to be destroyed by NRT. If the absence of a project were decisive we would have to conclude that, by being the outcome of a 'project' a baby born through NRT has an intrinsic value which is less than that belonging to one born after rape.

Since in these arguments there are many locutions such as 'end in itself', 'intrinsic value' and 'dignity', usually their conclusions are justified by reference to Kant's second formulation of the categorical imperative, according to which we ought to consider humanity always as an end and never as a mere means. So the idea is that having a child as a result of a project depending on our (human) will would be contrary to the future person's dignity because it would mean treating her as a mere means and not as an end in herself.[19]

Those who appeal to the Kantian argument often simplify Kant's view, attributing to him the idea of imposing on moral life an impossible constraint, to wit that we should consider humanity always and only as an end. As is commonly argued, what Kant actually requires is that all humanity (myself and others) should never be considered a mere means, but also and at the same time as an end. It is clear that all our life is interwoven with relationships in which persons are at the same time both means and ends: what is important is that they are never only means. The difference between a truthful promise to repay money borrowed and a false one does not consist in treating the other as a means in order to satisfy my need of money: in both cases I do use the other as a means (as a source of money). But in the second case I treat the other *only* as a means and not, at the same time, as an end. And I can discover this by considering the fact that the person receiving the false promise cannot agree with my way of treating him and cannot accept the end of my action. Kant asks each of us to try a thought experiment, to put ourselves in another's shoes, and on this experiment depends our awareness of having treated others only as a means or also as an end.

I would like to do the Kantian thought experiment in the case of a baby born through NRT, who is very likely loved by his/her parents and lives in a stable and wealthy family environment. I ask whether this child - once informed about the modalities of his/her birth - could or could not agree with his/her parents' choice to achieve his/her conception through NRT, accepting that he or she is the end of his/her parents' project, but being treated at the same time as an end in itself, having a peculiar 'intrinsic value'.

5. Conclusion

I do not claim that my suggested thought experiment will certainly be in favour of NRT. It is enough, for holding my position, that it should provide a reasonable probability of a favourable response. This is because, in this case not only do we not have any negative consequence for the child's wellbeing, but also there is no procedure contrary to the child's dignity. If this is so, then I think we can conclude that there are no compelling reasons for limiting reproductive freedom in case of NRT. Of course, this is a *logical* analysis, and I am aware that there may be psychological or sociological reasons for such a limitation, but which, however, do not seem to have any rational foundation.

In brief: if my arguments are sound, then I think they suggest that legislation concerning NRT should be minimal, and allow procreative choices to be left to people to decide on and take responsibility for autonomously. If we accept - at least as a matter of fact - that there is a plurality of ethical communities living within our societies, then legislation cannot legitimate a specific ethical community's view against the others. In matters such as the one concerning us, which engage our deepest beliefs concerning life and death, legislation ought to put itself forward as an instrument for fostering coexistence among different ethical perspectives, so that besides the traditional 'rights of political citizenship' there will be soon also 'rights of bioethical citizenship'.

Notes

1. From now on 'NRT' indicates the techniques which substitute for one or more stages of the process of reproduction which normally (or 'naturally') happens by means of sexual intercourse. I do not consider separately specific issues concerning different techniques (artificial insemination by husband (AIH) or by donor (AID), *in vitro* fertilisation (IVF), gamete intra-fallopian transfer (GIFT), etc.) since the philosophical debate seems to be focused on such oppositions as natural/artificial, or biological/social, or randomness/purposiveness, all of which involve more general questions.

2. Council of Europe Committee of Experts on Bioethics (CAHBI) *Procréation Artificielle Humaine* Strasbourg, Division des Publications et des Documents, 1989, p.11. (Translation by the editors.)

3. Chadwick, Ruth F., 'Having children: introduction' in Chadwick, Ruth F. (ed.), *Ethics, Reproduction and Genetic Control* London, Routledge, 1992, pp.3-43, p.3.

4. On this cf. Rawls, J., *A Theory of Justice* Cambridge, Mass., Harvard University Press, 1971, section 17.

5. Bobbio, Norberto, *L'età dei Diritti* Torino, Einaudi, 1990.

6. Hare, R.M., 'Abortion and the golden rule' *Philosophy and Public Affairs* 4 (3), Spring 1975, pp.201-222, p.203.

7. If we want to give an empirical meaning to the expression 'voice of the blood' we can refer to the biological relationship of 'natural' parent and child, i.e., the transmission of genes. In this sense we should distinguish different techniques of NRT, since some of them allow for a full genetic relationship, while others prevent it partially or totally. For an analysis of some problems on this issue and the difference between the "genic" and "genetic" relationship, see Alpern, K.D., 'Genetic puzzles and stock stories: on the meaning and significance of having children' in Alpern, K.D. (ed.), *The Ethics of Reproductive Technologies* Oxford, Oxford University Press, 1992, pp.147-169. In any case, my basic idea is that the 'voice of the blood' can have and has a moral meaning only within a responsible plan of parenthood, however pursued.

8. Cf. 'Reproductive technologies: ethical issues' in Reich, W.T. (ed.), *Encyclopedia of Bioethics* Vol. II, New York, The Free Press, 1982, pp.1454-1464, p.1456.

9. When Jonas views parental obligation as a model of the principle of responsibility, he claims that it is simply 'self-evident' that a parent has an obligation toward his/her child. In similar vein he claims that Hume's law is falsified in at least one case, namely that of a newborn whose being (existence) imposes an 'ought' on her carers; and even here Jonas holds that the mere being of an entity produces a duty on others in a self-evident way. Cf. Jonas, H. (transl. Portinaro, P.P.), *Il Principio Responsabilità* Torino, 1990, pp.162ff (*Das Prinzip Verantwortung* Frankfurt a. M., Insel Verlag, 1979). For a philosophical analysis of the concept of teleology, mainly concerning biological processes, cf. Mayr, E., 'The idea of teleology' *Journal of the History of Ideas* LIII (1), 1992, pp.117-135.

10. Kant, I., *Die Metaphysik der Sitten* (The Metaphysic of Morals) Part 1, Chapter 2, Section 3, para. 24. It is interesting to observe that after a few passages (para. 28) Kant holds that the obligation to care for the child depends on the fact that by *choosing* to procreate we create a being without its consent: I think that this remark is very interesting because there is no reference either to any 'physical operation' (as Kant calls it) involved in procreation, or to any natural bonding.

11. Lauricella, E., 'Sterilità e procreazione: l'opinione di un medico' in Ferrando, G. (ed.), *La procreazione artificiale tra etica e diritto* Padova, Cedam, 1989, pp.323-333, p.325.

12. Cf., for instance, Kass, L., 'Making babies revisited' in Shannon, T.A. (ed.), *Bioethics* third edition, Mahwah, N.J., Paulist Press, 1987, pp.453-480, pp.456ff.

13. On this cf. Radin, M.J., 'Market inalienability' in Alpern (ed.), *op.cit.*, pp.174-194.

14. Cf. Macklin, R., 'Artificial means of reproduction and our understanding of the family' *Hastings Center Report* 21 (1), Jan-Feb 1991, pp.5-11.

15. Cf. Ruyter, Knut W., 'The example of adoption for medically assisted conception' in this volume; and Thévoz, Jean-Marie, 'The rights of children to information following assisted conception' also in this volume.

16. It is interesting to note that the Austrian law passed in 1992 does not allow donation in the case of IVF, but does in the case of *in vivo* insemination. Moreover, AID is allowed only if male semen is infertile, and it is forbidden if the male can transmit a genetic disease, so that the couple has a troublesome dilemma because the choice is between not having any child and having a possibly unhealthy child. It is not easy to understand the reasoning behind a position such as this one.

17. On this point, cf. Lafollette, H., 'Licensing parents' *Philosophy and Public Affairs* 9 (2), 1980, pp.182-197.

18. O'Donovan, O., *Begotten or Made?* Oxford, Oxford University Press, 1984.

19. A negative feature of introducing NRT is the fact that having children 'naturally' becomes only one way (among others) which is instrumentally chosen in order to reach a goal within a human project, and therefore even 'procreation' is included in the category of what is 'instrumentally made' (cf. O'Donovan, *op.cit.*, pp.82ff).

11. LEGAL APPROACHES TO MOTHERHOOD IN HUNGARY

Judit Sándor J.D. LLM
Central European University
Budapest College
Hungary

1. Introduction

For a long time motherhood was regarded as a continuum from the 'moment' of conception, through pregnancy, delivery, and feeding and raising the child. The female contribution to the child was thought to be limited to providing shelter (the womb) and care for the baby, since the actual material contribution of the woman was proved only in the early nineteenth century. Now we face many fragmented forms of motherhood which may compete with one another. An egg donor is a genetic mother, a surrogate mother is considered an obstetric mother while the applicant mother in the IVF centre is considered to be the 'social mother'. Parallel to technical developments, the number and the combinations of the different mother roles is increasing. In order to assemble governing principles one should be aware that a pregnant woman's right to self-determination dates back only a few decades and is still considered a very vulnerable, 'young' right.

One of the possible solutions to the problem of summarising the sources of this right is to look at some leading cases in American jurisprudence and compare the issues with the statutory law in Hungary. Since in Hungary the current statutory law framework is incomplete in the field of assisted procreation, I shall refer to non-legal sources and also attempted legislation.

If one looks at the origin of women's right to decide whether or not to carry the child to term, one cannot avoid mention of the *Roe v. Wade* case. Whether or not it was the intent of the *Roe v. Wade* Court[1], women's constitutional right to privacy in choosing to terminate pregnancy before the end of the first trimester has been recognised since this case. This right is based on the due process clause which was found broad enough to encompass a woman's decision of whether or not to terminate her pregnancy. The abortion problem, in addition to privacy, raises issues of sex discrimination. Unwanted pregnancy places such a burden on a woman, severely restricting her life. For this reason, criminalisation of abortion at any stage of pregnancy would constitute discrimination against women on the grounds of sex.

Roe v. Wade is still the leading American case, the principle it established having been maintained for more than twenty years. The Court did not share the argument of the appellant that the right to privacy of women is absolute and as a consequence the

D. Evans (ed.), Creating the Child, 157–166.
© 1996 *Kluwer Law International. Printed in the Netherlands.*

pregnant woman is entitled to terminate her pregnancy at whatever time, in whatever way, and for whatever reasons she alone chooses. "Where certain 'fundamental rights' are involved, the Court has held that regulation limiting these rights may be justified only by a 'compelling state interest' and that legislative enactments must be narrowly drawn to express only the legitimate state interest at stake."[2] There is still much debate on the further reasoning of the court in making a distinction between three stages of pregnancy in determining in what specific period of pregnancy "compelling" state interest must be respected.

The legal frontier of the woman's right to choose, however, has been questioned on both biomedical and philosophical grounds, and even the law recognises the legitimate state interest in potential life at the compelling point of viability.

In *Webster v. Reproductive Health Services Inc.*[3] the Supreme Court upheld state laws banning the use of tax money for abortion consultation, and public hospital or public facilities to perform abortion. While the judgement affirms the view that a woman's choice is a private matter for her which is within the right to privacy, no state action is required to ensure this right. The right to privacy is clearly a negative right.

In *Casey* a great number of provisions of the Pennsylvania Abortion Control Act were challenged.[4] The Pennsylvania law required a special informed consent procedure 24 hours before the abortion. Disclosure had to involve, among other things, the risks of abortion, a description of the 'unborn child', and information about the medical agencies where prenatal care and neonatal care might be available. The Pennsylvania Abortion Control Act also included requirements for parental consent and spousal notice. Under the law a married woman had to give notice to her husband about her intention to have an abortion.

The Casey Court realised that the judicial act of line drawing may seem arbitrary but stated that "... there is no line other than viability which is more workable. ... The viability line also has, as a practical matter, an element of fairness".[5]

The Court held in its joint opinion that it is not unconstitutional to require physicians to present "truthful, non-misleading information" before abortion.[6]

The essential elements of the American judicial approach to unwanted motherhood can be summarised in the following way:

- recognition of the right of women to choose to have an abortion before the foetus is viable and to obtain it without undue interference from the State;

- before viability the State's interests are not strong enough to support a prohibition of abortion;

- the State has legitimate interests in protecting the health of the woman and the life of the foetus.

The main features of the abortion debate in the United States, and particularly the problem of conflicting rights, also constitute the major characteristics of the Hungarian legal approach. The differences between the two legal systems (on this question) are partly due to the continued strong positive protection of human rights and the close link between the concept of rights to life and human dignity in the Hungarian law. Since 'family planning' in other than the negative and ultimate form of termination of

pregnancy is still not a legislative issue in Hungary I will briefly mention the political, social and legal framework in which the potential new legislation may appear.

2. Positive v. Negative Protection of Basic Human Rights

Countries in Central Europe have very different constitutional traditions but some common elements appeared under the previous socialist political regimes. These include the enactment of welfare rights on the one hand, and positive state obligations on the other. Since the first democratic elections, constitutional issues have become prominent political and legal questions and a number of private law matters have become constitutional issues.

The main features of the positive protection of human rights have not changed despite important changes at the level of constitutional amendments in 1989-90 and the adoption of the human rights provisions of the UN Covenant and the European Human Rights Convention. Authoritarian traditions, the positive and 'provided' rights may strongly influence the processes of legislation, adjudication, and especially of government practice. As the Hungarian Constitutional Court has reaffirmed in its decision on termination of pregnancy (64/1991. (XII.17.)) protection of basic human rights does not encompass only passive protection or the state's refraining from certain activities, but also includes active protection and mechanisms to ensure human rights.

Within the scope of the rights of the person it is necessary to examine the degree to which personal autonomy is respected (e.g. the pregnant woman's right to choose, the patient's right that the treatment be subject to the constraint of his/her informed consent).

In order to highlight the Hungarian legal attitude toward assisted procreation, I will use a comparative method.

With respect to personal self-determination American jurisprudence has relied upon the principle of substantive due process under the Fourteenth Amendment of the U.S. Constitution. This approach supports a passive right of protection which is most apparent in the paradigm of privacy. By this, an individual has a right to be left alone in his private decisions, and the state recognises this right by being silent on these questions. This approach represents laissez-faire thinking as a dominant idea.

Other legal systems apply the civil law concept of the 'inviolability' of human beings. In Europe, and more specifically in Central Europe, however, there is also a strong tradition of positive protection of individual rights, or rights provided by the state. That is one of the reasons why the right to privacy in its American form is still an alien right in the Central Eastern European region. Nor does the Hungarian Constitution contain a general privacy-protection clause. It recognises, however, some specific 'privacy type of rights', such as the right to have personal secrets, to the confidentiality of correspondence, and to the protection of personal data.

3. Artificial Insemination

Artificial Insemination can be performed with the sperm of the husband (homologous insemination - AIH), with a donor's sperm (AID), or with a combination of donor's and husband's sperm (AIHD). AIH does not usually provoke any legal debate while AID raises questions of confidentiality and the right to personal identity.

Historically, the first legal question which had to be solved here was whether the use of donor semen technically amounted to adultery. In 1958 in a British case (*MacLennan v MacLennan* 1958 SC 105) the court held that adultery required the act of intercourse between two people one or both of whom were married to another person at the time that the intercourse took place. Transfer of semen could not amount to adultery.

Other possible limitations on the use of artificial insemination are imposed on the basis of marital status, age and sexual orientation of the woman.

The current Hungarian law regulates grounds for divorce with a *general clausula* in which adultery is not considered sufficient grounds for divorce. It follows that in the Hungarian law the relevant question is not the moral obstacle of technical adultery (unification of the egg and the sperm) but whether the legislator can justify the prioritisation of married women. Under the current regulation unmarried women do not have general access to artificial insemination although the technique is available in most countries with a donor's sperm.

There are serious terminological problems in the Hungarian law since the term 'artificial conception' is used when what in fact is being referred to is artificial insemination. The exact Hungarian term for artificial insemination is rarely used.

In Hungary 12/1981.(IX.29.) EuM r., amended by 7/1989.(III.22.) SZEM r., artificial insemination is available for a woman who:
1. is married and lives with her husband,
2. is not older than 45,
3. is legally competent,
4. has a permanent address in Hungary
5. and who according to expert medical opinion cannot have a child in the natural way.

The law demands an additional procedural requirement: the joint request of husband and wife for the therapy.

In 1992 the Hungarian Health Science Council (Egészségügyi Tudományos Tanács) adopted an *Ethical Guideline on New Methods of Human Reproduction.*[7] The *ad hoc* committee which produced the report analysed sixteen alternative possibilities based on the different possible sources of the gametes. The committee applied three different moral principles to the carrying out of assisted reproduction. These were: (1) respect for the individual which included special references to (a) autonomy and (b) protection of the handicapped; (2) the duty to provide assistance and support (that is not only *primum non nocere* but also provide active help); and (3) justice.

Assisted reproduction can be carried out only in specially appointed institutions where the technical and personal conditions mentioned in the next section are fulfilled.

3.1. CONDITIONS FOR AIH

1. Access to these techniques is based on medical indication.
2. The techniques are available only to married couples.
3. Before the performance of AIH informed consent has to be obtained from the couple.
4. The circumstances of the conception need not be revealed unless the law requires it.
5. In special circumstances (for instance before surgical radio- or chemo-therapy) the frozen sperm of the husband may be used for AIH.

3.2. CONDITIONS FOR AID

1. The technique should be available not only for married couples but also for heterosexual couples who live permanently together.
2. Sperm can be used for the purpose of AID only after it has been frozen and stored for at least 180 days.
3. The maximum number of successful inseminations from one donor is five.
4. Inseminations performed must be registered and these files must be preserved for at least 25 years.
5. Before the performance of AID the couple (recipient) must be informed about the technique and must give their written consent to the treatment.
6. If twelve unsuccessful procedures have been conducted with due care, then a further examination of the infertile couple is required in order to determine the possibilities of using another reproductive technique.
7. The donor's name should not be disclosed.
The committee also specified health criteria for donors.

4. *In Vitro* **Fertilisation and Embryo Transfer**

In vitro fertilisation (IVF), as the term suggests, involves the creation of an embryo outside the woman's body. The IVF technique, although well established in the modern world, still stimulates many legal debates. One of the most difficult legal issues, owing to the use of hormone therapy and to the IVF itself, is the production of spare embryos. The legal questions of property and custody are still unsolved, although, in most recommendations, those who contribute to the creation of the spare embryo are said to have a right to give or refuse consent to further usage of their gametes or to restrict in some way their further employment. In Europe the altruistic element is dominant in donation of embryos. Since the 'best interests' of the embryo are understood as the interest in being reimplanted into the maternal womb and since this presumption is almost always automatically considered, the only question left open is whether the woman is willing to accept the implantation or not.

Although various forms of IVF have already been used the conditions for requesting these medical interventions still are not regulated by law in Hungary. Two of the major questions are: Who should have access to this procedure? Should the age, marital status and sexual orientation of the woman matter?

Once the age limit appears in legislation, there follow the problems of how to treat equally women having very different reasons for requesting IVF. These include (a) women of normal childbearing age but who have premature menopause e.g. due to a gynaecological operation, (b) woman after and before menopause who were never capable of having a child, (c) women who were capable of bearing a child, albeit that when they were physically capable of having a child their marital or social status did not allow them to have a child and (d) women who chose not to have a child whilst at child bearing age for other reasons (e.g. pursuing a career).

Concerning marital status, it is difficult to justify the law's considering unmarried parents or single women as less capable of raising a child (even though they are willing to take an inconvenient, comparatively expensive and risky way to get a child) than those who, although living in marriage, raise unwanted children.

An additional series of problems appears in the conflict of changing the birth entry (registration), the anonymity of the procedure and the child's right to know the identity of its genetic forbears.

5. Surrogacy

Some forms of the new reproductive technologies require a form of surrogacy agreement between the social parents and a woman other than the woman who will raise the child. "Surrogacy is that arrangement in which a woman carries a child to term intending at the initiation of the pregnancy for another woman to raise the child as the social mother."[8] Fertilisation may take place through normal coitus or it may be a consequence of artificial insemination, *in vitro* fertilisation or embryo transfer. While the genetic father is often the husband of the woman who expects to raise the child as its mother, that need not be the case. While the genetic mother is usually the pregnant woman, that is not required. It is possible to take the sperm from one source, the ovum from another and place the subsequently developed embryo in the uterus of a third person. Surrogacy often requires a contract between the biological father and/or mother (who would like to raise the child) and the surrogate mother. It includes the agreement that after delivery of the child the parental rights of the surrogate mother will be terminated, and the biological father (mother) will be entitled to custody.

As with *in vitro* fertilisation the main legal questions in connection with surrogacy agreements are the following: Should the law impose restrictions on this procedure based on the age, marital status and the sexual orientation of the women engaged in the surrogacy agreement on either side? Can surrogacy agreements be enforced? What happens if the parties involved change their minds? What is the scope of the surrogate mother's liability? Can the choice to carry another woman's baby to term on a

commercial basis be regarded as a rational choice, or should the state intervene as *parens patriae* protecting individuals from the consequences of such self-destructive behaviour? Should commercial and/or altruistic surrogacy be regulated by the state?

Although the Hungarian Parliament still has not enacted a law on assisted procreation (except on artificial insemination), different approaches can already be demonstrated by the different terms applied in the Hungarian literature: 'beranyasag' and 'dajkaterhesseg'. One refers to the altruistic element of carrying a child to term while the other indicates the commercial character of the agreement about the child.

All pregnancy involves risk and inconvenience which may amount to physical harm and long term psychological harm. And this raises a fundamental question: Is surrogacy a degradation or, on the contrary, an appreciation of pregnancy?

In the British case *A v C*[9] the Court held that it is against public policy to make an agreement between a father and a woman who, based upon a contract, would conceive a child by artificial insemination and carry it to term. According to the court it was a purported contract for the sale and purchase of a child.

One of the most well known arguments in this field can be found in the judgement in the U.S. case of Baby M.[10] The Court held the surrogacy contract to be invalid in this case because it was in conflict with the laws prohibiting the use of money in connection with adoptions, laws requiring proof of parental unfitness or abandonment before termination of parental rights is ordered or an adoption is granted, and laws that make surrender of custody and consent to adoption revocable in private placement adoptions.

The woman who enters into a contract with the commissioning parents and surrenders her custodial rights even before the child is even conceived must offer her womb and her body for use either for money or out of altruistic motives. A question clearly arises as to whether what she does represents a degradation of motherhood, or rather the contrary. If motherhood is fragmented into distinct isolated phases - conception, sheltering the growing embryo, delivery, and child-rearing - does this mean that motherhood itself has been reduced to a chain of different jobs which women may be hired to do, providing a convenient solution to the problems of a woman who becomes a mother (in some sense) but intends to continue with her already existing activities. Such questions have strong gender implications, since surrogate mothers are necessarily women.

One of the biggest moral problems with surrogacy contracts is that the surrogate mother (who carries the child to term) is irrevocably committed to giving the child away before she knows the actual strength of her bond with her child. Many states have therefore adopted a regulation that only those women can enter into surrogacy contract as natural mothers who have already had a natural child.

One of the most heatedly debated issues in the ethics of assisted procreation is whether legislators or ethics committees should draw a sharp line between commerical and non-commercial surrogacy. Commericial surrogacy ('womb leasing') takes place when the commissioning couple wish to have a child but the future social (and/or genetic) mother cannot (or does not wish) to carry the child to term and seeks the assistance of another woman (surrogate mother) to carry the child to term through a commercial transaction.

In other words, this is a contract where the surrogate mother is motivated not be altruistic intent but rather monetary considerations. The arguments which support banning commericial surrogacy include the following: first, there is a parallel between baby selling (which has been outlawed this century) and making a contract concerning a child whose birth is expected; second, women cannot freely consent to provide their wombs for an infertile couple when the reward for their services goes beyond compensation for her expenses and losses.

Under many legal systems such a surrogacy contract would be considered void as it is 'contrary to public policy' or 'contraire aux bonnes moeurs'. If a new regulation is to come into force in Hungary it will probably follow the German *Embryonenschutzgesetz* of 1990 which outlawed all commercial surrogacy. Interestingly enough, the British law (the *Surrogacy Arrangements Act* of 1985 and the *Human Fertilisation and Embryology Act* of 1990) does not forbid commerical surrogacy explicitly.

Separation between procreation and implantation creates the possibility of selecting embryos with special features. While request for resemblance to the parents and the avoidance of hereditary diseases can be morally justified, other demands should be disregarded. There is little doubt that prospective parents now practice 'private' eugenics through prenatal selection. And this suggests the need for an exact definition of the service.

In Hungary legal questions around assisted procreation still remain untouched after the political transition. One of the main features of these unchanged laws is that a single woman cannot request these interventions.

Under the Hungarian Health Minister's Order (Sic!) No 12/1981 (IX.29.) Artificial Insemination may be performed upon the request of the married couple for the woman married and living with her husband, who is younger than 45, is legally competent and who, in medical opinion, cannot bear a healthy child in the natural course of things.

As for the possible future regulation of assisted procreation one has to refer again to the *Ethical Guideline* of the Hungarian Health Service Council.[11] I will summarise very briefly the main views and requirements of this guideline.

1. The Council supported both partial and full surrogacy[12].
2. A psychological examination of the couple and the surrogate mother is required.
3. Genetic and necessary medical testing is required.
4. Evaluation of the family's stability, particularly with regards to the future prospects of the planned child, is required.
5. Clarification of the intent of the surrogate mother, and arrangement of possible discussions between the couple and the surrogate mother are required.

6. Insurance Aspects

Questions regarding access to the new reproductive technologies, and problems of allocation and financing of the techniques of assisted procreation have not been brought before the Hungarian public. Under the Hungarian Act II in 1975 (as amended by the

Act 1992:IX 5.) those who are insured[13] are entitled to up to three treatments, entirely free, of artificial insemination, where this is medically indicated and within the legal limits. However, medical experts have generally held that three attempts financed by health insurance is not sufficient for the success of the procedure.

In vitro fertilisation is briefly mentioned in the Ministry order in 1994.[14] A Ministry order in 1993[15] recognised the techniques of assisted procreation by providing them codes and points which constitutes the basis for financing them.

7. Conclusion

It is true for all the procedures of assisted procreation that they do not serve curative purposes, but rather can be considered as palliative. Legal questions around these procedures arise in different fields. Among these are:

human rights (right to self determination, right to privacy);

property law (who has custody rights over the gametes and embryos stored);

family law (adoption, divorce[16], and in the case of surrogacy issues around (again) adoption and custody);

birth registration (on the one hand, a child born through assisted procreation has a right to know his identity, on the other hand this right may be in conflict with the parents' efforts to create a new family which frequently involves their changing the birth certificate and marking the commissioning parents as natural parents in the register);

allocation of resources (assisted procreation is expensive since it often involves lengthy preliminary hormonal treatment and numerous attempts to achieve successful fertilisation and embryo transfer);

medical secrecy (in respect of the genetic parents, the social parents, and of the child).

Once we recognise the complexity of the problem and its interrelation with other legal fields it will become clear that it is insufficient to apply mere ethical guidelines and some insurance law provision in the field of assisted procreation. After some years testing out transitory ethics guidelines it is inevitable that comprehensive legislation in the field will need to be introduced. There is a Draft Patient Rights Bill in Hungary which would provide general conditions for these treatments. However a general patients' rights bill, even with some special provision, could not fulfil all the requirements of an Act on assisted procreation.

Legislation should focus on access to these services, the quality assurance aspects of the assisted procreation centre, as well as arranging the various details of the procedures and the possible legal consequences. It is very hard to avoid having to strike a balance between the different persons playing the fragmented roles of motherhood. Conflict between egg donors, surrogate mothers and social mothers will occur, as the relatively short history of jurisprudence in this field has already demonstrated.

Notes

1. *Roe v. Wade* 410 U.S. 113 (1973).

2. *Roe v Wade op.cit.* Mr Justice Blackmun's opinion 410 U.S. 113 (1973).

3. *Webster v. Reproductive Health Services Inc.* 109 S.Ct 3040 (1989).

4. *Planned Parenthood of Southeastern Pennsylvania v. Casey* 112 S.Ct. 2791 (1992).

5. Justice O'Connor, Justice Kennedy and Justice Souter opinion part IV in *Planned Parenthood vs Casey op.cit.* in *United States Law Week Supreme Court Opinions* Vol. 60, No. 51, 1992, p.4805.

6. The Pennsylvania Abortion Control Act of 1982 (amended in 1988 and 1989) prescribes that, except in a medical emergency, at least 24 hours before performing an abortion a physician has to inform the woman of the nature of the procedure, the health risk of the abortion and of the childbirth, and the probable gestational age of the unborn child.

7. Hungarian Health Science Council *Ethical Guideline on New Methods of Human Reproduction* in *Lege Artis Medicinae* 2 (6), 1992, pp.554-565.

8. Furrow, Barry R., Johnson, Sandra H., Jost, Timothy S., and Swartz, Robert, *Health law Cases, Materials and Problems* second edition, St Paul, Minn., West Publishing Co., 1991, pp.974.

9. *A v. C* 1985 FLR 445.

10. Supreme Court of New Jersey, 1988. 109 N.J. 396, 537 A 2d 1227.

11. Hungarian Health Science Council, *op.cit.*

12. Full surrogacy is a procedure in which the commissioning couple provide the gametes and the surrogate mother her womb to carry the commissioning parents' child to term. In the case of partial surrogacy, fertilisation (accomplished either through consensual intercourse or by *in vitro* fertilisation) is of the surrogate mother's own oocytes, and she carries a child genetically her own to term.

13. The Hungarian health insurance system is based on mandatory contributions by employers and employees. Any patient who receives medical services is considered to be insured.

14. 6/1994. (1V.l.) NM r.

15. 9/1993. (1V.2.) NM r. on some questions concerning financing of some specialised health care treatments.

16. Divorce may create numerous legal problems, especially when one or both parents seek an abortion or prohibition of the further usage of stored embyros. Problems arise particularly when one of the genetic parents requests custody of the embryos, while at the same time the other parent seeks the prevention of implantation of embryos produced partly by his or her gametes.

12. THE INTERACTION OF RATIONALITY AND FREEDOM OF CONSCIENCE IN LEGISLATION ON CONTROVERSIAL BIOETHICAL ISSUES

Prof. Erwin Bernat
Department of Civil Law
Graz Law School
Heinrichstrasse 22
8010 Graz
Austria

The following considerations deal with the question of how a legislature may or, more precisely, must solve fundamental bioethical problems. First, I shall briefly focus on the question of determinant factors that should be included in the legislature's decision. In the first part of my discourse I shall in quite general terms deal with the relation of ethical principles, constitution and legislature[1], so as to be able to examine in the second part whether the Austrian legislature followed the essential dictates of rationality when it passed the *Act on Procreative Medicine* (1992).[2]

Thesis 1: The legislative decision has to be in accordance with paramount constitutional determinants, i.e., civil and human rights. Furthermore, legislature is bound by international conventions.[3]

In the context of interest to us there can be mentioned, if only by way of example, the rights to life, freedom of research and science, as well as the 'general right to personality' (*Allgemeines Persoenlichkeitsrecht*) in all its various forms. The legislative realisation of such judgements as manifest these fundamental liberties is difficult for at least two reasons. On the one hand, even value judgements laid down in fundamental liberties can come into conflict with each other, as has been shown in the well-known example of abortion and its resolution by the German Constitutional Court in 1975[4]: how must we proceed when the foetus' right to life collides with the pregnant woman's right of self-determination, and when one has to proceed on the assumption that both legal positions are safeguarded by the constitution?[5] On the other hand, the construction of the constitution's ethical determinants becomes more difficult if the intellectual content of their meaning is unclear. Is the embryo (foetus) from the time of its conception covered by the word 'everyone' in the sense of the original wording of the European Convention for the Protection of Human Rights and Fundamental Freedoms (art. 2, para.1, sentence 1)? Or is it rather the case, as was held by the Austrian Constitutional Court in 1974, that only the born human being falls under the scope of the provision, and that therefore the foetus does not partake in the protection

D. Evans (ed.), Creating the Child, 167–173.

of life provided by the fundamental rights?[6]   I shall now turn my attention to this problem of interpretation.

Thesis 2: If the intellectual content of the system of fundamental rights is uncertain, it should be supplemented with principles of a rational ethic.[7] Yet, often no amount of effort will suffice to achieve this ideal.

Let us resume the afore-mentioned consideration of the embryo's protection by fundamental rights. If the wording of a constitutional provision leaves undecided the question whether a right to life has been conceded, then a legislature should first aim to adopt an interpretation consistent with principles of a rational ethic. One therefore has to endeavour to find a reasoning which can claim to be universal, i.e., one that is comprehensible for, and evident to, everyone.[8] If the interpretation of a legal rule is founded only on religious convictions, the decision made is not a rational one. Nonetheless, though the judgement be non-rational, this does not necessarily mean that the content of the norm is irrational. It merely means that the content of the norm is not founded upon universally evident grounds, that is upon grounds which are plausible for everyone. Yet this does actually not preclude the existence of such grounds: a Jehovah's Witness' decision to refuse a blood transfusion appears to be irrational at first sight, yet it conforms with this sect's belief. Hence, one can speak of a non-rational decision only.[9]

According to the view set forth above, it would be indefensible for a legislature to presume a constitutionally granted right to life of the foetus simply because such a right to life is usually inferred from a divine revelation by Christian Churches.[10]   God's existence and his commandments, after all, can be explained only on the basis of metaphysical suppositions - hence they can be explained only non-rationally. However, at this point of the argument we encounter barriers to rational legal substantiation that are inherent to the Austrian constitution. Freedom of faith and conscience (art. 14 of the Constitutional Act on Fundamental Liberties [StGG 1867], as well as art. 9 European Convention for the Protection of Human Rights and Fundamental Freedoms) also means that the legislature has to respect the individual conscience of every person and must not confront the individual with decisions which would be emotionally and, normally, also intellectually overburdening.[11] If, for instance, the majority of the population intuitively presumes a right to life for the foetus, because the majority of the population has socio-cultural roots in Christianity, then much can be said in favour of including the 'man on the Clapham omnibus' valuation into the procedure of legislative decision-making. In other words: it should also be a task of legal policy to achieve a fair reconciliation - within the framework of the constitution's ethical determinants - between the ethical convictions in society, which are often polarised.[12] In this context it is also essential to infer constitutional protection of persons committed to no or other religious denominations.[13]

Thesis 3: The rationality of the legislative decision becomes more comprehensible, the more the strong points of a simple compromise wording are made transparent.

In the process of decision-finding, legislatures should therefore openly point out the 'mere compromise' of the statutory rule.

A very recent and illustrative example is the reformulated version of sec. 218a of the German Penal Code.[14] It has solved unequivocally the question whether the exemption from punishment of abortion also provides a ground for its justification[15] - a point formerly at issue in doctrine. Termination is not unlawful under the conditions defined in the provision, and is therefore allowed. I find this provision to be a sound compromise between those who intended to legalise abortion completely[16] - i.e., until birth - and the advocates of a model based on medical, ethical, social etc. grounds for abortion (the 'indication model') which is still more restrictive than the one which was in force until 1992.[17] From an intellectual point of view, this solution can be seen as satisfactory only if one is aware that it represents a compromise. Adopting the attitude of the 1975 judgement of the German Constitutional Court, which means approving of the foetus' right to life, it is *prima facie* hardly understandable why the pregnant woman's mere right to self-determination is seen to eliminate the unlawfulness of the foetocide.[18] Only an awareness of the legislative compromise makes this comprehensible. Doctrinal reasonings attributing rationality to the thesis of lawful defence *per se* are unconvincing. At least, they fail to convince me.

Thesis 4: Legislative solutions based on a compromise which as such cannot be rationally substantiated are inadmissible since they contradict the dictate of reasonableness.

The Austrian Act on Procreative Medicine contains illustrative examples of legislative compromises which cannot be substantiated universally, and thus are unconstitutional, as they contradict the dictate of reasonableness.[19] I will give four examples here.

Example 1: The act allows heterologous insemination *in vivo*, yet it bans the corresponding treatment *in vitro*.[20] Distinctions are being made here that cannot be due solely to the higher technical efforts necessitated by IVF. Why is using third-party donor semen allowed in a case where only the prospective father suffers from *impotentia generandi*, but ruled out in a case where his wife needs extra-corporeal fertilisation as well? The provisions are as unreasonable as if the legislature intended to allow blind persons to receive information via radio but not by means of braille.[21]

Example 2: The Austrian Act on Procreative Medicine aims to repress eugenic issues in assisted reproduction. Consequently, heterologous insemination is allowed only if the prospective father's semen is not reproductive.[22] If he suffers from a transmissible genetic disorder, the couple may not use the semen donated by a third party. On the other hand, though, legislators have tried to provide for the genetic health of the prospective child. For this reason, examination of the donor and his semen - before heterologous insemination takes place - should ensure that, according to the present state of medical science and knowledge, no risks to the health of the woman and the prospective child are incurred by using donor semen. However, the legislators' aims to create genetically healthy children and to repress eugenic issues in the context of heterologous insemination are hardly compatible. There is a choice to be made here.[23]

Example 3: In line with the Swedish model, sec. 20 of the Austrian Act on Procreative Medicine establishes the child's right to know his/her genetic roots, a right generally granted from the age of 14 onwards. It is striking, therefore, how obscure appears the provision[24] amending the civil law which exempts the donor from all responsibilities in family and inheritance law. Has the mere knowledge of one's genetic roots been of higher value to the legislators than claims under family law and the law of inheritance? Through the provisions mentioned, the legislators have created a special family law and a special law of succession based solely on the fact that the insemination was carried out by a physician ('artificially') and not be sexual intercourse ('naturally'). The infringement of the principle of equality is indeed obvious.[25]

Example 4: The issue of the legal status of extracorporeal embryos was severely contested in parliamentary debate. Since the Social Democrats were afraid that the 1974 statutory solution allowing terminations of pregnancy on demand of the woman within the first three months[26] might be at stake, if the embryo *in vitro* were better protected than one *in vivo*, a statutory definition was agreed upon which obscures rather than clarifies. Extracorporeal embryos are now called "developable cells" (sec. 1 para. 3 Act on Procreative Medicine). Hence, it appears rather inconsistent that mere "developable cells" are completely exempt from "destructive research".[27] Yet, the statutory rule in the given context is not very inclined to protection of life, either. Although cryoconservation has not been banned completely, it has been limited to one year.[28] After the elapse of that period, the legislators have given an indirect order for destruction: the embryos are to be disposed of. Why not then use them for scientific research?[29]

These four examples illustrate legislative compromises which seriously contradict the dictate of reasonableness. They lack a rational basis because their wording as compromises shows grave inner inconsistencies.

The sketch of thoughts presented here should be understood as a 'methodological guide' only. The question remains as to which ethical reasoning a legislature should adopt when it comes to closing the loopholes in the current law.[30] In particular, it will be necessary to clarify whether a more deontologically or a more teleologically oriented rational ethical system should be adopted as the basis of legal substantiation.[31]

Notes

1. On this topic, see also Bernat, E,, 'Biotechnologie, Rechtsethik und Gesetzgebung' *Ethik und Sozialwissenschaften* 3, 1988, pp.294-297.

2. 'Bundesgesetz mit dem Regelungen ueber die medizinisch unterstuetzte Fortpflanzung getroffen (Fortpflanzungsmedizingesetz - FMedG) sowie das allgemeine buergerliche Gesetzbuch, das Ehegesetz und die Jurisdiktionsnorm geaendert werden' *Official Gazette* 275/1992; cf. also Bernat, E., 'Towards a new legal regulation of medically assisted reproduction: The Austrian approach' *Medicine and Law* 11, 1992, pp.547-555; Morgan, D. and Bernat, E., 'The reproductive waltz: The Austrian Act on Procreative Medicine 1992' *The Journal of Social Welfare and Family Law* 1992, pp.420-426; Bernat, E. and Straka, U., 'A legal ban on surrogate mothers and fathers?' *University of Louisville Journal of Family Law* 31, 1992/93, pp.267-282;

Memmer, M., 'Eheaehnliche Lebensgemeinschaften und Reproduktionsmedizin' *Juristische Blaetter* 115, 1993, pp.297-308; and, recently, Pichler, H., 'Probleme der medizinisch unterstuetzten Fortpflanzung' *Der Österreichische Amtsvormund* 25, 1993, pp.53-55.

3. On fundamental rights problems see Loebenstein, E., 'Die Zukunft der Grundrechte im Lichte der kuenstlichen Fortpflanzung' *Juristische Blaetter* 109, 1987, pp.694-703 and pp.749-757; Schlag, M., *Verfassungsrechtliche Aspekte der kuenstlichen Fortpflanzung* Vienna, Braumueller Publisher, 1991; Bydlinski, F. and Mayer-Maly, T. (eds), *Fortpflanzungsmedizin und Lebensschutz* Innsbruck, Vienna, Tyrolia Publishing House, 1993; Losch, B., *Wissenschaftsfreiheit, Wissenschaftsschranken, Wissenschaftsverantwortung. Zugleich ein Beitrag zur Kollision von Wissenschaftsfreiheit und Lebensschutz am Lebensbeginn* Berlin, Duncker and Humblot, 1993; Morgan, D. and Nielsen, L., 'Dangerous liaisons? Law, technology, reproduction and European ethics' in Wheeler, S. and McVeigh, S. (eds), *Law, Health and Medical Regulation* Aldershot, Dartmouth, 1992, pp.52-74.

4. German Constitutional Court, judgement from 25 February 1975, *Juristenzeitung* 1975, pp.205-222.

5. Contrary to the judgement of the German Constitutional Court from 25 February 1975 (*op.cit.*), the Austrian Constitutional Court (Verfassungsgerichtshof - VfGH) has conceded to only born human beings a constitutionally granted right to life in its decision on the law allowing abortion on the woman's request within the first three months of pregnancy (Fristenloesungsentscheidung) of 11 October 1974, *Juristische Blaetter* 97, 1975, pp.310-316.

6. Within the Austrian legal system, a human right to life is constitutionally embodied in art. 2 of the European Convention for the Protection of Human Rights and Fundamental Freedoms only.

7. Rational is to be understood here in the sense of non-metaphysical. That an ethical system is non-rational, that is, metaphysically based, does not necessarily mean that its norms are irrational, but merely that their claim to validity cannot be derived from universally comprehensible grounds, i.e. from grounds plausible to everyone (Koller, P., *Theorie des Rechts. Eine Einfuehrung* Wien, Koeln, Weimar, Boehlau, 1992, pp.249ff.).

8. Birnbacher, D., 'Gefaehrdet die moderne Reproduktionsmedizin die menschliche Wuerde?' in Leist, A. (ed.), *Um Leben und Tod. Moralische Probleme bei Abtreibung, kuenstlicher Befruchtung, Euthanasie und Selbstmord* Frankfurt/M., Suhrkamp, 1990, p.266 and p.279.

9. On the problems from the point of view of German law see Court of Appeal Hamm (Penal Section) from 10 October 1967, *Zeitschrift für das gesamte Familienrecht* 15, 1968, pp.221-223; for Austrian law see Supreme Court from 3 September 1986, *Evidenzblatt* 90, 1989; on this point, see also Zankl, W., 'Eigenmaechtige Heilbehandlung und Gefaehrdung des Kindeswohls' *Österreichische Juristen-Zeitung* 44, 1989, pp.299-302.

10. Likewise Hoerster, N., *Abtreibung im saekularen Staat. Argumente gegen den § 218* Frankfurt/M., Suhrkamp, 1991, pp.114ff; 'Strafwuerdigkeit der Abtreibung? Alternativen und ihre Konsequenzen' *Universitas* 46, 1991, pp.19-26; 'Zur rechtsethischen Begruendung des Lebensrechts' in Bernat, E. (ed.), *Ethik und Recht an der Grenze zwischen Leben und Tod* Graz, Leykam, 1993, pp.61-70; see also Ruethers, B., *Rechtsordnung und Wertordnung. Zur Ethik und Ideologie im Recht* Konstanz, Konstanz University Press, 1986, pp.43ff.

11. On the freedom of religion and conscience in the light of the Austrian system of fundamental rights see in particular Ermacora, F., *Grundriss der Menschenrechte in Oesterreich* Wien, Manz, 1988, pp.176ff. as well as Adamovich, L. and Funk, B.-Ch., *Oesterreichisches Verfassungsrecht* third edition, Wien, New York, Springer, 1985, pp.411ff..

12. Cf. Birnbacher, *op.cit.*

13. Bernat, E., *Rechtsfragen medizinisch assistierter Zeugung* Frankfurt/M., Bern, New York, Paris, Peter Lang, 1989, pp.24ff..

14. That is the version of section 218a enacted in performance of the Unification Treaty (Einigungsvertrag 1992, *Official Gazette* I, p.1398) which has recently been set aside by the German Constitutional Court for alleged infringement of art. 1 para. 1, and art. 2 para. 2 of the Federal Constitution (the judgement is reprinted as 'Das Urteil des Bundesverfassungsgerichts zum Schwangerschaftsabbruch v. 28. Mai 1993' *Juristenzeitung* Suppl., 7 June 1993.

15. In favour of the thesis of lawful defence see, e.g., Eser, A., in Schöenke, A. and Schröeder, H. (eds), *Penal Code* 23rd edition, 1988, §218a marginal note 5; Harrer, H., *Zivilrechtliche Haftung bei durchkreuzter Familienplanung* Frankurt/M., Bern, New York, Paris, Peter Lang, 1989, pp.173ff.; Bernat, E., 'Gedanken zum rechtlichen Schutz des ungeborenen menschlichen Lebens - gezeigt am Beispiel medizinisch assistierter Zeugung' in Dirnhofer, R. and Schick, P.J. (eds), *Festschrift for W. Maresch* Graz, Adeva Publishing House, 1988, p.33, and pp.37ff; opposed to the thesis see, e.g., Belling, C., *Ist die Rechtfertigungsthese zu § 218a StGB haltbar?* Berlin, New York, de Gruyter, 1987, passim.

16. For instance the works of Hoerster, N., *op.cit.* (note 10) as well as the bill of the Member of the Bundestag, Blaess, P., *et al.* 'zur Legalisierung des Schwangerschaftsabbruchs und zur Sicherung von Mindeststandards für Frauen zum Schwangerschaftsabbruch' from 1 July 1991, *Bundestags - Drucksache* 12/890.

17. Bill of the Member of the Bundestag, Werner, H., *et al.* 'zum Schutz der ungeborenen Kinder' from 20th September 1991, *Bundestags - Drucksache* 12/1179.

18. For a different opinion, see Thomson, J.J., 'A defence of abortion' *Philosophy and Public Affairs* 1, 1971, pp.47-66. My valuation demonstrated in the text above is oriented on the principles expressed in the question of necessity (cf. e.g. section 34 German Penal Code) in current law.

19. The Austrian Constitutional Court sees the dictate of reasonableness as derived from the principle of equality (art. 7 of the Austrian Constitution - Bundesverfassungsgesetz - B-VG). For details of its jurisdiction see Klemens, C., *Die Judikatur des Verfassungsgerichtshofes zum Gleichheitssatz und zum Recht auf ein Verfahren vor dem gesetzlichen Richter* Graz, Leykam, 1987, pp.72ff..

20. Section 3 para. 1: "Ova and semen only of the spouses or cohabitants may be used in medically assisted reproduction". Section 3 para. 2: "In artificial insemination (Section 1 para. 2 no. 1), however, third-party donor semen may be used in case of infertility of the husband or the cohabitant". Section 1 para. 2 no. 1: "Methods of medically assisted reproduction in terms of para 1 are ... the insertion of semen into the procreative organs of a woman ... ".

21. Robertson, J.A., 'Decisional authority over embryos and control of IVF technology' *Jurimetrics Journal* Spring, 1988, pp.285-304.

22. Cf. Section 3 para. 2.

23. For details see Bernat, E., 'Das Fortpflanzungsmedizingesetz: Neue Rechtspflichten für den oesterreichischen Gynaekologen' *Gynaekologisch-Geburtshilfliche Rundschau* 33, 1993, pp.2-10, p.2 and p.7.

24. Section 163 para 4 Austrian Civil Code as amended by the Act on Procreative Medicine.

25. See also Bernat (1989), *op.cit.*, pp.168 and 203; Bernat, E., 'Das Recht der medizinisch assistierten Zeugung 1990 - eine vergleichende Bestandsaufnahme' in Bernat, E. (ed.), *Fortpflanzungsmedizin. Wertung und Gesetzgebung. Beitraege zum Entwurf eines Fortpflanzungshilfegesetzes* Vienna, Oesterreichische Staatsdruckerei, 1991, pp.65-121, p.65 and p.108, as well as Bydlinski, F., 'Zum Entwurf eines Fortpflanzungshilfegesetzes' *Juristische Blaetter* 112, 1990, pp.741-744.

26. Section 97 para. 1 no. 1 Austrian Penal Code.

27. Section 9 para. 1 Austrian Act on Procreative Medicine.

28. Section 17 para. 1 Austrian Act on Procreative Medicine.

29. Worth reading in this connection is Singer, P., Kuhse, H., Buckle, S., Dawson, K., and Kasimba, P., (eds), *Embryo Experimentation* Cambridge, Cambridge University Press, 1990.

30. For a general survey see Mappes, T.A. and Zembaty, J.S. (eds), *Biomedical Ethics* third edition, New York, McGraw-Hill, 1991, pp.4ff.

31. In favour of a deontological approach see Veatch, R.M., *A Theory of Medical Ethics* New York, Basic Books, 1981; and Beauchamp, T.L. and Childress, J.F., *Principles of Biomedical Ethics* fourth edition, New York, Oxford University Press, 1994. For utilitarian approaches to substantiation in particular see Singer, P., *Practical Ethics* second edition, Cambridge, Cambridge University Press, 1993; and Glover, J., *Causing Death and Saving Lives* London, Penguin Books, 1977; see additionally Glover, J., *et al.*, *Ethics of New Reproductive Technologies. The Glover Report to the European Commission* DeKalb, Northern Illinois University Press, 1989.

PART THREE

Assisted Procreation and the Interests of the Child

13. THE EXAMPLE OF ADOPTION FOR MEDICALLY ASSISTED CONCEPTION

Involvement of Society, Parent Suitability and Openness When Using Donors

Knut W. Ruyter
Center for Medical Ethics
University of Oslo
Norway

This paper will investigate whether adoption can serve as a paradigm for the use of medically assisted conception. If the example of adoption can be recognised and accepted as morally relevant, I will discuss in which areas and to what extent the experiences of adoption ought to be followed in medically assisted conception.

1. Adoption as Successful Problem Solving

In most cases adoption takes place when something has gone seriously wrong. Birth parents are either dead, or unable or unwilling to care for a child. The consequence is that children are abandoned, rejected or unwanted. For prospective parents the desire to adopt children usually comes after many years of trying have failed to produce children of their own, although some people adopt children, in addition to their own, for idealistic or political reasons. The situation is not ideal for any of the parties in this triangle. It touches often on sensitive and complex issues, in different ways for each of the parties.

Adoption is today characterised by the effort to rectify the situation of orphans or abandoned children by giving them a new set of parents. It is in the interests of these children that prospective parents are chosen as suitable and reliable. Another important characteristic is that openness is demanded. When children are adopted from the same country as their prospective parents, openness also entails the adopted children having access to the identity of their birth parents. In practice this right will hold good for children adopted from abroad only in exceptional cases. In addition, it is acknowledged that adoption implies many stress factors, related to abandonment, sorrow, concealment, and fantasies, which may be significant for a child's development and her or his adaptation to new circumstances and new parents. Some of the research on adoption emphasises the importance of the openness of parents, in order to help develop skills in mastering reality as it is. With these presuppositions, two recent surveys in Norway give a relatively positive picture of open adoption, presenting it as successful, especially

D. Evans (ed.), Creating the Child, 177–194.

in terms of the development of self identity and social adaptation.[1]

Under the given and less than ideal circumstances, adoption nevertheless represents the most acceptable solution for the parties involved. There are clear indications that adoption is a much better alternative than an upbringing in an institution or in a foster home, even when children are relatively old when adopted.[2]

It is important to note that the present solution represents a significant change from former practice. In many countries it is relatively new, dating from the 1970s.[3]

This change was primarily based on empirical research which substantiated the idea that secrecy about adoption had devastating effects on adoptees. The change was probably reinforced by the increase of adoptions from abroad, which occured simultaneously with drastic reductions in domestic adoptions, as a consequence of greater use of contraception, abortion on demand and improved social and economic arrangements for single mothers.

Even though the works of a few leading adoption researchers[4] substantially influenced the changes that have taken place, the changes also seem to reflect opinions that were relatively common among professionals from the 1950s, e.g. in Sweden and Norway.[5] The conclusion in both cases is that openness about adoption is a necessary condition for a harmonious development of identity and for psychological bonding and honesty in relations between adoptees and adoptive parents.

The key feature of this solution is that it gives primary consideration to the interest of the child. This is done in two ways. First, parents are chosen according to definite criteria, in order to judge their suitability and their capability to help and support the child.[6] Second, the child has a right to know about its origins.

Open adoption is now standard practice in all Western countries. It represents a relatively successful solution in a complex area. This does not mean that there is no further room for criticism or change. There is still a gap between ideal claims of openness and access to the identity of birth parents. Practical difficulties and institutional obstacles continue to make it cumbersome or impossible to fulfil the claim.[7] A further question is how rigid the requirements guiding the selection of adoptive parents should be, as well as which profession or agency is competent to make such an evaluation. In the broader perspective, much valid criticism may be raised against social injustices in adoption. In many cases birth parents relinquish children for adoption, not because children are unwanted as such, but as a result of social and economic pressures. Such criticism may be framed in terms of the sale of children, in which rich prospective parents (and countries) exploit poor parents (and countries).

2. Relevance for Medically Assisted Conception

At present there are great differences between adoption and medically assisted conception, especially in regard to openness, the psycho-social evaluation of parent suitability and the role the public plays in the process.

These differences are probably due to substantial disagreement about the relevance of

the example of adoption for medically assisted conception. We find a variety of contrasting positions, ranging from the view that adoption has no relevance for medically assisted conception to the view that the resemblances to adoption are so striking that medically assisted conception should be resolved and regulated in the same way.

Differering views on relevance are reflected in the differences that today exist between Sweden and Norway in relation to the use of donors in medically assisted conception. A Committee of Inquiry in Sweden accepted the analogy between adoption and donor insemination, and concluded that the needs of children must be adequately safeguarded. The child's interests must take precedence over those of prospective parents, donors or physicians.[8] A guiding principle in the report was that the same degree of openness that marks adoption practice today should be an objective in donor insemination.[9] The Committee recommended guidelines for the use of donors in insemination which are approximately identical to those applied to adoption, especially in relation to selection requirements for parents and the right of donor children to know the identity of their biological father when they turn eighteen.[10] Some other countries have also tended to favour greater openness with respect to donation practices in medically assisted conception, out of concern for the best interests of children, and sometimes with specific reference to adoption procedures.[11]

It is however not obvious that adoption is an appropriate precedent for medically assisted conception. Some say it has no relevance at all. This has been the majority opinion for example in Norway. In the preparatory law report in 1987 the analogy to adoption was explicitly refuted: "The question of secrecy of treatment in artificial insemination is to be considered as essentially different from the question of the duty of adoptive parents to tell their children about the adoption".[12]

Given that Sweden and Norway apply different norms, it is worth considering which elements in medically assisted conception are similar to adoption, and which are different. Even though disagreement about relevance has centered on the relation between donor insemination and adoption, I will address the question from the perspective of medically assisted conception in general.

3. Similarities and Differences

3.1. SIMILARITIES

Adoption and medically assisted conception are both ways of making *children* available in a non-ordinary way to couples who wish to have and raise children. They are in contrast to the ordinary or natural way of getting children.

These practices are non-ordinary in that adopted children and children of medically assisted conception are bonded to couples as a result of a non-sexual procedure. Both procedures help create *social* parent-children relations, relations which would otherwise not exist. In most cases adoption and medically assisted conception seem to be less

attractive solutions than having naturally born children. When this is not possible, adoption and medically assisted conception emerge as next best solutions, or as the last chance for getting children.

Adoption and medically assisted conception are also characterised by the *intervention of third parties*.[13] These act as intermediaries and have a supervisory responsibility, on behalf of or in cooperation with society. In both cases, society plays a necessary role in creating the relation between couples wishing to have children and children who are already born or may be born. With adoption, the third party is most often represented by adoption agencies (which mediate adoption), by social welfare offices (which judge parents suitable) and by a Ministry or other government agency (which approves adoption agencies and sometimes also makes the final decision on parent suitability). In medically assisted conception, the third party is represented by medical experts who perform their activities in clinics. The clinics are in turn, in some countries, approved by a Ministry and regulated by law or prescripts. Precisely because neither adoption nor medically assisted conception represent ordinary ways of getting children, the interaction involves a *social* dimension. This seeks to assure responsible activity, especially in regard to protecting the interests of the most vulnerable party, the child. The need for third party involvement may be more obvious in taking care of existing children and therefore in adoption, but medically assisted conception also undoubtedly includes an added moral responsibility, that of protecting the interests of children resulting from therapeutic interventions.

3.2. DIFFERENCES

The main difference between adoption and medically assisted conception can be described as follows: adoption helps existing children who are in need of parents, while medically assisted conception helps couples to have children and become parents.

Adoption takes care of existing children, who, for various reasons, are abandoned or unwanted. It intends to rectify a wrong. Adoption must deal with the consequences that the break from the birth parents may have for a child's development and adaptation. Medically assisted conception differs in this aspect because it originates in the natural desire of couples for an as yet non-existent child. Technology may make it possible to restore normal biological functions and help a woman to become pregnant and give birth to a child. This is a significantly different experience from adoption. The child comes into being as a result of a close physical relation to the mother, and this is also important for the development of the child's identity. Medically assisted conception does not imply any social break for the child, as is the case with adoption except in surrogacy using donated gametes (see below).

This difference may be expanded by looking into the relationship between adoption and various types of medically assisted conception. The clearest difference between these cases is when medically assisted conception utilises germ cells from the couple themselves and when adoption involves unknown and unrelated children. In the first case there is only one set of parents with their own children, united by blood ties. In

the other case there are two sets of parents, birth parents and adoptive parents, of which the latter are not genetically related to the child. The adoptive parents are socially bonded to take care of the child.

There are however a number of cases in which this difference is less conspicuous. This arises in medically assisted conception when external parties are recruited, such as donors or surrogate mothers. In adoption it involves cases in which one party adopts the spouse's child. The varieties may be presented in a diagram.

Genetic ties to social parents

	One tie	No ties
Adoption	Of spouse's child	Of unknown children
Donation	Semen/egg donation	Embryo donation
Surrogacy	Genetic and gestational surrogate mother	Genetic and gestational surrogate mother and semen donation

As the diagram shows there are no genetic ties in embryo donation in medically assisted conception. This method may also aptly be called preimplantation adoption. A remaining difference from adoption is nevertheless that women become pregnant and give birth. When a surrogate mother is used even this difference disappears. Surrogacy arrangements may be considered to be adoptions that are mediated before conception.

In a number of other cases the child has one genetic tie to its social parents. This applies to adoption of a spouse's child, and also to those types of medically assisted conception which utilise semen or egg donation, or in which a surrogate mother is inseminated with the semen of the spouse. Here too there is a remaining difference from adoption in those cases involving semen and egg donation by which women may become pregnant and give birth. In the case of surrogacy this difference disappears.

Since embryo and egg donation, as well as surrogacy, are prohibited by law in Norway, I limit my comments to semen donation, in which the child has one genetic tie to its social parents, through its mother.

On the one hand semen donation seems to resemble natural conception more than adoption, since the woman gestates the foetus and gives it birth. On the other hand semen donation implies a break between the genetic father and social father. A social father in this case can hardly be said to differ noticeably from an adoptive father. He may be compared to a husband who adopts his spouse's child(ren). In both cases there will be two fathers, one genetic and one social. This will also imply an uneven proportion in the parents' relations with the child. The express goal is, as in all

adoption, to give an already existing child a better and safer life than it would have had otherwise. In the case of semen donation it is much easier to conceal the break: medical experts make efforts to match donors with the prospective social father to minimise differences in appearance, and the child is born naturally. At the same time, however, the break is intended and created through the involvement of a third party. We have today only limited knowledge of the long term consequences for the relationship between the spouses and for the child itself.

It is sometimes emphasised that the advantage of semen donation over the adoption of unknown children is that it gives couples the opportunity to have their own children. This argument is however flawed, because it may be used in various directions. It is correct that the child has a genetic tie to the mother and that she gives birth to the child. These factors are often ascribed decisive moral weight in order to distinguish semen donation from adoption and thus justify a different treatment. Simultaneously, however, the argument implies that the other genetic tie has no significance, by concealing it and making it nameless. The genetic tie in itself is hardly the decisive factor distinguishing donation from adoption and in recommending one over the other. However, many may feel that semen donation is preferable to adoption, because these children may at least be said to be half your own. The other side of that coin implies that they are also half adopted. In today's practice of semen donation (except in Sweden and Austria) society, as the third party has not considered the moral import of the existing break when respecting the anonymity of donors and the secrecy of the infertility of the commissioning couple.

Even though there are important differences between adoption and medically assisted conception, the above demonstrates that there are also notable similarities.

The similarities are closely linked to the involvement of third parties, who function as necessary actors when it comes to mediation and control of adoption and medically assisted conception, through various groups of experts. In regard to donation there exists a common problem about breaks in the relationship between parents and children.

An important difference is that in most cases of medically assisted conception there is only one set of parents and the child is born naturally. In regard to donation the difference from adoption is weakened, since comparisons show that this type of medically assisted conception creates a break in the relationship between parents and children, while adoption intends to substitute the break from birth parents with a new set of parents, with the best interests of the child in mind.

4. Weighing the arguments

It is not easy to weigh arguments based on similarities and differences or to establish which considerations are important or reasonable.

In line with the experiences of present day adoption practice and the greater attention to the rights and interests of children, I attach greatest importance to the wellbeing of the child. This is a change in emphasis, and it has consequences for the evaluation of

medically assisted conception, traditionally considered part of medical practice. The change in perspective suggests that moral responsibility for the interests of children takes precedence over other interests. The difference in weight now given to arguments based on similarities apparently presupposes that people consider social parenthood to be at least as important as biological parenthood. It thus seems that some of the insights gained in adoption are transferrable to medically assisted conception, although not to the same extent in all areas.

Those who assign decisive importance to blood ties (with certain modifications in the case of donors) and to the experiences of pregnancy and childbirth (with the exception of surrogacy), however, may see these factors as constituting a substantial and morally relevant difference from the most common forms of adoption. This may imply that medically assisted conception should be treated differently from the example of adoption.

Nevertheless, if one accepts that adoption has a certain relevance for medically assisted conception, this has various implications. The analogy underscores the role of society in the practices, stresses the institutional and social characteristics of all parental roles, and emphasises the importance of openness in parent-child relations, when donors are used. The analogy thus opens the possibility of extending the example of adoption and applying it to the practice of medically assisted conception. The value of the analogy is not primarily to show that medically assisted conception should be treated exactly in the same way as adoption, but to help determine the extent to which the example of adoption may be relevant for medically assisted conception.

5. Intervention on the Part of Society

Morally relevant similarities in the involvement of third parties justify certain types of intervention and regulation on the part of society.[14] The responsibility of the third party as actor and mediator is based on the duty to protect the weakest party. Both adoption and medically assisted conception ought to be examined on the basis of the best interests of the child.

Past and present experience shows that societal regulation of adoption is necessary to reduce the likelihood of exploitation of children. Unregulated mediation of adoption often reveals a shady market in which poor parents sell their children, most often to foreigners who desire to adopt. Adoptive parents can then choose a child, according to their own preferences, at a negotiated price. In the worst cases children are bought for the purpose of being organ donors for other children.

The danger of exploitation of abandoned or unwanted children in adoption is obviously much greater than the danger to children born as a result of unregulated medically assisted conception.

In the medical domain there is a longstanding tradition of self-regulation. Physicians, as the third party, regulate their own activity in accordance with their own understanding of what constitutes responsible practice. Experience shows, however,

that self-regulation is difficult to achieve. There is also a tendency to relate primarily to the interests of adult patients. But even in the area of medically assisted conception, a number of factors may threaten the wellbeing of potential parents[15], and in turn may harm the interests of children.

When society becomes party to the conception of children by medically assisted means, it assumes a responsibility, as in adoption, for ensuring that this is done according to the interests of the children. It seems reasonable to assert that society has a duty to regulate both those who offer medically assisted conception and those who wish to avail themselves of the service.

Many countries have introduced regulation, through licensing authorities. In some countries medically assisted conception is also regulated by law (see appendix). The value of the analogy to adoption is that it can be used to justify some interference on the part of society, and to show that society should be hesitant in transferring sole responsibilty to the medical profession.

6. The Suitability of Parents

The second area I want to address is the specific issue of whether, in case of access to medically assisted conception, society should scrutinise prospective parents for suitability, as in adoption.

There are several reasons for suggesting that differences in this area are so great that the analogy has only a very limited application. In medically assisted conception the child is born into a family without its own preformed identity or characteristics. The subject of adoption is an abandoned or unwanted child, whose experiences have begun to form her or his identity and characteristics. Children for adoption often have special needs, and these are highly relevant in assessing which particular parents are most suited to take care of this particular child.

This represents a morally relevant difference, and one which justifies specific requirements for scrutinising prospective adoptive parents. The purpose of psycho-social scrutiny in adoption is to select suitable parents. The scrutiny sets more demanding standards than is required in normal conception and parenting. It has the function of licensing parents. It usually demands that certain standards be met: a stable relationship, age limits, economic wellbeing, good health, evidence of domicile, no criminal record and so on. Among these there are factors that may limit one's chances (such as poor education, poor economic status, religious belief and any specific preferences) or diminish one's chances (a history of unstable relationships, many children, serious disease or advanced age). Exceptions may rightly be made if there is a pre-existing and significant bond between the child and the person or persons seeking to adopt it.

Given the different nature of medically assisted conception, it seems reasonable to apply only the most general criteria for suitability to prospective parents.[16] This implies that medically assisted conception may not be available to everyone who desires it.

There will obviously be some disagreement about where to draw the line. However, one important factor in medically assisted conception may justify the imposition of specific requirements in relation to prospective parents: that society allows for and contributes to the creation of children who would not otherwise be born. As in the case of adoption, though to a lesser extent, one may consider the responsibility of the third parties to organise an activity in order to ensure good living conditions for children. This may imply certain requirements such as the existence of a stable relationship, good physical and psychic health and guiding age limits.

With regard to the ability of prospective parents to master circumstances that are from the outset less than ideal, the analogy with adoption also raises the question of the extent to which medically assisted conception should provide for counselling and other supportive services. With adoption the reasoning is clear. Less than ideal circumstances suggest that prospective parents should have access to counselling before adoption, and that adoptees and parents should have access to short-term counselling during the course of various developmental stages. If necessary, even long term psychotherapy should be available.[17] Several similar, less than ideal circumstances arise with medically assisted conception. Often something of a second best solution, it may leave substantial psychological and emotional stress. Concern for parents' ability to cope and for the wellbeing of children both suggest that counselling services ought to be available for those who avail themselves of medically assisted conception.

7. Secrecy and Anonymity When Using Donors in Medically Assisted Conception

The third area for consideration is the question of secrecy and anonymity in the use of donors in medically assisted conception. In comparison to medically assisted conception in general this comprises a relatively small number of cases.

The insights and experiences gained from the example of open adoption seem to have a greater degree of relevance to donation, even though due attention must be given to the fact that the discontinuities are of a different kind.

Even though the need to face reality took time to win approval in adoption practice, today it enjoys broad consensus. The opposite is usually true in regard to donors in medically assisted conception. In this area substantial efforts have been made to conceal realities, through secrecy, donor anonymity and even the destruction of medical records.

7.1. OPENNESS BETTER THAN CONCEALMENT

A fundamental insight from adoption seems to be that knowledge about the reality is better than concealment, even if openness also entails certain problems.[18]

The psycho-analytical tradition in particular has registered fantasies about adoption in the normal development of children. These fantasies often arise as explanations for disappointments or for discrimination between siblings. They can be an important factor in the child's development of an independent identity in relation to its parents.

The fantasies are, however, based on the certainty that in fact adoption has not taken place. The certainty that the factual circumstances are different from the fantasies, or that blood ties hold good whatsoever, is of enormous importance for the fundamental development of a child's identity and personality. Concealment of realities may have serious consequences for a child's development, when fantasies about adoption suddenly turn out to be real.[19] The premisses for the child's identification with its parents, itself an important foundation for its own personality development, will have changed dramatically. This does not imply that openness is unproblematic, but that it is preferable to concealment. Openness will give adoptees over time a better chance to master the difficult task of developing their own identity against the background of a known break with biological parents.[20]

Openness in adoption has also shown that adopted children have different fantasies from children raised by their own parents, because they also relate to another reality, namely the reality of a break.[21] The development of identity among adoptees builds on a complex reality involving both origin and experiences in the adoptive family. There is broad consensus that openness facilitates this development, because it gives the possibility of integrating the factual circumstances of life.[22]

When donors are used in medically assisted conception, the tradition has been to discount reality, concealing it behind the ideal of wanting the family to appear as a normal family. As was formerly the case with adoption, secrecy and anonymity seek to preempt possible social problems. This may involve the forestalling of possible charges of adultery or uncertainty of paternity, in order to shield the family from disapproval, rejection or stigma. Anonymous adoption once sought to conceal the shame of the young unwed mother and her illegitimate child. In donor insemination secrecy and anonymity can assure that both the infertility of the 'assisted' father and his possible sense of shame about this may be concealed.[23] None of these problems should be minimised, but the question remains of whether they are best resolved by secrecy or openness. The value of the analogy in this area is to remind us of the danger that concealment of reality may have serious consequences for the fundamental development of personal identity and wellbeing.

In this regard the consequences for adoptees are likely to be greater and more complex than for children born with the assistance of a donor, because adoptees must come to terms with the fact that their original birth parents did not want them or were unable to take care of them, while donor children know that their present parents actually wanted them. But I submit that this difference amounts only to a difference of degree, not of kind. A donor child too has an original, or genetic, father who does not want to acknowledge his offspring or take care of it.

As it once was in anonymous adoption, the socially regulated and constructed ideal of wanting to appear as a normal family, though built on a systematic lie, may cave in like a house of cards. This may in turn have serious consequences for the family generally and specifically for the child, for whom fantasies are no longer in opposition to realities, but actually come true.

Even though it is far more convenient to conceal the realities of using donors in

medically assisted conception than it ever was in adoption, there is always a substantial risk of details being disclosed. First, most professionals (such as psychiatrists and family therapists) are of the opinion that family secrets cause mental strains on the family, and that these increase rather than decrease over the years.[24] On the basis of work with couples with children conceived by donor insemination, a Norwegian family psychiatrist claims that concealment between family members may create invisible alliances, mental strain and undue burdens. In the long run, honesty reduces strain and allows for alternative ways of coping with the problems.[25] Under relatively stable circumstances most parents are likely to be able to cope with mental strain, but serious quarrels, crises or divorce (none of which is unusual) considerably increase the possibility that the reality will be divulged. Second, there is always a possibility that some close relatives or friends may suspect that the reality is not as it appears, or that parents at one point felt a need to ease the strain by confiding in close friends or relatives. The danger is that this type of information will one day be revealed to the child. Third, children are themselves very alert to hidden messages. They may intuitively understand or suspect that the reality is different from what it appears to be.[26] Since children frequently wonder and fantasise about origins and belonging as an important factor in their development, secrecy implies that parents must always give answers that do not reflect reality as it actually is. From studies of children and youths who were told about their origins, Snowden and others confirm that children prefer to be told the truth.[27] Fourth, the development of medical tests for all kinds of purposes makes it likely that donor children, at one point in their lives, will find out that their present father cannot have been their original, genetic father.

On the basis of an admittedly small sample of cases of disclosures[28], we know that the consequences for donor children can be grave. The breach of confidence in the parent-child relation is the same as in the known cases of disclosure of previously secret adoptions. The apparent reality proved to be false; this created insecurity and doubt about fundamental questions about origins, belonging and confidence. As with adoption a fundamental precondition for the healthy development of identity and personality is that parents answer children's questions truthfully and that they relate openly to reality as it is. For these reasons most non-medical professionals will advise against secrecy and in favour of openness.

Adoption research and clinical experience show that one factor characterising adoptees is a longing to retrace their roots and to learn about their origins. The process from the initial awakening of interest to actual steps to seek out the birth mother or father may take a very long time. It may also imply disappointments. Nevertheless, most professionals believe that the orientation towards reality helps strengthen the development of identity and clarify and integrate what Sants once called genealogical bewilderment.[29]

Another element of the analogy to adoption is important in evaluating the use of donors in medically assisted conception. It involves the changes that led to the new adoption paradigm. Some of the same changes can be noted in relation to changing attitudes to the use of donors. These changes may help reduce the need for secrecy.

The traditional charge of adultery has faded considerably, and it is in any case indefensible, given that adultery presupposes that a spouse is unfaithful through having a sexual relation with another. This is not the case when donors are used in medically assisted conception. But it remains a reality, and for some a serious problem, that spouses cannot escape a feeling of unfaithfulness because of the fact that a strange man has been implicated.[30] The question of paternity is resolved legally, if the husband consents, in accordance with the *pater est* presumption. There is still some uncertainty about paternity where consent has not been obtained or where the woman is not married. There also seems to be more openness about infertility nowadays. This is seen in many ways. In the first place, couples demand more information about the prospective donor. Secondly, in connection with relatively new forms of donations, such as egg donation, women usually prefer to use known donors. Thirdly, some empirical studies about the attitudes of donors show that a great majority are willing to allow the child access to non-identifiable information, while just less than fifty percent would be willing to let the child gain knowledge about the donor's identity at the age of eighteen.[31] Growing social acceptance may of course help reduce the need to conceal the use of donors behind an idyllic facade.

What provisional conclusions may be drawn about the use of donors in medically assisted conception from these comparisons? To the best of my judgement the analogy to adoption is particularly relevant in relation to openness and orientation towards reality, as these are fundamental conditions for confidence in the parent-child relationship and for the healthy personality and identity development of children born with the assistance of donors. Even though this entails that donor children will appear different from other children, the difference nevertheless reflects reality. Openness about factual circumstances should not imply greater problems for donor children than for other children who are different. A child conceived by use of a donor does not, for instance, have to come to terms with the problem of having once been abandoned. It must however also cope with the fact that the genetic father will not acknowledge his offspring. Like an adopted child, a donor child will wonder why the original father does not want to relate to 'me' or get to know who 'I' have become. A decisive point in favour of openness may be that there is a certain degree of social acceptance for this type of donation and that the original reasons for secrecy are reduced or eliminated.[32] As with adoption, openness in the case of using donors in medically assisted conception also requires will and imagination in resolving the related problems.

Two initiatives can be useful in coping with the challenges of openness. First, many parents will find support through sharing their experiences with others in relation to when it is advisable to tell the child and how this may be done. On the basis of their work with couples who have availed themselves of donor insemination, the Snowdens believe that the earlier one begins to tell the child, the better, even though the child may not at first be able to comprehend what the information means. The open information is included as a story in the natural history of the family, so that when the child becomes an adult she or he can say: 'I wasn't told; I just always knew'.[33] To assist in mediating the reality of donor insemination, a group of parents at a hospital in

England developed a children's picture story book called *My Story* which explains donor insemination in a way a young child can understand.[34] Furthermore, experiences from open adoption show that it is important for parents and children to have access to various kinds of counselling or supportive services, if the need arises.

7.2. DISTINCTION BETWEEN OPENNESS AND ACCESS TO IDENTITY

The form of openness described in the previous sections may not necessarily imply that donor children ought to have access to *the identity* of the donor at the age of eighteen, as is the case with adoption today. Even with adoption it is still an open question whether knowledge about the *identity* of birth parents is decisive for the personality development of adoptees. It seems however beyond doubt that knowledge about their status as adopted is crucially important. Two arguments particularly support the distinction between openness and identity, relating respectively to secrecy and anonymity. In the first place, results of research and clinical experience are unanimous in regard to the child's need for openness about factual circumstances. In regard to access to identity, a far more complex picture emerges. Some feel that knowledge about the donor's identity contributes to improved mastery and self-respect. Being denied information of identity represents an undue burden for the child.[35] Others emphasise that knowledge about the donor's identity can lead to confusion, disappointment and reduced self-respect.[36] After adoptees gained access to the identity of birth parents, experiences indicated that most are interested in acquiring general knowledge about their origin, but not necessarily specific knowledge about the actual identity of birth parents. Knowledge of identifiable information does not necessarily mean that adoptees have a need or desire to seek out the birth parents.[37] This may suggest that knowledge about a certain reality is more important than knowledge about actual identity. I therefore presume that the most important issue for the child is knowledge about the real circumstances of its origins, as a decisive component of its inner development of self-respect and personality. This inner adaptation of a complex reality in order to build one's own personal identity cannot adequately be answered on the basis of knowledge of the identity of birth parents. It can be developed only in relation to the actual social circumstances which give rise to one's own self-understanding. Knowledge of the identity of birth parents may contribute to this process, depending on a variety of factors, but does not seem to be necessary. In the second place, there is a notable disparity (and sometimes even a contradiction) in the practice of adoption, between the ideal right of access to the identity of birth parents and the many institutional and practical difficulties in obtaining records.[38] This is of course especially difficult with adoptions from abroad. However, if knowledge of the identity of birth parents would represent an undue burden on adoptees, one could reasonably surmise that open, but anonymous, adoptions could hardly be morally justified. However, given the non-ideal circumstances surrounding adoption, this is probably acceptable, because the question of access to the identity of birth parents is subordinated to the need of abandoned or unwanted children for parents who can and

will take care of them. It is probably also acceptable because the development of the
adoptee's own identity and personality is not dependent upon knowing the identity of
birth parents who could or would not take care of them.

For these reasons the analogy to adoption has limited application in relation to the
question of access to the *identity* of donors. It depends on how important one considers
knowledge of blood ties is for the development of identity. It does not seem reasonable
to use the discontinuation of anonymity in adoption as a basis for rescinding the policy
of anonymous donation in medically assisted conception, as has clearly been done in
Sweden, without reservation and regardless of situation. Given uncertainty about the
importance of knowing the identity of birth parents in adoption, an uncertainty which
is even greater in relation to donors in medically assisted conception, it seems
appropriate to proceed with caution.

In regard to blood ties, one area remains in which we know that knowing the identity
of the donor may be of central importance for donor children and their parents: the
medical domain. It can be important to have knowledge of the donor's heredity and
physical characteristics when certain diseases occur in donor children. This can be of
vital interest to the parents in their care of the child, and it can be of interest to the
child when as an adult she or he plans to start its own family. In countries like
Norway, in which secrecy has entailed the destruction of medical records, no
consideration is given to this legitimate interest in openness, despite the formidable
development of medical genetics.

My provisional conclusion is that the new adoption paradigm of openness and access
to identity of birth parents is especially relevant for the use of donors in medically
assisted conception when it comes to openness, but is less relevant and has certain limits
in relation to access to the identity of donors.

If it is acceptable to distinguish between openness (secrecy) and access to identity
(anonymity), as I propose in this paper, this must imply that children born with the
assistance of donors can rely on the openness of parents to inform them about the break
in their origin and about their complex reality. To assist in this process it seems
reasonable that third parties arrange for counselling and supportive services to be made
available for parents and children, if needed. The distinction also implies that
identifiable information about the donor must be recorded and kept, and that the
woman's medical record must include details which enable the recorded information to
be linked to the donor child. This procedure does not necessarily mean access to the
identity of donors. One can, as is presently the case in England and the U.S., protect
against access to identifiable information of donor, while allowing access to non-
identifiable information such as year of birth, eye colour, hair colour, height, weight,
place of residence, profession, marital status, hobbies, and so on. When medical needs
arise, physicians may request access to the donor's record.

In the long run openness about the use of donors can clarify whether knowing the
identity of a biological parent is of central importance for the development of a donor
child's identity and personality. If research and clinical experience substantiated such
a claim, anonymity ought to be lifted. In that case it would seem reasonable that the

rescinding of anonymity would take effect at the time the decision is made, though without being given retroactive force, as was the case with adoption.[39]

8. Provisional Conclusion

My provisional conclusion is that the analogy to adoption is morally relevant and appropriate, though some differences regarding genetic linkage and gestation may call for solutions that limit the extent of applicability.

The value of the analogy with adoption for medically assisted conception is primarily to emphasise that the interests of children ought to take precedence. The practices of adoption and medically assisted conception must be evaluated on the basis of this fundamental concern. The analogy underlines and justifies the role of society in regulating these practices in order to protect the interests of the weakest party.

The experiences leading to the new adoption paradigm are therefore relevant and valid for medically assisted conception. This holds true for the attempt to establish the proper degree and extent of regulations for medically assisted conception in relation to society's involvement, scrutiny of parent suitability, and claims to openness.

Acknowledgements

The author wants to thank Andreas Føllesdal, Reidun Førde, Øystein Magnus, Eamonn Noonan, Lars Christian Opdal, Jan Helge Solbakk, as well as the members of the philosophy group in the European Commission Research Project 'Fertility, Infertility and the Human Embryo: the Ethics, Law and Practice of Assisted Procreation', for thoughtful comments on earlier drafts, and the Norwegian Research Council for its financial support.

Notes

1. Cf. Dalen, Monika and Sætersdal, Barbro, *Utenlandsadopterte barn i Norge. Tilpasning - opplæring - identitetsutvikling. Empirisk undersøkelse og teoretisk videreutvikling* Oslo, Spesiallærerhøgskolen, Universitetet i Oslo, 1992; and Bodvar, Pål Ketil *Ny sjanse i Norge. Utenlandsadoptertes oppvekst og levevilkår* Oslo, Diakonhjemmets høgskolesenter, 1994.

2. Brinich, Paul M., 'Some potential effects of adoption on self and object representation' *Psychoanalytical Study of the Child* 35, 1980, pp.107-133, p.109.

3. There were exceptions, e.g. in Scotland and Finland. For an historical overview of how abandoned children were taken care of in Europe, see Boswell, John E., *The Kindness of Strangers: The Abandonment of Children in Western Europe from Late Antiquity to the Renaissance* New York, Pantheon, 1988.

4. Cf. Kirk, H.D., *Shared Fate: A Theory of Adoption and Mental Health* New York, Free Press, 1964; Kirk, H.D., *Adoptive Kinship* Toronto, Butterworths, 1981; Kirk, H.D., *The Collected Adoption Papers* Washington, Ben Simon Publications, 1988; Sants, H.J., 'Genealogical bewilderment in children with substitute parents' *British Journal of Medical Psychology* 37, 1964, pp.133-41; McWhinnie, Alexina, *Adopted Children. How They Grow Up* London, Routledge and Kegan Paul, 1967; Triseliotis, J., *In Search of Origins: The Experience of Adopted People* London, Routledge and Kegan Paul, 1973; Triseliotis, J., *New Developments in Foster Care and Adoption* London, Routledge and Kegan Paul, 1980; Triseliotis, J., and Russel, J., *Hard to Place: The Outcome of Adoption and Residential Care* London, Heinemann, 1984.

5. Cf. Hesselman, Stina, *Så kom du hem til oss* Uddevala, Bohusläns Grafiska, 1951; and Barnelovutvalget (Committee on the Children Act), commentary on law proposal in 1956, cited from Odelstingsproposisjon nr. 40 (1984-85) *Om lov om adopsjon* (Odelsting Bill on the Adoption Act).

6. The criteria which should guide the selection of parents are still disputed, especially in regard to arbitrary limits for suitable age, social and economic status, and to limitations on adoptions of children of other cultures or races. The Ministry of Children and Family in Norway has decided on guidelines that are relatively wide, compared to other countries: the marriage must be stable, the adoptive parents should be less than 50 years old, their economic status should be secure, there should be no serious disease and the adopted child should be the youngest in the family. There are no restrictions on transracial or transcultural adoptions.

7. Cf. Kirk (1981), *op.cit.*, pp.136-141, and Haimes, Erica, "Secrecy': what can artificial reproduction learn from adoption' *International Journal of Law and the Family* 2, 1988, pp.46-61, pp.52-56

8. Justitiedepartementet (Ministry of Justice), *Barn genom insemination. Huvudbetänkande av inseminationsutredningen* SOU 1983, 42, Stockholm, Justitiedepartementet, 1983, p.57.

9. *Ibid.*, p.58.

10. *Ibid.*, pp.162-164. The recommendations were passed into law in 1984. A few years later the health authorities prepared detailed guidelines, including criteria for selection of suitable parents and recommendations about how parents may attend to the needs of children for honesty and openness. In both areas the guidelines assert that it is helpful to judge them in the same way as in the practice of adoption (cf. Socialstyrelsens författningssamling, *Socialstyrelsens föreskrifter och allmänna råd om inseminationer* SOSFS 1987, 6, Stockholm, Socialstyrelsens författningssamling, 1987, p.15). The only other country to have lifted anonymity is Austria, where the donor child may request information about the identity of the donor from the age of 14 (cf. Morgan, Derek, and Bernat, Erwin, 'Austrian law on procreative medicine' *Bulletin of Medical Ethics* 83, 1992, pp.13-16).

11. See e.g. the Australian report (The National Bioethics Consultative Committee, *Access to Information. An Analogy Between Adoption and the Use of Gamete Donation* Australia, The National Bioethics Consultative Committee, 1988); the referendum in Switzerland in 1992 (cf. Thévoz, Jean-Marie, 'The rights of children to information following assisted conception' in this volume); the preparatory draft of an Artificial Insemination Act in the Netherlands in 1993 (cf. Hubben, J.H., 'Regulations governing the storage, management and provision of the personal particulars of donors of semen for artificial insemination. Lower House, Dutch Parliament, June 18, 1993' unpublished manuscript); and changes in practices in England towards openness as a result of research (Snowden, Robert and Snowden, Elizabeth, *The Gift of a Child. A Guide to Donor Insemination* second revised edition, Exeter, Exeter University Press, 1993; Haimes, *op.cit.*; and Morgan, Derek, and Lee, Robert G., *Blackstone's Guide to the Human Fertilisation and Embryology Act 1990* London, Blackstone, 1991, pp.162-168).

12. Sosialdepartementet (Ministry of Social Welfare), Odelstingsproposisjon nr. 25 *Om lov om kunstig befruktning* (1986-87) (Bill on artificial reproduction) p.32. When the Act was revised in 1994, the Government did not see any reason to reevaluate the questions. The majority of the Storting concurred.

13. For further discussion of this feature see Martyn Evans, 'A Right to Procreate?' in this volume.

14. See Evans, *ibid.*, for a more detailed justification.

15. For instance the unregulated use of donor semen, unregulated repetition of ineffective stimulation cycles, unlimited numbers of embryo transfers, etc.

16. See Evans, *op.cit.*

17. Auestad, Anne-Marie, 'I am father's baby - you can have the turtle - psychotherapy in a family context' *Journal of Child Psychotherapy* 18, 1992, pp.57-74, p.73.

18. Personal communication from psychiatrist Lars Chr. Opdal; cf. also Salonen, Simo, 'Facing reality: castration anxiety reconsidered' *Scandinavian Psychoanalytical Review* 10, 1987, pp.27-36; Lord, Ruth and Cox, Catherine E., 'Adoption and identity' *Psychoanalytic Study of the Child* 46, 1991, pp.355-67; Haimes, E. and Timms, N., *Adoption, Identity and Social Policy* Aldershot, Gower, 1985; and Toynbee, P., *Lost Children* London, Hutchinson, 1985.

19. Opdal, *op.cit.*

20. *Ibid.*

21. Cf. Kirk (1964), *op.cit.*; Sororsky, A., Baran, S. and Pannor, R., 'Identity conflicts in adoptees' *American Journal of Orthopsychiatry* 45, 1975, pp.18-27; Stein, L.M. and Hoopes, J., *Identity Formation in the Adopted Adolescent* New York, Child Welfare League of America, 1985; Rosenberg, Elinor B. and Horner, Thomas M., 'Birthparent romances and identity formation in adopted children' *American Journal of Orthopsychiatry* 61, 1991, pp.70-77.

22. Opdal, *op.cit.*

23. Cf. Baran, Annette and Pannor, Rubin, *Lethal Secrets: The Shocking Consequences and Unsolved Problems of Artificial Insemination* New York, Warner, 1989, p.107; Snowden, R., Mitchell, G.D. and Snowden, E.M., *Artificial Reproduction: A Social Investigation* London, Allen and Unwin, 1983; and Daniels, K.R., 'Artificial insemination using donor semen and the issue of secrecy: the views of donors and recipient couples' *Social Science and Medicine* 27, 1988, pp.377-383.

24. Karpel, M.A., 'Family secrets' *Family Process* 19, 1980, pp.295-306.

25. Guttormsen, Gro., 'Familieforhold ved donorinseminasjon. Om psykologisk effekt av hemmeligholdelse' *Tidsskrift for den norske lægeforening* 113, 1993, pp.2824-26; cf. Vandik, Inger Helene, 'Donorinseminasjon: Hvordan ivaretar vi barnets behov?' *NEM-NYTT* 4, 1993, pp.3-4; Snowden, R. and Mitchell, G.D., *The Artificial Family* revised edition, London, Allen and Unwin, 1983, chapter 5; Sokoloff, D.Z., 'Alternative methods of reproduction. Effects on the child' *Clinical Pediatrics* 26, 1987, pp.11-16; and Klock, Susan C. and Maier, Donald, 'Psychological factors related to donor insemination' *Fertility and Sterility* 56, 1991, pp.489-95.

26. Vandik, *op.cit.*, p.3; Haimes and Timms, *op.cit.*, p.97.

27. Snowden, R., Mitchell, G.D. and Snowden, E.M., *Artificial Reproduction: A Social Investigation* London, Allen and Unwin, 1983.

28. Baran and Pannor, *op.cit.*; Snowden and Mitchell, *op.cit.*; Lasker, Judith N. and Borg, Susan, 'Secrecy and the new reproductive technologies' in Whiteford, L. and Poland, M., *New Approaches to Human Reproduction. Social and Ethical Dimensions* London, Westview, 1989, pp.133-144; and Streitfeld, David, 'Secrecy and the sperm donor' *The Washington Post* 28 November, 1991, section C, p.5.

29. Sants, *op.cit.*

30. Baran and Pannor, *op.cit.*; Klock and Maier, *op.cit.*

31. Rowland, R., 'Attitudes and opinions of donors on an artificial insemination by donor (AID) programme' *Clinical Reproduction and Fertility* 2, 1983, pp.249-259; Daniels, K.R., 'Semen donors in New Zealand: their characteristics and attitudes' *Clinical Reproduction and Fertility* 5, 1987, pp.177-190; Daniels, K.R., 'Semen donors: their motivation and attitudes to their offspring' *Journal of Reproduction and Infant Psychology* 7, 1989, pp.121-127; and Mahlstedt, Patricia P. and Probasco, Kris A., 'Sperm donors: their attitudes towards providing medical and psychological information for recipient couples and donor offspring' *Fertility and Sterility* 56, 1991, pp.747-53. These findings seem to be confirmed by some semen banks in the US which offer both an open and an anonymous programme. About half of those who request donor insemination opt for the open programme. Openness includes access to donor's identity. The directors of these banks claim that it is equally as difficult to recruit donors to the anonymous programme as for the open programme (Herman, Robin, 'When the 'father' is a sperm donor. A new look at secrecy' *The Washington Post* Health Section, 11 February, 1992, pp.10-14).

32. Haimes, *op.cit.*, p.59.

33. Snowden and Snowden, *op.cit.*, p.134.

34. *Ibid.*, p.137. The picture story book *My Story* is available from the Infertility Research Trust, University Department of Obstetrics and Gynaecology, Jessop Hospital for Women, Sheffield SR 7RE, UK.

35. Guttormsen, *op.cit.*

36. Toynbee, *op.cit.*

37. Triseliotis (1973), *op.cit.*; Snowden and Snowden, *op.cit.*, p.137.

38. Kirk (1981), *op.cit.*, pp.136-141; Haimes and Timms, *op.cit.*; and Haimes, *op.cit.*, pp.52-54.

39. One may of course consider a number of practical arrangements which are varieties of the middle course proposed in this paper. There is much to be said in favour of the Dutch law proposal for an artificial insemination act, which encourages greater openness and gives the donor child the possibility of tracing the identity of its genetic father, without his consent, if the child's vital interests would be harmed if identifiable information was withheld (Hubben, *op.cit.*, p.4).

14. THE RIGHTS OF CHILDREN TO INFORMATION FOLLOWING ASSISTED CONCEPTION

Jean-Marie Thévoz
Fondation Louis Jeantet de Médecine
C.P. 277
CH-1211 Genève 17
Switzerland

1. Introduction

In this paper I would like to present and review some issues surrounding the information children ought to receive or have access to following assisted conception. The main issue is secrecy and anonymity in case of gamete donation, but also the kind of information parents should provide their children about their conception in a truthful relationship.

This reflection is conducted under specific local circumstances which give it a sense of concrete concern. On one hand, in May 1992, the Swiss people voted to accept a constitutional article about genetic engineering and assisted procreation which asserts that everyone has a right to know data concerning his or her ancestry. This might mean that children conceived through artificial insemination by donor (AID) will have a right to know the donor's personal identity (see Appendix I, p.205). On the other hand, in France, the new 'Bioethics Laws' of July 1994 secure full anonymity for sperm donors (see Appendix II, p.206). This highlights the importance of reflecting on the rights of children to information following assisted conception.

2. Initial Remarks

2.1. VARIETY OF SITUATIONS IN ASSISTED CONCEPTION

There are several means of getting a child through medically assisted conception, from hormonal stimulation to embryo donation or surrogate motherhood. The issue of providing one's child with some information about its origins arises differently according to which method is used.[1] These various means have different repercussions on family life and different implications for bonds and relationships inside the family. The most significant difference appears between the methods that use only the couple's gametes and those which resort to gamete donors. Why is this difference more significant than all the others?

195

D. Evans (ed.), Creating the Child, 195–209.

When the medical procedures use only the parents' gametes, the genetic bond between both parents and their child is unchanged as compared with natural conception. The medical assistance has been confined to a definite time period of the couple's life. The child is not different from one who could have been born to this couple through natural conception. Medicine is a mere instrument employed to obtain their own child, much as forceps are means of getting children out of the womb in cases of birth difficulties. The medical act changes nothing as compared to a natural conception, except of course that the child is born inspite of the couple's infertility. Moreover, in this case, the medical intervention is an episode in the couple's life, not in the child's.

Consequently, the question of whether to tell the child of the medical assistance received at the time of conception is quite unproblematic. It is left to the parents discretion to tell the story of his conception or of his birth, just as it is their choice to relate the story of their encounter, romance or marriage. All these events are in some form related to the present being of the child, but are of no necessary significance for his life. The questions of secrecy, withholding of information and anonymity are of no relevance here. They arise only in the case of gamete donation.

In this latter case, the role of the gamete donor changes the situation. First, the genetic ties between the parents and the child are broken. The infertile parent has no genetic tie with his/her child and has to develop another kind of bonding. Second, the effect of the medical intervention is long-lasting, life-long for the child. Third, the medical assistance is no longer restricted to a short episode in the life of the couple, but represents an intervention in the child's life. He will bear the consequences of the decisions of his parents and the help of the health care professionals. Consequently the issues of secrecy, withholding of information and anonymity of the donor arise here.

Discontinuity in genetic links does occur in other situations too, namely adoption or adultery. Adoption has many similar features with AID and in many aspects they can be treated alike. In fact, for the sake of consistency, these similar aspects of AID and adoption should be treated alike, as we shall see. The case of adultery is different since there is deception from the beginning. Adultery, contrary to adoption or AID, occurs without the consent of the husband or partner. Thus secrecy is a component of the family relationship and cannot be handled in the same manner as in adoption or AID. The cases of one-parent families is also different. I will not discuss these questions further, except to mention that maintaining secrecy in adoption or AID risks giving the child a vague hunch that his conception is as suspicious as if he were born of adultery.

In this paper, I will tackle primarily the right to information of children issuing from AID. My consideration of AID can in certain cases be extrapolated to other types of gamete donation, but not to all of them. For example, oocyte donation by an infertile woman undergoing IVF herself can not be treated in the same way, because, in a case where she never gets pregnant herself, it would certainly be psychologically devastating to her to know later that her gift resulted in a child.[2]

2.2. TYPES OF INFORMATION

The debate about secrecy and anonymity in case of gamete donation is extremely polarised. This polarisation is generally reflected in the national legislations or guidelines regarding artificial insemination. On the one hand, some advocate total secrecy (see Appendix II), on the other side total information (see Appendix I). Actually there is no need to come out either in favour of a right to or a black out on all and every piece of information. We are rather facing a continuum. The question then is where to draw the line between the kind of information a child has an absolute right to, that is the kind he has an interest in knowing and the kind that can, in special circumstances, be withheld.

Therefore, it is of paramount importance to distinguish at least three types of information that can be given to or demanded by the children of assisted conception and see that they mark a progressive disclosure process.

(i) information about the fact that assisted conception with gamete donation was used: I call this issue the problem of secrecy vs openness. Several surveys of patients attending artificial insemination programmes show that most of them wish not to disclose the gamete donation to their child. I have seen no follow up study of those families nor have I seen any data on how many have changed their minds and finally disclosed the information.

(ii) information about the medical and genetic condition of the donor: I will call this medical information. In general, centres do screen the donors and make up files with health data and physical information. In some cases this information, namely the medical record of the donor, can be useful for the child's own personal medical anamnesis.[3]

(iii) information about the donor's identity, i.e. the issue of anonymity. The protection of anonymity is often a condition required by the potential donors for going through with the donation.

It is clear that these data are linked in a progressive series, one has to reveal (i) to speak of (ii) and so on; and speaking of (i) may create a need or demand to know of (ii) or (iii) (Cf. 4.3.)

Usually, secrecy is justified with the argument that informing the child will harm him. Knowing that one parent is not at the same time one's genetic author is said to be distressing. So parents prefer to avoid telling their children. A further argument says that parents would suffer if the child knows, and are afraid it would break their family relationships. Truth-telling would go against the principle of non-maleficence.

Anonymity is often justified with the same kind of arguments. It would distress the family if the child wanted to know his genetic progenitor personally. The parents would fear meeting the donor through their child's initiative. The donor would no longer be able to live quietly if he can be reached at any time by his (multiple) genetic offspring. The upholding of anonymity is necessary to preserve quietness and inner peace. Anonymity benefits donors and parents.

2.3. MALE AND FEMALE PERCEPTION OF GAMETE DONATION

The most frequent gamete donation occurs in case of male infertility. The only recourse for fully infertile and many hypofertile males is artificial insemination with donor (AID). Apart from Sweden, Germany, Austria and foreseeably Switzerland and the Netherlands, all other countries protect the anonymity of sperm donors.

Oocyte donation is quite rare. It occurs mainly indirectly through surrogate motherhood (when the surrogate mother is inseminated with the sperm of the husband of the couple wanting a child), sometimes with oocyte donation between women undergoing IVF procedures. Frequently, oocyte donation happens between related women. One can observe that the rule of anonymity is less stringently applied in cases of oocyte donation. Often women want to know to whom they are giving their oocytes or whom they are getting them from. Embryo donation is a special case, often viewed as a form of adoption as both parents are on an equal level of parenthood *vis-à-vis* the child.

According to these factual observations one might formulate the following hypothesis: secrecy about gamete donation and donors' anonymity is a male (patriarchal) concern to protect male pride (property) in hiding male infertility and non (biological) paternity in a pluralistic society. Secrecy and anonymity are needed in order to hide what is considered a failure, *viz.* the inability to pass one's genetic heritage to one's offspring. This reveals an emphasis given to the biological side of procreation that might be typical of our present western culture. In this sense, artificial insemination by donor can be interpreted as the breaking of a cultural taboo, requiring to be covered by means of secrecy and anonymity.[4] Whilst considering genetic ties as important might lead to letting children born as a result of AID know about their genetic origin, eventually the more significant an infertile man considers genetic links, the more he will try to conceal the absence of this link!

The problem remains whether it is good to give so much weight to the genetic ties in families and whether the sociological importance given in our western culture to these ties of blood are to be encouraged, discouraged or seen as indifferent. I have dealt with this subject in my book *Entre nos mains l'embryon*[5] arguing in favour of letting social and emotional bonds prevail over biological and genetic ties as is the case of many less patriarchal societies, past and present.

On the other hand, we can observe other attitudes shown by women. First, they are better prepared to deal with infertility. Until recently infertility has always been considered to be a female problem. Indeed, mythology as well as literature always shows infertility in women. To my knowledge, no infertile male figure appears as such in fiction or in history. Hence women are more prepared to come to terms with infertility. It does not mean that it is less painful and distressing, only that society is more compassionate toward infertile women than men. Moreover, in the case of oocyte donation, the experience and timespan of pregnancy is a significant period in establishing a very special bond with the expected child. This relationship established between mother and foetus during pregnancy can prevail over the lack of any genetic

tie.

Regarding oocyte donation, women often prefer collaboration and openness in gamete exchanges. Newspapers have reported how sisters (and even a mother and daughter) have exchanged oocytes or assumed surrogate motherhood for one another. Some women, rejecting anonymity in oocyte donation, simply travel to other countries to get the medical procedure they want with the donor they have chosen.[6]

3. Theoretical Issues

3.1. WHAT IS TRUTH IN ASSISTED CONCEPTION WITH GAMETE DONATION?

There is no need to write here one further defence of truthfulness in relationships. I will start with the presumption that truthtelling is a fundamental moral duty and the foundation of common trust, necessary for all relationships and life in society, and so much the more in family relationships. The exceptions some authors try to justify in emphasising the principle of beneficence[7] don't diminish the importance of and need for truth for trust and true relationships. Regarding the AID issue, the first question to ask is what is truth in this situation?

(i) What is truth after AID? It might appear nonsensical to ask what truth is. It is not in the context of AID, because that is exactly the unsolved question. As Thielicke says "truth is not adequately defined simply in terms of the agreement between a statement and objective reality".[8] This is, firstly, because we cannot know "objective reality" outside thoughts, words and meanings which do not belong to this reality; and secondly, because we choose between thoughts, words and meanings to make our statements. Which of these statements is true in the case of AID: a) the man living with you is not your father, because someone else gave his gamete to allow for your conception; b) the man living with you is your father, although someone else gave his gamete to allow for your conception. What is true paternity? This is a matter of discussion.[9] I have argued elsewhere[10] that we cannot exclude emotional and social adoption as a kind of true fatherhood. This fatherhood without genetic ties is actually possible only after going through grief for one's own unborn children and relinquishing one's hope for genetic authorship. If this hope is not fully given up, a child born after AID will not be greeted as a gift, but be the permanent pointer to one's own secret failure to father one's child. It is not impossible that the failure to get through this narrow path to adoptive fatherhood is one of the reasons why so many people want to keep secrecy and anonymity. In these cases, what parents consider as truth is too reminiscent of their failure. Surely, this can be seen as threatening and frightening and therefore not disclosable to anybody, above all not to the child. That is the standpoint of the parents.

Surely, the donor considers himself not to be the child's father. More precisely, the donor wants anonymity in order to escape any fatherly role or duties. For him, genetic ties don't establish fatherhood; he doesn't want to be involved any more after donation.

To disclose his identity might involve him again in a role he doesn't want to assume. His truth is that he is not the father of this child, but he fears that other people might have another 'truth' and burden him with an unwanted fatherhood.

What the truth for the child himself is, I will try to uncover in the next point (3.2). Let me conclude this point before doing that. In summary, the 'truth' about conception will change according to the agent and the idea they, or society at large, have of true fatherhood. Ethnological studies have demonstrated how parenthood links are culturally constructed.[11] They also show that most societies have means of giving children to infertile couples.[12] In these cases they favour openness about filiation. They do not deny that the blood ties differ from the family bonds established by adoption or child transfer.

(ii) A second series of questions that arise are: what kind of information about conception ought parents to give their children in order to tell them the truth? Do parents have to tell their children all about their mode of conception, when, where, how, why and so on? No, parents certainly have a right to privacy about their sexuality, even when it happens to concern the conception of a child. On the other hand the child will certainly benefit from hearing his parents say that his conception was a time of enjoyment, that he was wanted and awaited. One must establish a balance between a right to privacy of the parents and their duty to be beneficent to their children. Thus, one has to distinguish between intimacy of the act and information concerning feelings and intentions. The 'truth' a child needs is not mere facts but veracity in the relationship, not crude factual information but sensitive disclosure of some knowledge, meaningful for the construction of his personality and identity.

Factual information and meaningful knowledge will not be easily severed from one another in assisted conception. Actually, information about the genetic links in the family will inevitably be tied up with some facts, namely the medical procedures and the reasons parents have needed them. Thus we are to move from 'truth' to 'truthfulness'. The significant thing is less the content of the information than the truthfulness of the relationship. Secrecy leads to omission, elusive answers and finally to deception. It can not only poison family relationships, but also break the confidence children place in their parents, even outside assisted conception. As Mitchell contends "knowing that AID families almost invariably refrain from telling the child or anyone else, children in normal families can never be sure of the truth of any answer they are given."[13] If society expects the family to have an important role in shaping the moral values of children, then it ought to promote truthfulness in family life and encourage disclosure and communication about family ties, be they biological or not.

3.2. IS THERE A NEED TO KNOW ONE'S ORIGIN?

Now let us take the child's standpoint. What is truth for him if he has been conceived through AID? What knowledge does the child need regarding his origins?

Truth for the child is what he sees, what he feels, lives and learns from his surroundings. As attitudes are more perceptible than genetics, he will adopt the man

at home as his father as long as the latter behaves like a father. From my point of view, this is good. Then, why change anything and make it more difficult by interfering and asking for disclosure? Because secrecy can have deleterious effects.[14] Children soon sense that the family is concealing something from them. "Child psychiatrists and psychoanalysts' clinical experience shows that every secret hanging upon a child is in fact a lie and produces a pathogenic effect".[15] The child will realise that something is kept secret, but not what it is. Thus he will no longer distinguish between true and false statements and suspicion will grow and destroy the relationships the secret was meant to protect.[16] Because secrecy has these deleterious effects on children, it is therefore no more possible to legitimate it for its usefulness and benefits toward the family. Secrecy is no white lie.

What is needed to avoid this deterioration? It is possible to identify various needs. The first and most basic need is for genuine relationships. This means that the parents, in our case especially the father, have gone through the narrow path of relinquishing their need for genetic authorship and fully accepted that they are foster parents. In other words they must deeply believe in their parental capacities. When they have reached this stage, it won't be difficult to live with this reality and they will be able to talk of it to their children in a supportive way. Once the child knows of his double lineage, he will have questions about his unknown progenitor.

During the teenage years, there is a need for personal identification and distance from one's father. There is a search for the ideal father, one who can meet all expectations, a quest to understand the origin of all things. In the normal process, the father at home fails to meet this ideal standard, and consequently the teenager is forced to continue his fundamental quest elsewhere. It is possible that one can get through to some 'transcendental father' only after the experience that no earthly father can match one's personal image of the 'ideal father'. Being prevented from meeting one's progenitor could be an obstacle to that kind of 'spiritual' quest. Often, the mere security of being aware that there is a possibility of knowing who the man is is enough to stop one's looking for him.[17]

Later in life, there might be a need for pertinent medical information. As medicine develops, namely genetic testing and predictive diagnosis, it will become more and more important to be able to give a true account of past diseases in the family. Unfortunately, people not told of their 'half adoption' will report inaccurate data to their physician. Some will be put at risk by this deception. It is then in the interests of the child, not only to know about his double lineage, but also, at least to receive some data about the donor, or better, to have a means, for instance through a third party, to get up-to-date information directly from the donor.

In brief, we see that there is a need to live true relationships, which is incompatible with secrecy; a need for factual medical information later in life and a need not to be deprived of access to the identity or person of the donor, which are incompatible with full anonymity. Do these needs create a right to know and on the other side a moral obligation of disclosure?

3.3. AUTONOMY, BENEFICENCE AND BALANCE OF INTERESTS

We have seen that donors, parents and children have divergent interests regarding secrecy and anonymity. The performance of AID includes a fourth party, the health care professionals. They have their own core of professional ethics which deals with duties of confidentiality, truth-telling, and anonymity.

Assisted conception with gamete donation is an area where those principles conflict. Truth-telling in the physician-patient relationship is now the rule. It is based on the principle of respect for autonomy of persons. This latter principle requires that physicians disclose all relevant information to their patients in order to allow them to take adequate decisions. Confidentiality is turned against third parties and protects both the privacy of the patient and the trust in patient-physician relationships. In one area of medicine, organ donation, anonymity has been instituted as a rule (very stringently enforced in Europe).

Which rule applies to AID? Anonymity between donor and receiver, as in organ transplantation? Respect for autonomy and therefore a right of access to information for the child? Confidentiality of any information concerning the donor and the parents with respect to any third party, including the child?

There are some specific features about gamete donation that do not allow it to be compared with organ donation. First, there are two receivers: the parents on a temporary basis and the child permanently. Second, the end result is the existence of a new autonomous human being. If the starting point is almost the same as in organ donation, the final situation has essential dissimilarities. This adds to the complexity of the issue but might also bring about some elements of a solution, by taking time as an essential key.

Secrecy occurs between the parents and the child, anonymity in a four-way relationship between physician/institution, donor, parents and child. Moreover, there is a contract between physician/institution, donor and parents about the way of handling information concerning the child. The contract is concluded unilaterally, without any representation from the offspring or advocacy of the child's interests, because only the donor and the parents are autonomous people. It's sure that, at the time of the contract, i.e. before conception, the child does not exist, and thus has no autonomy to justify any claim. But, the contract is only meaningful if a child is born and grows. He will thus gain autonomy. Furthermore, in any case, the contract is made about someone who will later be an autonomous being with rights originating from this autonomy.

Is the autonomy of a future person to be respected? The debate on the status of the embryo shows that the potentiality to become a person is not sufficient to give rights to the embryo - at the time it is an embryo. But in the issue at hand, the question is different since the claim (to know one's progenitor) is made when the child has eventually become autonomous. Therefore the contract about anonymity made before conception restricts the child's autonomy at the time of the claim. As the contract has been agreed to benefit the donor and the parents, there is a conflict between the principle of beneficence to some and the principle of the autonomy of another.[18]

Some would argue that the contract is also made for the child's benefit: he is better off as long as he doesn't know. Although I doubt that there is a benefit for the child, even if it were true, there would be a conflict between beneficence decided by others, that is paternalism, and the child's autonomy. If the child is of age, paternalism is no longer justified; he doesn't need to be protected against himself any more. He must be allowed to act autonomously, e.g. to choose whether to know or not, even if he will be hurt.

My conclusion is then, that there is no ethical argument to legitimate a hard-and-fast rule for withholding important information regarding the ancestry of an adult conceived by such means from him if he wants to know. What kind of implications has this conclusion for practical issues?

4. Practical Issues

4.1. WHO IS TO BE PROTECTED? WHOSE INTERESTS TO PREVAIL? INTERESTS, NEEDS OR RIGHTS?

In the above discussion, it has been argued that the child's autonomy must prevail over the benefits parents and donors get through secrecy and anonymity. This should be the normal ordering of principles in AID cases. In other words, it can be said that the child's right to have its autonomy respected is preponderant. Nonetheless this right cannot be absolute. All parties have some interests to be protected on different grounds. I therefore prefer to speak only of a *rightful interest* of the child in being told about his origin.

This rightful interest must be balanced against the interests of the parents and of the donors, specifically according to the type of information and the age of the child. Indeed, the child's interest is different according to each type of information I have outlined in 2.2. The child's interest weighs more as regards non-secrecy and less so for personal information. Information about fatherhood is needed early in childhood to be well accepted, but information as to personal identity only much later and only on request. Ordinarily the interests of the child to know will override the interests of parents in maintaining secrecy and of donors to remain anonymous.

This conclusion has also been reached regarding adoption. Parents have a duty to tell their adopted children of their double ancestry. Often, children have some rights to get information, even identifying information, about their genetic parents. Consequently, the best solution would be to establish the same rule with AID as with adoption, considering gamete donation as a form of adoption, and just as honorable.

In practice on the one hand, it would mean that parents are encouraged to speak to their children in order to allow them to develop their autonomy. This presupposes a change in mentality regarding gamete donation, male infertility and genetic bonds. On the other hand, the state must create an office to handle demands for information about one's origins. The best choice would be to appoint a judge to this office. His duty

might be to contact all parties to find out whether they oppose the release of the requested information, and on what grounds. Finally, he might balance the different parties interests and take a decision. With such an office and procedure, each major set of interests could be protected and society would be seen as valuing truth-telling in family and social relationships.

4.2. THE PARADOXICAL QUEST FOR MORAL PERFECTION

One puzzling effect of lifting anonymity is the possibility that there will be so few donors that no programme of assisted conception with AID can be maintained, with the effect that no child will be brought to life through this means any more. This paradox is often put forward by physicians opposing legislative steps toward the ending of secrecy and anonymity. In this case - and in order to escape this side effect of an ethical requirement - can we balance the wrong being made if no children are available to infertile couples and the wrong being made if information is withheld from children? To put it in a more theoretical form: can we drop deontological principles (tell the truth in every circumstance, respect the autonomy of the grown up child) to avoid bad consequences (no more donors).

This question could be answered by opposing utilitarians who would accept such a proposition and deontologists who would refuse to subordinate principles to consequences. This would please philosophers, but not the public or policy makers. One principle often used in discussion about reproductive technologies is that the child's rights takes precedence over the right to get a child. This principle should apply here as in every policy regarding reproductive technologies[19], even if it means fewer children through AID programmes.

However, this paradox is constructed on a false premise. Banning anonymity does not necessarily dry up the source of donors in the long term. Undoubtedly recruitment is made more difficult, but the experience of Sweden shows that AID programmes do continue, even if with a decreased activity. "Because of the difficulties in finding donors several centres have had to close their AID activity and the remaining five centres, with the exception of Malmö, decreased their activity." Moreover, "the new donors are NOT qualitatively different from the old ones recruited under the previous law. It was strongly claimed [by the Centres contacted] that the alleged difference was a fiction created by the mass-media".[20]

4.3. PERVERSE EFFECTS OF LEGAL OBLIGATION TO LIFT ANONYMITY

The conclusion which emerges from the above discussion is that there is a moral duty to promote supportive acceptance of male sterility in society, openness and truthfulness in family relationships and respect for the child's autonomy. These are ethical demands, i.e. ideals to aim at. Therefore, it is nearly impossible to convert these moral requirements into a legal obligation. There is a wide gap between ethical recommendations and legally enforceable norms[21] and this is particularly striking in the

context of AID.

As most surveys show, parents are reluctant to tell children about their conception through AID. Their reservations grow as the information gets closer to the donor's identity.[22] If the law were to grant the child an unconditional right of access to the donor's identity, it is more than likely that parents will feel less inclined to speak about the means of conception.[23] Maintaining secrecy would be the safest way for parents to prevent the child from knowing even of the existence of a third party involved in his origins. Therefore, the law must seriously take into account this feeling of insecurity. It must grant the parent an appropriate degree of protection along with the respect of the child's autonomy and rightful interest to information. It follows from this that it is preferable that the law does not take sides, either guaranteeing an absolute right of access to the donor's identity to children (as in Sweden) or in letting anonymity be an unbreakable rule (as in France). It must instead create a procedure for a just review and balancing of interests of all parties prior to granting or refusing information to the child. A conditional legal right to know, acknowledging a rightful interest of the child to get information, would protect simultaneously the interests of parents, donors, and children and reassure them.

Appendix I. The Situation in Switzerland

The situation in Switzerland changed completly on the 17th of May 1992. On this day the Swiss people voted to accept a constitutional article about genetic engineering and reproductive technologies. Along with other prescriptions aiming strictly to limit assisted conception, Constitutional Article 24novies (Pt. 2, lit. g.) contends that "the access of a person to data relating to his/her descent is guaranteed".

Beforehand, assisted conception was ruled only by professional ethical guidelines, namely those of the Swiss Academy of Medical Sciences (SAMS).[24] The SAMS issued guidelines on AID for the first time in 1981 and reviewed them in 1991 together with those on IVF in order to draw up a single document on assisted conception.[25] The SAMS always took a firm stand in favour of anonymity, though never taking sides on the issue of secrecy.

Now Switzerland happens to be in a period of uncertainty. Most medical practitioners have momentarily given up AID, unable as they are to give any guarantee of anonymity to the donors and patients. The Constitutional article provides merely a general legal framework and is not enforceable before the acceptance by the parliament of a final text. The Federal administration issued a first draft in June 1995. It has been distributed to various institutions and political lobbies for consultation. Although it is not possible to know what the Swiss people meant when they voted for this constitutional article - particularly the above mentioned sentence about anonymity - because the multitude of themes and different points included in Art.24[26], the first draft gives an absolute right to children over 16 years of age conceived through AID to know the identity of the donor. If the donor doesn't what to meet the child, the latter would

be informed of the donor's right to privacy and desire to be left alone, but the child would nevertheless receive identifying information about the donor. After this first consultation, the draft will have to be discussed by the Swiss Parliament. The debate will be very controversial as there will indeed be proposals for amendments from both conservative and liberal sides.

Appendix II. The Situation in France

Since 1973, artificial insemination with donors has been organised and practised mostly by the so called CECOS (Centre d'étude et de conservation des oeufs et du sperme). Until 1988 they covered up to 90% of AID activity. Since then legislative changes have had the unintended consequence of opening this activity up to many other centres and laboratories.[27] Right at the beginning of their practice, the CECOS established their own ethical code. The major principles are gratuity of donation, anonymity and couple to couple donation.

The gratuity principle is the application of the principle of the non-commercialisation of human tissues and organs to gametes. This should come as no surprise, as France is a vocal champion of the non-commercialisation of human body parts. In practice, it means that the donor receives no payment for his sperm and that AID programmes are run as non-profit making organisations. This rule is also seen as a guarantee of increased medical safety.[28]

Anonymity is the second principle. It is applied without any exception.[29] The reason given in favour of anonymity is the protection of all parties against unwanted interferences. Anonymity should protect the child against disputes between his parents and the donor.[30] But this principle is widely discussed and criticised outside the CECOS (mostly by psychiatrists.[31]

The third principle is specific to the CECOS and France. It rests on the idea that the 'gift of life' must be given by one couple to another. The donor must be the father of at least one child and have the consent of his wife/partner. This requirement has two goals. On the one hand, the couple do not have the fantasy of an imaginary stallion, but think of another couple willing to share the joy of parenthood. In addition, the procedure followed by the CECOS eliminates infertile bachelors and donors motivated by weird fantasies.

These three principles have been included in the 'Bioethics Laws' passed in July 1994 by the French Parliament (Laws 94-548, 94-653 and 94-654).

Acknowledgment

The author wishes to thank Marina Mandofia Berney and Søren Holm for providing useful information, Maurizio Mori and Alex Mauron for their thoughtful comments on earlier drafts. This paper is part of the 'Bioethics Project' of the Louis Jeantet

Foundation for Medicine.

Notes

1. I will use the word 'child' to designate the offspring issuing from assisted conception, whatever his age. Later in this paper the 'autonomous child' will refer to an adult offspring.

2. This is one of the reasons for which I favour spare embryo donation more than oocyte donation, cf. Thévoz, Jean-Marie, *Entre nos mains l'embryon* Recherche bioéthique, Genève, Labor et Fides, 1990, (Le Champ éthique 17), pp.158-159.

3. Genetic information could be secured without further recourse to the donor if a specimen of the donor's DNA were collected and stored. This material could be made available to the child, on request, with no direct threat to the donor's privacy. Nevertheless, such storage would create other ethical problems.

4. This point is supported by the fact that in other patriarchal societies not open to pluralism, AID is simply outlawed or considered highly immoral. That is the case in many Islamic countries.

5. Thévoz, *op.cit.*

6. Petit-Pierre, Marie-Christine, 'Pour les Suissesses, la route des ovules passe par Paris', *Journal de Genève* 26 mai 1993, p.15.

7. Jackson, Jennifer, 'Telling the truth' *Journal of Medical Ethics* 17 (1), 1991, pp.5-9.

8. Thielicke, Helmut, 'The truthfulness of a physician' in Lammers, Stephen E. and Verhey, Allen (eds), *On Moral Medicine, Theological Perspectives in Medical Ethics* Grand Rapids, Mich., William B. Eerdmans Publishing Company, 1987, pp. 537-543, p.538a.

9. See Delaisi de Parseval, Geneviève, *La Part du Père* Paris, Seuil, 1983.

10. Thévoz, *op.cit.*

11. Delaisi de Parseval, Geneviève and Janaud, Alain, *L'enfant à tout prix* Paris, Seuil, 1983.

12. Lallemand, Suzanne, *La circulation des enfants en société traditionelle. Prêt, don, échange* Paris, L'Harmattan, 1993, (Connaissance des hommes) and Lallemand, Suzanne, 'La circulation des enfants en société traditionelle' *Lettre du Comité Consultatif National d'éthique pour les sciences de la vie et de la santé* 28 mai 1993, p.14.

13. Mitchell, G.D., *'In vitro* fertilisation: the major issues - a comment' *Journal of Medical Ethics* 9 (4), 1983, pp.196-199, p.197.

14. In saying this I do not take a utilitarian position, I am just stating that the non application of a deontological principle had deleterious effects and thus could not claim to be an application of the principle of beneficence (a beneficent lie).

15. Delaisi de Parseval, Geneviève, 'Le désir d'enfant géré par la médecine et par la loi', in Parizeau, Marie-Hélène (ed.), *Les fondements de la bioéthique* Bruxelles, De Boeck Université, 1992, pp.91-102, p.98 (my translation).

16. Delaisi de Parseval, Geneviève, 'Réflexions d'une psychanalyste sur la question de l'anonymat du donneur de sperme dans l'insémination artificielle (IAD)' *Cahiers médico-sociaux* (Genève), 37 (2), 1993, pp.173-177, p.176.

17. Delaisi de Parseval (1992), *op.cit.*, p.97.

18. Anonymity remains a valuable principle between patients and donor, as long as they both state it in their contract. Lifting anonymity between child and donor does not imply automatically that parents may have access to the donor's identity.

19. Thévoz, Jean-Marie, 'PMA: L'enfant comme pierre angulaire d'une législation cohérente' *Cahiers médico-sociaux* 37 (2), 1993, pp.149-157.

20. Holm, Søren, personal communication, June 1993.

21. Durand, Guy, 'Ethique, droit et régulation alternative' in Parizeau (ed.), *op.cit.*, pp.63-75.

22. In answer to the question 'What is for you the best solution (with respect to secrecy and anonymity)?'; 52% said that the child must not be told (secrecy), 25% that the child must know there was a donor but not his identity, 11% that the child must know the identity of the donor; and 12% gave no opinion ([2] p.128, my translation).

23. Mandofia Berney, Marina, 'La garantie de l'accès d'une personne aux données relatives à son ascendance. Commentaire de l'article 24novies al. 2 let. g de la Constitution' *Cahiers médico-sociaux* 37 (2), 1993, pp.165-171, p.168.

24. For details about the SAMS and its status in Switzerland, cf. Thévoz, Jean-Marie, 'Research and hospital ethics committees in Switzerland' *Health Care Ethics Committee Forum* 4 (1), 1992, pp.41-47.

25. Swiss Academy of Medical Sciences guidelines are available from: ASSM, secretariat, Petersplatz 13, CH-4051 Basle.

26. Thévoz, Jean-Marie, and Mauron, Alex, 'Génétique et procréation dans la Constitution: des choix éthiques importants en perspective' *Plädoyer* 5, 1992, pp.50-54.

27. Cf. Comité consultatif national d'éthique pour les sciences de la vie et de la santé, Ethique et recherche biomédicale, *Rapport 1990* Paris, La Documentation Française, 1991, p.26.

28. It should be noticed that this principle was applied in the case of blood donation, but did not provide more safety from HIV blood contamination than in other countries where blood donors were paid. Cf. David, Georges, 'Don et utilisation du sperme' in *Actes du Colloque: Génétique, Procréation et Droit* Arles, Actes Sud, 1985, pp.203-224, pp.211-212.

29. *Ibid.*, p.214.

30. Alnot, Marie-Odile, Labrusse-Riou, Catherine, Mandelbaum-Bleibtreu, Jacqueline, Pérol, Yvonne and Rosenczveig, Jean-Pierre, *Les procréations artificielles* Rapport au Premier Ministre, Paris, La Documentation Française, 1986, (Collection des rapports officiels), p.83.

31. For example, Tomkiewicz, Stanislaw, 'L'insémination artificielle par donneur' in *Actes du Colloque: Génétique, Procréation et Droit* Arles, Actes Sud, 1985, p.546.

15. DONOR ANONYMITY IN THE DUTCH DRAFT OF AN ARTIFICIAL INSEMINATION ACT[1]

Joseph H. Hubben
Professor of health law, Nijmegen University,
The Netherlands

1. Introduction

Not knowing and not being able to find out who your father and mother are has profound implications for a child. Knowledge of one's origins provides a basis for deeper insight into oneself. Generally speaking, a child knows who his or her mother and father are. Some do not, or later discover that the person they thought was their mother or father is not their biological parent. The number of such cases has grown over the years with the increased use of artificial insemination (AI). The question which arises in all these cases is whether there are compelling grounds for withholding information about parentage from children who lack this knowledge, sometimes urgently desire to have it and are therefore so vulnerable.

The Dutch bill aims to regulate the provision of information about parentage to children conceived by means of AI. It will also contain rules on the storage and management of such information. The bill does not, of course, cover all aspects of access to such information. Problems may also arise in situations where children are put up for adoption, particularly when they come from abroad. Under present practice, information concerning the parentage of children from distant countries given up for adoption by their parents is kept for a long period of time. The Child Care and Protection Boards will endeavour to extend the period during which such information is stored (at present thirty years). Within this group problems sometimes arise with data collected in the past relating to mothers who have put their children up for adoption, once those who provided the information can no longer be found, have reached old age or have died. In such cases the files are often stored privately.

Finally, there is a very small group of cases - that is, small at present - where eggs or embryos have been donated. Such cases are in some ways similar to instances of sperm donation with which this bill is concerned. Egg-cell donation is different at present in that in virtually all cases the donor is known to the woman receiving the fertilised eggs. It is sometimes combined with surrogate motherhood and on occasions it is a relative, for example a sister, who is asked to donate an egg. Embryo donation may also be combined with surrogacy.

D. Evans (ed.), Creating the Child, 211–216.

2. Main Points of the Bill

2.1. HOLDING OF INFORMATION

Information on donors will be kept centrally by the AI Donor Information Centre, which is supplied with data by those carrying out AI. Failure to register such information or to provide it to the Centre will be an offence (Section 13). The obligation to register and provide information rests on every person or institution performing AI, i.e. not only the centre providing AI but, for example, also a general practitioner who collects semen from a centre and offers AI in his practice. The nature of the information concerning the donor which must be provided is described in Section 2, subsection 1. It includes:

1. certain medical information which may be of importance to the child, such as the donor's blood group, or diseases which occur in his family;
2. certain physical characteristics, such as colour of eyes and hair, height, weight, colour of skin and a number of other features as indicated by the donor.

In fact, these are the elements that have been described as a "donor passport". Information on the religious, philosophical or political convictions of the donor is not included. Finally the donor's surname, forenames, date of birth and address are also provided to the Centre. In order to be able to link this information to the biological child of the donor at a later date, the Centre must know the identity of the woman who was inseminated with his semen and on what date. Since many AI centres do not know if insemination has led to a successful pregnancy, it will be necessary to adopt a method whereby information later provided by the child, such as his mother's particulars, his date of birth, details of the birth (e.g. if it was premature) and, for example, his blood group and that of his mother, can be used to identify the biological father. Children who come to the Centre with questions will probably suspect that their fathers - if they have a father in the legal and social sense - are not their biological fathers. In some instances they may in fact know this because their parents have told them. The fact that they have come to the Centre means that this may be taken for granted. They will therefore not be asked to provide proof that they are AI children. It is known that at present, parents rarely tell their children that they were conceived through donor insemination, nor can they be obliged to do so. A number of AI centres discuss the desirability of frankness on this subject with parents, and a number say they will inform the child in due course. Whether they do in fact do so is unknown. It would seem advisable to ensure that parents receive sufficient information and, where necessary, counselling on this subject in the future. In addition to the technical aspects of AI, parents need to know more about how they can inform their child about conception, the donor as a person, and the possible psychological effects of learning about these things. The way in which to tell the child these facts and when could also be discussed. The objective of this bill is also to encourage greater openness with regard to such information.

2.2. PROVISION OF INFORMATION AND COUNSELLING TO PARENTS

The Dutch Parentage Foundation is of the opinion that the provision of information and/or counselling to parents should be made compulsory, as it is to the parents of adopted children. Leaving aside the question of whether the comparison with adoption is a valid one in this context it would not be appropriate to incorporate such an obligation in the present bill. It should be noted that the provision of information to parents constitutes from a medical point of view one of the due care requirements relating to AI laid down in a protocol. The Dutch Health Council suggested that it is important for couples to come to terms with the problem of infertility or subfertility before resorting to AI.[2] This does not prevent emotional problems arising during pregnancy but the prognosis is better. A period of two years between the diagnosis of infertility or subfertility and undergoing AI would seem desirable from the point of view of helping people come to a definitive decision. Such a waiting period would also have the effect of natural selection, as it does in adoption. Furthermore, it may reassure parents that if their child learns how it is conceived it will not regard them any the less as parents. This would also foster openness about donor insemination. The proposal that the AI centre should give the parents information about the donor which provides an idea of what he is like (without revealing his identity) can be regarded in the same light. They can then use this information in bringing up their child, part of which may involve making the child aware of and comfortable about the way in which he was conceived. At present, parents are sometimes given such information. It seems to be useful only if the parents have asked for it and if insemination has resulted in a birth. These conditions are laid down in the bill. If the parents do not ask for such information, the child will be able to do so from the age of twelve. In such cases the parents will also be sent information which does not identify the donor at their request, provided the child has not reached the age of sixteen (Section 3, subsection 4).

2.3. PROVISION OF INFORMATION TO THE CHILD

When a younger AI child comes with questions, he will initially be informed about the physical and other characteristics of the donor. Since the medical details are not of primary importance to the child - after all, what he wants is to form a 'picture' of his biological father - they will not be provided. Should it become necessary to ask for medical details, perhaps because the child is exhibiting otherwise inexplicable symptoms, this may be done through the general practitioner. From experience with adopted children, it would appear that many children who have been able to form an idea of what their parents are like are content with that. The desire to go further and contact the person in question is rarely present in young children. Therefore it is inadvisable to give the name of the donor to children between the ages of twelve and sixteen. If the child later decides that he wishes to know the name of the donor, this may be given with the donor's permission. Should he refuse, and if the child is suffering psychological damage as a result, then it will be possible under the bill to give

the name. Older children and adults will also initially be given only the information which enables them to form an impression of the donor. As in the case of young children, the identity of the donor will only be revealed if he gives his permission, or if vital interests - e.g. of a psychological or physical nature - of the person requesting information would be harmed if it was withheld (Section 3, subsections 1 and 2). Anyone claiming that they are suffering serious harm as a result of not knowing the identity of the donor must provide evidence that this is so. The criterion of 'vital interests' is taken from family law, in which the interests of the child usually determine the decision reached by the court. For example, Article 161a, paragraph 3(c) of Book 1 of the Dutch Civil Code refers to the "vital interests of the child".[3]

It is hardly necessary to state that the identity of the donor will be revealed if he gives his permission. If a minor child of sixteen or over, or a child over eighteen wishes to know who the donor is, the latter will first be contacted and asked for his permission. In situations where the donor has died or cannot be traced, it will be assumed that permission has been refused, and his identity may be revealed only if the child's vital interests require it. This rule is in line with the obligations which, according to the European Court of Human Rights, are imposed on States under article 8 of the European Convention for the Protection of Human Rights and Fundamental Freedoms. These are dealt with in greater detail in the Gaskin judgement.[4]

2.4. THE INTERESTS OF THE CHILD

The assessment of the child's vital interests (which takes place only if the donor refuses permission to reveal his identity, is dead or untraceable) is done initially by the Centre's Board. If the request is dismissed on the grounds that it has not been sufficiently established that the child's vital interests are at stake, the latter may appeal under the Dutch Administrative Decisions Appeals Act (AROB). The anonymous donor may play a role in such appeal proceedings as an interested party. It will be obvious that care must be taken to preserve his anonymitiy at this stage and the donor is permitted to appoint an authorised representative. If the Centre decides that his identity should be revealed, the donor will be promptly informed so that he is able, if he so wishes, to lodge an objection with the Centre, and, if that is dismissed, to appeal under the Administrative Decisions Appeals Act. The objection lodged by the donor may place the child's vital interests in another light. The donor will receive notification of the decision to release the information accompanied by the grounds on which it was taken. He will not of course be informed of the identity of the child at that moment. The notice of the decision will naturally inform the donor that he may lodge an objection. His identity will be revealed only once the period in which an objection may be lodged has expired.

Since learning the identity of the donor may have serious emotional consequences for the child there is an obligation for the Centre to ensure that there is expert assistance available when the information is handed over. This may consist of one or more sessions before the information is given and any follow-up care which may be

necessary, especially if particulars of a personal nature have been passed on. The Centre's duty is to ensure that there is a network of specialists who can take on counselling so that no one in these circumstances will be without assistance. It is not obliged to provide such counselling itself and may make use of existing agencies, such as the social services.

It is assumed that apart from the medical particulars, information concerning a donor will be given personally at the Centre and not through the post (recorded delivery). Use of the mail might lead to the information accidentally falling into the hands of a person other than the addressee.

The request for information made by a minor comes from him and not from his parents acting on his behalf. This is such a personal matter that it seems proper not to provide for representation of the child by the parents or guardian. A request from the parents may be complied with only if the child has already received the information in question and has not yet reached the age of 16. The rules governing the provision of information to parents are largely the same as those incorporated in the bill containing amendments to the Civil Code and other legislation in connection with the incorporation of provisions concerning medical treatment contracts.[5]

The Centre will keep a donor's particulars for eighty years - the average life expectancy in the Netherlands. Such a long period is necessary in order to achieve the aim of registration, i.e. to store and provide information on parentage. As long as the direct biological descendant of the donor is alive, the information must be kept. Requests for information may be made only by AI children and not by their children (with the exception of requests for medical particulars which may be made by a GP).

2.5. OTHER PROVISIONS

The remaining provisions of the bill contain, *inter alia*, rules governing the composition of the Board of the AI Donor Information Centre. It is particularly important that the Board's members be carefully chosen because they have primary responsibility for deciding whether information which will identify donors is to be supplied. Procedures regarding the provision of information will be laid down in the Centre's regulations.

Finally, the transitional arrangements are of great importance. These determine that the information regarding donors and insemination with their semen now held by AI centres and others will be transferred to the Centre. Where this includes medical particulars, these may already be provided according to the procedure laid down in the bill. The government announced a publicity campaign which will inform donors that, following the entry into force of the Act, they will have a year in which to notify the Centre that they do not wish the information relating to them which is stored there to be passed on to the child in question, his parents or others. Should a request be received which relates to a donation made before the Act entered into force, and the donor has notified the Centre as outlined above, the information will not be passed on. If he has not notified the Centre to this effect, he will be asked for his permission. If he refuses, the information will be withheld. Absence of permission due to the death

of the donor or because he cannot be traced is deemed to constitute refusal. In this way the interests of donors who assumed that their anonymity was guaranteed are protected. It was considered whether the transitional arrangements should be based on a questionnaire. However this would have meant that every donor who donated semen before the entry into force of the Act would have been confronted with a letter containing this question. Some of these men will have donated semen long ago and their personal circumstances may have changed. It does not seem right to invade the privacy of donors by asking for permission to reveal their identity to others. In order therefore to protect the privacy of donors as far as possible the bill has chosen to offer them the opportunity to respond to a general appeal to contact the Centre. Since the deciding factor determining whether information is passed on or not will always be the views of the donor before the Act came into force, I think the bill offers sufficient protection of donors' privacy.

3. Conclusion

In my opinion, this bill will create a balanced system for accommodating the wishes of AI children to learn about their biological father. It tries to balance the justifiable wishes of the children concerned against the need to prevent an 'open season' on donors and the public health interest that is served in having an AI system which functions properly.

Notes

1. Regulations governing the storage, management and provision of the personal particulars of donors of semen for artificial insemination. Lower House, 1992-1993, June 18 1993, 23207, nr. 1-2. In November 1995 this draft was still pending in the Lower House. It is questionable if there will ever be a majority for this proposal.

2. Dutch Health Council (Gezomeiheids Raad) *Kimstmatige voorplanting, in het byzomder in vitro Fertilisatie en draagmoederschap* Den Haag, 1986.

3. Dutch Civil Code (Burgenlÿk Wetboek).

4. *Gaskin vs. United Kingdom* 13 November 1987; cf. *Dutch Law Reports* 1991, nr. 659.

5. Lower House, 1990-1991, 21561, nr. 17.

16. ANONYMITY OF THE DONOR IN THE SPANISH ACT ON TECHNIQUES OF ASSISTED REPRODUCTION

Jaime Vidal Martínez
Profesor Titular de Derecho Civil
Departamento de Derecho Civil
Universitat de València
Spain

1. Introduction: The Spanish Act on Techniques of Assisted Reproduction

At the end of 1988, two Acts were published in Spain, concerning Techniques of Assisted Reproduction (ATAR) and the Donation and Utilisation of Embryos and Foetuses, their cells, tissues and organs (Acts 35 and 42 of the 22nd November and 28th December 1988 respectively).[1] These established detailed regulations on the subjects, which, however has remained in need of further statutory development for seven years.[2] The aforementioned Acts were the object of an Appeal before the Constitutional Court in 1989, which is still pending resolution.

The said Acts have as a precedent the Report issued by a Special Commission appointed by the Congress of Deputies (Lower Chamber) in 1986.[3] The Report and the Propositions of the Bill, which led to the present legislation, draw analogies with the Warnock Report.[4] The ATAR regulates the reproductive techniques which have been scientifically and clinically deemed to be suitable and are applied by authorised centres, with the fundamental aim of treating human infertility. However, the techniques can also be used in the prevention and treatment of transmitted diseases, and last, but by no means least, can be authorised for use in research and experimentation using gametes and fertilised ova, which is also controlled by the ATAR. The most important features of this regulation are its use of the concept of the *pre-embryo* which, however, is not defined in the legal text, but only in the preamble of the ATAR[5]; and the possibility it allows of donating human gametes and pre-embryos, using, with legal support, the genetic forces of a third person, who has nothing to do with the relationship of filiation established.[6]

In our opinion, another important aspect of the regulation established by the ATAR, is the anonymity of the donor of the gametes or pre-embryos, to which the following loose translations of legal texts more or less refer:

> The donation of gametes and pre-embryos for the purposes authorised by this Act is a free contract, formal and secret, concluded between the donor and the authorised Centre. (art.5.1)

D. Evans (ed.), Creating the Child, 217–228.

The donation will be anonymous and the details of the identity of the donor will be kept guarded in the strictest secrecy, under combination lock in the respective banks and in the National Register of Donors.

The children born as a result of this process have the right, either themselves or through their legal representatives, to obtain general information regarding the donors, which does not include their identity. The same right is given to the receivers of the gametes.

Only exceptionally, in extraordinary circumstances, which constitute a proved danger to the life of the child, or arise in the course of a judicial inquiry into a criminal practice, can the identity of the donor be revealed, and then only if the said revelation is indispensable in order to avoid the medical danger or to obtain the intended legal purpose. In such cases, it will be carried out in accordance with art. 8, clause 3. The aforementioned revelation will be as limited as possible and will in no circumstances involve the disclosure of the identity of the donor. (art. 5:5)

The revelation of the identity of the donor in alleged legal breaches of (art.5.5.) of this Act, will in no circumstances involve the legal determination of filiation. (art.8.3.)

All the information relative to the utilisation of the ATAR must be collected in individual clinical histories, which must be treated with all the reserves demanded and with the strictest secrecy as regards the identity of the donors, the infertility of the users and the circumstances contributing to the origin of the children born in this way. (art.2.5.)

The government had a legal, bounden duty, within a year of the publication of this Act, to regulate the creation and organisation of a computerised National Register of the donors of gametes and pre-embryos, intended for use in human reproduction, with the essential guarantees of secrecy in the form of combination codes (Final disposition 3).

The National Register will likewise record each child born from the different donors, the identity of the couples or receiving women and, wherever possible, their geographical location at all times. (Final disposition 3a)

With reference to the donation of gametes, the ATAR alludes basically to the donation of semen, because the freezing of ova for assisted reproduction is not authorised, owing to there being insufficient guarantees of the viability of the ova after they have been thawed (art. 11.2.). It forbids the fertilisation of human ova for whatever purpose other than human procreation.[7]

It is worth emphasising that in the context of the ATAR any woman can use these

techniques, provided that she expresses her consent freely, verbally and in writing, is at least 18 years of age and fully fit, physically and mentally, and is aware of all the possible risks (art. 6-1 and art. 2b ATAR). If the woman is married, she must have the consent of her husband and such being the case, neither she nor her husband can contest the filiation of the child born as a result of the application of the ATAR. The single male companion can also give his consent, in an authorised centre, for the fertilising of the woman with donor sperm, and this consent works as a recognition of paternity made in the Register of civil status, although the action for claiming legal paternity remains alive (art. 8, 1-.2 ATAR).[8]

So, the ATAR, by nature an administrative healthcare regulation, is also concerned with questions of paternity and filiation. In the case of surrogacy, it is enacted that such a contract will be completely void; the legal mother will be the woman who gives birth and the biological father can claim legal fatherhood (art.10).[9]

The ATAR consigns the application of sanctions to the General Health Act. Among the most serious breaches is the disclosure of the identity of a donor, except in the exceptions given in ATAR (art 20.2.B.j.). However, and despite detailed regulation, there are many doubts in the interpretation of even the most basic questions, due to faulty drafting (from a legal point of view) of the Act and, in our opinion, because of deep contradictions with constitutional and civil rules and principles, even as regards questions of filiation and the regulation of anonymity of the donor.

2. The Anonymity of the Donor in Techniques of Assisted Reproduction

The legal answer to the numerous questions raised by the new forms of human reproduction has been conditioned by the conception people have of the human being and law. This, together with the concrete valuation people have of the the aims towards which the techniques of reproduction are working, means that there is a desire to favour the utilisation of new methods of human reproduction. Given that in many countries assisted reproduction is qualified not only as that which requires the intervention of medics and embryologists, but also includes the use of the 'genetic forces' of a third person, alien to the relationship of filiation established through artificial insemination or *in vitro* fertilisation (IVF)[10], so the utilisation is judicially defined as a 'donation' of gametes or human embryos, considered as generic things to be traded. It is curious however, that a legal decision demands that a rigid secrecy has to be maintained as to the identity of the 'donor' - leading to his total anonymity.

Some authors locate the origin of the doctrinal construction of anonymity in the analogy with medical practice elsewhere and thus require that a potential semen donor, in case of legal consequences, fills out consent forms for Assisted Insemination (AI) similar to those completed by hospital patients before undergoing surgery, despite the clear differences between the two situations. Medical practitioners were seeking to ensure that the conditions of acceptance were those most convenient to their clients and themselves.[11] The draft Recommendation of the Council of Europe of the 5th March

1979 considered the anonymity of the donor in AI essential[12] in the interests - so the Council argued - firstly of the donors, whose donations otherwise would become practically non-existent, and secondly, supposedly, in the interests of child, ensuring its well-being.[13]

In various reports, drafts and studies, such as the Warnock Report and the Report of the Special Commission appointed by the Congress of Deputies in Spain, the principle of anonymity has been accepted as absolute. Among Spanish commentators and in those of the Latin countries in general, the case of complete anonymity has many prestigious advocates, although there are important exceptions. By contrast, the majority of Germanic authors are opposed to complete anonymity.[14]

A Commission appointed by the Swedish government presented recommendations concerning artificial insemination in September 1983[15], which, setting out from the parallels drawn between children born through AID and adopted children, with respect to knowledge of the identity of the biological father, drew attention to the fact that in Sweden, there were neither organisations to protect, nor studies conducted upon, children born through AID, who, as much as adopted children needed to know their origins, from both psychological and judicial standpoints. In the nuances of this report, however, there is the suggestion that it may be enough for the child simply to have the 'right of disposal' to information concerning their origins, without the need actively to pursue the right.[16]

Another aspect which caused difficulties regarding the child born through AID, was the fact that if there was no law to make a legal father of the man giving consent for fertilisation, then, this man might disclaim parental responsibility for the child at a later date. The German Federal Tribunal, in its judgement of 7th April 1983, reasoned that the question of paternity could not be resolved by a contract or agreement and that filiation could not be governed by private autonomy (arts. 1.593 and following of the BGB).[17]

Subsequently it has been pointed out that a Federal Constitutional Court's judgement of January 31st 1989, regarding the contesting of legitimacy, means that 'the right to know one's parentage' is now recognised as flowing from the general right of personality protected by the Constitution. Some commentators have concluded from the decision that the legislature is obliged to lay down a legal duty to document and to disclose information. Other authors are of the opinion that the decision does not prohibit the anonymity of the sperm donor, but only prohibits the withholding of available information.[18]

The Swedish Act of 24th December 1984[19] allows the married woman or a woman who cohabits with a man under marriage-like conditions, who has the written consent of the cohabiting man, to be inseminated with the sperm of another man, but the Act also states that this applies only when the donor has provided sperm before March 1st 1985. Where the donation has been made after this date, the child born as a result will be entitled to inform himself, on reaching sufficient maturity, of what has been registered in the hospital record regarding the donor of sperm. He or she will be entitled to the full support of the local Social Welfare Board. In a case of controversy

concerning paternity, anyone else with access to information about the donor's identity will be obliged to deliver it to the court on demand.[20] The example set by the Swedish Act was greatly to influence the doctrine on new forms of human reproduction.[21]

In order to widen the study of the question of the anonymity of the donor in AID some authors reason that the maintenance of reserve or secrecy is not the same as anonymity, and that, in the case of AID filiation, there are similarities with adoption - a judicial construction which, moreover, is being constantly modified.[22] The donation of gametes is seen to be a very delicate matter, and the CAHBI (Council of Europe Committee of Experts on Progress in Biomedical Sciences) has recommended that it should be licensed and controlled by a public authority. Where anonymity is concerned, although the majority are in favour of the concept, it is well known that it can prejudice the child born in this way.[23]

Although Acts like the 1988 Spanish Act of TAR have accepted the maintenance of donor anonymity, what is certain is that there are other European countries with wide experience in regulation of TAR which are hesitant to give legal support to anonymity provisions in the medical practices of assisted reproduction. Such was the case in France before the enactment (July 1994) of new biomedical legislation[24], in the United Kingdom[25], and in Germany, whose legislation have not included the concept of donor anonymity.[26] In Switzerland a constitutional amendment was accepted by referendum (17th May, 1992). Article 24 novies, al. 2, lit.g, provides that "a person's access to the data concerning his (or her) ancestry is guaranteed".[27] On the other hand, in some Scandinavian countries (other than Sweden) regulations seem to accept more or less clearly the anonymity of the donor in the practice of AID.[28]

It has been pointed out recently by some Austrian writers that the government bill entitled 'Law on Procreative Medicine (Fortpflanzungsmedizingesetz - FMedG) 1991', in section 20, sets up the child's right to know of the identity of the biological father. This right of information is granted on the same grounds that the German Constitutional Court established in the significant decision of January 31st 1989. Human dignity and the right to develop one's personality demand that the individual know what determines his individuality.[29]

However, questions have been raised about these arguments that the disadvantage in the psychological development of the children who never get to know their biological parents is that they are prevented from making an absolute assessment of their individuality. According to the questioning opinion "the crucial point is that if section 20 FMedG remains unchanged, donor insemination will be shifted abroad and many couples will have to do without this treatment ... . Other legal systems regard donor anonymity as self-evident. The Australian states, Israel, New Zealand, Norway, Spain and the Republic of South Africa have explicitly confirmed this principle". Besides, it is argued, there are practical problems in the regulation of the right to information on one's genetic parentage.[30]

Diverse solutions are suggested for regulation concerning matters between the human being conceived through AID and the biological donor, from total anonymity to the possibility of giving legal paternity (or maternity) to the donor. The following

intermediary positions are also proposed:

(a) giving the child conceived through AID the possibility of knowing biogenetic details about the donor, basically to protect his right to health, but with no further claim on the donor.

(b) allowing the AID child the possibility of knowing the personal identity of the gamete donor, but without any judicial consequences.[31]

Thus, it seems that the Spanish legal opinion, with Constitutional support, is paving the way to recognising the right of the AID child to know the identity of the donor, considering this right as fundamental, while not allowing this knowledge of biological relation to determine the judicial relation. However, it bears in mind the fact that this is not the answer concluded by the TAR Act arts. 5.5 and 8.3, where there may be an Appeal before the Constitutional Tribunal.

Some Spanish authors, on the other hand, have tried to point out the contradiction where, formerly, with the hoped for reform of the right of filiation, an approximation between the law and biological reality was looked for, but latterly, with the T.A.R. openly favouring donor anonymity, there has appeared a dissociation between the biological truth and legal paternity. The donor of semen (or ova) cannot ignore the aims of donation, nor can they be judicially exempt from all responsibility for the act of donation.[32] However, according to other doctrinal stances, the overriding factor in this type of filiation is the will to have a child conceived through AID as one's own, thus considering it to be a social or civil paternity. We must add though that this doctrine avoids the control which must accompany the creation of a legal paternity/maternity.

3. Conclusion

The Spanish Act of TAR repeatedly seeks to impose the anonymity of the donor in AID, maintaining the strictest secrecy surrounding these 'donations'. Under no circumstances, should the Civil Register reflect the fact that a child has been born through TAR (article 7.2 ATAR).

For our part, we have maintained that the anonymity of the donor in AID is an *ad hoc* construction, which, contrary to defending the interests of the people most directly involved - the child and his basic rights - looks fundamentally to the fulfillment of the interests and elimination of responsibilities of the other people involved in AID, thus impeding the child from defending his moral and material rights and interests.[33]

We understand that anonymity of the donor in AID contravenes the rules and principles of the Spanish law, both from a constitutional and civil standpoint, although it has been incorporated in the legal system by an administrative health Act relating to TAR.[34] We think that, according to these rules and principles, the child conceived through AID has the right to know the identity of the donor. First of all because, otherwise, the child is not considered as a person but as a thing, in contradiction with article 10-1 of the Spanish Constitution.[35] Second, because the child has, as every

person, inherent and inviolable rights, among them the right of not being discriminated against (art. 14, S.C.), the right to personal and familiar intimacy (art. 18, S.C.), and the right to know his own origins (in our opinion, the last one can be included in article 10, S.C.). In the third place, donor anonymity contravenes other constitutional principles contained in article 39, S.C. such as the integral protection of children[36], and the possibility of investigating paternity.[37] Finally, but most important, it remains an open question whether or not the Spanish Constitution permits one person to use the 'genetic forces' contained in the germinal cells of another person, whilst at the same time leaving the donor free of all legal links or responsibility.

The legal answer to the problems posed by AID is dependent on many factors. We believe that under no circumstances should there be any juridical decision at the expense of the child, whose interests are paramount according to Civil Law, given that children (and handicapped people) in order to be equal to other citizens, need special protection. Therefore, it seems appropiate to register all details concerning AID, so that the child can demand his rights and, if the need arises, apportion responsibility in the case of malpractice, especially if he is left without a legally determined mother or father. All details registered are subject to the rights of privacy, which imposes reserve, but a different sort of reserve from that of the absolute secrecy imposed by the anonymity of the donor.[38]

According to the Spanish Civil Code (art. 108 C.C.), filiation may be determined naturally or through adoption. The latter seems the more suitable, with necessary adaptation, for resolving problems arising through AID.[39] We think that these techniques in themselves are individualistic and depersonalised, therefore we do not see that there is any reason to favour AID with the donor anonymity. But, on the other hand, basic values, principles and rights such as freedom, the right to the scientific and technical production and creation, the free development of one's personality and maternity protection (arts. 1,10-1, 20, 39, S.C.) oblige the acceptance of the development of the new forms of human reproduction as long as the centre of gravity of the corresponding regulation is placed in the human being, free and responsible, as expressed in the juridical concept of person.[40]

Nowadays, scientific development in new forms of human reproduction shows that the main problems are genetic ones, concerning the human embryo, and the knowledge of human genome. By these human genetic science is achieving an enormous importance which affects many other scientific fields. Therefore, we understand that in the practices known as assisted conception or procreation, particularly in the sophisticated techniques of IVF, it is becoming necessary to protect the dignity and freedom of a person from the moment of the conception of the human being, without trying to transform the freedom to procreate into a 'right to a child', which supposes, among other consequences, a necessary restriction of freedom.[41]

We think that, medical assisted conception, as its name expresses, must try to protect the health of the women involved - and eventually that of their companions - who suffer from pathology in their natural capacity to procreate. In our opinion, only this medical assistance must be encouraged, without turning the medical intervention into a biological

one.[42]

We consider that law should never establish as a civil right the employment of the genetic forces contained in the human germ cells, because we consider these forces to be goods, the objects of personality rights, that cannot be transferred to other people.[43] In our opinion it may be particularly wrong and dangerous to establish a civil right over human embryos, regarding them as a property, because, taking the wider view, only what is truly valuable to the human being is also valuable for society.[44]

Finally, it is possible to argue that, if it is accepted that the consent of a donor in AID represents, from a juridical point of view, not a trade but only a basis to avoid judicial action against the authorised medical centres that employ germinal cells or human embryos, it must also result equally in the preservation all the rights and interests of the children born as a consequence of this type of donation.

In this context, we do not think there should be, in spite of some national legal texts or utilitarian arguments, any room for the juridical construction of blanket donor anonymity in future regulation of assisted conception, but only the protection of confidentiality concerning medical or biological assistance where personal and family intimacy would be adversely and seriously affected.

Notes

1. Published in the State Official Journal, 24 November 1988, and 31 December 1988, respectively.

2. See the final dispositions of the Act of TAR. Neither has it set up the National Commission on Assisted Reproduction (art. 21 ATAR). However, the enactment by two decrees-law of the statutory development forecast in the Act has recently been announced in the Spanish media (*El País* (Madrid) 7 November 1995).

3. *Informe de la Comisión Especial de Estudio de La Fecundación In Vitro y la Inseminación Artificial Humanas* Chairman: M. Palacios, Congress of Deputies, Spain, 10 April, 1986.

4. A decision of the Barcelona Territorial Court of Appeal of 12 November 1990, recognised the Warnock Report as a precedent of ATAR.

5. Group of cells resulting from the progressive division of the ovum, from fertilisation until approximately fourteen days later.

6. The expression 'genetic forces' was used by French legal commentator, Professor Cornu. Considering the genetic forces as goods of personality makes the possibility of transmission doubtful, at least from the point of view of the Spanish Constitution (cf. J. Vidal Martínez, *Las nuevas formas de reproducción humana: Estudio desde la perspectiva del Derecho Civil español* Madrid, Universitat de València, Editorial Civitas S.A., 1988. It is recognised however in the Spanish Act of TAR (art. 5) without any judicial intervention, and in an important part of the views of many, the undertaking of the contract relating to gametes and pre-embryos is also accepted.

7. Nevertheless, according to a recent newspaper article, a TAR centre in Barcelona solicited the donation of ova by means of financial compensation.

8. The insemination of a single woman (allowed implicitly, and it seems, in practice, in Spain) leaves the child with no legal father, and no possibility of knowing who his or her biological father is.

9. The Catalan Act of filiation (27 April 1991), which was also subject to an Appeal before the Constitutional Court, regulates also filiation in assisted procreation. A basic principle in Catalan law is that of permitting the child to investigate paternity and maternity. All children must, if possible, have a father and a mother (biological or juridical-social parenthood).

10. The 'assistance' received consists, in these cases, of the utilisation of alien genetic elements (semen, ova) or of human embryos obtained with those elements through the techniques of IVF. Some authors reason that the whole *raison d'être* of TAR resides in the substitution of the necessary faulty element or mechanism. Rivero Hernández, F. 'La investigación de la mera relación derivada de la fecundación artificial' in Gobierno Vasco, *II Congreso Mundial Vasco. La filiación a finales del siglo XX. Problemática planteada por los avances científicos en materia de reproducción humana* Departamento de Derecho Privado, Universitat del País Vasco, Madrid, Editorial Trivium S.A., 1988, pp.141-168, p.146.

11. Delgado Echeverría, J. 'Los consentimientos relevantes en la fecundación asistida. En especial, el determinante de la asunción de una paternidad que no corresponde' in *II Congreso Mundial Vasco (op.cit.)* pp.201-229, p.209 (quoting from Annas, George J., 'Fathers anonymous: beyond the best interest of the sperm donor' *Family Law Quarterly* 1980, p.6).

12. Pantaleón Prieto, F. 'Procreación artificial y responsabilidad civil' *II Congreso Mundial Vasco (op.cit.)* pp.295-317, p.296 points out the fact, quoting the opinion of Giesen (in 'Heterologe insemination - ein neues legislatorisches Problem?' *Zeitschrift fuer das gesamte Familienrecht* 1991, p.414) that the radical acceptance of the anonymity of the donor in the said draft was the result of a medical pressure group, concerned with the said practice.

13. Ruiz Vadillo 'Aspectos jurídicos de la inseminación artificial con semen de dador' in Marino, Simón and Portuondo, José Angel (eds), *Clínica Ginecológica* Salvat Editores, 1980, pp.113-147, p.117.

14. Cf. Rivero Hernández, *op.cit.*, pp.155-156.

15. Cf. Ewerlöf, G., 'Swedish legislation on Artificial Insemination' in *II Congreso Mundial Vasco, op.cit.*, pp.65-83, p.68.

16. *Ibid.*, pp.73-79.

17. Stoll, Hans and Fischer, Peter, 'Evolución del derecho privado aleman durante los años 1981, 2, 3' in *Revista de Derecho Privado* June, 1985.

18. Rainer, Frank, 'Federal Republic of Germany: new problems, new solutions' *Journal of Family Law.* 29 (2), 1990-1991, pp.375-6. See also Rainer, Frank, 'Germany: blood versus "mere" social ties' *University of Louisville Journal of Family Law* 32 (2), 1993-4, pp.335-344.

19. The Swedish Act was published on 22 December 1985.

20. See articles 4 and 5 of the Swedish 1984 Act. Cf. Ewerlöf, G., 'Swedish legislation of artificial insemination' in *II Congreso Mundial Vasco, op.cit.*, p.83.

21. At the end of the Report of the first day of work at the *Colloque Génétique, Procréation et Droit*, Professor Carbonnier pointed out that the doctrine of anonymity of the donor was being abandoned in the USA and above all in Sweden. 'Du Nord, la lumière?' *Actes du Colloque. Génétique, Procréation et Droit* Arles, Actes Sud, Hubert Nyssen, Editeur, 1985, p.84.

22. Labrusse-Riou, Catherine, 'Don et utilisation de sperme et d'ovocites' in *Actes du Colloque. Génétique, Procréation et Droit*, *op.cit.*, pp.255-276, p.266.

23. Hondius, F.W., 'The Council of Europe's contribution to solving problems raised by human artificial procreation' in *II Congreso Mundial Vasco*, *op.cit.*, pp.51-62, p.61.

24. Law number 94-653 of 29 July. Professor Claire Neirinck considers that the French Bills concerning biomedical ethics that establish anonymity of the gamete's donor reinforced by criminal offences, do not take account of the international commitments of France, as long as article 7 of the United Nations Convention establishes the child's right to know his parents and be brought up by them, if possible. Professor Neirink finds it difficult to admit that the French legislator is authorised to create an impediment to the child's knowing his origins. 'Commentaires des projets de lois relatifs à l'éthique biomedicale' *Les Petites Affiches* n° 75, 22 Juin 1992, p.7.

25. In line with the *Human Fertilisation and Embryology Act 1990*, a licensing body has been established concerned with the storage of gametes and embryos (the Human Fertilisation and Embryology Authority, HFEA) that is charged with maintaining a register of information concerning donors, treatment services and children born following the use of licensed services producing advice and information to centres and publishing a code of practice. Cf. Morgan, Derek, and Nielsen, Linda, 'Dangerous liaisons? Law, technology, reproduction and european ethics' in McVeigh, Shaun (ed.), *Law, Health and Medical Regulation* Aldershot, Dartmouth, 1992, p.57.

26. The German Act on the protection of the embryo does not include an exception right to oppose paternity of the husband who gave consent for the artificial procreation of the child of his wife. Cf. Deutsch, Erwin, 'The fetus in Germany. The Fetus Protection Law of 12.13.1990' *International Journal of Bioethics* 3 (2), 1992, pp.85-93, p.88. The German Bill guarantees the child - on demand - a right to receive information about the identity of his biological father on reaching maturity. See Bernat, Erwin, 'Regulating the artificial family: an Austrian compromise' *International Journal of Bioethics* 3 (2), 1992, pp.103-108, p.106.

27. Guillod, Olivier, 'Switzerland: everyone has the right to know his or her origins!' *University of Louisville Journal of Family Law* 32 (2), 1993-4, pp.465-474.

28. In Denmark donor anonymity is secured by administrative fiat, through the way in which the public donor bank functions; the child is not entitled to be informed of the identity of the father, nor of the fact that donor insemination has taken place. In Norway the principle of anonymity has been legally enshrined. However in Sweden the position is different. Cf. Morgan and Nielsen, *op.cit.*, p.61.

29. Bernat, Erwin, and Straka, Ulrike, 'Austria: a legal ban on surrogate mothers and fathers?' *University of Louisville Journal of Family Law* 31 (2), 1992-3, pp.267-282, p.279. Erwin Bernat considers the child's right to know his or her genetic roots in 'Austria: legislating for assisted reproduction and interpreting the ban on corporal punishment' *University of Louisville Journal of Family Law* 1993-4, pp.201ff.

30. Bernat and Straka, *op.cit.*, pp.280-282.

31. Rivero Hernández, *op.cit.*, p.154.

32. Delgado Echeverría, *op.cit.*, p.213.

33. We faced the question of the anonymous donor in AID in our study 'Las nuevas formas de reproducción humana: introducción y panorama general' *Revista General de Derecho* September 1986, pp.3685-3739 and later in our study *Las nuevas formas de reproducción humana: Estudio desde la perspectiva del Derecho Civil español*, *op.cit.*, pp.33 *et seq.*

34. The general characteristics of the TAR Act are stated in our study 'Choix de sexe: commentaire d'une décision judiciaire appliquant la loi spagnole sur les techniques de réproduction assistée' *International Journal of Bioethics* 3 (1), 1992, pp.5-12. Also recently in our comparative study with other European regulations on IVF 'Algunos datos y observaciones para contribuir a la consideración jurídica del embrión humano concebido *in vitro*' in *Estudios de Derecho Civil en homenaje al profesor Dr. José Luis Lacruz Berdejo* Vol. II, Barcelona, J.M. Bosch, 1993, pp.2077-2105.

35. Article 10-1 S.C. says: "the dignity of the person, the inviolable rights that are inherent to the person, the free development of personality, the observance of law and of other people's rights, are the ground of political order and social peace".

36. Marina Pérez Monge, from Zaragoza University, in her study 'El anonimato del dador en las técnicas de reproducción asistida: problemas de constitucionalidad en nuestro derecho' presented to the Symposium Europeo de Bioética, Santiago de Compostela, May 1993, considers that the ATAR 1988 breaks article 39.2 of the Spanish Constitution on paternity investigation and perhaps articles 10, 14, 15 and 39.3 S.C. We thank her for sending us a copy of this study.

37. The Spanish Constitutional Court in its decision of 17 January 1994 (published 17 February) considers it a child's basic right ("derecho primario"), in the protection of his or her interest, material and moral, to know his or her filiation when a blood test with a view to determining filiation has been ordered by the courts.

38. The Spanish Constitution considers fundamental the "derecho a la intimidad personal y familiar" (art. 18), a right which is different in profile from the 'right to privacy' in the USA. Vidal Martínez, J., *El derecho a la intimidad en la L.O. 5-5-82* Madrid, Editorial Montecorvo, 1984, pp.39-40.

39. The Tribunal of the "grande instance de Tolouse" in 1987, ordered a heavy fine to be paid to the benefit of the child, where a man consented to the AID of his companion and then later opposed his paternity. Mme Professor Rubellin-Devichi comments on this sentence, considering adoption to be the best way to give paternity to an AID child (*Revue Trimestrelle de Droit Civil* 4, 1987).

40. In our opinion *person* is the human being considered in a social context, and the capital article 10.1 S.C. is inspired by articles 1 and 2 of the German Basic Law. This article invokes the doctrine of ethical personalism inspired by Kant's philosophical system. Cf. Vidal Martínez, J., 'Algunas observaciones acerca del concepto de persona y de los derechos que le son inherentes (art. 10.1 Constitución Española), desde la óptica del Derecho Civil' in *Estudios en recuerdo de la profesora Sylvia Romeu Alfaro* Vol. II, Valéncia, Universitat de València, 1989, pp.1033-1045.

41. We argue for this in our *Communiqué à la 2ème rencontre internationale du groupe de Milazzo (Génétique)* Juillet 1991. Also, in *Revista General de Derecho* Sección de Derecho y Bioética, March 1993, pp.1941-42.

42. We argue for this in our 'Communication to the Plenary Meeting of the European Research Project, Fertility, Infertility and the Human Embryo' (Barcelona, 21-24 October 1994).

43. We support this juridical thesis of the existence of *inherent* basic rights (art. 10.1 S.C.) and particularly, in the article 1.3 of the Spanish Act 5-5 1982 protecting the right to honour, intimacy and control over images of oneself, that establishes in its context that these rights cannot be transferred to other people although consent to transfer may be an estoppel if there is later a claim.

44. This will be, in our opinion, a juridical instrument for stopping 'la poussée vers la chosification de l'humain' expressed by Dr. Jean Martin in *Enjeux Éthiques en Santé Publique* Genève, Médecine et Higiène, 1991, p.40, which follows clearly nowadays in assisted conception, but without restricting the basic freedom to procreate nor setting up rigid legal regulations that can hardly fit an ever-changing scientific and social context.

17. ASSISTED REPRODUCTION AND PARENT-INFANT BONDING

How Do New Reproductive Technologies Affect Parent-Infant Bonding and Our Understanding of the Family?

Karoly Schultz
Consultant Paediatrician
Tolna County Teaching Hospital
Department of Paediatrics
Szekszard, Hungary

1. Introduction

Many different opinions have been expressed about the ethical problems linked to assisted reproduction, but very few have addressed the problem: How do these reproductive technologies affect parent-infant bonding which is so important for normal harmonised family life.

The attachment between parent and newborn is a very complicated matter which has been extensively studied in the past two decades in the paediatric literature.[1] There has been an increased recognition and a greater appreciation of the importance of parent-infant bonding in Hungary, especially in the last few years. Paediatricians have recognised that this bonding is central to healthy family development. The increasing knowledge and technology in the care of sick infants has, in recent years, resulted in the development of neonatology and intensive care nurseries which have contributed further to the isolation of mother from newborn and family members from one another.

In children's hospitals, concern about protecting patients from contagious disorders has led to what today appear to be bizarre policies of isolation and separation. But now a critical re-examination of these practices is taking place and new directions helping the development of early parent-infant attachment are being charted.

The importance of mother-infant attachment has become the focus of perinatal care in Hungary. This means careful management of the pregnant woman and her husband during pregnancy, natural childbirth, early mother-infant contact (starting immediately after delivery), rooming-in for the mother and infant for the early postnatal period, and liberal visiting hours at the hospital for family members.

2. Parent-infant Bonding

The bonding of parents to their children may is a very strong human tie. According to

D. Evans (ed.), Creating the Child, 229–238.
© *1996 Kluwer Law International. Printed in the Netherlands.*

Klaus and Kennell this relationship has two distinctive characteristics.

> First, before birth, the individual infant gestates within a part of the mother's body and, second, after birth she ensures his survival while he is utterly dependent on her and until he becomes a separate individual.[2]

In the course of our professional activities, paediatricians have the opportunity to observe the mothers of healthy infants as well as those separated from sick infants. Two of the main questions which arise from these observations are: 'What is the normal process by which parents become attached to their infants?' and 'What triggers or disturbs a parent's bond to his or her infant?'

To answer these questions we may gather information from various sources, from clinical observations and from naturalistic observations of parenting. From such observations we can then piece together the components of the bonding process between a mother and her infant, and determine the factors that may influence its formation.

A number of events are important to the formation of the mother-infant bond.[3]

Prior to pregnancy:
  planning the pregnancy.
During pregnancy:
  confirming the pregnancy;
  accepting the pregnancy;
  the acceptance of the coming infant by the partner, and the support of the partner;
  foetal movement;
  beginning to accept the foetus as an individual.
Labour.
Birth.
After birth:
  seeing the baby;
  touching the baby;
  giving care to the baby;
  accepting the infant as a separate individual;

2.1. PRIOR TO PREGNANCY (THE IMPORTANCE OF THE FAMILY AS A MODEL FOR MOTHERING)

Child development literature suggests that children use adults, especially loved and powerful adults, as models for their own behaviour. Adults may respond to how they themselves were mothered, or what they observed. That is, long before a woman herself becomes a mother, she has learned through observation, play and practice a repertoire of mothering behaviours. Women will unconsciously repeat these learned behaviours when they become parents. So, the way a woman was raised greatly influences her behaviour toward her own infant.

An important example is the observation that, often, mothers who batter their children

were beaten when they were young. Hall *et al*[4] studied women who had come from disrupted families. Where one, or both, of the mother's parents had died, or her parents had divorced or separated, single mothers interacted significantly less with their babies than women whose parents were alive and the whole family was together.

2.2. PREGNANCY (THE FAMILY DURING PREGNANCY)

A woman experiences developmental changes during her pregnancy. These changes are physical and emotional changes within herself and the sensation of the growth of the foetus in her uterus. These changes can vary widely according to whether she planned the pregnancy, is married or single, is living with the father or not, and her desire for a baby.

During the first stage of pregnancy a woman realises that she will be a mother. The second stage of pregnancy starts with the feeling of foetal movement, at which point the mother becomes aware of the fact that her baby is in the uterus as a separate individual.

The acceptance of the coming infant by the father, and the support of the father, is extremely important during pregnancy. Positive marital relationships affect the woman's attitudes during pregnancy and the first year of motherhood, and positively affects parent-infant bonding. (The infant's mental development was greater at 1 year of age when the father was more satisfied with his marriage and supported his wife during pregnancy, according to research carried out by Grossmann.[5])

Lumley[6] explored the feelings of 30 Australian primigravidae during their pregnancies, and found that the feelings of bonding were inhibited when the woman's husband was not interested in the foetus, or when the husband did not provide his wife with emotional support. It is important to point out that the father and the extended family are of vital importance to the early development of parental bonding.

2.3. LABOUR, BIRTH AND BONDING (CONSTANT SUPPORT OF A WOMAN BY HER HUSBAND, BIRTH ENVIRONMENT, EARLY CONTACT WITH THE NEWBORN BABY)

The events of labour and birth also affect the woman's early perceptions of, and interactions with, her infant. The woman's birth experience is the second most significant variable predicting the variance of maternal attachment. At the present time, sweeping and fundamental changes in maternity practices relating to labour, birth and the early postnatal period are under way in Hungary. These changes have already taken place in the western European countries over the last ten years. The following is a list of some of the practices presently undergoing change. These practices all affect the process of parent-infant bonding.

- Constant support of a woman during labour (husband, family member).
- Birth environment (home births vs hospital births).
- Early contact with the newborn (in the delivery room).
- Rooming-in for the mother and infant in the early postnatal days.

Hospital policies in Hungary in the recent past did not permit any family member or friend to be present in the labour and delivery rooms, apparently as a consequence of strict hygiene rules and the limitation of space.   But this practice appears to be changing.   Anthropologists studied 150 different human cultures, and showed that, during labour, usually a family member (both grandmothers, the husband and occasionally the father-in-law or a friend - usually a woman) remained with the mother.[7] But studies have shown that not all companions are equal[8]; a husband, for example, might make a better support person during labour and birth, than a stranger.   The continuous support provided by the husband to his wife in labour, will positively affect the developing mother-infant and father-infant bonding, so that when the infant is born, at the same time, a 'new family' is born.   In sharp contrast to the woman who delivers in the hospital, the woman giving birth at home seems to be in control, is an active participant, immediately picks up the infant after birth and breast feeding starts within five minutes.   All these elements are important in the developing attachment to the infant.   Caesarean section, premature birth and the early separation of the infant from the mother, increases anxiety and later depression in the mother and negatively affects the bonding process.

2.4. THE EARLY POSTNATAL PERIOD (ROOMING-IN FOR THE MOTHER AND INFANT)

The early postnatal period (the first days of life) is a very sensitive period for parent-infant contact.   In many biological disciplines, these moments have been called 'sensitive periods', 'vulnerable points', or 'susceptible periods', which may alter the parents' later behaviour with that infant.[9]

During this enigmatic period, complex interactions between mother and infant help to lock them together.   (This must be distinguished from another sensitive time later in the first year, during which the infant establishes a stable, affectionate relationship with his mother.)   There are several studies supporting the hypothesis that close contact between the mother and full term infant in the first minutes, hours and days of life, alters the quality of the maternal-infant bond over time.[10]   Studies of the effects of rooming-in (in which the mother and infant are kept together in the hospital room) have also confirmed the importance of contact during the early postnatal days.[11]   Mothers who have rooming-in are more confident, more competent in caregiving, less anxious, more sensitive to the crying of their infants, and more attached to their own infants, than mothers who do not have rooming-in.

3. Assisted Reproduction and Parent-Infant Bonding

Assisted reproduction technologies do not cure a disease or solve the medical problem of infertility.   Rather, they circumvent the problem.   These procedures can tremendously influence the stages of the physiological parent-infant bonding process

described above. They can produce disruption of the harmony of family life. These disruptions are unavoidable in some forms or methods of artificial reproduction. These forms and methods are:

1. gamete (egg or sperm) donation;
2. embryo donation;
3. surrogacy (surrogate motherhood).

3.1. EGG (OVA) DONATION

This technique may be used when the woman suffers from an ovarian disease or genetic disorder. The donor is often a sister or a close friend of the recipient, because egg cryopreservation (freezing and storing frozen eggs) is problematic. The procedure may lead to several ethical problems concerning parent-infant bonding and the family. The mother, not being the genetic mother, may feel that the child is less hers than her husband's (if the husband is the genetic father). If another family member is the donor (a sister for instance) then the fact that the she is known as the biological mother within the family may later create uneasy feelings among family members. It is important to note that where donor eggs are used, the husband's support before and during pregnancy and at birth, and the fact that the gestating mother will experience pregnancy and will deliver the baby may help in the development of a normal mother-infant and father-infant bonding.

3.2. SPERM DONATION

Sperm donation may be used when the husband is sterile or has significantly reduced fertility or suffers from a hereditary disease. The child is biologically the wife's, and legally the couple's. In this case, cryopreserved sperm can be used from unknown donors. In this situation, the husband may feel that the child is less his than his wife's (who is the genetic mother). The husband may experience a sense of inadequacy. This might form a threat to the marriage, or lead to less support from the husband during pregnancy and at birth, and negatively influence the father-infant bonding process.

3.3. EMBRYO DONATION

This technique is used where both members of a couple are infertile. The embryo is a result of *in vitro* fertilisation of donor egg and donor sperm. The main argument for embryo donation is that it allows an infertile couple to have a baby, and experience the whole process of planning the pregnancy, carrying the developing foetus, and giving birth.

But it embodies many of the most important problems that arise from egg or sperm donation. How may the fact that the legal parents are neither of them the genetic parents of the infant affect parent-infant bonding? This situation can be viewed as a form of adoption (prenatal adoption).

3.4. SURROGACY

This is a reproductive technique in which a woman (the surrogate mother) carries a
baby for another woman (the rearing, social or legal mother). It is used where the
rearing mother has no uterus or suffers from difficult pathological conditions which
prevent pregnancy. The embryo is a result of *in vitro* fertilisation of donor egg and
donor sperm. In this case the legal parents may not be the genetic parents of the infant,
and (in any case) they do not experience the pregnancy or the birth process. Surrogacy
may also be viewed as a form of child adoption, then. This situation is the most
controversial from the ethical point of view, and raises questions about the bonding
process. How do feelinqs of attachment to the infant develop in the genetic, the
surrogate and in the rearing mothers?

4. Artificial Reproduction and the Family

There are many opponents of *in vitro* fertilisation and they express concerns about its
effect on the family. These concerns centre mainly on surrogacy arrangements. The
Roman Catholic Church, for instance, has said that "the practice of surrogate
motherhood is a threat to the stability of the family".[12]

4.1. THE MEANING OF 'FAMILY'

Before we try to analyse the consequences of new reproductive practices for the family,
let us answer the questions: 'What is our understanding of the family?' and 'What are
the determinants of the meaning of family?' Ruth Macklin gives a simple and objective
definition of the biological concept of family: "people who are genetically related to
one another constitute a family, with the type and degree of relatedness described in the
manner of a family tree".[13] Carol Levine gives us a broader definition: "families
should be broadly defined to include, besides the traditional biological relationships,
those committed relationships between individuals which fulfill the functions of
family".[14] Although the biological concept gives a very precise definition of what a
family is, it fails to capture other significant determinants of the meaning of family.
According to Macklin, in addition to the biological meaning, there appear to be three
chief determinants of what is meant by family.[15] These are: law, custom, and
subjective intentions. All three contribute to our understanding of the family.

4.2. THE MEANING OF MOTHERHOOD

The once simple concept of mother has been changed by the new artificial reproduction
techniques. *In vitro* fertilisation separates the process of producing eggs from the act
of gestation. Two different women to make a biological ccntribution to the creation of
a new life. The woman who provides the eggs (the egg donor) should properly be

called the genetic mother (a biological mother). The woman who contributes her womb during gestation should be called the gestational mother (or surrogate mother). She also is a biological mother. And further confusing the meaning of motherhood there is a 'third mother' (the rearing mother) who 'ordered' the pregnancy and the child, but who makes no contribution biologically to the creation of the new life.

So, which criterion should be used to determine who the 'real' mother is? Now that medical technology has separated the two biological contributions (producing eggs and gestation) to motherhood, some decisions will have to be made. It must be decided whether this technological advance calls for new terminology of motherhood.

The ethical question raised by the separation of the biological contribution to motherhood into genetic and gestational components is: Who has the weightiest moral claim to the baby after its birth in case of dispute, the genetic or the gestational mother?

The question may be answered in two different ways.

According to the first answer, the gestating woman (the surrogate mother) is the primary mother because the criterion is gestation. This position is adopted by George Annas and Elias, who have argued on the basis of "the greater biological and psychological investment of the gestational mother in the child".[16] A related reason is

> the biological reality that the mother at this point has contributed more to the child's development, and that she will of necessity be present at birth and immediately thereafter to care for the child.[17]

The related reason focuses on the interests of the child and also focuses on the importance of parent-infant bonding in this sensitive period.

In the second answer, the genetic contribution is viewed as determinative for motherhood, and the woman who makes the genetic contribution is the primary mother. There are two moral reasons that could be invoked in support of this position. The first stems from the notion that people 'own' their own genetic products, and it reflects the desire of each individual to have genetically related chidren. The second reason for assigning greater weight to the genetic contribution is a concern for the child. It is said to be in children's best interests to be reared by parents to whom they are genetically related.[18]

4.3. SURROGATE MOTHERS

Giving up their child may lead to profound emotional trauma and lasting consequences for surrogate mothers similar to those experienced by women who have given their babies up for adoption. Phyllis Chesler, who has written about custody battles in which mothers have lost their children to fathers, reports that many women never get over having given up their child for adoption.[19]

4.4. CHILDREN

There is very little data on the effects of artificial reproductive practices on children. Children born from surrogacy arrangements may have a greater of developing psychological problems than others. There is evidence from clinical studies indicating that adopted children seem more prone to mental and emotional disorders than non-adopted children.[20]

Snowden *et al* followed up 500 couples and their children produced by AID.[21] Normal, harmonious family life was observed by these authors, and most of the children's physical and psychological development was normal. Sudik pointed out that strict anonymity of a sperm donor is of vital importance for the wellbeing of the whole family; the couple must accept the child as wholly their own child.[22]

In contrast, the Swedish law[23] states that the child has the right to know not only the fact that he or she was conceived by AID, but also the identity of the donor.

5. Conclusion

The questions about how assisted reproduction techniques disturb parent-infant bonding can be answered from a wide range of sources of information. These include clinical observations during medical care procedures, naturalistic long term observations of parenting, and structured interviews with parents of infants born from pregnancies originated by these procedures.

Finally, the question arises as to whether, if the negative consequences of IVF techniques alter the traditional conceptions of the family, we have reasons for abolishing them. I think we need a great deal more evidence on a much larger scale before the conclusion can soundly be reached that artificial insemination procedures have such negative consequences for the family.

Notes

1. Cf. Klaus, M.H. and Kennell, J.H., *Parent-Infant Bonding* Toronto, C.V. Mosby Company, 1982; Klaus, M.H. and Kennel, J.H., 'Care of the mother, father, and infant' in Fanaroff, A.A. and Martin, R.J. (eds), *Behrman's Neonatal-Perinatal Medicine* Toronto, C.V. Mosby Company, 1983, pp.240-253; Jonsen, A.R., 'The ethics of pediatric medicine' in Rudolph, A.M. and Hoffman, J.I.E. (eds), *Pediatrics* Norwalk, Appleton, 1987, pp.9-16; Campbell, A.G.M., 'Ethical problems in neo-natal care' in Roberton, N.R.C. (ed.), *Textbook of Neonatology* Edinburgh, Churchill Livingstone, 1992, pp.43-48; Richards, M.P.M. 'Psychological aspects of neonatal care' in *ibid.*, pp.29-42.

2. Klaus and Kennell (1982), *op.cit.*, p.3.

3. The following account is taken from Klaus and Kennell (1983), *op.cit.*, p.241.

4. Hall, F., Pawlby, S.J. and Wolkind, S., 'Early life experiences and later mothering behaviour: a study of mothers and their 20-week old babies' in Shaffer, D. and Dun, J. (eds), *The First Year of Life* New York, John Wiley and Sons Inc., 1980, pp.77-89.

5. Grossman, F.K., *Pregnancy, Birth and Parenthood* San Francisco, Jossey-Bass Inc., 1980.

6. Lumley, J., 'The development of maternal-foetal bonding in first pregnancy' in Zichellen, L. (ed.), *Proceedings of the 5th International Congress in Psychosomatic Medicine in Obstetrics and Gynecology* New York, Academic Press, 1980, pp.5-13.

7. Raphael, D., unpublished data cited in Klaus and Kennell (1982), *op.cit.*, p.25.

8. Klaus, M.H., Kennell, J.H. and Soss, R., 'Child health and breast feeding: the effect of a supportive woman (doula) during labor and the effect of early suckling' (abstract) *Pediatric Research* 1981, 15, p.450.

9. Klaus and Kennell (1982), *op.cit.*, p.38.

10. Cf. Klaus and Kennell (1982) and (1983), both *op.cit.*.

11. Cf. McBryde, A., 'Compulsory rooming-in in the ward and private newborn service at Duke Hospital' *Journal of the American Medical Association* 145, 1951, pp.625-628; and Greenberg, M., Rosenberg, I. and Lind. J., 'First mothers rooming-in with their newborns: its impact on the mother' *American Journal of Orthopsychiatry* 43, 1973, pp.783-788.

12. Bolan, W.F., (Executive director New Jersey Catholic Conference) 'Statement of New Jersey Catholic Conference in connection with public hearing on surrogate mothering' *Commission on Legal and Ethical Problems in the Delivery of Health Care* Newark, N.J., 11 May 1988.

13. Macklin, R., 'Artificial means of reproduction and our understanding of the family' *Hastings Center Report* 21, 1991, pp.5-11, p.6.

14. Levine, C., 'AIDS and changing concepts of family' *Milbank Quarterly* 68, Suppl. 1, 1990, pp.35-37, p.36.

15. Macklin, *op.cit.*, p.6.

16. Elias, S. and Annas, G.J., 'Noncoital reproduction' *Journal of the American Medical Association* 255, 3 January 1986, pp.66-69, p.67.

17. Annas, G.J., 'Redefining parenthood and protecting embryos' in Annas, G.J., *Judging Medicine* Clifton, N.J., Humana Press, 1988, p.59.

18. Cf. Macklin, *op.cit.*, p.6.

19. Chesler, Phyllis, cited in *ibid.*, p.10.

20. For instance, Brodzinsky, D.M., 'Adjustment to adoption: a psychosocial perspective' *Clinical Psychology Review* 7, 1987, pp.29-31.

21. Snowden, R., Mitchell, G.D. and Snowden, E.M., *Artefizielle Reproduktion* (Bucherei des Frauenarztes Bd. 18) Stuttgart, Ferdinand Enke Verlag, 1985, p.15.

22. Sudik, R., 'Entwicklungstendenzen in der reproduktionsmedizin' *Zentralblatt für Gynekologie* 110, 1988, pp.129-137.

23. Swedish Governmental Committee Report, *Children Conceived by Artificial Insemination* (Law 1139) Stockholm, 1985.

PART FOUR

The Need for Regulation

18. PRIORITISING ASSISTED CONCEPTION SERVICES: A PUBLIC HEALTH PERSPECTIVE

Dr Jean Martin
Médecin cantonal (Cantonal Medical Officer)
Lecturer at the Faculty of Medicine
Cité-Devant 11, CH - 1014 Lausanne, Switzerland

1. Introduction: At a Juncture of Values

A society holds together by the rules that people are bound to obey. Human behaviour varies surprisingly from country to country and from era to era. But however bizarre it may appear to the outsider, it must always follow the constraints of biological reality. The trouble with science is that it changes biological reality.[1]

Health policymaking is always, and inescapably, an evaluative task. It is not only that value systems inevitably creep in to bias decision-makers, although they do. It is rather that policymaking logically requires a system of values. In large part those values are determined by culture.[2]

These quotations evoke well the context of the issues raised by assisted conception and related health care seen from a public health point of view. The questions which need to be addressed are related to several values and functioning rules to which Western societies are attached. These are some of the areas in which such questions arise:
- The role and structure of the family.
- The importance of filiation/descendance and its implications for property rights and their transmission.
- The happiness of having children, commonly referred to as the 'wealth of the parents and the nation'. This aspect has lost weight with the social evolution of recent decades and other enjoyments/pursuits/consumptions are sometimes preferred now. But having children remains a strong motivation, especially, it seems, among people who have difficulties begetting them.
- The right of individuals to maximise their wellbeing, as long as it is through licit means and does not infringe on the rights of others. With respect to this right, however, there are questions to be asked: Does the existence of a desire imply that it is legitimate (see below)? Or does the right not to have children (contraception, liberalisation of abortion, access to sterilisation) imply a right to have children whatever the circumstances?

D. Evans (ed.), Creating the Child, 241–253.

- The high esteem in which people hold scientific research and, more generally, progress. And, in spite of some serious questioning, the reluctance to put limits to researchers' freedom (even though some such limits now exist, for example in experimental genetics).
- The professional freedom of physicians, especially as regards choice of treatments (with the informed consent of the patient) and their liberty to accept (or decline) to treat a given person.
- The entrepreneurial freedom to act, to undertake, to trade.
- A certain Welfare State philosophy and/or practice as regards the role of the public hand in the health and social field. Yet, in a context where available monies do not grow as they used to, or even regress, it is imperative to make choices, which means some kind of rationing, preferably based on relevant, generally acceptable and mutually discussed criteria. In this regard, to what extent should public resources be used for debatable needs or optional care?
- From the same perspective, but more broadly, one has to consider the competition, in the public and private/household budgets, between health care, on the one hand, and other activities and sectors, which also have their own legitimacy, on the other. Should one sacrifice everthing else to health?

2. How Much Legislation? Which Legislation?

We consider here the role of the health authority, i.e. the competent Ministry of Health, which among other things has to present a budget and to judge whether to submit legal proposals to Parliament. The following excerpt of the Report of a Working Party of the Council for Science and Society (London) summarises the attitude we would have in Switzerland too:

> The appropriate regulation of the practices with which this report has been concerned is of two distinct kinds: a) Professional regulation as expressed by the codes of practice of the professional bodies. b) Regulation through the processes of the law. The former is preferable when medical practitioners have to decide what is for the best in the light of their patients' differing circumstances. It may also be preferable when the attitudes of society are changing so quickly that any new statute created by Parliament would quickly become outdated. Furthermore the law should be used sparingly in matters which concern people's private lives - if only because statutes which are unenforceable tend to bring the law into disrepute.[3]

3. The Roles of the Public Hand as Health Authority

When studying how the provision of assisted conception relates to the State's major areas of responsibilities, it is appropriate to recall what these are in the health field (I

am referring to the way they are seen in a context such as that of Switzerland):

3.1. CONTROL AND REGULATION OF HEALTH SERVICES

The mandate here is to insure 'good order' within the health system, in relation to:

- Credentials and competence of licensed/registered practitioners, disciplinary measures. (Part of this role might be entrusted, as in the British system, and in France through the "Ordre des médecins", to a professional body. In other countries however, this is a direct responsibility of the State.)

- Appropriateness of infrastructure and equipment in health institutions (hospitals, homes, etc.), be they public or private.

- Patient-physician relationships, respect for and implementation of patient rights.

In respect of ethical issues and problems, the public authority generally takes guidance from the codes of the professions. Up to a certain degree of severity of the problem, it can delegate this supervisory and disciplinary role, *de jure* or *de facto*, to organs/committees of the profession.

As regards rules of conduct in medico-ethical situations which have had growing importance and visibility in the recent past, great credit is given in Switzerland to the Guidelines and Recommendations of the Swiss Academy of Medical Sciences (SAMS), which has formulated statements in the following fields: experimental research on humans, ethics committees, (passive) euthanasia, transplantation, the definition and diagnosis of death, artificial insemination, sterilisation, and genetic examinations.[4] Concerning their legal and practical weight, Swiss Courts refer to these documents and, while they are not as imperative as laws would be, observers consider that they have a quasi-legal status.

3.2. PUBLIC HYGIENE (CONTROL OF MAJOR COLLECTIVE HEALTH RISKS)

This, along with health regulation, is a classical task of the State. For a long time, it had mainly to do with the control of communicable diseases. This has involved, in the past, the exclusion of and discrimination against leprosy patients, or quarantine in ports.

Presently, in industrialised countries, activities of the public authorities in this regard still cover infectious diseases (e.g., tuberculosis, rabies, hepatitis, especially when there are professional risks, aspects of sexually transmitted diseases, including AIDS) and the prevention of food-borne problems. But also, more and more, public institutions are concerned with the dangers linked to pollution and various man-made problems (chemical products, radiation, noise), as well as planning for emergency relief and care in case of disaster (natural or man-made).

3.3. COMMUNITY HEALTH

This is a major component of public health, especially in what can be called the British approach. The goal is not only to avoid certain dangers, but to insure that available resources are used in the way most favourable to the wellbeing of the community in general (the main concern is for the best possible health of the forest - figuratively speaking - rather than that of one given tree).[5]

One should avoid opposing community/collective health, evaluated through statistical indicators, to personal health; but it is essential to realise that saying that what is good for an individual must always be good for the group is simplistic and far from being always true. There are often tensions or conflicts between the benefit one or a few might get from a certain action, and the possibility of negative effects on the larger group. Some failures in medical assistance to developing countries have shown that particularly well, but it applies to our more prosperous conditions too.

Given its goals, this part of public action should include significant work in forecasting and planning, as well as in the evaluation of the programmes carried out.

3.4. HEALTH PROMOTION

This (newer) dimension refers to a more active, positive view of health. Not only does one try to preserve or maintain it, but also to promote it, to have it blossoming, by convincing people to adopt more favourable lifestyles and supporting them in doing so. One is here at the interface between, on the one hand, a desirable prevention and, on the other hand, individual freedom (including the freedom not to behave in a healthy way). Given this, the role of governments can be only a limited, proportionate one. However, health promotion includes also environmental measures conducive to the better health of the population. In this latter field strong, determined public action is called for.

3.5. SOCIAL PAYER

Especially since World War II, most of Western Europe has developed major social health insurance schemes ('Sécurité sociale" in France), leading in several countries to Welfare State situations, confronted today by serious crises. In no case can public means made available for health care grow indefinitely. Efforts to master expenses aim particularly at a rational and as economical as possible use of resources, avoiding unnecessary diagnostic or therapeutic measures. Debates in this regard occur for aspects of routine care as well as when new biomedical technologies are introduced, especially when they require more specialised personnel and infrastructure.

TABLE 1. Assisted conception (AC) and public health

Public health tasks	Benefits brought by AC	Risks (in part potential) introduced by AC
Health services control and regulation Ordered functioning of the health system Control of professionals and institutions Protection of the citizen/ patient		* Insufficient supervision of AC practices * Commercialisation * Insufficient attention to the rights of the persons involved and to the undesirable/unforeseen consequences of the commitments made * Unanswered issue about the anonymity (or identification) of gamete donors
Public hygiene Control of collective health risks (e.g. epidemics and, more and more, man-made risks)	Circumvention of sterility and, in certain cases, of hereditary diseases	* Choice of child sex and possibly of other characteristics * Socio-demographic imbalances in the long run
Community health (including prospective and planning function)	Satisfaction of the needs/ desires of a group in society	* Comfort medicine (médecine du désir) * Choices to be made about the use of collective resources: evaluation of the health gain brought by AC as compared with tackling other important problems (drug addiction, needs of children, adolescents and elderly, traffic accidents, environmental damage)
Health promotion	Parenthood made possible for sterile couples and related joys/fulfilments	* Psychosocial disorders among adults concerned, caused by conflict situations or personally ill-integrated issues in relation to AC * Ulterior psychosocial risk for the child (especially if there has been conflict among adults) * Right of the child to know (precisely) of all the adult partners involved in his birth?
"Social payer" role		* Contribution to the growth ('explosion') of health care costs * Is it a duty of the State to pay for AC? If yes, for all or part of the expense?

4. Assisted Conception and the Public Health Mission of the State: Which Benefits, Which Risks?

A phenomenon like the emergence of artificial procreation should be looked at in relation to the above described tasks. *Table 1* presents a summary of our analysis.

We have dealt only succinctly with the gains (in terms of health and wellbeing): they are relatively evident and usually get sufficient attention. We thought more of potential undesirable effects which might need regulatory action. The following comments complement the table (several papers by other authors present analyses with similar or complementary considerations[6]).

4.1. CONTROL AND REGULATION OF HEALTH SERVICES

A major preoccupation of reports on assisted procreation, from the beginning (e.g., Report of the Warnock Committee of 1984[7]), is the protection of the patient. While being desirable, it is quite difficult in medical care for the user to judge the relevance and quality of the care he/she gets. Nevertheless, in a field which touches deeply the private sphere of individuals and families, one needs to implement measures of supervision which give sufficient guarantees to those requesting assisted conception. These guarantees include assurance about and control of the experience and skills of the practitioners, the techniques used, the equipment and organisation of the centres/clinics and, very important, the information given to all concerned individuals, that is the patient, her husband/partner and, as the case may be, a donor of gametes.[8]

In May 1992, in a general referendum, the Swiss people accepted the inclusion of a new article 24 novies into the country's constitution dealing with assisted procreation and genetic engineering. Several laws will have to be drafted on this basis, but had not been at the time of writing.[9]

4.2. PUBLIC HYGIENE/HEALTH

Even if such risks might come about only in the long term (and even if some remain hypothetical public health might be threatened in several ways through large scale practice of what Francophones call 'médecine du désir'.[10] One thinks for example, in the reproductive field, of a possible distortion of the sex ratio or other characteristics if parents are put in a position to choose them freely and were doing it in a biased way.

Some years ago, a commentator wrote, in relation to assisted reproduction, "The freedom to abort should lead to the one to beget" (without limiting factors).[11] Is this true? In view of the potential of some of the techniques developed, and of their practical and social consequences, we doubt that one can support totally such a claim. The collective wellbeing is clearly of concern here. Individual freedom cannot be absolute if it tends to alter indispensable balances, or cause 'perversions' in the composition of the population. It is very much an issue of collective (and public health) interest to know whether individuals should be allowed to decide what sort of people

there should be.[12]

Concerning the right to reproduce, several authors think that it usually refers to a subjective right and that "in its historical sense, it clearly does not and cannot include the infertile".[13] A WHO meeting report[14] says "Governments are under no obligation to ensure the availability of IVF to any person who might desire to have a child. Even if one acknowledges the individual's right to reproduce, this right cannot be extended automatically to those who do not have the capacity to reproduce".

4.3. COMMUNITY HEALTH

The (difficult) task is to evaluate, at the level of the group/population, the health benefits of assisted conception compared to the benefits the same resources would bring if dedicated to public health problems other than infertility (which deserve to receive more attention than presently given their acuteness and extension, for instance drug addiction, battered children/adults, including those suffering from sexual abuse, the needs of the elderly, AIDS care etc).

Such a task requires data collection, analysis and evaluation, and it implies value judgements, which cannot be made by health professionals alone, but must come through multidisciplinary bodies which include representatives of the general public. The public should be sensitised to the fact that, more and more in the future, it will not be possible to avoid making such choices, and that it is not acceptable to undertake programmes on a large scale in a given field (e.g., assisted procreation) without prior consideration of the consequences this might have for the satisfaction or non-satisfaction of other needs.[15]

4.4. HEALTH PROMOTION

Under this heading, we consider the potential risks for the health/wellbeing of concerned actors in problem situations which assisted conception might provoke:
- Issues of informed consent (one recalls that up to five adult "partners" might be involved: two social/legal parents, two gamete donors, and a surrogate mother bearing the pregnancy - plus the medical team).
- The 'right to repent', as former French Justice Minister Robert Badinter said, might be claimed at several moments, but it can be exercised only up to a certain stage - it does not seem that such a right should justify the interruption of an ongoing pregnancy (the position of the pregnant woman being reserved).
- There are also difficulties about data confidentiality, including as regards information as to the specifics of a child's conception, in particular the characteristics and possibly the identity of gamete donors.

4.5. THE STATE AS A 'SOCIAL PAYER'

Related aspects have been evoked above. One further point which needs to be

addressed is whether access to assisted conception (as opposed to infertility treatment) and payment for it through collective means (public funds, generalised health insurance) should be a right of every citizen. Or to what extent one might judge that, being in part 'médecine du désir' or 'comfort medicine', it should be left, to a lesser or greater extent, to the personal preference, means, and allocation decisions of the patient and his partner (as one decides to have a more or less prestigious car, or to take more or less exotic holidays).

Raising this question might be termed antisocial or discriminatory. A peculiar point is that such medical measures as assisted conception are undertaken in part in relation to somebody who does not exist yet (but the situation is similar in medical care for infertility). In Switzerland at present, the so-called social health insurance funds (subsidized by the State) are not bound to reimburse the costs of assisted conception care while they do pay for the treatment of infertility, on the grounds that in the latter case one is indeed treating an illness and not simply circumventing it.

Also, as assisted conception represents important demands on professional and other available resources, economic choices have to be made. At this time, in the whole of Europe and elsewhere, public budgets are subject to serious constraints, leading to more (at least implicit, sometimes explicit) rationing.[16] In the health field, will assisted conception be among the first areas of care to experience cuts or will it be seen more and more as care which should be accessible to all, whatever the circumstances? (The latter trend is not the one which has been witnessed in recent years in Switzerland[17].)

5. An example: The 1992 Dutch Report *Choices in Health Care*

In 1992, the Dutch Government released the report of a Committee which looked at the whole range of problems in the health services, in relation to the following areas:
- exploding advances and related diagnostic and therapeutic possibilities;
- limited means (the more so because of economic recession);
- the basic intention of preserving principles of social solidarity and quality care accessible to all;
- the desire to maintain and promote personal responsibility towards one's health (including in the sense of a contractual commitment vis-a-vis the community).

The Dutch Committee used as its working definition of health the ability to function normally in society, in making a useful distinction between the individual, professional and community approaches to health (*Table 2*). It thought that the community approach had to be given more weight in judging needs.

In ordering priorities the Committee proposed a system formed of a funnel with four sieves in which certain types of care will be retained while others fall through, according to successive criteria:
- the necessity of the care;
- the effectiveness of the care;
- the efficiency of the care;

TABLE 2. From health to necessary health care

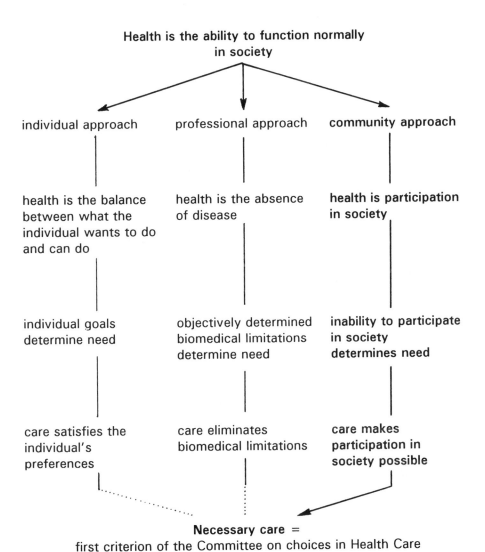

Source: Netherlands, *Choices in Health Care*, (1992) p. 50

- the question whether it can be left to individual responsibility.

Excerpts of the Committee opinion about *in vitro* fertilisation (IVF) are worth quoting:

> From the individual point of view of health and health care, *in vitro* fertilization is necessary if the woman concerned feels that it is. For one person, *in vitro* fertilization may be necessary care, and for another not at all. From the medical-professional point of view, it is defensible that *in vitro* fertilization is necessary. (...) From a community-oriented approach, the answer to the question of necessity would most probably be no. Undesired childlessness in the Netherlands poses no danger to the community, and it can not be said that childlessness interferes with normal function in our society.[18]

In addressing the question of whether IVF could be left to individual responsibility, it says:

> *In vitro* fertilization is a rather expensive treatment, for which many people could not pay. To make it available for everyone, it would have to be included in the basic package. Whether there are arguments in favour of compulsory solidarity with women who want *in vitro* fertilization is another question. One does not have a right to the ability to have children. Neither the interests of the community nor the norms and values of the society would seem to justify such a compulsory solidarity (...). From the medical-professional viewpoint, *in vitro* fertilization would be necessary care, reasonably effective and, compared to alternatives, reasonably efficient. From this point of view, there are arguments to limit the indications and to concentrate the treatment in a few centres. From the individual point of view, it could be considered necessary care with a reasonable cost-effectiveness. Those who need *in vitro* fertilization would have reason for solidarity, but a broad, not to mention a compulsory, solidarity would not seem to be justified, so that *in vitro* fertilization will not be included in the basic package.[19]

A report from a Swedish Parliamentary Commission with objectives similar to the Dutch one has been issued recently.[20] This Commission also dealt with IVF. In a 1993 preliminary document, it had proposed that IVF should not be paid for through the publicly supported health care system. However, in view of the reactions to that proposal following a wide consultation in the country, the Commission finally included IVF in a borderline category, for which the public purse might pay.

6. Concerning Needs and Wishes

'A need is a wish/desire for which one is not willing to pay anymore.' This sentence is heard in debates on health policy, sociology, and economics. The issue of the right

19. ARTIFICIAL INSEMINATION IN ITALY

The Current Legal Situation and Discussion of Possible Future Legislation

Gilda Ferrando
Associate Professor of Private Law
University of Genoa
Italy

1. Introduction: A General Overview

Medical intervention in procreation (contraception, abortion, assisted procreation) increases the range of personal decisions and choices in a way unknown in the past.[1] A couple's sterility, which had previously to be accepted as an inescapable necessity imposed upon the partners or as a design of providence to be borne with patience, can now be overcome or circumvented by those who want to complete their lives by giving birth to and taking responsibility for the raising of their own children. Physicians can now intervene not only to prevent and cure many kinds of sterility or infertility which were incurable until quite recently, but also to make a pregnancy possible even in more difficult cases of sterility.

In this field as in others, scientific progress allows human control of matters that were not at one time the object of choice, and therefore, since now these matters, like many others, depend on human decisions, it also increases the range of an individual's responsibility. The result is a need for 'rules' by which to select those decisions that are socially acceptable, that is which are coherent and compatible with a more general frame of values expressed by a given community. Such 'rules' are urgently needed in order both to guarantee that the individual's new freedom is exerted within a framework of fundamental rights, and to regulate human conduct and its possible consequences. The urgency of the need for such 'rules' was stressed in the late spring of 1995 by the Italian Medical Association (Federazione Italiana degli Ordini dei Medici), which approved a new Code of Medical Deontology[2] forbidding some medical interventions such as artificial insemination (AI) performed on people who were not members of a stable heterosexual couple, or on a woman over 50, or after a partner's death, and forbidding any form of surrogacy. This measure was taken in order to stimulate the Italian Parliament to legislate on this issue, while at the same time acting as 'surrogate' legislators for the inactive Parliament.

It is the role of legislators to provide such rules as are needed, whenever new problems arise out of social reality. This legislative task should be perceived as a necessary and pressing one whenever basic interests and rights of the persons are at

D. Evans (ed.), Creating the Child, 255–266.

stake. And in this case we are dealing with the following fundamental rights: to life, to health, and to freedom and autonomy of choice concerning one's personal life. There are also the rights of the new born and future people, with whose lives we ought to be concerned; the rights of the woman who is the real leading character in procreation, and especially in assisted procreation, where she shows a strong desire to become a mother and in order to reach her goal is willing to bear a great amount of inconvenience and risk.   It should not be forgotten that the new reproductive technologies are often quite painful and stressful, and that they are not without physical risks for women.

For these reasons, many countries neighbouring Italy or which have a culture and experience similar to the Italian, are legislating or proposing regulations for assisted reproduction.[3] Some countries have chosen what might be called 'minimal' legislation or regulation, limited to defining the status of the newborn.   This is the solution preferred by Switzerland (art. 256 civil code) and by the USA (art. 5 of the Uniform Parentage Act of 1975), where each State provides specific control over different aspects of assisted reproduction. Other countries have chosen 'fragmentary' legislation, among them the UK, Sweden and Germany. In these places there are regulations only for those aspects on which a strong need of control was socially perceived. Accordingly, in the UK, because of the intense emotions raised by Baby Cotton case, the Surrogacy Maternity Act (1985) became law, forbidding commercial surrogacy; and only later, in 1990, was the Human Fertilisation and Embryology Act enacted, aimed at regulation of assisted conception services and embryo experimentation, and protection of the embryo. In Sweden there are two statutes regulating parent-child relationships (n. 1139/1984, and n. 712/1988), one concerning *in vivo* insemination (n. 1140/1984) and another concerning *in vitro* insemination (n. 711/1988). Germany promulgated a law guaranteeing special protection to human embryos (13 December 1990). Yet other countries have chosen what might be termed '*systematic*' legislation, Spain and France for example. In Spain there is a law regulating all aspects of the issue (law of 22 November 1988, n. 35); while in France an even more ambitious project was attempted, since there is a law concerning the general protection of the human body and the person's dignity in relation to medical activity (laws n. 653 and 654 of 29 July 1994).

Different though these approaches to legislation might be, in each can be seen a passage - which in Italy has not yet occurred[4] - from ethics to law concerning assisted procreation.[5] This means a passage from subjective rules informed by personal values and conceptions of the right and the good, to objective rules which are valid for all citizens. This represents a complex evolution, and the main challenge for lawyers lies in the request for there to be such objective rules. Usually this request is justified by the observation that there is a normative gap which allows too much freedom both to physicians and infertile people, so that they do whatever they like, pursuing their own individual interests and disregarding any general interests, such as those of the prospective newborn and of future generations. And, indeed, as a matter of fact, in the absence of a specific law, we can see that other existing forms of regulation - which are in force and acting as substitutes for legislation - are inadequate, since they cannot

balance opposing interests and are defective either as far as efficiency or justice is concerned.

2. A Short Analysis of the Current Italian Situation

Here, a brief summary of the existing substitutes for proper legislation which presently regulate the Italian practice, will be given. Regulation is at present provided by the following sources: medical deontology, administrative regulations, the principle of 'private autonomy', and trends in decisions in the Courts.

2.1. MEDICAL DEONTOLOGY

The new code of medical deontology approved in the late spring of 1995 contains some rules valid only for the members of the profession, but they are not binding on other citizens, for which reason this code cannot be a source of legal rights and obligations imposed upon others. Nevertheless, the new code is an advance on the previously existing one. That code, the 1989 deontological code, as far as artificial insemination was concerned, established only fragmentary regulation, and was not fully satisfactory. On the one hand, in article 46 the code stated that the goal of any medical act directed to an "intervention on sexual and reproductive problems" was the "protection of health", while, on the other hand, it stated that the aim of *in vitro* fertilisation was that of "obviating sterility" (article 47). There are also two other general deontological principles which are relevant to the issue of this paper: the principle concerning informed consent, which constitutes the necessary prerequisite of any medical act (arts. 39 and 40); and the prohibition of any doctor advertising his/her activity (arts. 61 and following). However, the presence of these deontological norms did not prevent some bizarre events taking place, which received widespread attention in the media, and resulted in the general discrediting of the whole practice. Worried by these negative effects the Italian Medical Association (Federazione nazionale dell'Ordine dei medici), on the first occasion at its meeting of 2 April, issued certain prohibitions which have since been included in the new Code of medical deontology which was approved in June 1995. Article 41 of the new Code presupposes a prudential attitude by establishing that the goal of assisted reproduction is to meet the necessity of "overcoming sterility in order to reach the legitimate end of procreation". On this basis article 41 sets out a series of prohibitions (mentioned much earlier) aiming at protection of an expected newborn's interests. These prohibitions are of any form of surrogacy, of artificial insemination outside stable heterosexual couples, of artificial insemination in the post-menopausal period - fixed at the age of 51, since it so happened that in recent years a natural pregnancy did occur at that age - or after the death of the partner, and of any commercial and industrial exploitation of human gametes and embryos. The only positive prescription is that the practice of artificial insemination has to be performed in institutions satisfying "apt requirements".

The new Code of medical deontology has at most a exhortatory efficacy for the members of the Medical Association and for the legislator, who in this way is pressed into issuing new legislation, an outline of which is suggested by the Code. However, this Code also raises the problem of how far self-disciplinary rules can be extended without violating persons' rights and liberties. It is clear that only through a democratic process is it possible to guarantee the respect of all the interested parties, and therefore only State legislation can provide the basis of an acceptable solution of the problems involved.

2.2. ADMINISTRATIVE REGULATIONS

As for regulative sources of an administrative nature, there have been only two prescriptions (circolare) issued by the ministry of health. The first one (Circolare ministero sanità of 1 March 1985) states that only homologous artificial insemination is allowed within the national health service; the second one (Circolare ministero sanità of 27 April 1987 integrated with another one of 10 April 1992) makes mandatory examinations and controls on sperm in order to avoid possible disease transmission. Prohibition of heterologous insemination within a public context (i.e. within the National Health Services) has certainly contributed to a rapid growth and flourishing of private centres; and in this private field there are many very serious professionals, but unfortunately also some who do not seem to be as scrupulous as is desirable. For this reason it is nowadays quite commonplace to speak of there being an 'uncontrolled market' in assisted insemination, so that Italy appears to be entirely without rules, which attracts people to Italy who could not get a child in other countries where artificial insemination is more strictly regulated. The absence of rules and control procedures, together with the fact that there is no official scientific empirical research concerning the frequency or success of assisted conception practices, has stimulated a 'market of hope' which certainly involves a great amount of money without offering any guarantee that women's and newborns' rights will be respected.

2.3. THE PRINCIPLE OF 'PRIVATE AUTONOMY'

In the situation outlined above, the basic regulative principle of relationships between the various parties involved in artificial insemination is that of 'private autonomy'. Within this framework the prospective child has no voice unless adults are willing to speak for him or her. The 'autonomy principle', i.e. private individual's freedom of self-rule as far as his or her conduct is concerned, is certainly a fundamental principle of the Italian law. It is one of a person's basic rights as stated in article 2 of the Italian Constitution, and it is the grounds of both personal freedom (protected by art. 13 of the Constitution) and of privacy. When the principle is applied to family relationships it is specified by saying that the family has a peculiar 'natural' character (art. 29 of the Constitution), meaning that governmental decisions cannot intrude into family life; and when it is applied to health relationships, the 'autonomy principle' makes informed

consent a necessary justification in any medical treatment (art. 32 of the Constitution). Of course, the principle is limited by the need to respect others' significant interests, such as the basic values necessary for a civil social life.

In Italy, the 'autonomy principle' is the basic rule as far as artificial reproduction is concerned. Seen from the stand point of individuals asking for reproductive assistance, the principle allows all persons to pursue in an optimal way their individual choices. On the other hand, the principle also fits optimally with other ethical and social rules since it guarantees to each citizen freedom concerning his or her life-plans and goals.

However, the autonomy principle implies also freedom concerning economic enterprise, and in this field its application makes possible an uncontrolled growth of both private centres and many other related developments. In this connection, the rules of the market and individual informed consent (which is the core of the autonomy principle) are not sufficient to guarantee an adequate or balanced response to all the interests at stake. Informed consent, on the one hand, does not seem able to protect the interests of those subjects who do not take part in the action, but are involved in its consequences (foremost here the prospective newborn). On the other hand, informed consent seems only formally to guarantee the equality of individual agents, because cognisance has also to be taken of the unequal distribution of knowledge, information and power which is typical of patient-physician relationships whereby prospective parents resorting to artificial reproduction are peculiarly weak and vulnerable. For this reason, even informed consent has to be carefully analysed and decoded.

However, in the absence of a specific law, these doubts and qualms about the adequacy of the 'autonomy principle' (and informed consent) as a basic rule for assisted reproduction cannot be put into any concrete form *before* taking up assisted conception services. The only possible control over an individual's exercise of his or her 'private autonomy' comes *after* the procreative action, when, in the case of conflict, for example, a judge has to make a decision. Judges' decisions are inevitably fragmentary and mostly unpredictable, because - in absence of specific rules - the judge has to apply to the specific case some rule which originally was about different issues, or has to resort to the general principles of law. As a result, a judge ends up creating new rules *ad hoc*, as they are needed to fill a void in existing legislation.

2.4. TRENDS IN DECISIONS IN THE COURTS

In order to understand how control depending on courts' decisions works, two different exemplary cases will be examined. The first is the Monza surrogacy case, and the second is the Cremona paternity case.

In the Monza surrogacy case, after the newborn's birth the surrogate mother refused to give the baby to the commissioning couple, and the matter ended up in court. The Monza court[6] decided the case by means of a very straighforward argument, *viz.*, all surrogacy agreements are null and void, since they are "contrary to law, public policy and morals". There is, then, neither a valid obligation to bring pregnancy to term for others, nor to give the child up to the commissioning couple. Consequently, the

commissioning couple has no right to claim the child, and the surrogate mother has no right to claim the promised payment. All the issues concerning the child's status have to be solved on the basis of current legislation, rather than on the basis of the private rules of the surrogacy contract. So, as far motherhood is concerned, the mother is the woman who gave birth to the child (art. 269 of civil code); and as far as fatherhood is concerned, the biological father (the male of the commissioning couple who gave his sperm to have a child) can 'recognise' (riconoscere) a child born in this way, and if he does so, then he becomes the 'natural father'. At this point, since the mother and the natural father do not live together, the judge has to decide to whom to entrust the custody of the child and this decision has to be made according to the 'best interests of the child'. That is to say, in a particular case the judge has to evaluate whether it is better for the child to be raised by the mother or by the father and his wife. In the Monza case the judge decided that the child was to be brought up by the father.[7]

What emerges from this case and its judicial handling is that appealing to general principles of law such as the indisposability of the human body, the protection of public policy and the maintenence of morals, and to the application of civil code norms concerning parenting, allows an Italian judge to reach a rational conclusion. Within the judgement, on the one hand, certain fundamental principles are restated, and, on the other hand, the newborn's interests in having a certain status (i.e. being definitely a child of someone) and in having a normal family, are protected in a satisfactory way. The judge's decision seems acceptable even in respect of its consequences for policy considerations, since it discourages the practice of surrogacy. This is because, when private contracts concerning commercial surrogacy are declared void because they are contrary to public policy and morals, the hope of gaining any profit the surrogate mother and other parties may have had vanishes (since they cannot enforce payment) and at the same time the commissioning couple cannot claim the restitution of any amount of money given in advance to the surrogate if the contract is not completely or is only in part fulfilled.[8]

The second example is the Cremona paternity case, in which a husband disclaimed his paternity of a child born to his wife after having given his consent to heterologous insemination.[9] In this case the Cremona court decided that the husband's disclaiming of paternity had to be accepted, because his previous consent to donor insemination had no legal validity. It had no legal validity because the legal *status* of a child (for instance its status as the genetic child of a man) is something of an indisposable nature which cannot be derogated by consent. Moreover, *impotentia generandi* is one of the express cases in which, according to article 235 of the Italian civil code, it is possible to disclaim the paternity of a child, given which the husband's action has to be accepted if impotency is proved. I have already noted, however, that the Court could have given a different interpretation of current rules, so as to reach a quite opposite conclusion denying admissibility to the husband's disclaiming of paternity.[10] In my opinion, a too strictly 'formalistic' approach was followed by the court in Cremona, probably dependent on the fact that many judges evaluate heterologous insemination negatively, and a judgement of this kind would certainly have some influence on decisions in such cases

as faced the court on this occasion. But the Cremona approach seems unacceptable because it permits the husband to escape a responsibility he accepted beforehand through his consent to donor insemination, and does not guarantee a clear status to the child born because of that consent.

In general, a judge's decision has the advantage that it avoids a final and definitive delegitimisation of the values held by the losing party, as it is always possible that another judge will reach a different conclusion; but this has the concomitant disadvantage that it does not always permit the proposal of efficient and acceptable rules. Moreover, the principle of private autonomy is an important and basic value, sanctioned by the Italian Constitution and regarded as ethical since it permits choice to the individual; yet sometimes it does not seem to protect sufficiently weaker subjects, the general interest or future generations. For these reasons a law on these matters is urgently needed in Italy.

3. The Debate Concerning Future Legislation

The preceding short analysis of the current legal and regulatory situation in Italy shows the source of a deeply rooted need for specific legislation on artificial insemination. There is now a general consensus that the legislator's intervention is a necessity. But, although there are no doubts on what the source of any new regulation should be (i.e. the Italian Parliament), there are many doubts on when to enact such legislation, on how to do it, and on its content. In other words, the question which needs to be answered is: what rules should we have for assisted reproduction? How should we make the passage from ethics to law in a field which involves so deeply the individual's life and challenges some of the basic values of personal and social coexistence? Here we have to balance very different values such as those relating to sexuality, procreation, the disposition of someone's body, a person's dignity, respect for people's privacy, and the protection of health and of future generations. Moreover, we know that Italian society is pluralistic in which there are many divergent moral views about life, sexuality, birth and family relationships. What, then, is needed is legislation permitting the peaceful coexistence of a plurality of conceptions.

The existence of this ethical plurality is recognised also by the Italian National Committee for Bioethics in the preface to a statement ('Parere') issued in order to suggest some basic guidelines for regulation of the whole field.[11] Moreover, this document includes statements of quite different positions on some of the most controversial issues, suggesting that the National Committee recognises both an equal dignity for each different outlook, and that, where an outlook is a 'minority' outlook, its dignity should not be diminished by a majority vote. Accordingly, informed by a "frank and tolerant debate" the Committee's members "finally intended to confirm a pluralistic methodology which is respectful of different moral positions".

It is true that contrasting views were held about crucial issues, such as the acceptability of heterologous insemination, of surrogacy, of artificial insemination of a

single woman, of anonymity of donor, etc. But it is also true that the Committee's members found their views converging on many significant points such as: the idea of having a definite system able to give licences to centres for artificial reproduction and to control their activity; the idea that to each newborn we must guarantee a status which is certain and non-discriminatory; the idea of having an 'informed consent' statement and a good deal of information available to women applying for artificial insemination; the idea of forbidding any practice of artificial insemination informed by racial prejudice; the idea of forbidding any collection of gametes or embryos without the explicit consent of the interested persons; the idea of forbidding any commercial and industrial exploitation of gametes, embryos or embryonic tissues, and (relatedly) prohibition of any form of payment or advertisement; the idea of prohibiting the creation of embryos for experimentation and research; and the idea of prohibiting any division of the early embryo, cloning, ectogenesis and interspecies insemination for reproductive or research purposes. These agreed principles have been referred to by some later documents such as one by the Guzzanti Commission (21 December 1994) established to study the problem and propose regulation concerning qualitative medical standards to be required by assisted conception centres, and the preliminary draft of the Italian Medical Association Code.

Since it will involve some very basic and personal rights, if we want it to be of any use and respected any law concerning artificial reproduction must be grounded on a wide social consensus. Such a consensus can be achieved through a serious and calm public debate among those taking different positions, which must certainly be different from that stimulated by extraordinary cases highlighted by the media. Very likely, the National Committee for Bioethics is an apt institution in favour of finding the sort of consensus which will be required. Whether it is or not, however, recognition of ethical pluralism implies respect for different positions, and to maintain that respect it is necessary to avoid a majoritarian logic according to which rules supported by a majority can be rightly imposed upon minorities. The rules needed for ethical pluralism are those permitting and guaranteeing the peaceful coexistence of different views of life and reproduction, while expressing other common principles of more fundamental character.

The task of any legislation which holds peaceful coexistence on such issues as artificial reproduction dear, is not, then, to assert any principles of an 'ideological' nature (such as an abstract idea of the 'ideal' family or of the dignity of human sexuality), but to suggest rules that will be effective and respected. It is necessary, then, that penalties under the law should be proportionate to the gravity of the misconduct, and must be provided for acts which it is possible to control through public legislation. As Mary Warnock says "the law is not, and cannot be, an expression of moral feeling. It must apply to everyone, whatever their feelings; it must be both intelligible and enforceable".[12]

What is needed, then, is 'soft legislation', i.e. legislation aiming mainly to regulate medical intervention in order to ensure, first and foremost, the health and privacy of women, newborns, and donors. The kernel of such a 'soft' legal framework should be the licensing and controlling of the centres of artificial reproduction, with the aim of

ensuring homogeneous and adequate qualitative standards and avoiding heinous forms of advertising and commercialisation of gametes and embryos as well as of medical activity itself or of the parental desires and hopes of couples. Another key stone of such new legislation should be the constitution of an independent authority appointed to control an assisted reproduction centre's activities and to revise quality standards. This new institution would be able to play a significant role in protecting the rights of persons in a field where the evolution of knowledge and technology is extremely rapid and where effective protection requires a flexibility which cannot be provided by any legislation.

Even the rule of informed consent should be carefully revised in order to fit the specific requirements of the artificial reproduction situation. So women in particular should be informed of the real likelihood of success of a therapy (according to some controlled standard), of the risks and complications for health connected with proposed treatments (if any), and of the legal consequences. (This special attention to informed consent does not depend on woman's peculiar psychological situation regarding pregnancy, a fact that might be a source of endless discussions, but on the weighty consequences of making a choice to have certain kinds of treatment.) Moreover, it would be right that women should have access to a standard sterility treatment before resort to new reproductive technologies.

Any legislation should devote special attention to the legal conditions of children born through artificial reproduction: rules are needed that guarantee equality to all children independently of the different ways in which they have been conceived and born. Each child has a right to a stable and certain family relationship and not to be subject to any sort of social discrimination. From this viewpoint, the donor anonymity rule - even if it is so controversial - seems to me consistent with current principles of Italian law concerning filiation[13]: though donor anonymity does not entirely disregard the relevance of biological data, it pays greater attention to the psychological and affective aspects of filiation in the sense that the current law favours the ascertainment of biological paternity only when this permits an effective assumption of responsibility regarding the child.[14] On the other hand, those who are against donor anonymity, arguing that there is a right to know one's biological origins, have to be prepared to hold to such a claim not only for children born throughout artificial insemination, but for any child (including, for example, those born within valid marriages as a consequence of an adulterous relationship and adopted children).

As far as access to assisted procreation techniques is concerned, I have suggested that, given the end of peaceful coexistence of a plurality of divergent moral views, any legislation should be 'soft' and should propose 'soft' rules. With this pluralistic end in mind, the recent French law is certainly not the model to be followed in Italy: it sets down too many prohibitions and a too heavy an apparatus of sanctions, which in some cases would be unenforceable, or at least enforceable only with extreme difficulty, and which in other cases are hardly respectful of individual autonomy. Moreover, 'soft' legislation on assisted reproduction needs to make allowance for the time factor, in the sense that any proposal must include a mechanism for a periodic revision of legislation.

The proposal for a new institution appointed to control the assisted conception centres and to study various problems has a central role in the whole process in any 'soft' law. Only through such an institution would it be possible to keep rules which move with the rapid changes both at the technological and at the social level, and avoid the risk of obsolescence of the statutes.

At present (November 1995) there are many bills which have been presented to the Italian parliament and are waiting to be discussed. In addition, a new Commission - chaired by Busnelli, professor of civil law at the University of Pisa - was appointed in early 1995 by the minister of Justice to prepare a proposal for the cabinet, but at the time of writing, the Commission's report is not yet available. However, even a glance at the various bills which have been presented reveals that they propose both a wide range of legal techniques and arise out of and express a diversity of underlying values. Some bills are limited to the regulation of specific issues, such as those aiming only at protection of the newborn's status and therefore forbidding any disclaimer of paternity after consent to heterologous insemination.[15] Another bill (Senato, n. 1070/1994) contains rules intended to guarantee a high standard regarding the organisation of assisted conception centres (but with no other aims apart from this).

The remaining bills propose a global or systematic control of assisted procreation.[16] All these bills concur in admitting a need for some regulation of the assisted conception centres, and all propose that an independent authority be appointed to control the centres' activities. Moreover, all forbid any form of commercialisation and advertising of human gametes and embryos, and all stress the relevance of women's informed consent and favour the protection of embryos, proposing that they should be created only for procreative goals (and never for experimentation). Most of these bills support donor anonymity and protect the child's status by banning later disclaiming of paternity. Finally, there is a high level of agreement on some basic prohibitions such as those concerning pregnancy in older women, *post mortem* insemination and surrogacy. Differences emerge among the bills with wider scope on the following issues: a) the permissibility or otherwise of heterologous insemination, it being allowed in all bills but those presented by Fuscagni and Alberti Casellati; b) the permissibility of artificial insemination (as well as of married couples) also of stable though unmarried couples and single women, which would both be banned under some proposals (bill presented by Mussolini), would be allowed to the former but not to the latter (in the bill presented by Mazzucca), and would be allowed both to the former and the latter (in the bills proposed by Chiaromonte and Melandri).

The controversial issues turn out to be some of the crucial problems in the whole area, but there is also wide agreement on a number of topics. It is not impossible, then, that in the near future even the Italian Parliament will promulgate new legislation concerning artificial reproduction.

Notes

1. On these issues see Zatti, P., 'Natura e cultura nella procreazione artificiale' in Ferrando, G. (ed.) *La procreazione artificiale tra etica e diritto* Padova, Cedam Editore, 1989, pp.176-181.

2. Federazione Italiana degli Ordini dei Medici, *New Code of Medical Deontology* obtainable from the Federazione Nazionale degli Ordini dei Medici, Chirurghi e degli Odontoiatri, Piazza Cola di Rienzo 80/A, 00192 Roma. An annotated edition came out at the end of 1995 and is distributed upon request.

3. For a remarkable collection of different legislation, see the report published by the Comitato Nazionale per la Bioetica, *La legislazione straniera sulla procreazione assistita* Roma, Poligrafico dello Stato, no date (published in 1993).

4. None of the bills presented to previous legislatures succeeded in being discussed in the parliament. For an analysis of these proposals, see Ferrando, G., 'La procreazione artificiale: verso la regolamentazione per legge' *Politica del diritto* 1986, pp.501-574.

5. On this, see particularly Rodotà, S., 'Introduzione' in Rodotà, S. (ed.), *Questioni di bioetica* Roma-Bari, Laterza, 1991, pp.vii-xii; and Rodotà, S., 'Strategie per legiferare in bioetica' *Bioetica. Rivista interdisciplinare* II (2), 1994, pp.122-125.

6. Tribunale di Monza, sent. del 27 ottobre 1989, in *Foro italiano* I, 1990, col. 298ff, with a comment by Ponzanelli.

7. Moreover, according to some jurists, the fact that former surrogacy contract is null does not prevent the father's wife adopting such a child according to a 'special adoption case' as stated by art. 44 of the Italian adoption Act (Law No. 184/1983). However, we do not know what happened in the Monza case.

8. For a defence of surrogacy, see Shalev, C., *Birth Power: The Case for Surrogacy* New Haven, Yale University Press, 1989.

9. Tribunale di Cremona, sent. del 17 febbraio 1994, in *Giurisprudenza italiana* I (2), 1994, col. 996 with a comment by Ferrando (and also in *Bioetica. Rivista interdisciplinare* II (2) 1994, pp.382-396, with comments by Guarneri e Ferrando).

10. This is the solution accepted by French jurisprudence: see Cour d'Appel de Paris 29 March 1991, *La Semaine Juridique* 1992, J, 21855, with a comment by Dobkine.

11. Comitato Nazionale per la Bioetica, *Parere Sulle Tecniche di procreazione assistita. Sintesi e conclusioni 17 June 1994* Rome, Presidenza del Conciglio dei Ministri, Dipartimento per L'informazione e L'editoria, no date.

12. Warnock, M., 'Introduction' in Warnock, M., *A Question of Life* Oxford, Basil Blackwell, 1985, pp.viii-xvii, p.x.

13. See Ferrando, G., [entry] 'Filiazione legittima e naturale' in *Digesto IV discipline privatistiche* Vol. VIII, Torino, Utet, 1993, pp.298-369.

14. In this connection see, Corte costituzionale, 20 luglio 1990, n. 341, in *Giurisprudenza italiana* I (1), 1991, col. 625, with a comment by Tria; and Corte costituzionale, 27 novembre 1991, n. 429, in *ibid.*, col. 385, with a comment by D'Amico.

15. Cf. Camera (the Italian House of Representatives), n. 799/1994; Camera, n. 1363/1994; Camera n. 1952/1995; and Senato, n. 1484/1995.

16. The bills making global and systematic proposals are: Camera, n. 1879/1994, presented by Mazzucca; Camera, n. 1124/1994, presented by Melandri; Camera, n. 908/1994, presented by Basile and Mussolini; Camera, n. 1043/1994, presented by Chiaromonte (with a corresponding bill in the Italian Senate, Senato, n. 116/1994, presented by Salvato); Camera, n. 1978/1995, presented by Fuscagni (with a corresponding Senate bill: Senato, n. 1394/1995 presented by Mancino); and Senato, n. 1550/1995, presented by Alberti Casellati.

20. BIOETHICS AND NEW REPRODUCTIVE TECHNOLOGIES IN RUSSIA

Dr. Ivanyushkin Alexandr Yakovlevitch
Principal Scientific Researcher
Institute of Man
Russian Academy of Sciences
Moscow

1. Background: Attitudes to Abortion

The first work devoted to the problem of artificial fertilisation as a cure for female infertility in Russia occurred before the October Revolution.[1] But the mass use of artificial fertilisation has developed only since the 1980s. The comprehension and awareness of the humanitarian (moral, legal, philosophical, religious and theological) aspects of this medical practice is closely linked with the attitudes of the community to sexuality, child-birth, family and, particularly, to birth control and family planning. Birth control in Russia is still performed substantially through abortion. According to one questionnaire, only 22% of women of child bearing age within the borders of the USSR regularly used contraceptives in 1990, while 57% never used them at all.[2]

A radical solution of the abortion problem in this country was produced immediately after the Russian Revolution in 1917. In 1920 Soviet Russia became the first country in the world to legalise abortion. One of the early founders of the Soviet health care system, Z.P.Solovyev, has called the resolution of the Health Ministry and the Ministry of Justice in the Government of Soviet Russia which abolished the penalty for carrying out abortion an 'historic document'. This is a just appraisal, for two reasons. First, some dozens of years afterwards, similarly liberal laws in relation to abortion were adopted in many other countries. Second, the 1920 law determined the demographic politics of the Soviet State for many years.

The abortion problem has ranked as a political question in the USSR from the very beginning. On the one hand, the abortion ban in other countries was described as 'bourgeois hypocrisy and lies', while on the other the legalisation of abortion by the Soviets harmonised with the struggle against religion, coincided with the nihilistic attitude to the family (which was spread particularly in the 1920s), and reflected the class approach to the 'female question'. In 1924 an 'abortion commission' was created which had the right selectively to permit a free-of-charge abortion, based on class criteria.

From 1936 to 1955, when totalitarian power in Soviet Russia was at its most stable, abortion for non-medical reasons was forbidden (as it was during the reign of fascism in Italy and Germany, and in Ceausescu's Romania). The re-legalisation of abortion

D. Evans (ed.), Creating the Child, 267–277.

for non-medical reasons in 1955 in the USSR was one of the first signs of 'defreezing'. The subsequent forty years have been marked by changes of the law and public opinion in the direction of lifting social prejudice and prohibition in relation to abortion. The abortion article in the Russian Federation Law On Health Care is brief and stipulative, stating "A woman may make her own decision concerning child birth in cases where her health is jeopardised".[3] Typical is the Decree of the Health Ministry No. 1342 accepted in 1987, which allows the interruption of pregnancy earlier than 28 weeks for non-medical indications in cases where the husband has died during pregnancy, where the woman or her husband are in prison, where a woman has more than five children, or a handicapped child, already, and so on. In 1993 abortion was finally anchored in the law (in the Basic Law of the Russian Federation on the Health Care of Citizens) in which abortion is permitted up to 22 weeks gestation according to the wish of the mother for social (non-medical) or medical indications, and thereafter according to the wish of the mother for medical indications.

In the course of the seventy or more years since the Revolution, a veritable abortion industry was established in USSR[4] Moreover, an abortion culture appeared demonstrating to the whole world a negative experience in demographic and social politics in the field of women's rights and artificial abortion.[5]

This negative experience can be summarised as follows. First, the main role in family planning politics was played by the administration, allowing, prohibiting, and permitting anew artificial abortion. Second, abortion has become a regular, everyday matter. Sociologists note that a woman in this country undergoes four to five abortions on average (some women undergoing as many as eight to twelve abortions). Up to the end of the 1960s the number of abortions in Russia presented a stable growth pattern, reaching eleven or even twelve million a year (out of fifty million world wide), accounting for 180 cases per 1,000 women of childbearing age. This figure has dropped a little in recent times.

Third, in the former USSR, 3,500 doctors were fully occupied with pregnancy interruption. Taking all the gynaecologists in the country into account, each of them spent, on average, one third of his working time performing abortions.[6] Taking into account the complications which may arise after surgical intervention, one can say that gynaecologists spent a very substantial amount of their time with patients seeking such help. Moreover, the high percentage of tubal infertility in Russia (31.4%) is connected to the high abortion rate.[7]

Of special interest in further discussion of the moral and legal problems of the new reproductive technologies is the attitude of doctors and the population to abortion. Although the USSR has been the leader in abortion provision for many years, the issue has remained taboo in the national consciousness. Abortion was regarded by society as a pragmatic instrument for controlling the birth rate, and the moral context of the phenomenon remained largely neglected. For instance, the moral dimension of abortion was practically untouched in medical discussions; when speaking with patients doctors drew their attention only to the iatrogenic character of complications connected with this medical intervention.

The attitudes of doctors to abortion were shaped by the official position of the State, specifically of the Health Ministry. Out-of-clinic abortions (illogically called "non-medical" though as a rule performed by qualified doctors) were strictly punished by the State. On the other hand, the freedom of access to abortion in Russian clinics is unprecedented. Medical indications for artificial pregnancy interruption have always been very broad. If we take for instance the Health Ministry Decree No. 234 of 1982 or number 302 of 1993 we find the following reasons accepted as justification for artificial termination of pregnancy of up to 28 weeks (in 1982) or at any point in gestation (in 1993): amputation of four fingers in a woman, and all forms of chronic alcohol addiction in the father (including the first stage when there is no physical dependence on alcohol). We believe that this concept of 'medical indications' of artificial termination of pregnancy appeared in the USSR after 1936, when abortion on demand was prohibited and legal and safe abortion remained accessible only where there were 'medical indications'.

The whole history of the attitude toward abortion in Russia since 1920 convinces one that the problem was treated in an extremely one-sided manner, from the view point only of the health of the pregnant mother and her right to opt for motherhood. It becomes clear why 'medical indications' of artificial termination of pregnancy in Soviet and post-Soviet times appear too general and a caricature of medicine. For all this time, society as a whole, and doctors in particular, failed to see, or pretended to overlook, the other side of abortion - the right of the foetus to life. The extensive list of medical indications mentioned would not be so vast if the doctors compiling it had been aware of the profound philosophical, religious and moral issues surrounding the life of the foetus.

Modern Russian society is marked by the appearance of the abortion abolitionist movement. In Moscow, for instance, several associations have been registered - 'Life', 'For Life', 'Right to Live' and so on. Recently representatives of the Russian Orthodox Church expressed their opinion in connection with the acute problem of abortion in Russia. The position of the modern orthodox writers concerning abortion remains within the boundary of the general Christian approach: the conception of an oocyte is regarded as an act of God's will and God's creation, and the embryo bears, at any stage of its development, human dignity and therefore is covered by the Biblical commandment "Thou shalt not kill". It follows that neither a real danger to the woman's life, nor rape, nor pregnancy in adolescence justify abortion.[8]

So, the initial philosophical problem relating to the whole clinical practice of artificial fertilisation, that is the problem of the ontology and moral status of the human embryo, has been ignored for decades or at least underestimated by Russian doctors and by society in general. In order to overcome the aforementioned deformation of professional consciousness, it will be necessary to invoke international ethical and juridical norms and standards in this field of professional activity. Increased awareness of the problem of the ontological and moral status of the embryo in the community as a whole is already occurring as a result of the revival of religious approaches to abortion.

This, then, is the general moral background, the overall social ethical atmosphere accompanying the spread of the practice of artificial fertilisation in Russia.

2. The Use and Regulation of Reproductive Technologies

Between 1981 and 1983, in Moscow, Leningrad and Kharkov, gynaecologists carried out a clinical experiment to evaluate the efficiency of artificial insemination (AI) as a cure for infertility. The method has been shown to be effective in 28% to 85% of cases, depending on the nature of the infertility treated.[9] The final modification of the method, refinement of indices, and analysis of failures took some years, and only in 1987 did the Ministry of Health of the USSR issue its first decree regulating artificial human reproduction in Russia - Ministry of Health Order No. 669 of 13th May, 1987. This juridical act allowed the extension of the clinical experiment to five Russian and two Ukrainian cities, as well as to Tblisi (in Georgia) and Kishinev (in Moldova). As an annex to this order, Instructive and methodical recommendations for the application of women's artificial insemination method have been approved.

The Ministry of Health Order No. 568 of 10th October, 1989 expanded the experiment to a further 22 obstetric and gynaecological institutions (in 14 cities of Russia, and additionally in Azerbadzhan, Kasakhstan, Turkmenistan, Kirgiziya, Latvia, Lithuania and Estonia). Now some 45 centres using artificial insemination methods are active on the territory of the Russian Federation.

The clinical experiment concerning the implementation of AI thus took more than ten years, reflecting the fear of the medical beaurocracy of taking a final decision permitting clinical manipulations with human gametes (donor's or husband's sperm), this fear being understandable in a society which has almost completely lost the tradition of philosophical comprehension of the ontological and moral status of the embryo and foetus.

The initiative in the implementation and clinical application of the *in vitro* fertilisation (IVF) method has been taken by researchers working with the Moscow Scientific Centre for Gynaecology, Obstetrics and Perinatology of the Russian Academy of Medical Sciences (SCGOP RAMS). As early as 1965 a scientific group for the study of early embryogenesis was set up, and in 1973 the laboratory of clinical embryology headed by B.V.Leonov was established there. It was in this laboratory in 1984 that IVF was implemented in Russia and in 1986 the first test-tube baby in Russia was born. IVF is now successfully used in 4 clinical centres in Moscow, and in several other Russian cities including St. Petersburg and Krasnodar. The method is also used in the Ukraine, in Kiev and Kharkov. Altogether in Russia, over 2,000 children have been born by means of IVF. The success rate for IVF in Leonov's laboratory is as high as 15% for one embryo transfer. Most cases in which IVF is applied are of women's infertility resistant to other therapy, and involve the use of the husband's sperm. Russian doctors boast of success in the use of IVF with patients who have exhausted ovaries, that is using donor oocytes. SCGOP RAMS convened a seminar for doctors and other

specialists from many cities of Russia and other independent countries in May 1994 after a decline of interest in the C.I.S. in the application of IVF. In 1994 Russia's first professional association of specialists in the field of human reproduction was established, with V.M. Zdanovski as its President.

In the context of the growing use of IVF in Russia one is struck by the lag in philosophical comprehension of and legal backing for the clinical practice. Until 1993 there existed in this country virtually no standard acts (either juridical or ethical) to regulate the application of IVF.

In the summer of that year, the Russian Parliament passed the *Basic Law of the Russian Federation on the Health Care of Citizens* which states, in article 35 on 'Artificial fertilisation and embryo implantation' that "any mature woman of fertile age has the right to artificial fertilisation and embryo transplantation".[10]

Also in article 35 we find the following regulations.

> Artificial fertilisation and embryo implantation is to be performed only in institutions which are licensed for this kind of activity, and where the permission of the married couple (or single woman) has been obtained in writing. Data concerning the performance of any artificial fertilisation or embryo implantation, including the donor's identity, is to be subject to medical confidentiality. The woman has the right to be informed about the procedure of artificial fertilisation and embryo transplantation, and about the medical and legal aspects of its consequences, about medical and genetic follow-up studies, and about the appearance and nationality of any donor. This information is to be provided by the doctor performing the medical intervention. The illegal performance of artificial fertilisation and embryo transplantation is regarded as a criminal act to be prosecuted according to the law of the Russian Federation.[11]

In December 1993, the Health Ministry of the Russian Federation adopted Order No. 301 allowing the extensive use of both AI and IVF. As an annex to this order the *Manual for the application of artificial insemination of women with donor sperm for medical indications (AID Manual* hereafter)[12] and the *Manual for the application of extracorporeal fertilisation methods and embryo transfer to the uterine cavity for female infertility treatment (IVF-ET Manual* hereafter)[13] are attached.

3. Bioethical and Philosophical Reflection and the New Reproductive Technologies

With respect to bioethical reflection, Russia has advanced much more in such areas as psychiatric practice, transplantology, and biomedical research using human beings as subjects than in the new reproductive technologies.

On the legal side, in 1993 two important juridical acts were adopted in Russia. These were the Russian Federation Laws on Psychiatric Treatment and Securing the Rights of Citizens in the Giving of Such Assistance, and on Organs and Tissue Transplantation.

The preparation and adoption of these legal documents have become possible because of a kind of 'brain-storming' in which not only well-known medical specialists, but also lawyers, philosophers, and representatives of public social movements (for instance members of the Independent Psychiatric Association) participated. The entire process took place in the context of the general democratisation of society and a consequent discussion of acute socio-economic problems in Russian psychiatry and transplantation.

Unfortunately, analogous fears have not been expressed in regard to the most important unsolved problems in the application of the new reproductive technologies. The lag in philosophical comprehension, juridical regulation and ethical control of this medical practice appears to be quite unacceptable considering that the number of children born through artificial fertilisation can be counted in thousands, while heart, liver and lung transplantation (which commenced at the same time as IVF, that is in the mid-80s) take place on a comparatively restricted scale (under 100 operations between 1986 and 1995).

Moreover, a consideration of the normative juridical acts presently regulating artificial fertilisation practice in Russia reveals serious contradictions. Compare the opening of article 35 of the Basic Law of the Russian Federation on the Health Care of Citizens ("any mature woman of fertile age has the right to artificial fertilisation") with the *AID Manual* and the *IVF-ET Manual* mentioned earlier. The titles of these two manuals emphasise the idea that the criteria for applying donor insemination or IVF and embryo transfer are restricted to medical indications. Let us imagine a situation where a medical institution which has a licence for the application of artificial fertilisation is attended by a lesbian woman asking for AI by donor sperm. According to the Basic Law, doctors have to perform this medical intervention, while according to the Ministry of Health's Manuals they have to reject the woman's request: lesbianism is not included in the list of medical indications for artificial fertilisation.

There is a greatly increased possibility that unmarried women will resort to AI having been given this right since 1993. According to the Instructive and methodical recommendations for the application of women's artificial insemination of 1987 (mentioned earlier) the matter was to be decided positively rather than negatively. This document stipulates as indications for the application of AI either the husband's pathology (azoospermia, etc.) or the wife's pathology (abnormal uterus position, etc.). A separate section reads: "The matter of performing insemination of unmarried women is to be decided individually by a commission headed by the chief administrator".[14] This is a very complicated procedure, involving, on the one hand, the risk of discrimination against many women, and the violation of civil rights, and on the other hand, the fear of jeopardising the fate of the future child by condemning it to live in an incomplete family. The responsibility for such decisions is left to the mercy of the life experience and common sense of people who are (professionally) nothing more than administrators.

In the aforementioned Manual on AI with donor sperm of 1993, the same medical indications from the husband's or wife's side are listed, together with words allowing the artificial insemination with donor sperm of an unmarried woman of child-bearing

age, where the request comes from the single woman. Taking the literal meaning of these words, we can conclude that an unmarried woman with her uterus in an abnormal position, or with immunological failure, or with uterus neck infertility (all medical indications) are entitled to resort to donor AI, while women who are unfortunate enough to be healthy are refused this right.

The brief opening statement of article 35 of the Basic Law (quoted above) evokes quite naturally the question whether or not the Russian law opens new possibilities for various eugenic projects - a fear not unreasonable bearing in mind that the scandalous programme set up in the U.S.A. aiming to create a bank of Nobel prize winners' sperm to be donated to women volunteers was connected with these very artificial fertilisation methods. The worldwide criticism of the programme forced its creators to stop publishing information concerning it.[15] Looking ahead, we can imagine that the realisation of contemporary programmes of human genome mapping would provide a new impetus towards the creation of a new social context for eugenic hopes. This possibility makes it crucial to work out and discuss philosophical aspects of the new reproductive technologies.

A more immediate problem reflecting the every day application of artificial fertilisation methods is connected with gender selection. Determining what the child's sex is before birth is unconditionally ethically justified if there are reasons for presuming an incurable inborn pathology in an unborn child. From the ethical point of view, it appears questionable when some Russian doctors perform pre-birth determination of the child's sex on request of the parents solely because they already have three children of the same sex. In the *AID Manual* the issue of sex choice is mentioned only once, and then only implicitly, when an unfavourable medical and genetic prognosis regarding the offspring is given as a ground for medical intervention. In the *IVF-ET Manual*, the matter of sex choice is unfortunately totally omitted.

Let us now consider matters connected with gamete donation. The regulation for sperm donation already worked out in 1987[16] envisaged the following conditions for donation and use: age between 20 and 40 years; absence of urological, venerial, andrological and genetic diseases; a thorough medical examination; the possibility of using both non-frozen and frozen sperm; consideration of the wishes of the parents with regard to the nationality and appearance of the donor (height, colour of hair and eyes, shape of face and nose) etc. A special Application-Liability form is to be signed by the donor stating that he will "make no effort to determine the identity of the recipient or of the child born through fertilisation by his sperm".[17] We believe that this statement imposes a moral but not a legal obligation on the donor because currently there are no norms in Russian Law forbidding a pretension to fatherhood in such cases.

The physical ease with which sperm can be donated (compared with obtaining other organs and tissues for transplantation purposes) only emphasises the difficulty many people have overcoming social barriers to becoming donors of gametes. One of the first researchers into artificial fertilisation methods in Russian medicine remembers that there were cases where young people donated on the one day, but came back the next day and asked that their now frozen donated sperm be destroyed.[18] The most acute

moral and ethical contradictions are rooted in the term "active donor" which plays a prominent role in both Ministry of Health Manuals on artificial fertilisation (1987 and 1993). The "active donor" is a donor regularly donating his sperm. He may be active not longer than five years with a monthly donation of as many as five ejaculations (giving a maximal figure of about 300 donations per active donor). According to the *AID Manual* the efficiency of this method is about 35%.[19] In other words, an "active donor" can give birth to 100 children. Unfortunately, neither the issue of possible incest between such children after 20 or 30 years, nor the issue of the right of the person born through artificial fertilisation to know the details of his origin or to look for his blood relatives when he reaches his majority, has been discussed in modern Russian society.

A sperm donor, in Russia, gets a remuneration. Ethical judgements regarding this practice differ. If we consider the fee for one donation, it is not large (US$8-10) and can be regarded as compensation for transport expenses and inconvenience experienced, which means we can take it as ethically acceptable. If we consider the low economic level of the life of the people acting as sperm donors (and make the rough calculation that the remuneration which can be obtained by an 'active donor' in a month equals two thirds of the average wage in the country) the informed consent of many donors to give sperm can hardly be judged as voluntary, because it is coerced by need. Such considerations makes one sceptical of the seriousness of regard for the following stipulations in the Application-Liability form signed by the donor, *viz* that he will give truthful information concerning his heredity and will keep to the regimen prescribed by the doctor. *A propos* which, the authors of the *AID Manual* do not conceal the fact that the renumeration paid is in fact for healthy sperm. The donor is warned that "the sperm sample will not be paid for during donation if the spermogram characteristics do not comply with standards".[20]

We believe that the gamete donation issue is one of the most complicated bioethical questions comparable with such difficult questions as active euthanasia, the moral justification of abortion, and so on. Unfortunately, the topic of sperm or oocyte donation is very rarely discussed in a philosophical and moral context today in Russia.

To date, we have not experienced in Russia any case of the application of IVF in a surrogate mother. In the relevant normative documents regulating artificial fertilisation this subject in not mentioned at all. The pioneer in using IVF, Leonov, has frequently expressed his opinion in the mass media that he sees no ethical objection to this practice. When speaking with the author, he stressed that 'surrogate motherhood' should be allowed but must not contradict the International Federation of Gynaecologists and Obstetricians declaration concerning the ethical aspects of human reproduction.[21]

IVF is hardly accessible for the majority of the Russian population, though about 3 million people within the territory of the former USSR need the treatment.[22] SCGOP RAMS, the largest centre for artificial fertilisation boasting over 1500 'test tube' children encompasses with its IVF-ET programme about 1,000 women annually. The state spent US$0.5m on the organisation of this artificial fertilisation centre. The issue of distributive justice arises all over the world in connection with IVF, and is very acute

in Russia because IVF is not a method offered free-of-charge. The cost of treatment compared with other countries is not high - between US$300 and US$1,000 - but many families simply cannot afford to pay. For some categories of the population, for socially unprotected women for example, SCGOP RAMS provides IVF free.

We have to face the very important and at the same time difficult problem of the evaluation of the physical and psychical health of children born with the help of IVF. Notwithstanding the fact that there exist over 20,000 test tube children in the world, their long-term follow-up has been very restricted. Some data indicate that the risk of abortion of foetuses conceived through IVF is three times the normal, that the risk of inborn defects in such foetuses is twice the normal, and that perinatal of mortality is three to four times the normal.[23]

From 1989 to 1993, at SCGOP RAMS, paediatrician V.O. Bachtijarova carried out a complex evaluation of the health of children born with the help of IVF (group I - 82 children) and AI (group II - 60 children). Of the mothers of the first group, 46% were aged from 25 to 30 years, and 51% from 31 to 41 years. In the second group, 18% were aged from 25 to 30 years, and 82% were aged from 31 to 41 years. 24% of the women had reached between the ages of 35 and 40 by the time they became pregnant. The duration of infertile marriages varied between 1 and 15 years (between 1 and 5 years for 45% of the women in group I. 51% of those in group I suffered from absolute tube infertility, while all the women in group II were fertile, donor sperm being used. In 86% of group I, and in 54% of group II, delivery was performed through caesarean section. Major child development anomalies have been observed in 5% of group I and in 4% of group II children. Altogether, severe congenital anomalies accompanied by cerebral defects have been observed in 5 out of 142 children followed up. Four of these have been transferred to specialised facilities. 127 children have been taken home in a satisfactory condition. 15 children (slightly more than 10%) showed severe damage of the central nervous system or other organs - resulting in their transfer to specialised institutions or clinics. Data was not available for 27 of the children taken home. Examination has been performed for 100 children from both groups aged between 1 and 3, and the health state has been normal in 92% of these cases.[24]

Analysis of the health of children born through AI has been carried out in Russia since 1987, thus supplying the authors of the *AID Manual* (1993) with evidence enough for the conclusion that "the duration of pregnancy, delivery, and health of newborns after artificial insemination does not differ from ones in the general population".[25]

4. Conclusion

We will soon mark the twentieth anniversary of the introduction to Russia of the treatment of infertility by IVF. Leonov, sharing the opinion of the most radical specialists, believes that from both the clinical and economic point of view, IVF is to be considered as the best prospective cure for various forms of infertility.[26] However,

WHO representative M. Wagner noted, in 1989 at the sixth International Congress for
In Vitro Fertilisation that the results of this method are regarded, in epidemiological
terms, as rather poor.[27] Any solution of this dispute obviously demands an
interdisciplinary approach to the problem of artificial fertilisation. The present article
should be regarded as one of the first steps of the young Russian bioethics in this
direction.

Notes

1. Iljin, F., 'Artificial insemination as cure for female infertility' *Journal of Obstetrics and Female Diseases*
1 (2), 1917, pp.45-54.

2. Popov, A.A., 'A brief history of abortion and demographic policy in Russia' *Family Planning in Europa*
1, 1994, pp.5-7.

3. The Russian Federation Law on Health Care *Isvestia Sovetov Deputatov Trudjashihsja USSR* Moscow,
1971, p.29.

4. Avdeeyev, A.A., 'Abortions and birth rate' *Sociological Survey* 3, 1989, pp.54-68.

5. Popov, *op.cit.*

6. *Medicinskaja Gazeta* 17 January 1990.

7. Manuilova, I.A., *Modern Contraceptives* Moscow, Malaja Medveditsa, 1993.

8. Smirnov, Rev. Dmitrij, '"Difficult" Questions' in *Save and Preserve* Moscow, The Orthodox Medical-
Education Centre 'Shizn', 1994, pp.25-34.

9. Leonov, B.V., *Alone Together* Moscow, Sovjetskaya Rossia, 1991, pp.1-68, p.38.

10. Basic Law of the Russian Federation on the Health Care of Citizens *Vedomosti Verhovnogo Soveta R.F.*
1993, No. 33, St. 1318, p.2308.

11. *Ibid.*, pp.2308-2309.

12. Health Ministry Order of 28 December 1993, No. 301, *Manual*, pp.4-13.

13. *Ibid.*, pp.15-27.

14. Health Ministry Order 13 May 1987, No. 669, *Manual*, pp.8-15, p.8.

15. Drgonec, Jan and Holländer, Pavel, 'Moderná medicinia a pravo' *Obzor Bratislava* 1988, p.164.

16. Health Ministry Order 13 May 1987, No. 669, *Manual, op.cit.*.

17. Health Ministry Order 28 December 1993, No. 301, *Manual*, p.14.

18. Leonov (1991), *op.cit.*, p.38.

19. Health Ministry Order 28 December 1993, No. 301, *Manual*, p.4.

20. *Ibid.*, p.14.

21. Leonov, B.V., '*In vitro* born' *Tchelovek* 3, 1995, pp.69-76.

22. Leonov (1991), *op.cit.*, p.6.

23. Vandelac, L., 'The other side of artificial reproduction' in Vasetsky, S.G. (ed.) *Gens. Sex. Man.* (translated into Russian by Ginsburg, A.S., Lushnikova, A.A. and Svetchnikova, V.V.) Moscow, Mir, 1993, pp.94-104. Originally *La Recherche* 20 No. 213 (special edition *La Sexualite* Paris, September 1989).

24. Bachtijarova, V.O., '"Artificial" children' *Tchelovek* 4, 1995, pp.120-122.

25. Health Ministry Order 28 December 1993, No. 301, *Manual*, p.4.

26. Leonov (1991), *op.cit.*

27. Vandelak, *op.cit.*

might be known to the couple, has no rights with respect to the child. This presumption is derived from the above mentioned Section 1463 of the Civil Law which refers mainly to non-assisted reproduction, but can also be applied to the technique of assisted reproduction, which was known to the legislator at the time of the drafting of the law, although he chose to legislate only on the matter of disputed fatherhood.[11]

As regards surrogacy, under the Greek legal system, any agreement between a couple whose gametes are used and a woman who agrees to carry and bear a child of that couple could not be legally permitted and would not be valid, even if there were no payment involved, because any such agreement is considered to be against good mores.

As far as fatherhood is concerned, the husband cannot, as has been indicated, dispute fatherhood if he gave his consent to the artificial fertilisation. The law does not specify that this consent should be written, however it would be better for doctors to require written consent to avoid disputes in court.

With regard to a donor, he cannot sue for legal fatherhood if the mother was married and her husband gave consent for artificial fertilisation. Similarly, in cases of adultery, the biological father cannot seek legal fatherhood if the persons who have the right to dispute the legality of the child do not do so.

As regards the child born by sperm donation, it is difficult to decide whether it has the right to dispute fatherhood if the mother and her husband gave their consent for the child to be born in their marriage. The consent of the husband of the mother to have a child with the techniques of artificial fertilisation by donor, has introduced a new type of fatherhood into Greek law, stronger than fatherhood by adoption. Since it is clearly presumed that the father or the mother cannot dispute their fatherhood or motherhood, it is accepted that the Greek legal system recognises a social fatherhood which cannot be disputed by any member of the family in which the person was born. Of course, there is always the chance that when the child grows up it might raise the issue of its biological parents and could go to court. In this case the court will be asked to issue a decision which will be judge these issues for the first time in Greece.

From the point of view of the Criminal Law, artificial reproduction by donor could be considered an offence to family status, since Section 354 of Penal Code states among other things that the supposition of a child (that is the presentation of the child as the child of the husband or wife when it is not in fact biologically connected to him or her and he or she has not consented to the presentation of the child as such) is punishable by imprisonment.

When the child is conceived with the consent of both parents *in utero* or *in vitro*, and with their gametes, there is no offence. The same is true if the conceptus is a result of donated gametes, provided that both members of the couple have given their consent. However, where only the wife has given her consent for artificial fertilisation *in utero* or *in vitro* with her or donated ova and donated sperm, without the consent of the husband, or contrary to his will, there is an offence because we have the supposition of a child. In this case the husband can dispute fatherhood and ask for divorce. In the rare case where the wife has not given consent or opposes these techniques but the doctor acts anyway, according to the will of the husband, for example when the woman

is unconscious during an operation or an examination, more offences are committed, such as illegal violence, abuse of an incompetent woman and supposition of a child.

3.2. OTHER MATTERS

Concerning other matters which could be discussed in the context of the new reproductive techniques, such as product liability, insurance, anonymity, publication of clinic success rates, the role of ethics committees, the limits of applications of the new techniques etc. one can note the following with respect to the situation in Greece.

3.2.1. *Product liability and insurance*

The provisions of Civil Law on the deposit of goods might be applied by analogy. The depository/unit holding the sperm, gametes or embyros would then be responsible for any minor or serious fault, if there were an agreement for remuneration; otherwise the depository would have an obligation to care as for his own. Insurance could be a solution for sperm banks, however in Greece private insurance is just being developed and for the time being there is no prospect of such insurance being available.

3.2.2. *Donor anonymity*

As was said above, in the decision of the Central Council for Health, donor anonymity is respected, and gamete donation and storage are permitted on condition that the anonymity of donors and recipients be respected. However, in the same document it is stated that all relevant data should be kept secret but accessible for a possible genetic need and also for the protection of the right of the child to find out in the future of the mode of his conception and maybe the identity of his genetic parents. Of course we do not know the exact way in which the legislator is going to regulate this matter; however there would be a major problem if there were a provision for possible disclosure of the identity of the donor.

3.2.3. *The role of ethics committees*

Ethics Committees do not yet function in Greece (though there are a very few exceptions) despite a Ministerial circular of 1978 providing for their establishment in all hospitals.[12] The new law 2071 of 1992 on the Modernisation and Organisation of the Health System provides for the establishment of a National Ethics Committee which will draw up policy on matters of medical and professional ethics, give an opinion on other relevant matters, and also give an opinion, at a second level, to help remove disagreements among the local ethics committees when they start fuctioning. The same law provides for the establishment, by ministerial decisions, of ethics committees in all public and private hospitals. These local ethics committees will give an opinion to the Board of Directors of the Institution on matters of medical and professional ethics and

also oversee the application of the rules of medical and professional ethics. The above mentioned decision of the Central Council for Health speaks about there being ethics committees in each assisted reproduction unit. However, it is still unknown when and how exactly these provisions will be put into effect.

3.2.4. *Sex selection and success rates*

Sex selection is not allowed according to the Decision of the Central Council for Health, except when a serious hereditary disease linked with the sex is to be avoided. However, since there is still no control by the State (since the Presidential Decrees mentioned in Law 2071/1992 have yet to be passed) anything can be done in the private sector. Further, since there is no state control, success rates claimed by the various clinics are very high, perhaps higher than the ones of the best Centres in the world.[13] Scientists themselves see the need for the establishment of a National Registry of all births achieved with the techniques of assisted reproduction.

4. Conclusion

The techniques of human artificial reproduction are already part of our lives. Scientific and technological progress cannot be stopped or strictly directed. However, the time has come to do something and some regulation is needed. Maybe there is no need to legislate on each minor detail yet, since things change so fast, but - in Greece at least - framework legislation is urgently needed.

Such legislation will need to be able regulate these techniques in a way which can be applied in practice, because in Greece there are many laws which are not applied at all, or are badly applied. On the other hand, what is also needed, even more than legislation, is the building, mainly through education, of a 'moral conscience' which will help not only scientists but all persons to keep the fragile equilibrium, and utilise the progress of science and technology in a prudent way which will not harm mankind, but will, on the contrary, benefit it.

Notes

1. Informal review of the daily press of Athens from 1986 to 1992, carried out by the author for the purposes of this paper.

2. Quoted by the secretary of the Committee on Laws and Rules of the Holy Synod, Mantzouneas, E., in Goudeli, N., 'Is or is not the production of high-technology children a form of racism? Views of Greek scientists and other important persons on artificial fertilisation and eugenics' *Messimvzini* (daily newspaper) 7 January 1987 (translated by the author).

3. Anonymous Archimandrite, quoted in Gavza, P., 'She will give birth to her brother' *Eleftheros Typos* (daily newspaper) 20-21 June 1987 (translated by the author).

4. Vacaros, D., quoted in Telides, C., 'Borrowed mother' *Ikomes* (periodical) 4 September 1991, pp.45-47 (translated by the author).

5. Ginis-Papthanassiou, J. (Chief Secretary of the Synod) quoted in Katsanopoulou, M., 'Are test-tube children illegitimate?' *To Vema* (Sunday newspaper) 4 March 1990 (translated by the author).

6. Decision No. 9 of the 56th Plenary of the Central Council for Health, 5 July 1988 (translated by the author).

7. Committee of Experts on Progress in the Biomedical Sciences (CAHBI), *Human Artificial Procreation* Strasbourg, Council of Europe, 1989.

8. Interviews with a number of people of letters and science on the issue of sex selection revealed a variety of views (of which a few follow). One geneticist said that very few couples would choose a sex-selected ferti- lisation, and for this reason the real danger was small. An IVF specialist said that in Greece, where the 70-80% of people prefer to have boy children, many people would take advantage of the possibility of sex selection. An ex-parliamentarian said that the female sex would lose, in the sense that fewer girls would be born taking into account the existing ideas in Greece; and one professor of law said that a dangerous racism would rise in the name of eugenics.

9. Law 2071/1992 on the Modernisation and Organisation of the Health System' *Ephimeris tes Kyberniseos* 123A 15 July 1992.

10. Translated by the author.

11. Androulidaki-Dimitriadi, I., 'Legal problems arising from artificial reproduction (problems of civil law)' *Nomiko Vema* 34, 1986, pp.10-17 (in Greek).

12. Ministry of Social Services, Ministerial Circular No. 3061 of 5 June 1978; cf. Koutselinis, A. and Michalodimitrakis, M., *Medical Responsibility* Athens, Gutenborg, 1984, p.148.

13. Cf. Kontopoulos, V. (a professor of gynaecology) quoted in Katsanopoulou, *op.cit.* and Theocharatos, C., 'Fertile business' *Ethnos* (daily newspaper) 7 January 1992.

22. THE LEGAL SITUATION OF ASSISTED REPRODUCTION IN SPAIN

Jaime Vidal Martínez
Profesor Titular de Derecho Civil
Departmento de Derecho Civil
Universitat de València
Spain

1. Background

At the end of 1988, two Acts were published in Spain: on Assisted Reproduction Techniques (ARTA) and the Donation and Utilisation of Embryos and Foetuses, their cells, tissues and organs (Acts 35 and 42, 22 November and 28 December 1988). They established detailed regulations on the subjects, which have been, however, for seven years in need of subsequent statutory development.[1] The aforementioned Acts were the object of an Appeal before the Constitutional Court in 1989 and that Appeal is still pending resolution (at the end of 1995).

2. Regulation of Practitioners

By the ARTA, the Government is supposed to establish a National Comission of Assisted Reproduction with wide powers, but this has not been constituted as yet.

  Also, according to the final dispositions of the ARTA, the Government should have brought forward regulation, within a six months period, on the following issues concerning assisted reproductive techniques (ART):
- necessary requirements for the authorisation of ART centres;
- protocols for the information of donors and users;
- protocols on studies of donors and users;
- genetic diseases that can be detected by means of prenatal diagnosis;
- rules for transport of gametes and pre-embryos;
- a computerised national register of gamete and pre-embryo donors (to be brought into operation with a year).
  The continued non-fulfillment of these obligations seven years after the Law's enactment casts doubt on its application.

  The centres that implement the ARTA in Spain have, up to now, based their protocols on their own regulatory frameworks taking into account the regulations expected to emerge when the government fulfils its obligations under the ARTA.

D. Evans (ed.), Creating the Child, 287–289.
© 1996 *Kluwer Law International. Printed in the Netherlands.*

3. Criteria of Access to Services

According to article 2.1 in the ARTA, any woman over eighteen who is physically and psychically healthy who is fully competent to act can receive or make use of the techniques mentioned above (art. 6.1.). In cases of married, non-separated women, they need their husband's consent.

The medical teams that implement the ARTA are responsible for the choice of donor, and must guarantee that the donor has the utmost phenotypical and immunological similarity/compatibility with the recipient and her family (art. 6.5).

It is stated in the Act's Preamble that the woman's wish to procreate must not be restrained when it is assumed to be free and responsible.

4. Consent Procedures

The ARTA obliges medical teams properly to inform and advise potential users of ARTs about possible implications, outcomes and risks (art. 2.2.). Consent to allow the use of these techniques must be formally stated and written down (art. 6). The donation of gametes and pre-embryos is regarded as a free, formal and secret contract, arranged between the donor and the authorised centre (art. 5.1). The donor must be informed of the aims and consequences of the donation (art. 5.4).

5. Methods of Treatment

The regulation foreseen for ARTA has not been developed yet, and the Registers have not yet been set up.[2] The Spanish Society of Fertility is attempting to gather data about application of ART in Spain.

In the 1991 World Collaborative Report, the data for which were submitted to the 7th World Congress on IVF and Alternate Assisted Reproduction, Kyoto, Japan (12th-15th September 1993), only one Spanish Centre took part. It had carried out 762 procedures, with 120 births, 625 oocyte retrieval cycles, 100 in vitro fertilisation (IVF) treatments, no gamete intra-fallopian transfers (GIFT), 206 thawed transfers, 25 micromanipulations and 28 oocyte donations.

According to data provided by the Valencian Infertility Institute the figures for 1993 were: (for treatment cycles) 2106 IVF and 108 other procedures, and (for clinical pregnancies) 328 through IVF treatments, of which 249 resulted in live new-borns, and 29 through procedures other than IVF, each giving rise to one or more live births.[3]

6. Prohibitions

Article 3 of ARTA expressly forbids insemination of human ova for any purpose other

than human procreation. From art. 4 the illegality of transferring to the womb more pre-embryos than those strictly necessary to produce pregnancy can be inferred.

From article 5 of ARTA several prohibitions can be inferred: of the donation of gametes and pre-embryos for commercial or money making purposes, of giving the identity of donors except for cases contemplated by law, and of employing as donors people suffering from genetic, hereditary or transferable diseases. No one donor is allowed to be the genetic parent of more than six children.

Cryopreservation of ova for the purposes of reproduction is not authorised as long as there are no guarantees of their viability after the thawing process.

There is detailed regulation on diagnosis, treatment, research and experimentation with pre-embryos. The last is expressly forbidden, either in the womb or in the fallopian tubes (art 16.4 ARTA). There exists a long list of serious offences (art 20.2 B ARTA) committed whenever legal regulation is trespassed to any extent or where pre-embryo research projects are conducted without the necessary licences having been granted.

7. Rules of Parentage

Specific rules of parentage are included in articles 7-10 ARTA which complete and modify rules foreseen by the Civil Code; the Civil Register must not contain data from which it can be inferred that reproduction has been assisted.

The husband's consent prevents him objecting to filiation through marriage where a donor has contributed to the child's conception. On the other hand, non-married males are permitted to recognise as their own the child had by the woman. The woman is the legal mother of the children she has given birth to. Any contract for pregnancy by surrogacy will be considered void.

Notes

1. The forthcoming enactment of two decrees-law has now been announced by the media (*El País* (Madrid) 7 November 1995). These concern the requirements for the authorisation of ART Centres, protocols of donors and users, and registers of donors and of preembryos.

2. But see note 1.

3. We would like to thank Dr Barri of Epuipo Dexeus, and Dr Pellicer and Dr Remohi of the Valencian Infertility Institute for their help in obtaining these figures.

23. PATIENT PERCEPTIONS OF ASSISTED CONCEPTION SERVICES

Maria Dolanska
Genetic Counselling Centre
Thomayer University Hospital
Prague
Czech Republic

Donald Evans
Centre for Philosophy and Health Care
University of Wales, Swansea
Singleton Park
Swansea
Wales

As part of the European Commission research project on *Fertility, infertility and the human embryo* an empirical pilot project was executed to collect certain data relevant to the design of assisted procreation services and their regulation. The project took the form of a questionnaire distributed to patients of infertility clinics in Bulgaria (BUL), the Czech Republic (CZR), Hungary (HUN), Italy (ITY), Poland (POL), Russia (RUS), Spain (SPA) and the United Kingdom (UK).

1. Background to the Questionnaire

The project attempted to ascertain the attitudes and perspectives of patients towards their infertility and the possibility of assisted conception services. It was interested to ask whether attitudes on specific aspects of the services vary from country to country. The project was also concerned to try to discover how couples seeking assisted conception services planned to behave in the event of a successful clinical intervention using the new technologies in order to assess the adequacy or desirability of regulations of the services to protect the interests of the resulting children, the commissioning couples and the donors of gametes. Finally the project endeavoured to discover whether male and female patient perceptions of numbers of factors in the implementation of such services differed in important respects.

Consequently members of couples were asked to reply independently to a questionnaire which contained just six questions. The first concerned their willingness to employ either donor sperm, donor oocytes or donor zygotes in resolving their childlessness and further, whether there were preferences for which of these they would

D. Evans (ed.), Creating the Child, 291–301.

be willing to employ. The second concerned questions of anonymity of donors and the disclosure of information to the children born by these means about the nature of their origins. The third concerned the willingness of the couples to pay for assisted conception procedures, the fourth concerned the provision of counselling. Sex selection of and sex preferences for prospective children were the issues canvassed in the fifth question and the final question sought to discover whether the couples were willing to travel outside their own country to obtain such services as were unavailable in their own country.

2. Analysis

Most of the responses were obtained from patients who attended infertility clinics over a period of two months during 1994 and 1995. However the variety of patients makes general conclusions difficult to achieve. Some of these were presenting for the first time and had received little or no information from the infertility clinic about the possible modes of treatment. Others had already received some treatments, some successfully, and had returned for further help. In one case past patients were canvassed for their views. One of the institutions conducting the survey was an institute of genetics to which women with fertility problems were routinely referred. All the others were infertility clinics which offered the full range of assisted conception services. Some of the clinics offered services only on a private payment basis (including the Russian centre) whereas others offered both public and private services. On some occasions the male member of a couple failed to return a completed questionnaire when his partner had completed one. The numbers of people approached in the different countries also varied very greatly, depending on the size of the unit in question. The numbers of completed questionnaires were as follows:

	BUL	CZR	HUN	ITY	POL	RUS	SPA	UK
Female	65	37	84	17	15	50	29	75
Male	65	37	84	17	15	50	27	48
Total	130	74	168	34	30	100	56	123

The differences in numbers and characters of the patients and the variety of institutions at which the patients presented make it impossible to draw generalisable conclusions about the comparative character of attitudes of infertile couples in the different countries. Nevertheless the figures are suggestive of certain conclusions which are significant for the drawing up and enforcement of regulation of assisted conception services and as such may suggest the worthwhileness of a more exhaustive empirical study designed to produce definitive answers to the questions concerned.

3. Employment of Donor Gametes or Zygotes

Patients were asked whether they were willing to consider the use of donated gametes or zygotes in seeking assisted reproduction services. If they were willing to do so they were given the choice of using:

(1a) either donated sperm, oocytes or embryos as required;
(1b) donated sperm only;
(1c) donated oocytes only;
(1d) donated embryos only.

The responses were as follows:

Question (1a): If you decide to seek assisted reproduction will you agree to the use of either sperm or oocyte or embryo donation if necessary?

	BUL	CZR	HUN	ITY	POL	RUS	SPA	UK
male	41	29	64	7	10	30	19	21
female	48	33	65	7	9	32	20	42

Question (1b): If you decide to seek assisted reproduction will you agree to the use of sperm donation only?

	BUL	CZR	HUN	ITY	POL	RUS	SPA	UK
male	3	4	12	5	2	12	1	7
female	6	3	3	4	2	10	3	2

Question (1c): If you decide to seek assisted reproduction will you agree to the use of oocyte donation only?

	BUL	CZR	HUN	ITY	POL	RUS	SPA	UK
male	2	3	8	1	1	8	1	1
female	4	0	16	3	2	8	3	3

Question (1d): If you decide to seek assisted reproduction will you agree to the use of a donated embryo only?

	BUL	CZR	HUN	ITY	POL	RUS	SPA	UK
male	16	1	0	0	2	0	0	3
female	5	0	0	0	1	0	0	3

The totals of respondents prepared to use donated gametes or zygotes were as follows:

Totals

	BUL	CZR	HUN	ITY	POL	RUS	SPA	UK
male	62	37	84	13	15	50	21	32
female	63	36	84	14	14	50	26	50

From the sample questioned there were only very small percentages from all countries except the United Kingdom, Spain and Italy who were opposed to the use of donors altogether. 33.3% of the British male respondents were so opposed and 33.3% of British females respondents as opposed to 22.2% of Spanish males and 10.3% of Spanish females on the one hand and 23.5% of Italian males and 17.6% of Italian females on the other hand. It must be remembered that the total number of Spanish respondents was much smaller than the UK number and the Italian numbers were the smallest of all. However the overwhelming majority of respondents were in favour of some form of donor assisted conception with percentages varying between countries from 66.6% to 100% with five countries being well above 90%. The overall figure for all respondents in favour of donor assisted techniques was 91%. For the most part there seemed to be little evidence of male and female preference for sperm only or oocyte only donation except for Hungary where 14.2% of males preferred sperm donation only (four times as many as the female respondents) and where 19% of female respondents preferred oocyte donation only as opposed to 9.5% of males. The Bulgarian figure of almost 25% of male respondents preferring embryo only donation was out of character with all other group responses.

4. Disclosure of Information

Question 2 asked whether the commissioning parents wished to know the identity of the donors of gametes or zygotes (2a), whether they wished the resultant child to know the identity of the donor (2b) and finally whether they intended to tell the child the nature of its origins if donor gametes or zygotes were employed (2c). The responses were as follows:

Question (2a): If donor gametes are used would you wish to know the identity of the donor?

	BUL	CZR	HUN	ITY	POL	RUS	SPA	UK
male 'yes'	25	12	15	4	2	12	1	6
male 'no'	35	16	32	11	13	26	23	31
female 'yes'	30	10	6	4	2	12	1	13
female 'no'	27	26	78	11	12	28	25	54

Question (2b): If donor gametes are used would you wish your child to know the identity of the donor?

	BUL	CZR	HUN	ITY	POL	RUS	SPA	UK
male 'yes'	7	0	0	4	0	1	1	6
male 'no'	31	29	24	10	15	49	23	30
female 'yes'	9	0	2	0	0	2	1	8
female 'no'	29	36	82	14	14	48	25	53

Question (2c): If donor gametes are used would you tell your child that donor gametes were used in its creation?

	BUL	CZR	HUN	ITY	POL	RUS	SPA	UK
male 'yes'	4	4	0	8	0	2	7	16
male 'no'	26	29	56	6	15	48	15	21
female 'yes'	8	8	24	9	0	1	7	35
female 'no'	23	27	61	4	14	49	17	27

The issue of anonymity of donors of gametes has been extensively discussed in those countries which have passed legislation or are preparing legislation for the regulation of assisted procreation services. The Swedish law has been amended to remove the original anonymity provision[1] whereas elsewhere it is still a binding condition of the acceptance of donor assisted services. The dissonance between legislatures on this point has led to at least one difficult case which is still going through the courts concerning the rights of a mother and the child born to her in Sweden by means of sperm donated in Denmark.[2] Whether such dislocation will produce many more difficult cases as more legislation emerges is a moot point. However there is certainly potential for such an increase in the absence of harmonisation of regulation in this and other aspects of the law governing reproduction. Thus it is worth asking whether the issue of donor anonymity is important to prospective parents (2a) and, as is canvassed in question (2b) whether it is considered by those parents to be important for the resultant children. The amendment of the Swedish law is a possible precedent for other countries which have initially built anonymity into their legislation, such as the United Kingdom.[3] Perhaps the most important basis on which such changes should rest is the welfare of the children concerned. Apart from the comparison with the rights of adopted children in countries such as the UK to access information about the identity of their genetic parents, a right in this case which was hard won after prolonged argument and evidence gathering about the welfare of such children, the most compelling basis for change would be evidence of harm to the children produced by long term follow-up of families resulting from assisted procreation programmes. But in order for such research to be possible the children must be identified. Question (2c) seeks the views of prospective parents about their willingness for this to occur. If they intend to keep their infertility a secret from the children then the children cannot be properly followed up without

breaching the confidence which their parents are guaranteed by laws such as the UK Human Fertilisation and Embryology Act 1990. That Act does guarantee to children access to genetic data about their genetic progenitors when they attain maturity. But if such children are totally ignorant of the nature of their origins they will not know whether to seek such information. A general refusal by parents to divulge to their children the fact that they were produced by means of donated gametes renders the provision of the Act somewhat ineffective.

An analysis of the responses shows that the numbers of prospective parents who would like to know the identity of the donors varies from less than 3.5% in Spain to 42.3% in Bulgaria. That is, in all countries only a minority of people desired such information – indeed in most cases a small minority. When we ask whether such people would wish their children to know the identity of their genetic progenitors the numbers shrink almost to vanishing point. The highest percentage of people who did so wish was 12.3 % in Bulgaria but the remainder varied from 0% in two countries to 11.4% in the UK. The reticence to share information about the identity of the donors with the child also extends to information about the use of donor gametes at all in the origins of the children. The highest proportion of people who were willing to divulge this information was Italy where 50% said yes, though it has to be remembered that this was the smallest sample used in all the countries. In most countries either no respondents or very small proportions of them said 'yes', for example 0% in Poland and 1.5% in Russia. The Hungarian and UK figures present an interesting response pattern in common. Both countries involved a similar proportionately large number of respondents and parallel contrasts between male and female affirmative responses was noticeable in them. In Hungary 0% of men and 28.57% of women expressed an intention to tell the child that donor gametes were employed in its creation, in the UK the male numbers were 33.3% men and 46.6% women.

5. Public and Private Provision

In most countries in Europe some provision of assisted conception services is funded out of the public purse. This is usually supplemented by a much larger volume of services which are purchased privately by patients. Some authorities refuse to purchase the services out of public funds because they regard it as a luxury service rather than a service which meets a pressing clinical need. The willingness of patients to make considerable sacrifices to obtain help in overcoming infertility may offer some indication of whether it is proper to regard infertility merely as the frustration of a capricious desire for a child or rather as constituting a genuine health need. For example, that so many presenting patients in the survey live in former Eastern Bloc countries and are subject to considerable economic disadvantages but are nevertheless willing to pay for assisted procreation services indicates something of the seriousness with which they regard their condition. In the Russian Centre, for example, where the service is provided only as patients pay for it themselves, the cost of one cycle of IVF is

equivalent to more than a year's average wages. The aggregated male and female responses to the question 'Will you decide to seek assisted reproduction even if you have to pay for it?' (3a), and 'Will you use assisted reproduction if it is offered free of charge?' (3b) were as follows:

Question (3a): Will you decide to seek assisted reproduction even if you have to pay for it? (in this country it likely to cost about.....)

	BUL	CZR	HUN	ITY	POL	RUS	SPA	UK
'yes'	77	67	128	18	28	97	52	82
' no'	6	1	4	6	0	3	0	11
'don't know'	12	5	36	11	2	0	0	24

Question (3b): Will you use assisted reproduction if it is offered free of charge?

	BUL	CZR	HUN	ITY	POL	RUS	SPA	UK
'yes'	130	64	168	32	30	100	48	90
'no'	0	2	0	0	0	0	0	5
'don't know'	0	4	0	3	0	0	4	11

Numbers of patients who responded 'don't know' to (3a) gave their reason for so doing as being that they simply did not have the necessary money. Thus it is the 'no' reponses to (3a) which are most revealing about the intensity of the desire for a child felt by infertile patients. In all cases except Italy (the smallest sample) the proportion of 'no's' is below 10%.

6. Counselling Services

In many countries it is accepted that the provision of counselling services for potential users of assisted conception services and for donors is a necessary feature of good clinical practice. Indeed in some cases, the United Kingdom for example, it is enshrined in the legal regulation of the treatment.[4] Respondents were asked whether they had been offered genetic counselling (4a), whether they had been offered any other kinds of counselling (4b) and whether they had found such counselling helpful (4c). The aggregated male and female responses were as follows:

Question (4a): Has genetic counselling been offered to you in dealing with your fertility related problem?

	BUL	CZR	HUN	ITY	POL	RUS	SPA	UK
'yes'	33	32	53	7	2	11	24	0
'no'	60	10	111	19	26	89	20	0

Question (4b): Has any other kind of counselling been offered to you in dealing with your fertility related problem?

	BUL	CZR	HUN	ITY	POL	RUS	SPA	UK
'yes'	15	16	124	5	13	54	19	33
'no'	27	18	38	21	15	46	23	89

Question (4c): Have you found such counselling helpful?

	BUL	CZR	HUN	ITY	POL	RUS	SPA	UK
'yes'	19	59	142	12	9	48	19	12
'no'	19	0	12	1	16	0	4	2

The figures suggest that there is still a good way to go to provide a proper cover of counselling services in most of the countries in the pilot survey. However it should be pointed out that appearances may deceive for numbers of the respondents were attending the clinics for the first time and it might be that counselling is offered at a later stage in the process of accessing assisted procreation services.

7. Sex Selection

There has been considerable discussion about whether sex selection should be permitted in assisted procreation now that we have the means to determine the sex of the pre-embryo before placement in the uterus of the prospective mother. Arguments against such freedoms have included the empirical claim that selection would lead to gross imbalances between the genders, it usually being assumed that the predominant choice would be for sons rather than daughters. Despite the very small proportions of children born by means of assisted procreation techniques the principle of freedom to select the sex of children born by these means may be thought to encourage an increase in demand for abortion on the grounds of the sex of the foetus, thus strengthening the claim. Of course slippery slope arguments of this empirical kind are open to challenge, if not refutation, by showing that there is no evidence to support the cited predictions. An examination of the wishes of infertile couples with respect to choice of the sex of the children they plan might offer some help in this regard. The respondents were asked 'If you plan a pregnancy would you like to be able to choose which sex the child should be?' (5a) and 'If your answer is *yes* which sex would you prefer?' (5b). The responses were as follows:

Question (5a): If you plan a pregnancy would you like to be able to choose which sex the child should be?

	BUL	CZR	HUN	ITY	POL	RUS	SPA	UK
male 'yes'	15	20	4	4	2	19	5	10
male 'no'	48	17	80	14	13	31	22	39
female 'yes'	15	14	2	2	3	14	4	6
female 'no'	46	24	82	15	12	36	25	67

Question (5b): If your answer is yes which sex would you prefer?

	BUL	CZR	HUN	ITY	POL	RUS	SPA	UK
male 'male'	14	10	1	4	1	12	0	6
male 'female'	1	10	3	0	1	6	3	5
female 'male'	4	5	0	0	0	5	0	2
female 'female'	9	7	2	1	3	9	2	2

The only group to show a majority in favour of sex selection were the male respondents from the Czech Republic. For the rest the overall 'no' vote from male respondents was 76% and from females 82%. This suggests that the pressure for sex selection in general is not overwhelming. It should be noted that the figures refer to couples the vast majority of which are seeking their first and maybe their only child. The desire for a healthy child of any sex clearly predominates. Whether the same would apply when a further child was planned is another matter. However such a change in wishes would not normally be expected to upset the balance between genders but rather to ensure it if the remarks of numbers of the respondents about question (5a) are used as a guide. Nevertheless the sizes of some of the minorities are such that the absence of firm guidelines on the matter will present constant problems for practitioners. The preferred choices of those who did signal a desire to select the sex of their children are interesting, though they are very small samples. Overall there are no startling contrasts between men and women in their choices, neither are there obvious imbalances between the sexes. The exception does seem significant, viz. Bulgarian men where the choice of a son rather than a daughter was fourteen to one.

The more powerful argument against sex selection is a moral one, viz. that to permit selection would be to bestow respectability on what is really a disreputable criterion for assessing the worth of people. Though some respondents expressed strong opinions against sex selection in the optional comments allowed for in the questionnaire which accorded with this view the empirical data concerning numbers in favour of or against sex selection are by the way with respect to this argument.

8. Procreative 'Tourism'

We have already alluded to one legal tangle which has resulted from the dissonance between legislatures in the regulation of assisted procreation services. It could, of course, be an isolated case. However if there was known to be a considerable willingness on the part of people to travel to another country for services which were either unavailable or illegal in their own country then such problems would be likely to multiply. Such a prospect would lend weight to the call for harmonisation of laws and regulations between countries, or at least call for the provision of some agreed mechanism of arbitration in the event of such tangles occurring. Additionally already there have been cases of people travelling beyond the boundaries of their own country to obtain treatment in countries where there is less rigorous control of assisted conception services. For example a fifty nine year old woman was refused such services in the United Kingdom on the basis of her age - in the United Kingdom all publicly funded services in the field set an age limit for the women treated which varies between thirty five and forty two years of age.[5] Additionally the Human Fertilisation and Embryology Authority which licenses all centres entitled to offer such services in the United Kingdom sets an age limit. The woman in question travelled to Italy where restrictions are currently almost non-existent and was successfully treated. It is not the purpose of this paper to adjudicate on such issues but simply to note that they occur and to enquire as to whether the custom is likely to increase. Thus the respondents were asked 'If assisted conception services are not available in your country would you be prepared to travel to another country to receive them?' (6) The aggregated male and female responses were as follows:

Question 6: If assisted conception services are not available in your country would you be prepared to travel to another country to receive them?

	BUL	CZR	HUN	ITY	POL	RUS	SPA	UK
'yes'	101	56	112	21	26	50	50	79
'no'	26	6	36	11	4	50	6	33

In every country at least half the repondents were willing to travel to receive treatment and in most large majorities were prepared to do this suggesting that the possibility of an increase in the sort of problems canvassed above is high.

Acknowledgements

Thanks are due to the following practitioners and researchers who carefully collected all the data in the project in their respective countries: Dr. Ilya Vatev, Sofia, Bulgaria; Mr. John Parsons, London, England; Dr. Pedro Barrie, Barcelona, Spain; Dr. Boris Leonov, Moscow, Russia; Dr. Marian Szamatowicz, Bialystok, Poland; Dr. Maria Dolanska, Prague, Czech Republic; Dr. Karoly Schultz, Szekszard, Hungary; Dr.

Marina Mengarelli, Bologna, Italy.

Notes

1. 'Law on Insemination' No. 1140, 20 December 1984, art. 4.

2. Cf. *The Independent* 17 June 1994.

3. See the Human Fertilisation and Embryology Act 1990, Section 31, 5.

4. See the Human Fertilisation and Embryology Act 1990, Section 13, 6 (c).

5. Wiles, R. and Patel, H., *Report of the Third National Survey of NHS Funding of Infertility Services* London, College of Health, 1995.

PART FIVE

Assisted Procreation and the Law

24. LEGAL CONSENSUS AND DIVERGENCE IN EUROPE IN THE AREA OF ASSISTED CONCEPTION - ROOM FOR HARMONISATION?

Associate Professor of Law Linda Nielsen, Dr. juris,
Faculty of Law, The University of Copenhagen
Denmark
Member of the Danish Council of Ethics

1. Introduction, Purpose and Legislative Approaches

1.1. INTRODUCTION AND PURPOSE

In this essay legal issues involved in the treatment of human infertility are analysed and the predominant legal views in various European countries are compared, to see whether some kind of consensus is possible. For this purpose the existing legislation in Europe is outlined.[1] To a certain extent existing practice described by national experts is also included.

The need for such analysis is initiated by the fact that there is legal - and ethical - dispute throughout Europe as to what should or should not be allowed in the practice of reproductive medicine. Many of the countries in Europe have either enacted or are in the process of drafting legislation to govern the activities of medical practioners and researchers. The result is that we have serious incompatibilities between laws of member states on matters such as assisted conception.

International approaches are called for by the fact that the new reproductive technologies make people cross national frontiers to achieve what they cannot have in their own country - access to *in vitro* fertilisation (IVF), donor insemination, egg donation, embryo donation, surrogate motherhood, etc. In today's modern 'global village', with its means of transportation and communication, the restrictions in one country regarding these possibilities may lead to a kind of 'procreative tourism'. This way citizens may exercise their personal reproductive choices in other, less restrictive countries.

There is a broad choice between aiming, on the one hand, at a uniform minimum threshold of law and regulation - thus emphasising individual freedom of choice - and, on the other hand, at a uniform maximum coverage of law and regulation - thus emphasising societal protection of future children issuing from assisted conception.

In the following the different legislative approaches are described and the areas of consensus and divergence on the different topics within assisted procreation are outlined together with some indications of what might constitute the reasons for the differences. Some remarks are made about the advantages and disadvantages of trying to reach consensus and finally some concluding remarks regarding the analysis are made.

D. Evans (ed.), Creating the Child, 305–324.
© 1996 *Kluwer Law International. Printed in the Netherlands.*

The survey includes *the UK, Germany, France, Austria, Spain, Italy, Greece, Norway, the Netherlands, Poland, Hungary, Sweden* and *Denmark*. The description is by no means exhaustive but suggests how and why some countries have a 'restrictive' attitude towards the area of assisted reproduction, whereas other countries hold a more 'permissive' attitude.

1.2. DIFFERENT LEGISLATIVE APPROACHES

Although the questions that arise with respect to law, medicine and bioethics are similar all over the world, there are differences of a philosophical, economic, social, political and religious nature which have led to different regulations. The legal solutions regarding these questions may be characterised as a) the prohibitive approach, b) the cautious regulatory approach, c) the liberal regulatory approach, and d) the laissez-faire approach. A number of examples may illustrate this:

1.2.1. *The Prohibitive Approach*

In *Germany* the attitude towards assisted reproduction has been restrictive, centred almost entirely on penal provisions but without forming part of the Criminal Law. The Embryo Protection Act[2] prohibits a) fertilisation other than for purposes of pregnancy, b) the fertilisation of a human egg cell for any purpose other than to start a pregnancy in the woman who produced the egg, c) the fertilisation of more eggs than may be necessary for transfer in one cycle, d) permitting sperm to penetrate an egg other than for the purpose of producing a pregnancy. Thus egg and embryo donation are prohibited. Gestation outside the womb is prohibited other than for achieving a pregnancy.

In *Austria* a range of prohibitions in relation to both assisted conception services and embryo research was enacted in 1992. Assisted conception is to be confined to married couples or stable heterosexual cohabitees, who are deemed to be able to provide a satisfactory home for the child. Storage may not exceed one year after which any stored embryos or gametes must be allowed to perish. All forms of *in vivo* assisted conception using donated gametes are prohibited with the exception of donor insemination. Donor sperm may also be used in the context of IVF but egg donation and embryo donation are not permitted. The semen of any given donor may be used for medically assisted reproduction in up to three marriages or cohabitant relationships. Semen donors do not enjoy rights of anonymity. Any child who may be born following the use of his sperm may, from the age of 14, request information regarding his identity. Clinics have a duty to keep records showing the name of donors, birth date and place, nationality, residence etc. Embryo donation is prohibited and ova and embryos may be used only for women from whom they are genetically derived. This ensures that donated embryos or gametes may not be used to establish a surrogate pregnancy.[3]

1.2.2. *The Cautious Regulatory Approach*

In *Denmark* donor insemination is not regulated. In practice the public hospitals normally treat women who are married or cohabiting, but not single women or lesbians, who may be treated in private clinics. Administrative provisions operated through the central Danish cryopreservation facility for sperm ensure that donor insemination (AID) will be undertaken only anonymously. Donor insemination can also take place in private clinics and without a doctor's involvement, which is not unlawful. IVF may be offered in the public hospitals or in private clinics. According to guidelines from the Minister of Health women over 45 years should not be offered IVF. Donation of human eggs is accepted.[4] Administrative regulations[5] specify that the donation of unfertilised human eggs should be undertaken only anonymously. Donation of fertilised human eggs is prohibited according to the 1992 Act.[6] It is permissible to cryopreserve human eggs, but according to administrative regulations only for a maximum of one year and aiming at treatment and research only in Denmark. According to special legislation[7] advertising and procurement of surrogacy are liable to punishment. A new bill on assisted procreation is expected to be presented in the 1995-99 session of the Danish Parliament.

In *Sweden* donor insemination is restricted to married couples, or those in a long standing relationship. Treatment requires written consent from the husband or cohabitant who will be regarded as the legal father of the child. The most radical aspect of the law is the section relating to information about the donor. It is decreed that the child should have the right to obtain identifying information about the donor.[8] The net effect of the change of attitude to donor anonymity represented in the law was, firstly, to reduce the number and change the types of donors available - older married rather than younger single men offered themselves as donors - and, secondly, a reduction in the demand for donor insemination. In fact, many Swedish couples seeking donor insemination seek treatment in other countries where donor anonymity is still guaranteed - e.g. Denmark. To be eligible for IVF couples must be married or living together in a permanent relationship (more than 2 years). Fertilisation outside the human body may be carried out only in a general hospital, unless the authorisation of the National Board of Health and Welfare is obtained. The use of donated gametes in the context of IVF or the donation of surplus embryos to another couple is forbidden. The reasoning is that donor insemination in itself constitutes a deviation from the natural biological process; a combination of sperm donation and external fertilisation represents an even greater departure from that process. Where the donation of ova is concerned it is considered that use of eggs from a third party is contrary to the human biological process.[9] Freezing of surplus embryos is allowed for up to one year with the couple's consent.[10]

In *Norway* artificial fertilisation may be carried out only in institutions specially authorised for this purpose by the Ministry of Social Affairs. The decision to undertake treatment with a view to artificial reproduction shall be made by a physician. The decision shall be based on medical and psychosocial assessment of the couple. Artificial

reproductive treatment may be carried out only in married women or women living in a stable partnership with a man. Donor insemination may be carried out only when the husband is infertile or if he himself suffers from or is a carrier of a serious hereditary disease or, in special cases, where the woman is the carrier of a recessive gene for which the man is also a carrier. The physician providing the treatment shall select a suitable sperm donor. The identity of the donor is to be kept secret. The treatment of sperm before procreation with a view to determining the sex of the child is allowed only if the woman is a carrier of serious sex-linked hereditary disease. Generally, IVF may take place only if the woman or her husband or partner is infertile or if they are, for reasons unknown, infertile as a couple. However, IVF may also be used in cases of serious hereditary disease. Such treatment may be carried out only with the gametes of the couples themselves - neither donor sperm nor donor eggs may be used in conjunction with IVF. The embryo may be used for implantation only in the woman from whom the eggs originate. The freezing of unfertilised eggs is prohibited. Only establishments which are authorised to carry out artificial fertilisation may freeze or store sperm or fertilised eggs. The latter may be utilised only for implantation in women and may not be stored for more than three years.[11]

In *France* new legislation was enacted in 1994.[12] According to this legislation both members of the couple must be alive, of an age to procreate and married to obtain medically assisted procreation. If not married, they must be able to prove that they have been living together for at least 2 years. Their consent to the transfer of embryos or insemination must be obtained. An embryo may not be conceived unless gametes come from at least one member of the couple. Both members of the couple may decide in writing that attempted fertilisation of a number of oocytes will necessitate the storage of embryos in order to fulfil their parental request within 5 years. Both members of the couple are to be consulted each year for 5 years, to find out whether they maintain their parental request. Exceptionally both members of the couple may give consent in writing for the stored embryos to be received by another couple. In the case of the death of one member of the couple the surviving member is to be asked in writing whether he consents to the stored embryos being given to another couple. Exceptionally a couple for whom medically assisted procreation without a donor would fail may receive an embryo. The receiving of an embryo is subject to the decision of a judicial authority, after obtaining written consent from the couple who originally conceived the embryo. The judge must carry out any investigation necessary to discover what the couple will be able to offer to the future child on a familial, educational, and psychological level. The recipient and the couple giving the embryo may not find out their respective identities. However, in the case of therapeutic necessity, a doctor may obtain non-identifying medical information concerning the donor couple. No payment whatsoever may be made to the couple giving the embryo. Medically assisted procreation with donor gametes may only be carried out as a last resort when medically assisted procreation within the couple has failed. Medically assisted procreation must be carried out under the responsibility of a named practitioner registered in each establishment or laboratory as authorised to carry out such activities. Moreover, there

are specific arrangements concerning the donation and use of gametes. The donor most be part of a couple which has already procreated. The use of gametes from the same donor may not deliberately result in the birth of more than 5 children.

1.2.3. *The Liberal Regulatory Approach*

In the *UK* the attitude towards assisted reproduction has been more liberal.[13] The Human Fertilisation and Embryology Act of 1990 (HFE Act) regulates infertility treatments, including IVF, donor insemination and egg and embryo donation. A statutory agency charged with a wide range of responsibilities - the Human Fertilisation and Embryology Authority (HFEA) - licenses clinics which undertake the storage of gametes and embryos and any infertility treatment which involves the use of either donated gametes or embryos created outside the human body. In addition the Authority is charged *inter alia* with maintaining a register of information concerning donors, treatment services and children born following licensed services, and providing information to donors, to potential patients and to children born following regulated services. The HFEA Code of Practice contains provisions which deal with the confidentiality of records, and detail appropriate laboratory standards and qualifications and experience of staff employed at licensed centres.

In *The Netherlands* legislation in the reproductive area is scarce. In *Spain* legislation concerning assisted reproduction has been made which has not been implemented. The 1988 legislation[14] is intended to regulate the donation and utilisation of embryos and foetuses, their cells, tissues and organs.

1.2.4. *The Laissez-faire Approach*

In *Italy* the legal approach towards assisted conception is omissive. Italy has not yet produced any statute regarding the issues related to artificial fertilisation, treatment of human gametes, human embryos etc., although proposals have been made. There is no legislation or formal regulation of IVF. Thus there are no age conditions and no legal provisions banning semen, egg or embryo-donation. Neither is there for the time being any central collection of IVF statistics and it is therefore not possible to obtain reliable information about the number of treatments carried out and their outcome. A more or less common code of practice has been agreed including e.g. that for a couple to be entitled to IVF they must be married and that donation of eggs or sperm is acceptable but IVF embryos should not be donated from one couple to another. Some clinics in Italy have been among the first to treat women who have passed the age of natural menopause.

Greece is another example of a country adopting the laissez-faire approach with almost no regulation. Artificial reproduction is not embraced by specific legislation. However, Law 2071/1992 provides for the establishment and function of Units for Artificial Fertilisation and authorises this regulation by a Presidential Decree.

In *Poland* assisted reproduction has not been regulated, either by laws dealing with

the practice of medicine, or by family code provisions regulating the problem of affiliation or other aspects of the legal status of the child. Furthermore, there exist no consistent professional guidelines referring to this issue.

In *Hungary* there have been only a few legislative attempts in the field of assisted procreation. Artificial insemination is regulated to a certain degree, whereas IVF is not. In 1992 the Hungarian Health Science Council adopted a report on the 'Ethics of new methods of human reproduction' which applied 3 moral principles, including, respect for the individual (autonomy, etc.) and justice.

2. Areas of Consensus and Divergence - the Different Topics

The following description is based on the different legislations and reports from national experts regarding existing practice. Not all of the countries are mentioned, when the national attitudes towards the different topics are outlined, but the survey presents a picture of the basic areas of consensus and divergence within the countries.

2.1. ACCESS TO ASSISTED CONCEPTION

2.1.1. *Married Couples, Cohabiting Couples, Single Women and Lesbians*

In *all* of the countries involved in the survey married people are entitled to assisted conception. In *Hungary* artificial insemination is available only for women who live in a marriage and have a permanent address in Hungary.

In most countries assisted conception is also available to couples in stable, heterosexual cohabitations. This goes for *Austria* (where no specific period of cohabitation required), *Denmark* (where, in practice three years cohabitation is required by the public hospitals), *Norway, Sweden, Holland, the UK, Germany, France* (where legislation requires two years cohabitation), *Italy* and *Spain*. It is also practised in *Greece*.

The main rule seems to be that single women and lesbians may not benefit from medically assisted conception. In *Spain* it is allowed as there is no legislation on the matter, which means that the question is normally decided by the clinicians. In *Denmark* single women and lesbians are excluded from IVF in public hospitals, whereas there is no regulation concerning artificial insemination in private hospitals.

2.1.2. *Post-Mortem Insemination*

In *Germany* post-mortem insemination is unlawful. In *Denmark* IVF after the death of a spouse or partner is prohibited, whereas there is no explicit regulation concerning insemination. In *France* both members of the couple must be alive and consent; posthumous insemination is banned.

2.1.3. *Age Conditions*

In *France* only couples in the procreative age group have access to assisted conception. In *Denmark* doctors are advised by administrative guidelines from the Ministry of Health to refuse treatment to women over 45 years. In *Hungary* a woman can receive artificial insemination only if she is not older than 45. In *Italy* there are no age limits outside of Medical Association guidelines.

2.1.4. *Number of Eggs Transferred*

In *Germany* transfer of more than three embryos during the same cycle is unlawful. In *Austria* a doctor may cause only as many eggs to be fertilised as are to be used in that treatment cycle. A number of countries have no provisions on the topic.

2.2. OFFERING OF ASSISTED CONCEPTION

2.2.1. *Practitioners*

In *Germany*, the law prohibits any but doctors from acting in this particular area. In *Austria* lawful assisted conception may be practiced only by obstetricians and gynaecologists.

2.2.2. *Licensing*

In *Austria* any practitioner, who intends to offer assisted conception, must apply for a licence. Similarly, doctors in *Germany* have to be licensed to carry out IVF. In *France*, *Norway* and *Sweden* there is also a licensing system regarding the clinics performing assisted reproduction.

In the *UK* a licensing statutory body - the Human Fertilisation and Embryology Authority - sets the terms regarding infertility treatment, storage and embryo research.

In *Spain* centres with the fundamental aim of treating human sterility require authorisation. In *Greece* a Presidential Decree will determine the terms for the establishment and function of units of assisted reproduction. In *Hungary* the Health Science Council in 1992 adopted a report stating that assisted reproduction can be applied only in specially appointed institutions where certain technical and personal conditions are fulfilled.

In *Denmark* there is a general authorisation of doctors but no specific licensing system of clinics.

2.2.3. *Financing*

In *Germany* social security covers IVF for married couples (3 attempts). IVF may be covered by private insurance. In the *UK* private health insurance does not cover

assisted reproduction and National Health Insurance does not guarantee the provision of assisted procreation services. In *Scandinavia* infertility treatment services are offered by public hospitals, but only a certain number of times (in Denmark, for example, 3 times), and the question of financing is being debated.

2.3. DONATION

2.3.1. *Allowed or Banned?*

In *Austria* all forms of assisted conception using donated gametes are prohibited with the exception of donor insemination *in vivo*.

In *Greece* donation of gametes is not regulated but is practised freely. In the *UK*, *Spain* and *Italy* donation is allowed. In *Poland* both insemination and IVF using semen from a donor is practised.

In *Germany* and *Austria* embryo donation and egg donation is banned. Also in *Norway* and *Sweden* egg donation and embryo donation is presently banned, but the situation is being reviewed. In *Denmark* egg donation is allowed, whereas embryo donation is banned.

2.3.2. *Consent to Donation*

In all of the countries storage and donation of semen and eggs to another infertile couple is conditional on consent to donation. Normally the requirement is for written informed consent.

2.3.3. *Paternity and Maternity*

In *Germany* heterologic and homologic insemination is permitted. A husband who consented to the artificial procreation of his wife's child by AID does not automatically give up his right to void his paternity later. A woman giving birth to a child is always considered the legal mother. In *Austria* an unmarried couple who request treatment services must first submit to advisory procedures before a competent court or public notary to have the legal consequences of the procedure explained. The most important of these is that the unmarried cohabitant has to acknowledge paternity of the child. The court or notary will issue a special licence to the couple which they must sign. In the Austrian legislation it is stated that the mother of the child is declared to be the woman giving birth. The legislation ensures that the donor of semen may never be established as a father of a child conceived following donor insemination.

In *France* no relation of filiation may be established between a child born through reproductive technologies and the donor of its gametes. Where one member of a couple consents to the use of reproductive technologies but will not declare the child to be his, he still has liabilities to the mother and the child. In *Norway* and *Sweden* consent from a spouse or cohabitant may also lead to legal paternity.

In *Greece* it has been proposed that donation cannot be revoked after the fertilisation. In section 1463, subsection 2 of the Civil Law it is stated that:

> the relationship of the person with his mother and her relatives is established by birth. The relationship with the father and his relatives is established by the marriage of the mother to the father or by affiliation, voluntary or judicial.

In this way, the legal relation of the child with the mother is not influenced by the fact that conception was a result of insemination (husband or donor), since the relationship between them is established by birth. In the same way it is not influenced in the case of IVF techniques whether the ova are donated or not. The child which is born belongs to the woman who carried it and gave birth to it. As far as fatherhood is concerned, the husband cannot dispute fatherhood, if he gave his consent to the artificial fertilisation. A donor cannot sue for legal fatherhood, if the mother was married and her husband consented to artificial fertilisation. Similarly, in the case of adultery, the genetic father cannot seek fatherhood if the persons who have the right to dispute the legality of the child did not do so.

In *Denmark* a Law Reform Commission on children and paternity has been established by the Minister of Justice with the task *inter alia* of making specific regulations on paternity and maternity regarding assisted procreation.

In *Spain* donation does not lead to filiation. In *Poland* no family code provisions regulate the problems of affiliation in connection with assisted reproduction using donated gametes. The Polish supreme court in 1983 stated that the husband cannot deny his paternity of the child born from donor insemination when he consented to this, as such denial could be considered as contradictory to the rules of social coexistence.

2.3.4. *Anonymity*

In the *UK*, *Italy*, *Greece*, *France* and *Denmark* there is donor anonymity. In *Hungary* the Health Science Council has stated that the donor's name should not be disclosed in cases of donor insemination.

In *Spain* the details of the identity of the donor are kept guarded in the strictest secrecy in the respective banks and the national register of donors. The children born as a result of this process have the right either themselves or through their legal representatives to obtain general information regarding the donors which does not include their identity. The same right is given to the recipients of the gametes. Only in exceptionally extraordinary circumstances which constitute a proven danger to the life of the child or as part of judicial inquiry into a criminal practice can the identity of the donor be revealed. In *France* donation is made anonymously except when therapeutic reasons justify the waiving of such a prohibition.

In *Sweden* anonymity was abandoned in 1985 - the first country in the world to adopt this position. This has together with other factors led to a decline in the number of clinics performing donor insemination and in the number of donations. In *Austria*

semen donors do not enjoy rights of anonymity. On donation the semen donor must consent that any child who may be born following the use of his sperm may from the age of 14 request information as to his identity. Clinics have a duty to keep records showing the names of donors, their birthdate, birthplace, nationality, residence and the names of the donor's parents. In *Germany* donor anonymity has been held to be unconstitutional.

In *The Netherlands* a Bill has introduced 'donor passports', keeping information on donors centrally and aiming at encouraging greater openness with regard to information about the donation. The child may - having reached the age of 16 - be given the name of the donor if the donor permits or if vital interests, for example of a psychological or physical nature, would be harmed if the identity of the donor were withheld. The decision is to be made by the AI Donor Information Centre.

2.3.5. *Limitations on the Number of Children by Donor*

In a number of countries there are limitations on the number of children which may be produced by a given donor. This goes, for instance, for *France* (5 children per donor) and for *Austria* (3 marriages or cohabitations).

2.3.6. *Other Questions*

In *France* advertising for donation is forbidden but public information in favour of donation is not included.

The screening of eggs, embryos, or donors are new areas of interest, especially preimplantation diagnostics. In *France* this method is available to a couple only if a qualified physician testifies that, regarding the family medical history, there is a high risk of the offspring being born with a particularly serious genetic disease for which there is no chance of therapy at the time of the diagnosis. In *Norway* preimplantation diagnosis may be carried out in case of serious, hereditary disease for which there is no cure.

2.4. SURROGATE MOTHERHOOD

The main attitude seems to be reluctance to accept surrogate motherhood. The contracts are normally looked upon as being unenforceable. Functioning as a surrogate mother is normally not a criminal offence. The methods of intervention and prevention differ between the countries.

In *Germany* a doctor's participation in surrogate motherhood is punishable. The surrogate mother who is to be the target of an assisted procreation and the foster father to be are exempt from criminal prosecution. The penal provisions do not automatically mean that the contract between a surrogate mother and the social parents is void. Advertising for surrogate mothers etc. is unlawful.

In *Denmark* a special law was laid down in 1986, according to which advertising and

procurement of surrogacy is liable to punishment. The act does not state that contracts of surrogacy are forbidden but it is presupposed that such contracts are invalid, and if payment is included in the contract the necessary arrangements concerning transfer of custody or adoption would not be accepted by the authorities.

In *Norway* and *Sweden* surrogacy is normally prohibited. The legislation provides, that the embryo may be used only for implantation in the woman from whom the eggs originate.

In *France* surrogacy is strictly prohibited, whether commercial or not. The child born through such an illicit practice cannot be adopted by the commissioning couple.

In *Hungary* the Health Science Council has stated that both partial and full surrogacy should be supported. A psychological examination of the couple and the surrogate mother is required, as well as genetic and necessary medical tests; evaluation of the family relations with special concern for the future prospects of the planned child; clarification of the intention of the surrogate mother and arrangements for the possible debates between the couple and the surrogate mother.

In the *UK* surrogacy is accepted, but specific regulation secures a non-commercialisation principle.

2.5. OTHER QUESTIONS

2.5.1. *No Commercialisation*

In *Scandinavia* a non-profit principle is practised in the public health service. In *France* sperm donation must be unpaid.

2.5.2. *Conflict of Laws*

The normal rules apply regarding private international law, that is family law, law of inheritance and contract. Some of the national regulations will come into play via the vehicle of *ordre public*. Some questions, for example the question of whether or not a natural (surrogate) mother may validly relinquish the rights to her child and whether or not such a child may be validly adopted by its prospective social parents, will probably rather be decided by looking at the best interests of the child.

3. Basic Areas of Convergence and Divergence

The areas of *convergence* are centred on the following basic principles:
a. Access to IVF is in all of the countries surveyed granted to married couples and in most countries also to cohabiting couples.
b. A licensing system is practised in most of the countries surveyed with the aim, for example, of securing the quality of services.
c. Donor insemination is offered in almost all of the countries surveyed. In the case

of donation the couple normally cannot select the donor.

d. When donation of eggs or embryos is accepted, legal motherhood is normally with the woman giving birth to the child.

e. A non-commercialisation principle is normally practised.

f. Surrogacy contracts are normally considered void and unenforceable. Often the legislation prohibits advertising.

The areas of *divergence*, where disagreement or national difference is more pronounced, are mainly centered on the following aspects:

a. Access to insemination and IVF by single women and lesbians

b. Access to information by children born following assisted conception

c. Donation of human embryos and eggs

d. Method of securing quality of services

The area of consensus is widespread, but the same goes for the area of divergence. Some of the differences are fundamental. Thus, the possibility of a comprehensive policy, or of legislation encompassing all of the problems related to fertility, infertility and the human embryo, in the different countries within the EU may never be forthcoming. It may also be questioned whether such comprehensive consensus and legislation is desirable. To investigate these questions further, some indications of the cultural, social, economic and religious reasons behind the current position in the various countries is necessary.

4. Possible Reasons for the Areas of Convergence and Divergence

In the following some indications of what constitutes the main similarities and differences in culture and regulation between the EU countries involved are pointed out. The purpose is only to present some snapshots of cultural concepts and behaviour in these countries, to begin to evaluate the possibilities of making regulations embracing countries of very different cultural backgrounds. Further elaboration and corrections are necessary, but even small contributions to an understanding of the cultural differences seem worthwhile.

4.1. SIMILARITIES - BASIC HUMAN VALUES

The basic human values concerning
- protection of life,
- autonomy,
- human dignity,
- protection of human rights, including the right to found a family,
- abandoning eugenics and discrimination
are common in the countries surveyed.

These similarities tend to make some harmonisation and perhaps common regulation a realistic possibility. The possibilities of achieving consensus on a European level are

reflected in the European Convention on Human Rights and the difficulties are reflected in the problems connected with the drafting of a Bioethics convention.[15]

4.2. DIFFERENCES - RELIGION, PUBLIC DEBATE, EXTENT OF REGULATION

4.2.1. *Religion*

Differences in religion must be respected. Problems in this respect may concern e.g. the status of the human embryo. However, the effect of the differences in religion is not - as one might expect - that Italy has the strongest rules concerning biotechnology, genetics and life. On the contrary, in this field this country has no statutory regulation. It may seem that attempts to introduce rules on these issues have been frustrated because of the (formal or informal) opposition of the Catholic party and the Catholic Church. These may consider any attempts at regulation a slippery slope leading to the appropriation by the State of matters that are properly the business of the church.[16]

A few examples may be illustrative:

In *Denmark, Sweden, Holland, Belgium* and the *UK* it is probably fair to say that religion for many people plays a minor role in their everyday life, but that christian thinking, and the moral values derived therefrom to a very high degree affects the way of living and of thinking as a fundamental part of their cultural inheritance.

Italy is the only country within the EU with a Catholic party as a majority party: in other countries, there are no Catholic parties as such or, if they do exist, their composition is more complex than in Italy (for instance, *Germany*). Nevertheless, there are no specific legal rules concerning the limits of the research and development of new technologies, the priority of public investments, or the protection from dangerous or uncontrolled implementation of genetic technologies by private institutions in Italy. This lack of regulation[17] has a twofold perverse effect: a) Public institutions (hospitals, health services, etc.) either do not offer any assistance, or, if they do, they often act at the risk of the doctors or the patients, without any protection of their respective rights; b) lacking any type of criminal as well as civil regulation, private health institutions are free to offer any type of intervention. This means that a highly speculative activity on the free market is now flourishing which is both extremely expensive and dangerous for women and for the newborn.[18]

4.2.2. *Public Debate and Openness*

The importance of public debate and openness in these sensitive areas must be noted. If the legislation is to be effective it must be felt as norm-setting and preferably reflect the State as a friend rather than a 'big brother watching you'. Knowledge and openness are preconditions both of such a norm-setting and educational function, and if the consent of the public to legislation is to play an important role.

Again a few examples may be illustrative:

In *Denmark, Norway, Sweden, Holland, France* and the *UK* the public debate is

widespread and extended. This must be seen in connection with people as very well informed populations. In the mass media there are lots of programmes including discussions, and one task of the Councils of Ethics is to create a debate amongst the population concerning ethical questions related to the life sciences.

In some of the countries in *Southern Europe*, the public debate is generally not as widespread and the State has no tradition of encouraging information and debate to the same extent about either ethical or medical issues.

4.2.3. *Women's Movements*

Women's movements are strong in some of the countries, e.g. the Scandinavian ones, and they have to a large extent been quite hostile towards the expansion of technologies concerning assisted human reproduction and genetic screening.

4.2.4. *Intensity and Extent of Regulation*

The differences concerning the intensity and extent of regulation must be taken into consideration. In the area of personal affairs and the area of health the difference does not seem overwhelming. There seems to be reluctance in most of the countries to legislate in the health area, and especially in the area of reproduction, which is seen as a private sphere. Nevertheless, legislation is now being enacted in these countries; but its extent and forms differ very much. One such contrast is between the very wide-ranging *French* legislation (on the one hand) and the *Italian* laissez-faire approach (on the other). Different legal and medical traditions are also of importance in this respect. For example, in the *UK* tradition professional guidelines are predominantly important, whereas the *Scandinavian* and *French* traditions lay much emphasis on substantial law as well.

4.2.5. *Public and Private Services*

The existence or non-existence of a public health service free of charge and the extent and quality of such public service compared to private health service provision is important. In this respect also systems of social security and insurance are significant.

For example, the welfare society in *Scandinavia* possibly makes many people consider the State as a provider of services and support; the 'public purse' offers help for the needy and often finances other services as well, e.g. public domestic help, kindergartens, etc. Similarly hospitals in Scandinavia have, until recently, been almost exclusively public institutions, free of charge and used by the vast majority of the Scandinavian population.

In *Southern Europe* the State also provides a wide range of public services (hospital, social services, etc.), yet the quality of the services provided is often very low; this encourages wealthy people to organise side-systems, like private hospitals.[19]

5. Is Consensus Desirable?   Some Pros and Cons

5.1. WHAT CAN WE LEARN FROM THE PAST?   (INTERNATIONAL PRIVATE LAW)

From the history of the origin of the Hague Conference[20], one can tell that the first Hague Conventions were built on the principle of nationality as the cornerstone of both public and private international law.   The concept of nationality was seen as distinctly cosmopolitical.   The world was seen as a community of nations, each with its own culture and legal traditions.   It was precisely because the legal diversity was valued that clear limits were seen as to the possibilities of unifying the various private laws of the world.   Certainly, the possibilities for unification of fundamental rules of universal justice were recognised - nowadays we would call them human rights.   But a complete unification of substantive private law was seen as an illusion.

This was true in particular for the laws relating to personal status, family and succession.   Unification of law in these areas was seen not only as an illusion but also as undesirable, because it would curtail human freedom.   The principle of nationality was thought to ensure that a person would retain a sphere of freedom when he travelled abroad - and this was in turn thought to be his destiny and mission, since he is born a cosmopolitical being.   Hence the utility of concluding multilateral conventions on the conflicts of laws which, provided they are based on the principle of nationality, will ensure personal freedom of the citizens of Contracting States when they travel around.

Another approach taken was more pragmatic.   The emphasis was on putting an end to any legal uncertainty, resulting from that variety of laws, which was prejudicial to individual interests.   Later one of the recurrent features of the Hague Conventions is the use of the concept of habitual residence by which a person living in Countries other than that of his or her birth could claim some of the rights given to citizens of those Countries.   Additionally, one of the important innovations of the last 20 years has been the introduction of a limited form of party autonomy in family law as a result of which the parties may decide on certain aspects of jurisdiction and choice-of-law by agreement.

The experience from the United Nations Convention on the Rights of the Child and the draft Bioethics Convention seems to be that consensus can be obtained as long as the Conventions are centred on broad principles.   However, as can be seen from the difficulties of the EU regulation on protection of individuals with regard to the processing of personal data and on the protection of biotechnological inventions (patents), achieving consensus over specific rights and duties is often problematic.

5.2. ARGUMENTS AGAINST CONSENSUS AND INTERNATIONAL POLICY-MAKING IN ASSISTED PROCREATION

a. When considering the content of international regulation, consensus carries the risk of 'harmonisation downwards', where the regulation is based on the lowest common

denominator.

b. Moreover, international instruments or international regulation may have difficulties in taking the local culture into account; may be too difficult to change in this unstable area; and may lack precision.

c. Finally, comprehensive EU regulation would face serious problems in stating the fulcrum of bioethical balance: Which is the position to which the plural system should be magnetised - towards a more restrictive or a more liberal approach? What institutional structures are necessary to articulate and effect the determinants of public choice?

From this point of view it is probably not feasible to produce a detailed set of guidelines to which all nations within Europe could subscribe. The differences of culture and legal systems seem to make this too difficult.

5.3. ARGUMENTS FOR CONSENSUS AND INTERNATIONAL POLICY-MAKING

a. International regulation or policy may for example improve the quality of services. Moral pluralism may carry the risk of underestimating the danger of infertility treatment to the concept of human dignity.

b. International regulation or policy-making would promote transnational equality.

c. Consensus is the only way of setting tangible limits which are likely to be followed broadly. The need for regulation and policymaking may be seen as a way of securing democracy in the bioethics field.

Justice Michael Kirby has made this observation about the dangers of the law failing to keep up with science:

> My chief point is a simple one. Science and technology are advancing rapidly. If democracy is to be more than a myth and a shibboleth in the age of mature science and technology and more than a triannual visit to a polling booth, we need a new institutional response. Otherwise we must simply resign ourselves to being taken where the scientists and the technologists' imagination leads. That path may involve nothing less than the demise of the rule of law as we know it. It is for our society to decide whether there is an alternative or whether the dilemmas posed by modern science and technology, particularly in the field of bioethics, are just too painful, technical, complicated, sensitive and controversial for our institutions of government.[21]

5.4. THE ROLE OF LAW AND INTERNATIONAL POLICYMAKING

Regulation may happen through informal or formal law. Either way, if law is seen as necessary or appropriate, regulation may have both different functions, and different levels.

5.4.1. *Functions of Regulation*[22]

A norm-setting function. This involves declaring certain values and interests as worth protection against any infringement (e.g. of human dignity or the best interests of the child born as a result of assisted reproduction). This function is based on the vision that law may be educational - a way of implementing ethics.

A protective function. This involves balancing the protected values against other interests, providing sanctions for abuses and minimising risks to patients and others affected by the application of infertility treatment (e.g. the children).

A regulative or declarative function. This entails securing clarity and certainty in handling controversial areas of bioethics, ensuring that the persons involved know what is acceptable and what is not acceptable so they can act accordingly. An example is denial of treatment to lesbians and women over a certain age.

5.4.2. *Levels of Regulation*

Object of protection: individual or society at large? This level includes the choice between pluralism and universalism. The trend in western culture has for a number of years been pluralism and individualisation, which tends to embrace ethics, too. This has lead to moral pluralism via individual autonomy administered by informed consent. A wish to obtain national and international solidarity may speak in favour of universal solutions.

Timing: ex post facto, current or anticipatory? This includes the dilemma of opting for the risks of a slippery slope versus opting for exaggerated legislation. Moreover, there may be worries as to the factual possibilities of control.

Location: clinic, Council of Ethics, government, international body? Professional control at clinics may ensure the quality of medical treatment, and independent Ethics Councils take into account broader ethical considerations. Problems of international private law may call for international instruments.

Form: prohibition, permission, criminalisation. The urgent need for flexibility in this area may make formal legislation less adequate. It is imperative that the legislation secures consequence, predictability and equity.

5.5. KEY ISSUES IN HARMONISATION

It would be a valuable gain to secure:
* the protection of human dignity, the (unborn) child-to-be, and the patient;
* the self-determination of the various countries in respecting differences of a cultural,

philosophical, social, economic, religious and political nature;
* freedom of research, freedom of contract and free movements between EU countries;
* the efficiency of medical care;

One solution is to accept that there is no need for absolute uniformity, but a need to try to establish broad, basic areas of harmonisation. We can perhaps profitably aim for international agreement on broad principles to guide the development and use of assisted reproduction and to give legal content to the moral concept of human dignity, autonomy, protection of the (unborn) child and quality of services.[23]

International measures may serve as safeguards *per se* and may serve as a basis for national measures protecting the values described above.

6. Conclusion

In my opinion the area of assisted reproduction calls for national legislative measures and should also concern the international community.

This conclusion is based on the fact that the wide-ranging consequences of the new possibilities are a matter of concern for society as such. It is also imperative to ensure that this sensitive area becomes part of the democratic process which will secure openness as to the use of the new biotechnologies and a broad debate and consensus in the area. This should also secure a public acceptance of the use of the new biotechnologies. Finally legislation may be necessary in certain areas to protect weak groups including the child-to-be and future generations. To a certain extent I think it advisable to declare a moratorium in certain areas until we are sure that any solution is well debated and widely acceptable.

These arguments, in my opinion, override the arguments stressing the privacy of reproduction. I also think they override the advantages of self-regulation between the professional groups.

Any international regulations or guidelines should be based on very broad principles, accepting that national differences be accepted on a large number of issues. *Nationally* the areas of legislation might include questions of access to assisted reproduction, licensing systems, restricting who is allowed to offer assisted reproduction, provisions on donation, anonymity, storage and surrogacy. These topics should be dealt with according to the local culture, legal traditions and medical practices of the respective countries.

Internationally questions of quality of services might be secured via codes of practice or the like. Moreover, international measures might be called for regarding procreative tourism, where persons seek assisted reproduction in other countries less restrictive than their own. Finally it might be thought advisable to make international provisions on broader themes connected with assisted reproduction, e.g. a non-commercialisation principle, questions of informed consent, prohibition against selection of donors based on the couple's wishes and maybe access to assisted procreation services. Some of these topics are partly dealt with by the draft bioethics convention, but others are not.

It is important to stress that privacy concerns and autonomy are vital in the area of assisted reproduction, but at the same time the nature and consequences of the new reproductive technologies make public intervention necessary in some areas - nationally and internationally. However, this intervention cannot free each individual from taking responsibility for choices made regarding the use of the new methods. We need responsibility from the individual, the different countries and the international community, for the sake of our children.

Notes

1. A comparison between Scandinavia, England and Austria and an analysis of different approaches to a number of topics are included in Morgan, Derek and Nielsen, Linda, 'Prisoners of progress or hostages to fortune?' *The Journal of Law, Medicine and Ethics* 21 (1), 1993, pp.30-42.

2. Embryo Protection Act (Embryonenschutzgesetz) of 13 December 1990.

3. Act No. 275 of 14 May 1992 on Procreative Medicine.

4. Act No. 503 of 24 June 1992.

5. Bekendtgørelse No. 392 of 17 May 1994.

6. In a court decision it has been established that donation of a human egg, and subsequently fertilising it with semen from a donor cannot lead to criminal sanctions.

7. Act No. 326 of 4 June 1986 - the ban has been included in the Adoption Act.

8. Act No. 1140 of 20 December 1984 on Insemination.

9. In a report from 1995 a majority in the Swedish Medical-Ethical Council has suggested that egg donation be allowed - but without donor anonymity for egg donors as well as for semen donors.

10. Act No. 711 of June 1988 on Fertilisation Outside the Human Body.

11. Act of 14 June 1994 on Medical Use of Biotechnology. Cf. the Norwegian bill with explanatory memorandum, nr. 37, 1993-94 on the Medical Use of Biotechnology, and the report this Bill is based on, Report No. 25 (1992-93), *Biotechnology in Relation to Human Beings*.

12. Law No. 94-654, 29 July 1994, on the Donation and Use of Elements and Products of the Human Body, Medically Assisted Procreation, and Prenatal Diagnosis.

13. The Human Fertilisation and Embryology Act 1990.

14. Act 35 on Assisted Reproduction Techniques of 22 November 1988; Act 42 on Donation and Utilisation of Embryos and Foetuses of 28 December 1988.

15. Council of Europe, *Draft Convention for the Protection of Human Rights and Dignity of the Human Being with Regard to the Application of Biology and Medicine: Bioethics Convention and Explanatory Report* Dir/jur (94) 2, Strasbourg, Directorate of Legal Affairs, 1994 (with amendments of 1995).

16. The following analysis is partly based on Nielsen, Linda and Nespor, Stefano, *Genetic Test, Screening and Use of Genetic Data by Public Authorities in Criminal Justice, Social Security and Alien and Foreigners Acts* Copenhagen, The Danish Centre for Human Rights, 1994.

17. During the legislative period which ended in 1992, there were 100 bills concerning the regulation of the Reproductive Technology, not one of which has been passed into law; cf. *ibid.* p.37.

18. *Ibid.*

19. *Ibid.*, p.39.

20. van Loon, Hans, 'The Hague Conference - its origins, organisation and achievements' *Svensk Juristtidning* 1993/4, pp.293-315.

21. Kirby, M., *Reform the Law* Oxford, Oxford University Press, 1983, pp.238-239.

22. Eser, Albin, 'Legal aspects of bioethics' in *Europe and Bioethics. Proceedings of the First Symposium of the Council of Europe on Bioethics* Strasbourg, Council of Europe Press, 1985, pp.41-42.

23. In the course of the reflections of the European Commission research project Fertility, Infertility and the Human Embryo, a preference for a uniform minimum threshold of law and regulation has emerged.

25. THE AUSTRIAN ACT ON PROCREATIVE MEDICINE: SCOPE, IMPACTS, AND INCONSISTENCIES

Erwin Bernat
Erich Vranes
Department of Civil Law
Graz Law School
Heinrichstrasse 22
8010 Graz
Austria

1. Introduction

On July 1, 1992, the Austrian *Act on Procreative Medicine*[1] came into effect after several years' discussion in expert circles consisting mainly of academics in the legal field, scientists, and physicians. This essay discusses the act's main principles, outlines its provisions - which cover both treatment and research - and indicates their possible impacts on assisted reproduction practice.

With respect to the latter, the discussion of the act itself is preceded by a summary of the results of an in-depth statistical survey on AID in Austria.[2]

As will be shown in the concluding outlook, the methodological conception of the Austrian approach differs widely from Germany's. On the other hand, both Austrian and German substantive law embody social values more conservative by far than England's regulations.

2. Empirical Data on Assisted Reproduction

In April 1986, Bernat and Schimek[3] conducted the first extensive statistical survey among all 707 gynaecologists registered in Austria at the time. The survey covered the distribution and relevance to their day to day practice of AID; the levels of information they had with respect to good clinical practice in AID and the legal situation; and attitudes of gynaecologists regarding this mode of procreation. Comparable data on *in vitro* fertilisation (IVF) and gamete intra-fallopian transfer (GIFT) are not available, since there is still no central register in Austria of gynaecologists practicing in the field of assisted procreation. The survey can be deemed representative in view of both its response rate of 54% and the composition of its respondents.

D. Evans (ed.), Creating the Child, 325–332.

2.1. DISTRIBUTION AND RELEVANCE

9% of the gynaecologists reported having carried out AID (hereinafter: "AID-experienced"). Only 12% said they had not yet been confronted with the question of AID, while two thirds of the AID-inexperienced gynaecologists had had inquiries by at least one patient.

It is worth noting that 45% of the AID-inexperienced gynaecologists point out the possibility of AID as a therapeutic method to their patients, when indicated, and according to the survey, 63% know colleagues who practice AID.

2.2. ATTITUDES

The fundamental social disagreement prevailing with regard to AID[4] is also seen among Austrian gynaecologists: 40% of the AID-inexperienced view medically indicated AID applied at the request of a married couple in a "very or rather negative" light, while 45% view it in a "very or rather positive" light. On the other hand, 91% of AID-experienced gynaecologists see AID as a "positive", which reveals vast ethical incongruencies both between AID-experienced and AID-inexperienced practitioners, and within the latter group itself. In contrast to the attitude expressed in the new regulation (see below), 62% of AID-inexperienced and 86% of AID-experienced declare themselves opposed to the child's right to know its genetic roots.

2.3. PRACTICE OF AID IN AUSTRIA

These statements and percentages refer to AID-experienced gynaecologists only. 74% reported fewer than 20 insemination patients (only three gynaecologists reported more than 100); the number of inseminations was on average 10 per gynaecologist. The average birth rate was 6. On the basis of the survey's findings it can be extrapolated that, up to 1985, 1115 children had been conceived by means of AID in Austria, 196 in 1985 alone, accounting for 0.23% of all live births in Austria that year.

2.4. DONATED SEMEN - ORIGIN, AND SELECTION CRITERIA

30% obtain semen from their colleagues or acquaintances, 30% from sperm banks, and 22% from college students, while 18% give other sources. The main selection criteria are noncontamination by sexually transmissible diseases or hepatitis B (25%), resemblance in phenotype (30%), sociocultural origin (15%). Only 37% declared that they usually document donor data: 31% stated this was impossible since they obtained semen from sperm banks.

The statutory provisions outlined below have considerable repercussions for several aspects of the gynaecological practice described above.

3. Prohibitions

In accordance with its conception as a comprehensive state regulation of medically assisted reproduction, the Austrian *Act on Procreative Medicine* (1992) seeks to answer all possible legal questions related to reproductive medicine. This aim is pursued through the following means: (a) the introduction of a wide range of prohibitions, (b) the regulation of the treatment services which remain lawful (this represents a 'partial U-turn' with respect to the right to liberty[5]), and (c) status and relationship stipulations.

3.1. LEADING PRINCIPLES

The core of the act can be found in those sections which stipulate the permissibility and the corresponding prohibitions of treatment. From these sections, two main principles can be deduced and summarised as follows:

(a) Reproductive medicine is permissible only within the boundaries of marriage or (heterosexual) cohabitation. Single women are not eligible (unlike in Israel[6], for example).

(b) Only those oocytes and sperm derived from the married couple or cohabitants may be used for their assisted reproduction. However, AID (*in vivo*) is allowed, though only when the husband's or cohabitant's gametes are not reproductive. Apart from this exception, all heterologous methods of assisted procreation are prohibited (resulting in inconsistencies[7]). This leads to the odd consequence that the use of donor semen continues to be prohibited in the process of IVF or GIFT, even where such *in vitro* treatment may be indicated by the wife's condition (of tubal sterility for example), so long as the husband's condition (azoospermia for instance) requires a donor.

3.2. SURROGATE PREGNANCIES

A legal ban on surrogate mothers is provided by the act in that it prohibits (heterologous) embryo transfer and embryo donation. Furthermore, ova are to be used only by the women from whom they have been derived. Finally, all treatment services may be carried out for the benefit only of a couple who suffer from sterility.

3.3. NONMARRIED COUPLES

Interestingly enough (in view of the drafters' otherwise more conservative approach), the act does not require a minimum duration of non-marital cohabitation.

3.4. *ULTIMA RATIO* CLAUSE

Besides the above requirements, medically assisted reproduction may be performed only if "according to science and experience, all other possible and reasonable treatments for inducing a pregnancy by means of sexual intercourse have failed or are deemed futile"

(translation by the authors).

3.5. SANCTIONS

The act seeks to prevent contraventions of these provisions by treating violations as breaches of administrative regulations, which incurs fines up to 500,000 Austrian shillings.[8]

4. Procedural Safeguards

4.1. LICENSING AND HOSPITAL STANDARDS

The standards are as follows.
(a) All forms of medically assisted reproduction declared permissible by the act's provisions may be performed only by a gynaecologist.
(b) With the exception of homologous artificial insemination *in vivo*, all treatments must be carried out in specifically licensed hospitals.
(c) Such licences are issued if appropriate personnel and equipment standards are met and if adequate psychological counselling or psychotherapeutic care are available in the hospital.

4.2. MORAL OBJECTIONS, DISCRIMINATION

The gynaecologist's and paramedical personnel's right to refuse to carry out or assist in the provision of assisted reproduction services is guaranteed by a conscience clause stating that neither group is under any obligation to perform such services. On the other hand, no one may be discriminated against in any way for either performing or declining to perform these services.

4.3. INFORMED CONSENT, COMPREHENSIVE COUNSELLING

The act states the following:
(a) Each treatment has to be preceded by detailed information on its risks, and, if deemed necessary by the doctor and not declined by the spouses/cohabitants, by psychological counselling or psychotherapeutic treatment.
(b) In any case, however, cohabitants must receive instruction from a court or public notary on the legal consequences of their consent. This is required of a married couple only if AID is to be applied.

4.4. PROHIBITION OF RESEARCH, LIMITED TREATMENT

'Destructive research' on pre-embryos and gametes is - unlike in England - absolutely

forbidden; screening and treatment, on the other hand, are allowed only in so far as is deemed necessary, from a medical point of view, for inducing a pregnancy.

4.5. LIMITED NUMBER OF EMBRYOS TO BE TRANSFERRED

The number of oocytes that a gynaecologist may fertilise at one time is restricted to the quantity necessary to achieve pregnancy according to the prevailing state of medical science (three to four, according to the government bill's official commentary[9]).

4.6. CRYOCONSERVATION, DURATION

Cryoconservation of gametes and pre-embryos alike may not exceed one year (compared with five years and the possibility of a five-year prolongation in Israel[10]). Although not explicitly stated in the act, it is clear from the explanations accompanying the draft that after this time has elapsed, the procreative material must be destroyed. This has been criticised[11] and an alternative proposal for 'prenatal adoption' has been put forward.[12]

4.7. STATE CONTROL

Extensive record keeping and reports to state institutions are required of gynaecologists and hospitals to enable sufficient state control.

4.8. OPTIONAL INFORMATION ON 'GENETIC ROOTS'

A child created by means of AID is given the right to be informed about his/her genetic roots from the age of fourteen, if desired. This obviously corresponds to the drafters' intention which rests upon the prospective child's best interests, although this approach has been heavily criticised[13], and the results of psychological and social research could indicate a different approach.[14]

4.9. SYSTEM OF SANCTIONS

Violations of any of these provisions (with the exception of unlawful cryoconservation) are prosecuted as breaches of administrative regulations, unless they constitute criminal offences, which fall within the jurisdiction of the criminal courts. Moreover, a physician who disregards these provisions risks being held liable under professional and disciplinary codes.

5. Rules of Parentage

5.1. MATERNITY

Although ovum and embryo donations are prohibited (see sub 3.1.), the act states that the woman giving birth to a child will always be regarded as its legal mother. The purpose of this rule is to subject illegally performed embryo transfers and those carried out abroad to appropriate family law regulation.

5.2. PATERNITY

A husband or cohabitant consenting to AID before a court or a public notary loses the right to contest his legally presumed paternity if the offspring is the result of this AID (and not the result of adultery, e.g.).

Moreover, the act stipulates that a third-party donor whose semen has been used for assisted reproduction can never be legally established as the father of a child thereby conceived (but see, on the other hand, the child's right to receive information on his/her 'genetic roots', sub 4.8.).

6. The Legislative Concepts of Germany and England

6.1. GERMANY

The German legislative solution (*Act for the Protection of Embryos 1990*[15]) reveals a conceptually quite different approach to that of Austria. It is based mainly on criminal law and does not furnish procedural safeguards - a fact which is all the more remarkable since both the Austrian and German approaches emphasise similar values: human dignity and best interests of the prospective child in both countries (with right of privacy being the third determining factor in Austria; right to life and freedom of science, in Germany).

Consequently, the act provides serious sanctions (up to five years imprisonment, or fines) for abuse of procreative techniques[16] aimed at the physician only. The donation of spare embryos remains lawful nevertheless.

6.2. ENGLAND

Setting out from self-determination as the prime factor, the English approach is based on a completely different weighing of values: The right of self-determination is to be understood as procreative autonomy, a value not even mentioned in the German official commentary.

Having ascribed no human dignity to the embryo *in vitro*, the English act[17] allows embryo screening and destructive research (e.g., for pharmaceutical industry purposes).

The Human Fertilisation and Embryology Authority (HFEA), set up by the same act, functions as a statutory licensing authority. It can also allow the purchase, export, and import of embryos.[18]

7. Final Remarks

As has been pointed out in various commentaries[19], the regulation of a matter which poses so many ethical and legal questions, and is prone to controversies, arising out of variation in people's fundamental ethical values, can be only a compromise trying to match prevailing social values within the legal community.

Whether or not this compromise has been achieved by the legislative attempts discussed here, it is safe to say (from the point of view of comparative law), that Austria (as well as Germany) does not lie within the mainstream of legislative approaches as far as the weighing of values - and corresponding legislative results - are concerned. Although following very different approaches (mere criminal law provisions in Germany; comprehensive administrative regulation avoiding criminal sanctions and including family law amendments in Austria), Austria and Germany emphasise similar values and therefore come to relatively restrictive laws.

The extremely liberal English approach, on the other hand, can be traced back to the underlying ethical concept which stresses procreative autonomy and does not grant the embryo the right of human dignity.

In other words, these vast legislative differences in the laws of Austria, Germany and England - all signatories of the European Convention on Human Rights - can be seen as results of, grossly speaking, divergent basic ideological questions: 'What should be allowed?' in Austria and Germany, *vis-a-vis* 'What should be prohibited?' in England.

Notes

1. Austrian *Act on Procreative Medicine*, *Official Gazette* 275, 1992.

2. Bernat, E.R., and Schimek, M.G., 'Kuenstliche heterologe insemination in Oesterreich' *Fertilitaet* 4, 1988, pp.112-120.

3. *Ibid.*

4. Bydlinski, F., 'Zum Entwurf eines Fortpflanzungshilfegesetzes' *Juristische Blaetter* 112, 1990, pp.741-744.

5. For a discussion of this point (and references to other discussions on the same point) see Schlag, M., 'Zur Regierungsvorlage eines Fortpflanzungsmedizingesetzes' in Bydlinski, F., and Mayer-Maly, T. (eds), *Fortpflanzungsmedizin und Lebensschutz* Innsbruck and Vienna, Tyrolia Publishing House, 1993, pp.65-80.

6. Schenker, J.G., '*In-vitro* fertilization (IVF), embroytransfer (ET) and assisted reproduction in the State of Israel' *Human Reproduction* 2, 1987, pp.755-760.

7. Cf. Schenker *ibid.* and Bernat, E., 'Das Fortpflanzungsmedizingesetz: neue Rechtspflichten für den oester-reichischen Gynaekologen' *Gynaekolisch Geburtshilfliche Rundschau* 33, 1993, pp.2-10.

8. For more details see Bernat, E., and Straka, U., 'Austria: A legal ban on surrogate mothers and fathers?' *University of Louisville Journal of Family Law* 31, 1992-93, pp.267-282.

9. Government Bill, 216 of the Appendices to the shorthand records of the National Council; 18th legislative period, 1991.

10. Cf. Schenker, *op.cit.*

11. Cf. Bydlinski, *op.cit.* and Bernat (1993), *op.cit.*

12. In Schlag, *op.cit.*

13. Bernat (1993), *op.cit.*

14. Snowden, R., Mitchell, G.D. and Snowden, E.M., *Artificial Reproduction. A Social Investigation* London, George Allen and Unwin (Publishers) Ltd, 1983.

15. German *Act for the Protection of Embryos*, *Official Gazette* 1990, 1: 2746-2748.

16. Bernat, E., 'Fortpflanzungsmedizin und Recht - Bemerkungen zum Stand der Gesetzgebung in Oesterreich, Deutschland und Grossbritannien' *Medizinrecht* 9, 1991, pp.308-315.

17. English *Human Fertilisation and Embryology Act 1990.*

18. Bernat (1991), *op.cit.*

19. Bydlinski, *op.cit.*; Schlag, *op.cit.*; Bernat (1993), *op.cit.*

26. ASSISTED PROCREATION IN GERMAN LAW

Prof. Dr. Drs. h.c. Erwin Deutsch
Faculty of Law
University of Göttingen
Germany

1. Introduction

The German law on reproductive medicine has several sources each covering a different aspect. Since 1985, the German Medical Association's *Model Code of Professional Ethics* (hereinafter MBO) deals with physician's rights and duties connected with reproductive medicine.[1] This code is supplemented by guidelines of the German Federal Medical Council (hereinafter BAeK guidelines) for the practice of gamete intrafallopian transfer (GIFT), *in vitro* fertilisation (IVF) and embryo transfer (ET) as therapeutic methods against human sterility.[2]

The Embryonenschutzgesetz (Embryo Protection Act) of 1990 (ESchG)[3] is the one German statute directly regulating reproductive medicine. The Act is a criminal law, making punishable a given number of techniques of artificial reproduction, protecting the embryo from commercial exploitation and experimentation and prohibiting the creation of hybrids and chimeras. At about the same time, the Law on Adoption Mediation was modified in order to prevent commercialisation of surrogate motherhood.[4] The modification of the Social Security Code V declared the medical treatment that is aimed at inducing pregnancy to be covered by the public health insurance.[5] The newest source is a draft law on organ transplantation, which might have an impact on reproductive medicine, too.[6]

2. Regulation of Practitioners

The Federal Doctor's Council has recently published revised guidelines for professional ethics concerning assisted procreation.[7] They are legally binding and enforceable by the Independent Professional Courts.[8] The ESchG had a considerable impact on the revision of these guidelines, as well as on the progress of science. The rules that have governed assisted procreation up until now are being modified and made absolute by the Act.

Section 9 ESchG reserved for doctors the carrying out of artificial insemination, IVF, ET, and GIFT, and the conserving of a human embryo or a human oocyte which a human sperm-cell has already entered or has been artificially introduced into. This

D. Evans (ed.), Creating the Child, 333–339.

guarantees that in this area scientifically founded medical expertise rules. The voluntary participation provided for physicians in section 10 ESchG, section 9 MBO and section 3.1 BAeK *Guidelines* is supposed to bolster the freedom of conscience guaranteed in art. 4 sub. 1 of the German Constitution (GG).[9] Some portions of the population supposedly are opposed to the creation of human life through artificial fertilisation for ethical reasons. The same is supposedly true for personnel immediately involved in the artificial creation of human life. After deciding to participate in reproductive medicine services, the physician has a duty to give notice to the medical board and to prove he or she meets the necessary professional requirements with regard to personal, professional and technical skills (sec. 9 Model Professional Code and sec. 3.5 BAeK *Guidelines*).

3. Criteria for Access to Services

Artificial insemination, IVF, ET and GIFT are generally regarded as being legally permissible. The ESchG quite on purpose does not offer all encompassing regulation of assisted procreation.[10] In view of the fact that in general everyone is free to act as they please, and that this liberty can be restricted by a law only if third parties' interests are violated, it is safe to say that this silence of the law hints that aided procreation is an area exempt from punishment. This concerns especially artificial insemination. This is permitted in all ways, be it through heterologic or homologic insemination. In legal political discussions the term 'heterologic', which traditionally describes IVF of a woman with sperm from a man other than her husband, has led to difficulties of interpretation.[11]

Unlike the ESchG, sec. 3.2.3 BAeK *Guidelines* generally confines these methods and new techniques like Embryo Intra-Fallopian Transfer (EIFT) and Zygote Intra-Fallopian Transfer (ZIFT) to married couples only. The basic rule is that assisted procreation is permissible only with the husband's semen. The use of semen originated from a third person for a married couple requires an exemption from a commission set up by the local provincial medical council. Commission control is also obligatory for cohabitants who intend to undergo homologous IVF or GIFT with the cohabitant's semen.[12] It is important to note that neither the *Guidelines* nor commission control are applicable to normal artificial insemination.[13]

Since 1990, reproductive medicine has been recognised as a form of medical treatment covered by health insurance. According to Section 27a of the Social Security Code Fifth Book (SGB V) the conditions of coverage are that:

a) The physician considers medically assisted procreation to be necessary.

b) It is likely that medically assisted procreation will bring about pregnancy; generally after four unsuccessful attempts the prospects are considered poor.

c) The prospective parents are married.

d) The medically assisted procreation is homologous, that is using ova and semen stemming genetically from the parents-to-be.

e) The prospective parents have been instructed about the medical and psychological aspects of this therapy by a physician other than the attending gynaecologist.

4. Consent Procedures

Sec. 4 sub. 1 ESchG declares assisted procreation by insemination, IVF or GIFT without informed consent of the donors to be prohibited and punishable. In the same way, Sec. 4 sub. 2 ESchG proscribes ET without informed consent. Pursuant to Sec. 3.4 BAeK *Guidelines* the doctor has the obligation to inform the patients about the scheduled operation, its several phases, its chances of success, the likelihood of complications and its costs. The informed consent must be given in writing and signed by doctor and both spouses.

5. Methods of Treatment

Sec. 3.2 BAeK *Guidelines* mentions the medical indications for assisted procreation. IVF and ET are always allowed with tubal blocking and tubal insufficiency. Some forms of male infertility and immunologically conditioned sterility are limited medical indications. GIFT and EIFT can be used with male infertily and immunologically conditioned sterility, when other methods including intra-uterine insemination have failed.

Under any circumstances, infertility with no certain cause is a medical indication for assisted reproduction only after the failure of all other diagnostic and therapeutic treatments. Further restraints on the use of assisted procreation include all absolute medical contra-indications of pregnancy, for example psychogenic sterility (i.e. sterility where the cause is not organic but rather mental) and serious medical risks for the woman's health or the child's development.

6. Prohibitions and Limitations

6.1. GAMETE AND EMBRYO TRANSFER AND FERTILISATION

Sec. 1 sub. I nos. 1-6 ESchG declares the following abusive uses of reproductive technologies to be prohibited and punishable: (a) the transfer of an unfertilised, extraneous oocyte into a woman's uterus, (b) the artificial insemination of an oocyte for any purpose other than to create a pregnancy, (c) the transfer of more than three embryos during the same cycle, (d) insemination through intratubary gametic transfer more than three oocytes, (e) the insemination of more oocytes than can be transferred to the woman over the course of one cycle, and (f) undertaking a genuine embryo transfer, or extraction of an embryo from a woman's uterus for any other purpose than

to keep it alive. By the same token, the artificial transfer of a human sperm-cell into a human oocyte for any purpose other than inducing pregnancy is punishable. In particular, research with human embryos is now prohibited, because an oocyte must not be fertilised for any other purpose other than to induce the woman whose oocyte is fertilised to become pregnant (sec. 1 sub. 1 no. 2 ESchG).

However, the protective effect of the law is always limited: A doctor who, in violation of sec. 1 sub. 1 no. 3 ESchG transfers more than three embryos to a woman during one cycle is not liable for damages in the way of maintenance if more than one child is born.

6.2. SURROGACY

Seemingly not quite within the law's scope is sec. 1 sub. 1 no. 7 EschG which prohibits and makes punishable undertaking the artificial insemination of a surrogate mother, or the transfer of a human embryo to a surrogate mother. Fortunately, both the person who wants to have the child and the surrogate mother are exempt from punishment, just as in the above listed cases the woman who donated the oocyte or the embryo, and the woman to whom the oocyte or the embryo is transferred are exempt from punishment. Thus, sec. 1 ESchG is basically a special penal provision for physicians, as the doctor's restriction in sec. 9 ESchG already prohibits non-doctors from acting in this particular area. A doctor who applies reproductive techniques in violation of sec. 1 ESchG is liable for the damage caused by his actions.[14]

7. Rules of Parentage

The general legal rules concerning the father's and mother's relationship with a child are as follows:

A child which is born to a woman who is married or at least was married during the 302 days before a birth is, by virtue of the regulations in section 1593 of the German Civil Code (BGB) qualifies as the husband's or ex-husband's child. The only way the husband or ex-husband can void his affiliation is by contesting his paternity. If he does not contest it, he remains the legal father.

If the child's mother is not married at the time of the birth and during the last 302 days before the birth, the child is regarded as illegitimate. The child's legal father is the man who either acknowledges his paternity or whose paternity is established by a court of law, section 1600 a BGB. The true state of things, that is the genetic affiliation of either an acknowledging father or of a father whose paternity is established by a court of law, does not play a role in this context.

The rule of *mater semper certa est* has relieved the legislator of the task of establishing criteria for a mother's affiliation with a child: A woman who gives birth to the child automatically qualifies as its legal mother. The only way a natural mother's affiliation with the child can be changed according to current law is by adoption of the

child.

These basic rules also apply in the context of reproductive medicine. A child which is born to a woman as a result of artificial insemination, irrespective of whether this was by heterological or homological insemination according to German law, is always legally this woman's child. If the mother is married or was married during the last 302 days before birth the husband or ex-husband qualifies as the child's legal father. In the context of heterological inseminations the biological or genetic truth of this qualification is not taken into account. The mother's husband or ex-husband can destroy his affiliation with the child only by contesting his paternity at the time stated by law. The child itself also has a limited right to contest its affiliation to the legal father.

A child which is born to an unmarried mother as a result of assisted procreation always qualifies as an illegitimate child. The semen donor's paternity can either be established by a court of law according to the general section of 1600 a BGB, or, which will rarely be the case, by the semen donor acknowledging his affiliation to the child. A legal father/child relationship can also be established by a man's acknowledging his paternity with the consent of the child (sec. 1600 a Abs. 1 BGB and Sec. 1600 c BGB). In this context, too, the biological or genetic truth of this legal affiliation is not taken into consideration.

In a surrogate motherhood context, these general rules lead to the same results: The surrogate mother who gives birth to the child by law becomes the legal mother of the child, irrespective of whether she became a surrogate mother through AI, IVF, ET, or other means. The only fact that counts is that she is the one who gives birth to the child. If the surrogate mother at the time of birth or at least 302 days before the birth was married, her husband or ex-husband according to sec. 1593 qualifies as the child's legal father. If she was not married, the prospective father, that is the husband of the couple who 'ordered' the child, can acknowledge his paternity or can be established as the legal father by a court of law (sec. 1600 a BGB). He then becomes the legally acknowledged father of the child. The same is possible if the husband of the surrogate mother successfully contests his affiliation with the child his wife bore.

The German Supreme Court decided[15] in 1983 that a social father who initially consented to his wife's being artificially inseminated with the semen of another man by giving this consent does not automatically give up his right to void his paternity later. In certain cases the Supreme Court denies the social father's obligation to provide maintenance because the inherent basis of the transaction might have changed.[16]

8. Donor Anonymity

In contrast to many other countries the anonymity of the semen donor is considered unconstitutional. In 1989, the German Constitutional Court, in a case involving a child's right to void a determination of affiliation, decided that a child in principle has the right to know who his or her father and mother are.[17] The court held this to be part of a person's right to privacy, which is guaranteed in art. 2 sub. 1 and art. 1 sub. 1 of

the German Constitution, and is a result of the very close connection between the execution of one's right to self-determination, that is one's right to determine one's own individuality, on the one hand, and information about the factors constituting this individuality, on the other hand. Constitutionally, this is not, however, an absolute right but rather one that is granted only within the framework of the constitutional regulations.[18] The legislator can thus limit this right through regulations insofar as such limits are not formulated for unconstitutional purposes and under the totality of the circumstances this is a proportionate regulation. One constitutionally valid limitation of the child's right to know who his or her true father and mother are, is to maintain a peaceful relationship in the social (adoptive) family.[19] This constitutional background means that anonymous donation or semen cocktails are prohibited. A promise to the donor to keep his identity a secret is void.

Notes

1. German Medical Association, 'Model Code of Professional Ethics' *Deutsches Aerzteblatt* Vol. 91, 1994, pp.B-39

2. German Federal Medical Council, 'Guidelines' *Deutsches Aerzteblatt* Vol. 91, 1994, pp.B-44.

3. Embryonenschutzgesetz Bundesgesetzblatt 1990 I: 2746. The literature on the legal and legal-political aspects of reproductive medicine is boundless. For relevant opinions cf. Günther, H., 'Criminal prohibitions on embryo research' *Medizinrecht* Vol. 8, 1990, pp.161-167, and Kamps, H., 'Law of reproductive medicine - a survey' *Medizinrecht* Vol. 12, 1994, pp.339-348.

4. Bundesgesetzblatt 1990 I: 2017.

5. *Ibid.*, 1211.

6. Cf. *Ethik in der Medizin* Vol. 5, 1993, p.211.

7. German Federal Medical Council, *op.cit.*, pp.B-44.

8. Verwaltungsgerichtshof Baden-Wuerttemberg, *Neue Juristische Wochenschrift* 1991, p.2368; Bundesverwaltungsgericht, *Neue Juristische Wochenschrift* 1992, p.1577.

9. Bundestags-Drucksache, 11/8057, p.17.

10. Bundestags-Drucksache, 11/8057, p.12 *et seq.*.

11. The Federal/State Commission 'Reproductive Medicine' in its quest for comprehensiveness tried to solve this problem also. According to art 2, sec. 1 sub. 2 of the raw draft the criminally prosecuted "donor ... is not the man who lives with a woman in a relationship designed to be permanent".

12. Ratzel, R. and Lippert, H.-D., *Model Code of Professional Ethics* Berlin, 1995, p.77.

13. *Ibid.*, p.79.

14. For civil liability of the apparent father see French Apellate Court of July 10, 1990 *Recueil Dalloz Sirey* 1990, *Jurisprudence* p.517.

15. Entscheidungen des Bundesgerichtshofes in Zivilsachen, Vol. 87, p.169.

16. Bundesgerichtshof, *Neue Juristische Wochenschrift* 1995, p.2028 and p.2031.

17. Bundesverfassungsgericht, *Neue Juristische Wochenschrift* 1989, p.891.

18. Coester-Waltjen, D., 'Artificial procreation and civil law' *Zeitschrift fuer das gesamte Familienrecht* Vol. 39, 1992, pp.369-373.

19. *Ibid.*, p.373.

27. INFERTILITY, INABILITY AND RIGHTS: AN ENGLISH LEGAL CASE STUDY

Arlene Judith Klotzko
Research Fellow in Medical Law and Ethics
The London Hospital Medical College
England
Research Fellow
The Center for Bioethics and Health Law
Utrecht University
The Netherlands

1. The Case of X

A 67 year old man, diagnosed with prostate cancer, now in remission, desires to contract with an ovum donor and a gestational surrogate to produce a child using his sperm. The man is unmarried, is living with his mother, and is in a monogamous relationship with a married woman who has been abandoned by her husband. The married woman, in her early 40s, is seeking an annulment, but even if that legal proceeding is successful, the man has no intentions of marrying her. His two married sisters have children. But he states that he wants to carry on the family line with a child of his own. It is unclear whether the man has sufficient financial resources to care for a child, but he has mentioned that in the case of his death, Social Security would provide a survivor's benefit of $500 per month until the child is 18 years of age.

The ethics committee at the reproductive medical centre is asked to review the case and make a recommendation whether the centre should accept this man as a patient.

2. Commentary

Is it not lack of freedom not to fly like an eagle or swim like a whale?[1]

Infertility is a grief, not a disease. Those who suffer from it are not in pain and are not ill.[2]

Helvetius believed that technological progress is largely unproblematic; he was far too optimistic. Modern medical technology can remedy many defects and shortcomings of nature. Who has the authority to deem such transformations unnecessary, or even inappropriate? How and when may freedom be restricted?

D. Evans (ed.), Creating the Child, 341–346.

A person's freedom can be curtailed by constraints that are external (the coercive power of the law, for example) or internal (limitations such as those created by one's own physical constitution, for instance). One can call an internal constraint an inability, but not every absence of an ability is a negative constraint.

Perhaps, the most useful point at which to begin is an analysis of whether X has a genuine inability. There are three categories of infertility: physiological; social; genetic.[3] The physiologically infertile are infertile or sterile; the socially infertile are unwilling or unable to procreate through sexual relations with the opposite sex; the genetically infertile can transmit a genetic disorder.

X seeks to use his own sperm to father a child. His cancer is in remission, which suggests he has probably had oncology treatment. Even if such treatment has rendered him temporarily or permanently infertile, he has presumably stored his sperm. Thus, whether or not his sperm can be contemporaneously produced, he cannot be regarded as physiologically infertile. Rather, he is socially infertile, a condition that does not seem to rise to the level of a genuine inability. Moreover, a 67 year old single man not fathering a child is hardly "a striking deviation from a norm of expectancy or propriety".[4] Indeed, quite the reverse.

Freedom can be conceptualised as equivalent to autonomy, which can be viewed negatively, as noninterference, or more positively, a perspective that seems particularly apt in the European context. Two articles of The European Convention on Human Rights confer positive rights that are relevant to this case: Article 8 protects the right to private and family life; Article 12 protects the right to marry and found a family. However, neither of these provisions clearly supports a moral right of access to infertility treatment.

Moral rights exist prior to, or independently of, any legal or institutional rules. Human rights are moral rights that are fundamentally important and held equally by all. The right to procreate can plausibly be seen as both a moral and a human right, deriving from the principle of autonomy. But is it an absolute right? Feinberg posits three categories of human rights that could appropriately be seen as absolute: a positive right to a good that is not scarce; a negative right not to be treated inhumanely; a right not to be exploited or degraded.[5]

If one accepts this analysis, the right to procreate should not be viewed as absolute. And it is, of course, understood that society can legitimately restrict the liberty of some to protect other identifiable individuals. In the case of X, the party to be protected is the potential child.

Thus far, we have been looking at this case without regard to the larger social dimension, which is relevant in a general sense - because we should not ignore communitarian concerns - and specifically as well - because the UK has a public health care service. In such a context, the scarcity and expense of infertility treatment could be legitimate criteria for limiting access. In this case, the allocation issue is minimised because, in the UK, most infertility treatment is offered by private clinics.

The law can say nothing or it can say a great deal about contentious issues, such as those surrounding assisted reproduction, but generally two types of approaches can be

discerned. In the first mode, the state stands back and allows for private ordering; the legal regime is designed to give effect to the intention of the parties and prevent interference with their arrangements. This is the classic contract paradigm.

In the second mode - comprehensive legal regulation - the state actively intervenes and sets normative standards of conduct.[6] The UK Human Fertilisation and Embryology Act of 1990 (HFE Act), while seemingly belonging to the second mode, actually represents a third. Although it regulates donor insemination, storage of gametes, storage of embryos, and embryo research, it sets few normative standards. Nor does the Act solve existing moral disagreements. Instead, it establishes an institutional framework within which compromises can be worked out.[7]

And what does this institutional framework tell us about the existence of a legal right to reproduce? Must the state foster artificial reproduction or just not interfere with it? Under the HFE Act, the state facilitates assisted reproduction by removing any rules of law which prevent individuals taking steps to overcome their inability to have children. This is accomplished via the new status provisions which permit some of those who use assisted reproduction techniques to be defined in law as parents without recourse to a court.[8] But there is no right to reproduce, and thus no entitlement to assisted conception services.

The HFE Act imposes obligations on treatment centres to give information, provide counselling, and take into account the welfare of potential children. It sets up the Human Fertilisation and Embryology Authority - an organisation that is unique in the world - which is charged with implementing the statute. The Authority licenses treatment services and publishes guidelines in a Code of Practice. Of the four guiding principles that are set out in the Code, two set the parameters of our ethical discussion.

(1) "The right of people who are or may be infertile to the proper consideration of their request for treatment."

(2) "A concern for the welfare of children, which cannot always be adequately protected by concern for the interests of the adults involved."

Thus, the Code mandates that physicians take account of the interests of non-patients, and thereby address social questions with a strong value component.

X wishes to contract with an egg donor and a gestational surrogate. Use of an egg donor requires in vitro fertilisation (IVF), which is regulated by the Act and its Code of Practice. Because he also wishes to contract with a gestational surrogate, we must look to The Surrogacy Arrangements Act of 1985. While that legislation contains criminal sanctions on participation by intermediaries and a prohibition of commercial agencies, it explicitly exempts from criminal sanction the parties directly involved in the arrangement - the commissioning parents and the gestational mother. Further, payment of the surrogate is not illegal.

Granting X's request would not be proscribed by the surrogacy legislation. But, because he wishes to use IVF, a licensed activity under the HFE Act, we must look to the Code of Practice section 3.19, the provision on surrogacy:

The application of assisted conception techniques to initiate a surrogate pregnancy

should only be considered where it is physically impossible or highly undesirable for medical reasons for the commissioning mother to carry the child.

This section alone would probably cause a licensed centre to refuse to initiate a surrogate pregnancy involving X, because his inability is not medical - it is social.[9] Paradoxically, although absence of a medical problem would preclude a surrogate pregnancy through a licensed centre, it is important to realise that there is no medical reason for X to resort to licensed technology in the first place. He could contract with a woman to be both the gestational and genetic mother, and arrange for home insemination, all of which are out of the ambit of HFE Act.

Indeed, if X wishes to father a child by artificial insemination, he would have to make such arrangements himself. For section 13(5) of the HFE Act will preclude him from gaining access to infertility treatment at a licensed clinic.

A woman shall not be provided with treatment services unless account has been taken of the welfare of any child who may be born as a result of the treatment (including the need of that child for a father)....

This is the only section of the Act that addresses the question of access to treatment. It is significant that the Act deals with the ethical question of access in terms of an examination *only* of the welfare of the child. In the context of the HFE Act, this concept of the 'welfare of the child' falls obviously short of addressing the relative merits of existence and non-existence. Nor does it retain its usual meaning in the context of family law. Instead, the 'welfare of the child' is here conceptually equivalent to the suitability of the prospective parent or parents.[10] It should be noted that, despite this language, IVF is not unavailable to single women.

The Code of Practice contains the Authority's guidance on the interpretation of this provision. The Code highlights the factors that should be taken into account by the clinician, for example, who is intended to bring up the child (section 3.14), the needs of the child, and the ability of the prospective parents or parent to meet these needs (3.16).

Refusal of treatment is addressed in section 3.28:

... Treatment *may* be refused on clinical grounds. Treatment *should* also be refused if the centre believes that it would not be in the interests of any resulting child....(emphasis added)

When the Code's 'factors' are used as a lens for examination of our case, the decision of the clinician is clear. The child's need for a father is not met. Need for a mother, although not stated in the statute, is clearly implicit. No one seems prepared to act as a mother to this child: X's mother must be at least in her mid-80's, and there is no indication that his sexual partner would be willing to take on the responsibility. The small amount of money that would be available for the child until the age of 18 is

clearly inadequate. Finally, it is significant in a moral sense that X has made no real provision for the future of his child. This may well indicate that he views the child in an instrumental way - as merely a means to an end.

Who would be the legal parents? Under sections 27 and 29 of the Act, the gestational mother (the surrogate) would be considered the child's mother. X, because he is not the husband of the surrogate, would have to go through adoption proceedings. Under section 28(5)(a) of the Act, the surrogate's husband would be considered the father unless they were judicially separated or he can prove that he did not consent to the treatment.

As we have seen the Code sets out 'factors' to be considered by the clinician in making a judgement. Enormous discretion is vested in the physician. This accords with the prevailing English legal standard for decision making for incapacitated patients. That standard is the patient's best interests - which can be determined only by a physician.

The test for best interests that has been accepted by English courts is the *Bolam*[11] test, which was developed in relation to ascertaining whether a doctor has sufficiently departed from the required standard of care to be considered negligent. The test - resting on the reasonable body of medical opinion - has been borrowed from negligence cases and used to answer such questions as whether it is in the best interests of an incompetent girl to be sterilised[12], and whether it is in the best interests of a PVS patient to have artificial nutrition and hydration continued.[13]

Thus, looking to physicians to use their own norms and those of their colleagues to make decisions with profound moral and social implications is an accepted and pervasive aspect of British medical law and ethics. In the reproductive context, the doctor is free to use his or her values to determine whether a prospective patient would be a suitable parent. Such discretion was contested when Saint Mary's Hospital in Manchester refused IVF treatment to a woman who had a criminal record for prostitution; she had been rejected by the local authorities as a prospective adoptive or foster mother.[14]

The judge found that decisions denying IVF treatment are reviewable by the courts. He went on to hold that the determination by her physicians that she would be an unfit parent was a reasonable one. There is no legal right to assisted conception. And - as in the cases involving decisions for the incapacitated - in the matter of access to treatment, the locus of decision making rests squarely with the physician.

Acknowledgement

I would like to thank the Cambridge University Press for permission to reprint parts of this paper from my 'Commentary on "Immortality through the fertility clinic"' *Cambridge Quarterly of Health Care Ethics* 4 (3), Summer 1995, pp.380-383 and to use the case study of Mr. X ('Immortality through the fertility clinic' *ibid.*, p.375).

Notes

1. Helvetius, quoted in Joel Feinberg, *Social Philosophy* Englewood Cliffs, New Jersey, Prentice-Hall, 1973, p.8. The following discussion draws on definitions put forth by Feinberg.

2. Lord Kennet, HL Deb. vol 513 col 1028, 17 Dec 1989: quoted in Montgomery, J., 'Rights, restraints, and pragmatism: the Human Fertilisation and Embryology Act 1990, 54 *Modern Law Review* 1991, p.524, p.526.

3. Canadian Law Reform Commission *Working Paper #65: Medically Assisted Procreation* 1992.

4. Feinberg, *op.cit.*, p.13. This is one aspect of a genuine inability.

5. *Ibid.*, p.96.

6. Kennedy, I.M., and Grubb, Andrew, *Medical Law: Text and Materials* London, Butterworths, 1994, p.763, citing the report by the Ontario Law Reform Commission *Human Artificial Reproduction and Related Matters* 1985.

7. Montgomery, *op.cit.*, p.524.

8. Montgomery, *op.cit.*, p.526.

9. Obviously this section, like others in the Act and the Code, addresses the infertility of women and not men, but the criteria for treatment eligibility are clearly physiological.

10. Kennedy and Grubb, *op.cit.*, p.782.

11. *Bolam v. Friern Hospital Management Committee* [1957] 2 All ER 118 [1957] 1 WLR 582.

12. *Re F (Mental Patient: Sterilisation)* [1990] 2 AC 1 (1989) 4 BMLR 1 (HL).

13. *Airedale NHS Trust v. Bland* [1993] 1 All ER 821, (1993) 12 BMLR 64 (HL).

14. *R. v. Ethical Advisory Committee of St Mary's Hospital ex p. Harriott* [1988] I FLR 512.

28. FRENCH ASSISTED REPRODUCTION LEGISLATION

Judge Christian Byk
Associate Professor of Law
University of Poitiers
France

1. Regulation of Practitioners

In 1988, two governmental rulings (decret 88-327 and 88-328) installed an administrative licensing procedure for activities related to reproductive technologies. In order to obtain a licence, public or private hospitals should satisfy certain criteria (technical requirements). A national administrative board was mandated to advise the Minister of Health about the opportunity to licence the centres asking for application. Around 60 got approval, after these criteria (the technical qualifications) were applied together with the policy decision that it would be inappropriate to have more than one centre for one million inhabitants.

In 1994, Law 94-654 of 29 July explicitly expressed the existence of a monopoly for medically assisted reproductive technologies. Assisted reproduction can be performed only in public hospitals and in laboratories (generally, privately owned) doing biological tests. Moreover such hospitals and laboratories are obliged to obtain ministerial agreement for each of the activities (kinds of assistance) performed. The agreement is valid for 5 years and is given only after taking into account the opinion of the above mentioned administrative body: the National Commission for Biology, Reproductive Medicine and Prenatal Diagnosis. Further administrative regulations are however needed to implement these new provisions of the public health Code and to combine it with the existing 1988 licensing procedure governing prenatal diagnosis.

2. Criteria of Access to Services

Such criteria are provided for the first time in the above mentioned 1994 Act.

2.1. REGARDING MEDICALLY ASSISTED REPRODUCTIVE TECHNOLOGIES

These technologies ('methods of treatment') cover clinical and biological practices aimed at facilitating *in vitro* conception, embryo transfer, and artificial insemination as well as other techniques with equivalent effects (art L152-1 Public Health Code). They do not cover surrogacy which is strictly prohibited, whether commercial or not. The

D. Evans (ed.), Creating the Child, 347–349.
© 1996 *Kluwer Law International. Printed in the Netherlands.*

child born through such an illicit practice cannot be adopted by the commissioning parents.

Medically assisted technologies are accessible only for heterosexual couples facing a medical diagnosis of infertility or a particularly serious disease that could be transmitted to the offspring. The husband and wife must both be alive at the time of the insemination or at the time of the embryo transfer. Both partners should be of reproductive age. Finally they should have been married or prove that they have been cohabiting for at least two years (art L152-2).

2.2. REGARDING PREIMPLANTATION DIAGNOSIS

Preimplantation diagnosis is accessible for a couple only if a qualified physician testifies that, regarding the family medical history, there is a high risk of the offspring being born with a particularly serious genetic disease and with no chance of therapy at the time of diagnosis (art L162-17).

3. Consent Procedures

Regarding couples attending for reproductive technological assistance, consent shall be given by each member of the couple beforehand for insemination or embryo transfer (art L152-2). When reproductive technologies imply the use of gamete donation, specific consent is also given in the presence of a notary or a judge who will inform the members of the couple of the consequences of their will for the filiation of the expected child (art 311-20 Civil Code, and see below, section 5).

A specific procedure is also designated when a couple are to use the embryo of another couple. The written consent of all members of both couples is required but is not sufficient. A judge should finally decide the matter, basing judgement on the interests of the future child (art L152-5).

For preimplantation diagnosis, the two members of the couple should give a written consent (art L162-17).

Regarding the donation of gametes, the donor (man or woman) should be living within a heterosexual couple, and have children within that relationship, and the donation should procede only with the written consent of the other member of couple (art L673-2).

In all the above cases, consent can be withdrawn by any of the persons concerned before transfer or insemination (art L673-2).

4. Prohibitions

What is excluded by the criteria of access mentioned above is consequently prohibited: there is no right of access to reproductive technologies. Homosexual couples, single

persons, and cohabiting couples with less than 2 years living together, are excluded and posthumous insemination, surrogacy or the use of donated fresh sperm (as well as mixed sperm) are banned (art L152-2 PHC). With respect to donors, single persons as well as homosexuals and persons having no children are excluded (art L673-2 PHC).

Also outlawed are: Payments in relation to gamete donation and embryo 'adoption' (art L665-13 PHC); the use of the gametes of a single donor for giving birth to more than 5 children (art L673-4 PHC); and the limitation of access to gamete donation to couples who recruit donors (art L673-7 PHC).

Giving information that would identify the donors to the future parents and *vice versa* is prohibited (art L665-7 PHC and art L152-5 PHC). And so too is the procreation of an embryo for purposes other than medically assisted conception (art L152-3 PHC).

5. Rules of Parentage

The civil code has been modified as follows by Law 94-653 of 29 July 1994. No relation of filiation may be established between a child born through reproductive technologies and the donor of its gametes. Such prohibition concerns also any action concerning the civil liability of the donor (art 311-19). The consent given by a member of a couple to the use of reproductive technologies will secure him/her from any action regarding the filiation of the child except if it can be proven that the child was not born as a result of the use of reproductive techniques.

However, consent is deprived of any effect in case of death, divorce, or separation, where this occurs before insemination or embryo transfer. Consent can also be withdrawn in writing by either member of the couple (art 311-20).

One provision of the law is aimed essentially at the man of a cohabiting couple: it states that where one member of a couple gives consent to the use of reproductive technologies, but will not declare the child to be his, then he still has liabilities to the mother and the child. Moreover, a court can establish his paternity (art 311-20).

INDEX OF NAMES

INDEX OF SUBJECTS